The Kaliani Wind
& other
JUNGLE STORIES

Ashok Biswal

PUSTAK MAHAL®

J-3/16 , Daryaganj, New Delhi-110002
☎ 23276539, 23272783, 23272784 • *Fax:* 011-23260518
E-mail: info@pustakmahal.com • *Website:* www.pustakmahal.com

Sales Centre

- 10-B, Netaji Subhash Marg, Daryaganj, New Delhi-110002
  ☎ 23268292, 23268293, 23279900 • *Fax:* 011-23280567
  E-mail: rapidexdelhi@indiatimes.com
- 6686, Khari Baoli, Delhi-110006
  ☎ 23944314, 23911979

Branches

Bengaluru: ☎ 080-22234025 • *Telefax:* 080-22240209
E-mail: pustak@airtelmail.in • pustak@sancharnet.in
Mumbai: ☎ 022-22010941, 022-22053387
E-mail: rapidex@bom5.vsnl.net.in
Patna: ☎ 0612-3294193 • *Telefax:* 0612-2302719
E-mail: rapidexptn@rediffmail.com
Hyderabad: *Telefax:* 040-24737290
E-mail: pustakmahalhyd@yahoo.co.in

ISBN 978-81-223-1268-3

Edition: 2012

Printed at : Param Offsetters, Okhla, New Delhi-110020

Preface

The story starts with the death of a baby elephant due to electrocution; I was in pain even to bring the facts in writing. Love remains everywhere, animals are no different. A child always goes to the mother.

The animals should get some dignified space at present. They were a part of our past and should also get recognition for the future. In silence they speak their cause.

The stories touch the cultural sides and in the same extent the wildlife sides are touched; culture and tradition goes side by side; wildlife is an integral part of our life, our thought, our practice. Over the years, the human societies evolved, but the animals have not changed much, they are still living the same way as they were living thousands of years back. Still they hold a prominent place in our culture, in our imagination.

In some of my stories I have given vivid descriptions of the places, so many quick changes are occurring due to human activities, at least in future people will know about some places of the past. The feeling of being in the place, by reading the stories, will give more satisfaction.

While interacting with the front line forest officials engaged in the protection of the most primitive tribe – the animals, I want to name the wildlife as most primitive tribe as they are so stubborn to change their shape and attitude, the pain in their eyes are most apparent. By staying with the most primitive tribe of the world for decades, they turned primitive, are unable to express them in a proper way, only they merged with the nature, turned speechless like the animals in wild.

This book is dedicated to the front line forest staffs and Range Forest Officers, they have been working in most hostile conditions, and due to their constant effort still the wildlife is getting some breathing space; they work tirelessly, without getting proper recognition. This book is dedicated to Foresters like Meher who joined and retired in the same post after serving for more than 35 years. When I met him, at that time he was in service, only a smile was reflected on his face; this book is a tribute to the unstoppable souls like him.

The book deals with prominent wildlife areas of Orissa and also about the elephants of Jharkahand; Orissa and Jharkhand remained my main working areas; my experiences in those areas are reflected in the stories. With whomever I interacted, they all cooperated extremely well, be it the young fisherman on the Mahanadi waters, be it the old forest guard in the deep forests, all opened their hearts before me. Many factual details were gathered from them. They unfolded their heart, I tried to gather those words, the information on myths and the traditions are the offshoots of such interaction. The rural life is penned in detail, the wildlife stay in the countryside, in uninhabited areas, not in the towns; in the rustic life the animals peep from lonely corners.

This book is written in the form of stories, the facts, data were collected from different sources, and effort was made to keep the accuracy as far as possible. This book is however not a reference book, it is a collection of wildlife stories where imagination played a major role; there might be discrepancies in understanding the facts, the myths. This book is aimed to sensitize people; the stories are presented in a lucid manner to let the emotions flow. Some necessary facts about animals are given in the stories, to understand the animal, little information about it is necessary. The beauty of the nature will be better appreciated with little understanding of animals and nature.

The basic purpose of writing the book is to sensitize people for the cause of wildlife, for the cause of preservation; we need to preserve the speechless creatures for future.

Let everybody praise the beauty of the butterfly in the garden, the chirpings of the birds in the hide, the beautiful golden sun, the rain drops on the flowing water, the cool breeze, let there be dew drops on the green grasses.

Let us make small efforts, I turned speechless when I found my young daughter of three years rescuing the small turtle hatchlings. She was running and running and releasing stray turtle hatchlings into the sea waters; without getting tired.

Contents

The Silent Forest

(The story is written on the electrocution of three wild elephants in Chandragiri area, near Paralkhemundi town in Southern Odisha)

"He was my best friend, we moved together, played together, and you know, that day we trumpeted together for the first time." Raman, the baby elephant spoke to the rising moon, which was coming out from the Akashpakshi peak, the tallest peak of the area. The baby elephant was standing on a small earthen mound, surrounded by tall Sal and semi evergreen forest of the Deccan plateau, inside Lakhari Wildlife Sanctaury. The other trees mainly Piasal, Bandhan, Kasi, Sahaj, Bahada, Hariada, Sisoo, Sunari, Kusum, Jamun, Kendu, Mahua, and Amla were in a mixed group after the Sal forest. The terrain was mainly hilly with narrow valleys usually rugged except at the eastern strip, where the terrain was plain and had gentle slope. The hills with an elevation ranging from 300m to 1600m and above were the continuation of the eastern ghats, and were forming two plateaus featuring some of the high mountains – prominent among them were the San Tangri, Bada Tangri, Poipani Parvata, Ramachandi Parvata, Luhakhamba Parvata. The rivers, mostly seasonal, fast and furious flew through the sanctuary. Innumerable falls also dotted the vast land of the elephants.

A weak and exhausted Raman was staggering at a distance, alone, away from his mother; and was extremely depressed. The herd was standing silently, no movement of their huge ears and all were looking at the moon, with their trunks raised and eyes closed. By habit, the elephant herds are well-knit, every member is related to the other member. Mostly sisters, aunts and mothers apart from very young males constitute an elephant herd. In his herd, most of the sisters were much older and he was the only surviving young male member. They have a tradition, when some significant event ever happen with the herd, they all gather in a full moon night, near a big water body, inside the forest and convey their feelings to the rising moon. Gentle wind was blowing from the sal forest to the open space, where the elephants were standing. They were twelve in number and all were looking at the moon; their number reduced from fifteen to twelve only five days ago. The herd comprising of mostly young females and one baby, fondly called Raman; and he was the smallest, cutest and the most loved one.

The night was a full moon night and the uncut moon was coming slowly towards their head from the tall mountain top. They raised their trunks further, at the direction of the full moon. The herd was standing in the middle of a deep forest, bamboo patch on the left, Sal forest on the right and also on the back, and in the front, a big lake was extending right up to the foot of the tall mountain. The dull dark shadow of the forest was slowly disappearing with the rise of the moon. The moonlit trees, the reflection of the moon on the still water of the lake with the herd standing still in a group with their trunks raised, was giving impression of a vast canvass.

"You know, Jahnamama; Somesh and I were very good friends," Raman told to the rising full moon of Paralkhemundi forest. Raman and other elephants affectionately call the full moon "Jahnamama" the maternal uncle, eternal uncle of all animals of the forest. They would convey their feelings to their loving uncle whenever they were in trouble or when any happy event would take place. As the full moon rose from the mountains, casting the shadow of the trees on the dazzling water of the lake, the herd gathered and conveyed their feelings to their uncle. The herd, at the sight of the full moon, used to run, trumpets, then go into the lake and throw water, come to the mud, roll, come to water again and then make merry. But on that day, they were unusually calm, not even moving their ears, standing still and were raising their trunks at the direction of Jahnamama. Tear drops were rolling from their tiny eyes and then they raised their heads further.

"I still remember his young days. After birth, he was very tender, almost unable to stand. The whole group gathered around him, I pushed all, came to the front, only to find a young one staggering in his feet. In our group when a child is born, always the aunts and sisters take care of the child so that the mother can get a lot of food, but here for Somesh, he never wished to be away from his mother. The aunts, and sister of course, cared for him a lot, but he preferred to be with his mother. For months, the little Somesh walked in between the legs of his mother. After each half an hour, he would stop for mother's milk. Unlike others, he never liked to be away from his mother, never liked to be independent. You know, Jahnamam, in our herd, the mother loves the child so much, nurses the child for more than two years," Raman was recollecting the memories of his friend. He had to express his grief, open his heart, his feelings before his Jahnamama. That was the tradition. Raman had to narrate his deepest feelings.

"You know Jahnamama, he was my only friend in the herd. He was the smallest and I, only two months older than him, were very good associates. Wherever I went, he used to run after me, pull me by his trunk." Raman was speaking to the rising moon. He was sniveling and his voice was obstructed with sigh, and he paused for a while. He was unable to raise his trunk; in fact he did not have energy to do so for long. He took a little rest, raised his head again, raised the trunk; pain reflected on his forehead, tears was rolling continuously from the tiny eyes.

“Jahnamama, he was so loving so live, every one loved him. He would run a little, come back, hide below the mother’s belly, call me to touch him, then coil his trunk like a creeper with his mother’s and I never was able to pull their trunks apart. As I try hard, he used to hold his mother more tightly, and remain almost embedded to his mother’s body. After all he was the most loving child of his mother,” Raman was recollecting the behaviour of his friend. His eyes had swelled because of continuous weeping.

More than an hour had passed since the moon first appeared from the Akashpakhi peak and it was almost half way to the mid sky. The herd was standing with raised trunks since then. They were frozen, not even their tails moved, nor their ears moved; their dark structures looked like heap of stones, and the raised trunks appeared like the pre-historic flora raising form the bumpy earth. All, at one time took long breaths and drowned their trunks together.

Raman looked at his mother, at his aunts and then looked at the bright moon on the horizon and started saying, “He ran on that day, we were standing on the banks of the Ramanadi river. It was not a big river, rather a small one, but filled with water and had tremendous current. The lightning was dazzling in the right sky, rain drops as big as the areca nut fruits were dropping from the black sky continuously. But, he, instead of taking shelter below the big banyan tree, ran towards the mighty Ramanadi, stopped after a short distance and looked at me, moved his ears and raised his trunk. I understood his message. He was calling me to enjoy the first rain. I stepped forward.” Raman stopped for a while. He started crying, but controlled himself after a while, looked again at the moon and continued speaking –

“It was also my first rain. As the rain drops touched my hair, my body started shivering and at once, the energy of the rain ran in to my veins. It was so thrilling, so enjoyable. I ran towards my best friend, rather my only friend, and we ran here and there; touched each others body, raised our trunks and then went near the river bank. Our mothers cautioned us, but we did not listen and you know Jahnamama; we together touched the rain water, the mighty river water. Rain drops were pouring form the sky, the stream was full with the water; and the lightings were blazing on the sky, the deafening sounds of the thunders were coming from all the sides and we touched the flowing water, then filled our trunks, threw water at each other and raised our trunks, looked at the flashing lightning. The next lightning flashed its light, and simultaneously we trumpeted and the sound came from the forests of the hills. It was our first trumpet together, and you know, it sounded like the thunder from the sky,” Raman, the baby elephant started sobbing, sorrow within him was choking his lungs, his heart. He raised his little trunk and trumpeted and the sound of his heart echoed in the hillocks. The elephant herd near the forest understood his feeling and they raised their trunks further, all looked at the moon and then lowered their trunks.

Raman looked at the herd, they looked tired, dejected, and all had lowered their trunks and were silently looking at the small ripples in the water. The reflection of the moon moved with every ripple, after all their dear Jahnamama was moved by their sorrow, their misery. The tradition desires one to express his memorable moments of his departed friend; and all memories need to be unfolded for the last time. Raman bowed his head down, his eyes were shut, moved his head and again lifted his head up, opened his eyes , looked at the shining moon and started recounting –

"Would you believe, Somesh didn't know how to fill water in his trunks. He, that day, tried to lift his trunk for the first time, you know. We were playing inside a big pond, aunts were filling their trunks with water and then blowing the same to their bodies, some times throwing the waters at the others. It was so interesting. Somesh, as usual entered into the pond. He at that time was only four feet tall, still he entered till his belly touched the water, then dipped his trunk and instead of sucking the water, blew water through his trunks. Bubbles came out, but no water went inside the trunk, only it was a little wet. Then, he lifted his trunk and blew over his body. No water, only air came out. He was surprised. Again he dipped his trunk into the water, blew the air, raised his trunk and blew the air again onto his body. His body was not wet, no water was coming from his trunks. He was very surprised, repeated his actions again and again. Strangely, that day neither his mother, nor any of the aunts were helping him, rather they forgot to teach the water sucking method to Somesh. He called me to teach, and I went near him, dipped my trunk inside the water, sucked water in and then lifted the trunk and blew the water onto my body. Do you know what was his reaction," Raman paused a little. The evening was getting thicker and cooler, dew drops were accumulating over the leaves. The night, on that hour, was not alive with the howling of the jackals and hyenas, roar of the tigers and grumbling of the bears. The flying bats were also somewhat absent, and the owls were not flying over the head. In that silent night, the elephant herd was saddened at the demise of their friends. They were bidding farewell to their friends and were telling their heart to the lovable Jahnamama. In that quiet moment, Raman, the baby elephant was remembering his departed friend.

"His little eyes swelled like a balloon, he could not believe, how a child like me could make the trick? Again I did the same, and he was perplexed. He, looking at me, dipped his trunk inside, blew air into the water and lifted his trunk, but there was no water. He looked so unhappy, tear rolled from his eyes. Again he dipped his trunk inside, and I stopped him, asked him to suck through the trunks, and he did the same. He lifted his trunk it was heavy, and he blew the trunk over his body. Water came out. So much joy in his eyes! He was so happy! He hugged my trunk with his and we played with the water throwing game for hours, non-stop, did not listen to our mothers and aunts. The water throwing game used to be our most favourite game. Whenever we saw a water body, we used to play the water throwing game." The little elephant was recollecting his friendly days with his departed friend Somesh.

"Can you believe we wrestled a lot alongside the rivers. Wrestling alongside the river course turned out to be regular events for us. After sucking milk from our mothers, we used to go near the water course of the river and interweave our trunks, pushing each other. Most of the time, I allowed him to beat me, only to create interest in him. It made him cheerful, he loved the wrestling always. Our wrestling would continues thereafter followed by a good bath in the river along with our herd," Raman continued.

Raman was totally heartbroken, he in fact had lost his only friend in the vast forest. The moon was shining brightly on that evening and was about to reach the mid sky, the stars were twinkling from the black roof and the gentle cool breeze was blowing from the tall hills to the forest below. A couple of days back the herd had lost their vibrant members and the heartbroken herd was looking for solace amidst the hillocks and the tall trees. The herd had reconciled to the fate, but not the inconsolable small elephant Raman, and how could he be? Raman again recounted his most memorable moments with his friend to lovable Jahnamama.

"Do you know, Jahnamama; once we flew like birds, away from the ground," Curves formed on his forehead, and eyes glittered; he was recollecting his exciting days with his buddy. Soon his expression turned melancholic.

"That day we went to a huge tamarind tree, and tried to pull the branch, not from the base, but away from it, neat the tip. That branch did not break, we pulled ourselves further back, legs more entrenched to the earth. Suddenly my legs slipped and I lost balance. The next moment we were in air. The branch had pulled us up. All laughed at us, and we felt terribly embarrassed at our failure, tongues went deep into the mouths, eyes were down in anguish, in shame too. His mother came near, solaced him by putting her trunk over his body and demonstrated the technique to pull a branch. She put his trunks near the base of the branch and asked him to do the same. Somesh then put his trunk near his mother's trunk, more closer to the base. She then removed his trunk from the branch, and asked me to put my trunk there. I did the same and as per her direction pulled the branch together. To our utter surprise, the branch broke with a bang, and surprisingly, we were not in the air. At our success, everybody thumped the ground with their feet. We learned the behaviour from our mothers and aunts, together." His voice was loaded with sorrows of his heart. The silent moments of the night was getting lengthened quite abnormally, only the inaudible feelings of Somesh were in the air. The peaks, though moon-lit in that night were still not vibrant as were used to be. The bats, owls were not coming from their hides, and the jackals were not howling from the peaks, the depth of the Death Valley on that day was not that deep in the absence of the normal sounds of the wild animals. The light of the jackals, the ghost lights from the caves were not sighted that night, the sudden fleeing feet of the hunter and the to be hunted were not echoed from the mountains. The sound of the waterfall was not reaching the ears of the sorrowful elephants.

"You know, he and I moved and moved, together for weeks with our mothers. Our herd moved from forest to forest, from one hill to the other hill in search of food. Innumerable streams, big water bodies we must have crossed. The big watercourses turned smaller and smaller and we, baby elephants, found the time in the waters more enjoyable as we could cross the streams without taking help of our mothers and aunts. Those were great days for us, after all we are getting older, taller and stronger. The rivers, streams then got dried up and we missed the clear flowing water. We moved around the forest for the water points, and finally found some. Those water bodies were not that clean and cool like the river water, but we had no option, and slowly we liked the muddy water. All around we could see different animals, spotted deers, antelopes, jackals, porcupines, buffaloes, wild boars and even small rabbits. The birds of many colours and wings flock and then sail into the blue sky. We saw so many animals for the first time, you know. During our long journeys, when we moved and trumpeted, the animals used to hide themselves, but here the animals came much closer, since there was no water around." The little baby elephants was talking to the moon. The moon now had reached the centre of the sky and was slowly going down. His mother came closer and stood near him. She understood the grief of her son. Both the elephants raised their trunks and looked at the moon. Suddenly, the owls hovered over the head of the little elephant and the jackals started howling in a group, one after the another. The night was filled with their sound. The water drops were tickling down from the trees. Raman closed his eyes. The calls of the owls was as if entering into his body and chilling him within, the grief also had made him still within. He controlled himself, he had to open his heart before the Jahnamama, lest he would break the tradition. For elephants, breaking the tradition was an unforgivable sin and the Jahnamam will not listen to the voice of the violators in future. Also, more than tradition he wanted to open his heart, to reduce the grief within. Whom else he could speak? The herd was so helpless, so grief stricken. He took a long breath and continued –

"Once our herd was going through the forest, the time was noon, sun shining right over our back and we were very hungry. The members took food. And we, as usual, broke the branches as per the methods taught to us by Somesh's mother. We were enjoying the play, and went deep and deep into the forest without knowing. The forest turned calmer and calmer, no sound of the breaking of branches any more. We were very nervous, moved our sensitive ears to get the sound of our mothers, but no sound. We were terribly frightened. Then we stopped for a while and raised our trunks and moved the same to get any signal. Oh! Somesh's mother was calling. The message could not be gathered by the ears, but our sensitive feet and point on our forehead could receive the message of alarm. We traced the sound and stood still, and after some time, we listened the sound of the running legs. The whole herd gathered around us, everybody was nervous like us, eyes wide open in disbelief. Somesh's mother came forward, gave gentle slap on his back with her trunk. We should be careful, should never leave the herd. After all we were too small to survive in the deep and dangerous forest." Raman was recollecting his days with his close friend

"Slowly and slowly we turned more adventurous, and our duels were more frequent. Now we were climbing steep hills with ease, broke the thick branches with little effort. Strength came slowly to our legs, to our trunks. The days were so interesting. Our trumpet sounds reverberated from mountains and our voices turned much louder. We find it much easier to walk in our seasonal migration routes. No more we were that tired. After all we were growing." The sweet memories were filling his heart.

"The days turned warmer and warmer, and we felt very hot and thirsty and spent most of our playing times in the muddy water, plastering ourselves with black mud. We used to pour muddy water onto each other's body, then the mud plaster was formed as the skin got a little drier. The whole herd then used to join us and we play a lot." The little elephant was continuing. The cool breeze had stopped a little, the horizon was more clear. The memorable thoughts of his friend had lightened him considerably. He looked at the dearest Jahnamam. It was so sweet, so charming. The moon light was reflected from his little eyes and it was shining. But the mood did not last long, and it soon became gloomy. The thoughts, hazy, terrifying roamed around. He then looked at the mountains around, and they were sitting like old men in groups, backs bent and heads down and motionless. The night life was turning more terrifying. The vision got blurred further.

The herd were on the field for more than four hours, looking at the bright moon, performing the ritual by raising their trunks repeatedly with the movement of the moon. The night sky was getting brighter with the arrival of the moon at the centre, and the horizon was studded with sparkling stars. After some time the cool breeze started blowing with lots of mist; as a result, the horizon turned whiter and unclear in the east. The mountains on that side was also turning hazy, finally disappearing beneath the haze. The elephant herd looked exhausted and to some extent resigned themselves to fate and tried to retreat to the dense forest area to take rest for the night. But Somesh did not move, he, in fact did not wish to move even. He had not fully opened his heart to his much loved Jahnamama. The moon was slowly being covered with the white mist. The little elephant raised his trunk again, nodded his head, cool dew drops moistened his eyes further and his voice got clogged. He moved his head again and told Jahnamama in a melancholic voice –

"We played all through the day, were very tired, at the end. That afternoon was most thrilling. Bright golden sun was shining behind the peak, golden rays reflected from the broad sal leaves, giving forest the orange-golden tinge, birds calling from the hides and we were standing on the river bed, full with round pebbles. The water, like a serpent of the forest, was moving with rhythm, the crests of the ripples shining like the brightest stars of the sky before the deep blue background. His dusky skin silhouetting against the background, the rays of the orange sun were coming around his head, and he looked like a deity, garlanded around the neck, aura coming from the face. He raised his trunk and blew water into the sky and the falling water droplets appeared like molten crystals. He ran along the water course, and to me it appeared as if the afternoon sun was moving with him, the stars in the ripples were shining more brightly with his run. It was a superb view, eye catching, a lifetime memory. He called me as usual, and I without looking at my mother ran towards him, and both of us at once went into the river water. The water level was not much, depth only upto our belly level, both of us dipped our trunks, lifted water filled trunks, and threw water at each other. Most surprisingly the water jets met at the middle and the water instead of touching each other formed a pillar at the middle. Again blew water, the water jets met at the middle and a pillar was formed again. I looked at him, his eyes were deeply shut, ears wide open and the water jet coming from his trunk like an eternal spring. Though it was late afternoon still we played and played in the water and constantly formed the water jets and water pillars. But I did not know then that would be our last game together, we would never play again and he would not see the next morning sun," the little elephant moaned, his grief came as a blow of wind. The last memory of the lost friend had saddened him considerably, the slate coloured sky too increased its depth, made the forest more darker. The fireflies were glowing in groups at the side of the lake, near a dark bush. They were glowing one moment, the next moment there was complete darkness.

"That evening was cool and clear, the brightest stars came to the horizon much earlier. Light breeze was blowing from the mountain peak and our herd, instead of taking rest moved further. The forest was filled with sweet aroma, the cool breeze was increasing our appetite, after all we played throughout the afternoon, did not even eat a single blade of grass. The herd came to the forest, but most of the trees had shaded their leaves. Strangely the aroma didn't subside, rather it increased, so also our hunger. We moved towards the direction of the aroma, the scent of the ripened paddy and found one field full with golden paddy inside the Sal forest. The inflorescences of the plants were quite long, full with sweet paddy grains, juicy and tasty, and we ate till our stomach were full. Jahnamama, you didn't come early on that evening and you failed to witness the fateful events. Had you been around, you would have warned us early, but you did not arrive. The cloud and fog had covered you, your light was there, but we could not see you," Raman was narrating the final moments; agony was there in his tone. The flying bats had positioned themselves in the tall trees, hanging with their heads down and listening carefully to the recounting of the events from the little elephant. The howling jackals and their blue lights were no more around; the jungle had reached its quietest moment. The wind from the hills was also not blowing, the twinkling stars are peeping from the sky through the fog cover and the dearest Jahnamama had moistened its eyes. After all the elephants were so dear to him.

"Somesh as usual was bubbling with energy in that eventful evening. He ran around the paddy field, did not trample a single paddy plant, plucked the juiciest ones and offered me to eat. I was so happy; my little dear loves me so much. I, too plucked some juiciest paddy plants and offered him to eat. He ate merrily, lifted his trunk and trumpeted. I too trumpeted and our joint sound came from the tall mountains. We both looked at you, your light was there, but you did not peep from the sky, you were hidden behind the thickest fog," Raman narrated his story with little anguish in his tone at the careless attitude of his dearest uncle on that day.

"We went to the side of the forest, just adjacent to the paddy field and were taking rest for a while. Somesh was with his mother, a little away from the herd, plucking the rice plants and helping his mother to eat more. Both mother and the child were enjoying the meal, and they remained quite long inside the field. Then they came out, satisfaction in their faces from eating a great feast, their feet turned heavy like their stomachs and they did not wished to walk to a big tree. They went to a bald pole on a earthen mound , inside the field, and it looked like a dead stump, straight, without branches, to rub their bodies. That was the way we relax after a good meal, and they did exactly the same as we other members did in that evening. My mother was standing near a big sal tree, rubbing her back and others too were rubbing their bodies against the trees, but none against the bald pole. But, we didn't know of the grave danger stored in that bald pole, and how could have we imagined after all. No pole was a threat to us, maximum it would break during a strong rubbing due to lack of strength in its roots. Here the mother and the child would not get a good rubbing; after all they were so veracious eaters, lazy too. We had never seen a thin pole with so many leafless white creepers which were coiling its top, sagging and their other ends were not visible, lost beyond the big Sal tree. I did not look at Somesh and their mother, started rubbing my body against a strong Sal tree, near to the tree where my mother was rubbing her body. Suddenly the forest was lighted from the blinding spark of a lightening. No thunder followed, only a feeble cry, weak but nerve breaking, filled the environment. I didn't understand what happened in the forest so suddenly. How the lightning came so suddenly, and where from the feeble cry came. I looked at the other members; all were baffled, and they looked panicky. Little Somesh, he was standing alone, not near his standing mother. His mother had fallen in the ground, painful cry was coming out of her mouth, and she was shivering like a branch of a tamarind tree in a storm. And my dearest Somesh was totally perplexed, looking impassively at the falling mother. Instantaneously, my dearest one ran towards his mother, and how could he watch his mother falling on the ground, screaming in pain, kicking her legs."

"And Somesh touched his mother," Raman could not continue further and started crying. His mother Rani, then caressed her child Raman, moved her trunks over his tender skin, then embraced him tightly and the marching herd stood silent at listening his cry. The herd understood his feeling, after all the baby had lost his best friend and the tradition says to express one's heart to the Jahnamanma before leaving for the jungle. They came closer to the baby elephant, circled him and all looked at the departing moon, their hearts too were broken by the event. Tear rolled down from their eyes too, long breathings came from their lungs, and their throats got choked. Half of the sky was covered in the mist and white clouds were constantly moving over the Jahnamama. The aunts came further closer, caressed him, gave consolation for the irreparable loss. Raman again looked at the departing moon and took a very long breath and then spoke –

"Somesh touched his motionless mother and he too collapsed, felled on the ground, his trunk fell over his mother's trunk. No moan from his little mouth came, not a single hair of the little body shivered, not a drop of tear felled on the ground, not raised was the little trunk which was constantly creating trumpets in the jungle. The little one, at his last moment, touched the trunk of his dearest mother, Looking them falling on the ground, we understood something unusual had happened. The most powerful aunt of the group, Rina, came rushing towards them and tried to pull them up. And, as she touched the body of little Somesh, she trembled and collapsed like a free falling stone, scream came from her mouth and she, after few minutes, turned silent, before our eyes. And you know, we could not move even our eye lids. The earth, the sky turned silent at once. I could not believe my eyes. The delightful three were lying motionless on the ground, but we could not dare to come near them, rather we ran away from the site and hid ourselves in the dense forest." Raman looked at the horizon, eyes were totally blank. He did not speak a word for quite a long period and watched the white clouds moving in the dark sky.

"That was the last glimpse my best friend. The elephants never returned to our herd and we did not know why they fell on the ground at once, trembling and screeching in pain. The next night we went there, but no sign of the friends. We came to the spot and saw that bald pole uprooted, twisted, and the glazing white creepers which looked like strong ropes, covered it all over. I only looked at the twisted bald pole, my eyelids did not drop. I wished to touch that pole, to feel the touch of my only friend, my most valued friend, but my mother didn't allow, my aunts held me back and I cried there, cried there," Raman did not sob further, his eyes turned impassive, and his legs lost the strength to balance his body. The moon was disappearing behind the engulfing white mist.

"Now I am alone, all alone, without a friend. We will move to the forest, climb mountains, even reach the Akashpakhi peak, cross the mighty Ramanadi river, but there will be no one to play with me, to share my joy, to join me in adventure. Our trumpets will not siren together ever. The only friend felled on the trunks of his beloved mother, trunks together, his little body fell on the side." Sigh came gushing from the lungs.

The herd started moving towards deeper forest, and Raman had to leave. The bright moon was covered with dark cloud. The rituals had been finished, and now it was the time to depart for rest. Life has to continue further. They stepped together, with their trunks down, ears moving like big fans

"We will never trumpet together, the thunder will come, but we will never create the thunderous sound together." The voice of the little soul echoed from the tall mountain peaks. The Paralakhemundi jungle had sunk to its thickest darkness.

The Moonlit Sand

Turtle egg hatching – (Rishikulya river mouth)

We were walking to the Rushikulya beach, our vehicles parked at the last village on the sands. The coconut trees stood all around. The small huts sit below the trees like age-old men. I was listening to faint sounds from a hut, probably the grandmother was singing for the naughty child.

Oh! My dear child
Find the field with plentiful of ragi
Sleep in the field.

A child of an agrarian society dreams of the field of golden ragi, with plentiful of birds around. The trees are moving slowly, the grandmother hugs him in reality. The wind of the hand fan made of palm leaves gives a soothing touch to him and he dozes off to sleep. My legs stopped, I looked at those children in the early hours of the evening, some inquisitive ones gather around, those faces were innocent, curiosity in their eyes. We were disturbing their sleep at the evening. The rustic Odisha goes to sleep early in their thatched houses, surrounded by trees around, the night sky gets filled with silence. They were laughing, sweet laughs; their faces were glowing like glow worms in the moonlit night.

The gentle sea wind was blowing. With it came the lyrical songs of the grandmother once again. The old lady was singing once the naughty grandson was asking for more.

Rain drops fall
Seeds sprout.
Where my dear has gone?
Play the Telingi tune.

I returned to my childhood days. Once I was a young child then, my mother told me, I was naughty like the kid of the green fields, not listening to any one, and my grandmother used to take me in her laps and sang many songs.

Oh! Little rat, Little rat
Eat bountiful of paddy.
I am angry, I am leaving.

(This society is linked to paddy, the little rat is eating the paddy, it hurts the mother, she was angry. The child thinks of the black grey house rat, hidden at the darkest corner, comes out to steal the food, rat and the man live together.)

Those songs induced sleep in me then. Imagining the common creatures around, the lyric was hypnotizing me. The lap of the grandmother was so sweet, so soft, so comfortable, tears came to my eyes.

I moved forward, my team had gone ahead, I looked at the village, the half moon had come to the thatched roof of the hut, and the child was sleeping with the song. The grandmother was signing –

Swing dear boy, swing
Grow; brave air and water
Elephant move in the deep forest
To eat the pandnus shoot
Child cries for milk from the mother.

I imagined the scene. The child cries, doesn't listen. The grandmother sings the songs, she asks the mother to feed child, the child gets the solace and goes to sleep.

I sat for a while on the sand mound, gentle wind was blowing from the sea, my old memories were breezing past me. Those were soft like the mother's lap. I closed my eyes, the dim moonlight was creating my childhood world, the call of the jackal was coming from the pandanus bushes, I, a young child then, laughed at the jackal.

Oh! Dear Jackal, Dear Jackal,
Look back, look back
Don't run as if the house is burning

The jackal has a strange habit. When encountered with human beings, it runs away towards the bushes, hides behind it. The young child then laughed at the jackal, everybody tells him that the most cunning animal, the jackal always hides behind the bushes.

Those jackals are very interesting; somehow they are embedded into my memories. In a bright sunny day of the monsoon, the black cloud hovers on the sky, sun peeps from the tall hillock. The rainbow appears in the western sky after a drizzle, the new leaves dazzle in the bright sun, the children of the green horizon. I always remember the paddy fields extend up to the horizon, then the worldly boys remember the jackal. One boy starts singing –

It is sunny, it is raining,
The jackal is getting married

The other children laugh, clap their hands, the beautiful sun gets reflected from their faces.

Those animals are so close to the children of the muddy fields and bushy forests, I closed my eyes for a few minutes, then stood up and walked alongside the pandanus trees, the smell of the white flower was intoxicating.

I went ahead, the foot track was on the sand, the creepers covered the open sand on the way. The pandanus trees were stranding on the side, and were moving through this patch for some time. On the way there are some up and down sand forms, all were small. In between a small water channel was existing, through which the tidal water comes inland, the channel was small, during the time of our journey there was some water. The sound of the sea was louder now, the wetness of the sea water was perceptible, and the evening chill was bringing excitement to us, we were close to the beach, we were going to see the new life.

"Was it that interesting, the hatchlings will really come from the sand?" my young companions, Papun, my son, a child of eight, asked me.

"They resemble a blooming lotus; the bud comes out of the sand, then blooms," I spoke; the child looked at me with broad innocent eyes.

"If I will ask you to imagine a blooming lotus on a large pond, the bud is blooming in quick motion, the coming of the turtle hatchlings will resemble that, each individual turtle hatchling will be like a petal of the big lotus flower," I replied. He was silent for some minutes. Imagining a lotus, I was trying to draw similarity. For the first time he will be seeing a sea turtle hatchling.

"Whether they really look so beautiful, vibrant like a lotus?" he asked me, then paused for a while.

"Are the turtle hatchlings looking like petals? Are they pink in colour?" he continued.

"I'm going to give you a surprise, hold your breath for a few minutes." I wanted his excitement to continue.

The ever inquisitive child asked another question –

"Is the turtle world beautiful, if the turtle is so beautiful, then their world must be beautiful too?" he asked again.

"The beauty of the turtle world is inexpressible, the forage grounds in the coral world is unmatched. The forage grounds of the sea turtles remains in the coral world, all the colour in the world exhibit their magnificence in the uncanny structures of the corals, the sea reeds are moving with the sea current," I narrated.

We were approaching the sea. The moon light was soft, the sky was clear, the breeze was blowing from the sea side, the waves were dazzling in the moonlight. On our front, the villages remained far behind, the panadnus forest on the coastline was creating a dark wall, the limits the marine turtles understand. The white sand on the beach was illuminated.

Suddenly we saw a small dark object on the white sand. My daughter, a child of three bent down and looked at it keenly. I too looked at it, her brother too looked at it. It was moving, strangely it was moving. I knew instantly that we were in the grounds of the turtles, innumerable hatchlings were waiting for their time to come out of the sand and to proceed to the sea. Papun and Elli were surprised, it was their first encounter with the marine turtles, and they thought it to be worm of the sea coast.

I lifted the creature, around three-four centimeter long, the tiny flippers were moving in vein, to go to the sea. They looked at it keenly.

"Who recites those songs for them, they are without mother at the vicinity?" he asked, of course the question should haunt the young minds, they didn't know lives grow without mother in many species, and turtle is one. It is a natural way of evolution of life. At that age they of course should not know the complexities of the world, the world revolves round father and the mother.

"Can you sing a rhyme, the songs you learnt from your grandmother?" he asked, my song floated with the moisture of the wet sea, the mother then teaches us about the nature, the lives around us were so important.

Night breaks,
Crow calls
Get up, get up
Don't be late.

"No body, they were left to themselves. The wind of the night brings the first song, the first rhyme, the nature teaches them about the lives, rhymes around them. You can resemble." And then I recited the poem.

Dear weaver bird, dear weaver bird;
Mother went to graze the cattle
Will bring ripened Bel (Aegle marmelos)
Little girl will eat,
Mother will cuddle.

They listened to me, probably they were also listening it for the first time from me.

"Theirs is a strange way of life, the eggs remain buried in the sea-side sand for more than one and half months. Then the eggs hatch, the hatchlings comes out, and they listen to the sound of the mother sea. The reflection on the sea side gives them the direction, they follow the wetness of the huge water mass ahead, and they crawl towards the sea." I was explaining, they would be exposed to the real turtle hatchlings coming out of the sand.

We now crossed the green part of the beach, no more seaside grasses or any other vegetation was there on the white sand, the sea line was clearly visible, the children on seeing the white line ran towards the sea, they were highly excited.

We moved around on the beach, the beach was calm, the hatchlings were yet to emerge from the sand, our attention was diverted to the joy of the children, they found the crabs called Pavana Kankada in Odia, the small swift crabs of the sea shore. These crabs are very swift, they move as the living animals move towards them. They were found in large numbers just at the sand line which is touched by the water, not found few meters away from that, or inside the sea. We looked at them they were moving fast. Waves were breaking on the shore and the water comes a few feet inside. These crabs were dwelling at that line, when the children move towards them. They moved quickly away from the children. Ellie, the youngest member of our group chased those crabs. The crabs were looking at her steps. In that moonlit night we could see the movement of the crabs clearly, and the torch light with us was following the crab. Elli came closer to a big crab, around 3 cm long. It was keenly looking at Elli, its protruding eyes came out of the resting place. The crabs have a strange eye form. The eyes are not fixed into the body, rather they are attached to the main frame through an arm which has some movement, its colour was light brown, some whitish thick lines were drawn over the relatively flat top, its flippers were slim and looked almost transparent. As she came closer the crab stopped its movement, remained on its belly, watched Elli. She at once ran at it, but it moved faster, took a quick side movement, dodged Elli, but Elli ran after it. It finally ran here and there, and as she came close it slid into a small hole. It was a strange phenomenon, one could see numerous small holes on the waterfront, and these holes were made by these crabs, for their shelter. A big wave came, Elli ran for cover, the tide water covered the place. Ellie's footsteps were erased, the crabs hole was filled with water, the bubbles came out. Once the water retreated, the crab again surfaced, many other crabs also surfaced, the game continued.

A group of young people came from the darkness, they introduced themselves. The group were from the nearby villages. All young boys, aged between 15 to 20, the group was formed to protect the beach during the nesting period till the hatchlings comes out. The job paid them some money, apart from their regular income from fishing activities, they get some wages out of this work. They wore half pants and shirts or T-shirts, all dark in colour, thinly built, but were swift in feet. I looked at the moon, the moon had gone up, the night was getting deeper, the waves were breaking constantly.

The message of the first turtle emergence came; we could see the wavy movement of torchlight on the sea beach, the signal to reach the spot. Instantly we ran towards the spot. The sand was not in a heaped position. It was difficult to distinguish this land from other areas there, only visible difference was the minor depression there. Three four broken egg shells were lying nearby. We looked keenly, there was little movement. A small black stone was at the centre of the movement, and a tiny small black stone was getting constantly pushed upwards. Little golden and white sand particles were glued to two sides, also on the frontal depression little sand particles were also deposited. I looked keenly, the nose was like the beak of hawk. The beak was sharp, curved inwards a little, just above two nostrils were fixed. Its full head was visible now, small hexagonal with darker outer lines were marked over its body and head. Some were bigger, some smaller, and then the neck came. Many small hexagonal structures. The size of the hexagonal was very small, much smaller than the design on the head, the head portion was lighter in colour, the neck was much darker.

Now many heads were emerging from the sand, it was a strange phenomenon, the sand, the black rose petals were unfolding. The buds were opening slowly, it was like a flower opening in a super fast motion. Slowly the bodies came out, the sand particles were getting pushed away, many hatchlings were trying to come out at one time. The sand particles were falling from their heads. Their front flippers were visible now, they were moving the front flippers and the bodies were coming out of the sand with inward pressure created by them through their flippers. It was a superb event, all the hatchlings were trying to come out of the hole at one time, the eggs were laid in a half feet radius hole, so the hole was the centre of the movement. Dozens of heads now appeared on the sand mass, each hatchling was trying for space, their bodies were getting pushed up, some were half way upwards, some three fourths outside, some in the verge of emerging, turtle after turtle were coming out, with passage of every second. The second the scene was changing, many bodies were in the frame, their eyes, their bodies, their flipper, their full bodies now clearly visible. Some turtle hatchlings were now fully out of the hole, they now started dispersing in all direction. Their movement looked like a fire show, the particles in a show were dispersing radially out, in all direction. As the hatchlings started moving away, the circle got bigger and bigger. The hatchlings were crawling on their belly down, they were moving their flippers constantly. The movement gives them a push upward, they pushed the sand backward and they went forward, wait a little and then push the sand backward and go forward again and the movement went on. Slowly and slowly the hatchlings were dispersing, the centre was now diluted; there were many new comings, many formations were created. Sometimes they were in group, looked like the hatchlings touching each other's hands, sometimes two friends were strolling, however here no one was waiting for the companion, sometimes one hatchling was crawling over the other. The outer layer was now taking curve, their heads were now aligned towards the sea side, and the ones which were away from the sea now changed their position and were crawling towards the sea.

It was a very strange event, how they knew the location of the sea was strange. The hatchlings now almost formed a mat, the mat was moving towards the sea. At the sea front there was little depression due to the wave action, the hatchling now arrived at the water line, their movement was constant, no change in movement due to the wetness of the sand. A big wave came, washed the one line at the front into the sea, many were also wet. Water just touched them, and they continued their journey into the sea. Irregular lines were drawn on the wet sand, slowly and slowly all the hatchlings melted into the dazzling water, they reached the laps of the mother sea. I looked at the sea, waves after waves were crashing onto the white coast line, no sign of the turtle hatchlings any more, the moon was dancing with the new guests on the sea waters, the turtle generation was going ahead.

I became a bit emotional then, the event was creating a sense – a strange one. I witnessed the history, the evolution of a race from so close, and looked at my daughter. She was having a torch, she was trying to find out the turtle hatchlings which could be left out. She was carrying the hatchling to the sea waters, then releasing there, and as the hatchling was getting drifted away, her eyes were following it. The torch light was following the path, slowly and slowly the hatchling go into deep water, and with a bigger wave its presence was hidden from our eyesight. After the departure of the rescued hatchlings she came back again, searched for the stray hatchlings, rescued them once again and then released them into the waters. The moon was now much high in the sky, the night was denser, the sound of the sea was constant. The turtle hatchlings were coming frequently, pits after pits were now getting active. We watched many, my daughter went on rescuing the stray hatchlings, she had unbound energy, the hatchlings had to be protected, had to be rescued and the time went on. Suddenly I remembered the rhymes, the loved ones, I listened it so frequently.

Spin and whirl
My sister name Gaauri
Your sister name Shaauri
No your sister name Gaauri
No my sister name Shaauri
We swim the river
The boatman will rescue
Spin and whirl.

Ellie, my small daughter of three was constantly rescuing the hatchlings. She had unbound energy, her tiny legs were not tiring. Our eyes tired, she was singing the rhymes, the hatchlings turned to her friends, she was singing for them –

Flowers of ridge gourd blossomed
Flowers of cucumber blossomed
Little rat requested
Keep a fistful of rice

The turtle hatchlings were coming out, blooming like the flowers of Jahni (ridge gourd) which blooms in the night only.

I looked at her; moon rays were falling on her little frail body. At the back drop of the trees she was running and running, tirelessly, the little legs were not stopping, the joy of giving back the life was getting her immense satisfaction, giving her unending energy.

Turtle at Gahirmatha

One day, to see the real turtle world and understand it too, I listened so much of the turtle kingdom at Gahirmatha. Olive Ridley sea turtle is the prominent one, I collected materials before hand. To me, one of the most interesting events associated with the turtle nesting was the discovery of the nesting site itself, rather true scientific recording of the site. Bhitarkanika mangrove at its backdrop, the nesting site was known to the outside world along with the crocodiles in the channels of the mangrove forest...

The Olive Ridley turtles migrate en-mass from the south of Sri Lankan coast in the Indian Ocean, arrive in the shallow waters of continental shelf of Odisha coast for mating, and subsequent nesting. The whole process including the hatching of the eggs takes approximately eight months and is spread between October to May. The mating of turtles takes place between November to January, when they float for a prolonged period in the surface waters, thus making them vulnerable from fishing nets and trawlers. The nesting takes place between January to May, each female turtle lay on an average 100 eggs in the sandy beaches. The turtle eggs are white in colour, round in shape with diameter of about 4.0 centimeters. The shell is soft leathery and, looks more like a table tennis ball or a ping pong ball. The incubation period takes between 45 to 60 days depending upon the temperature.

Findings the Beach

Dr. H. R. Bustard, an Australian, a crocodile specialist of FAO/UNDP and a renowned discoverer, came to Bhitarkanika during 1975 in search of crocodiles. Odisha, at that time was infamous for the crocodiles in the distributaries of Mahanadi, Brahmani and other river system. The more notorious area was the dark forests of the Bhitarkanika but not much was known about the crocodile habitat there. When he came to Bhitarkanika, the mangrove forest was dense, innumerable number of inland channels criss crossed the entire area, the location was one of the best places for the crocodiles to live in. He searched and found many crocodiles. He proposed, in case the crocodiles are given appropriate protection, the population would increase considerably in the favourable habitat. He started his mission-protection of crocodiles of Bhitarkanika. All supported the project and the crocodile rearing and breeding centre was established with initial captive strength of 96 crocodiles. The number increased over periods, crossed 1000 number during 2006, a phenomenal growth and astounding success of conservation programme. After all that time he realised the potential of the crocodile protection.

During his research period, he noticed the mass turtle nesting called aribada, on the coastlines, which was located beyond the Bhitarkanika forests. He suggested for turtle conservation, and the State Government agreed and declared the place as a Gahirmatha sanctuary for higher protection of turtles.

Gahirmatha beach history

Gahirmatha coast, a land mass of around 30-35 km of shoreline extending between Dhamara river mouth to Barunei, the mouth of river Hansua, is famous for mass nesting of Olive Riddle turtles. Since ancient times, the erstwhile ruler of Kanika was collecting tax at the rate Rs.1.25 per boat load of turtle eggs. The turtle eggs used to find their way to markets at Calcutta. Adult turtles too were captured in the high sea and were marketed in Calcutta in earlier days, not too far back from now. The local people knew about such turtle nesting since long, before actual scientific recording by Dr. Bustard. But little was known to the outside world; and due to the great effort of Dr. Bustard, this massive phenomenon was known to the outside world. The government responded, research on turtle nesting started, information of turtle nesting was compiled. The turtle nesting found to occur not only at Habalikhati, the place where the research scholar was stationed, rather it was spread throughout the beach starting from Barunei to Dhamra mouth. But records of such mass nesting was hardly found, even during British India period, and just after that there was no report about such mass phenomenon. The existence of such a massive rookery came to lime light only during early 1970s.

Turtles in the Wild

There are seven species of marine turtles in the world, they are- i) the Flat back, ii) Green sea turtle, iii) Hawksbill, iv) Kemp's Ridley, v) Leatherback,

vi) Loggerhead and vii) Olive Ridley, out of which five species inhabit the Indian waters, and most significantly four varieties of marine turtles – the leatherback, the green turtles, the Hawksbill turtles and lastly the Olive Ridley turtles, frequent the coasts of Odisha. All the four varieties found in the Odisha coast are included in the Schedule-I of the Wild Life (Protection) Act and listed endangered under IUCN "Red Data Book". These turtles are also protected under the Convention on International Trade in Endangered species of Wild Flora and Fauna & also under the Convention on Migratory Species.

The Olive Ridley sea turtles, regarded as the most profuse sea turtle in the world, well known for their mass nesting, live in tropical warm waters of Pacific and Indian oceans. Their habitats spread in the waters of India, Arabia, Japan and Micronesia south to the southern Africa, Australia and New Zealand. In the Atlantic Ocean waters their presence has been found in western coast of Africa, coasts of northern Brazil, Suriname, Guyana, French Guiana, Venezuela. In the Caribbean sea they are found in the far north as Peurto Rico. In the Pacific Ocean they are found in the Galapagos island, from Chile to the Gulf of California. The Olive Ridleys are generally found in shallow marine waters with depth range 22-55 metre, mostly within 15 kilometers from the shore, they occasionally occur in open oceanic waters.

The Olive Ridley, deriving its name from the Olive Green heart shaped carapace of the adult, is the smallest marine turtle. Adult have an average size 2-3 feet in length, weigh between 35-60 kilograms. The adult female is heavier than the males, the turtle is primarily carnivorous, mainly feeds on shrimps, crabs, fishes and crustaceans. The carapace is heart shaped and is characterized by four pairs of infra-marginal scutes on the bridge, two pairs of pre-frontals and between five to nine lateral scutes per side – a unique characteristics of Olive Ridley. Each side of the carapace has 12-14 marginals. The head is medium sized, broad and triangular in shape, concave sides, and the snout is short. The colour of the carapace is grayish green olive in colour, sometime little reddish due to growing algae on it. The bridges and hingless plastron appear greenish white in younger ones and creamy yellow in older members. The mature adult males have thicker and longer tails than females which is used for copulation. The hooked claw on the front flippers of males allow them grasp the females during copulation, and also they have longer and tapered carapace where as the female has round dome like carapace. The males have more concave plastron – an adaption for pairing with females.

The Olive Ridley turtle hatchlings are dark grey in colour, with a pale yolk scar on the bottom, the hatchlings appear dark when wet, the carapace length is around 37-50 mm and weighs between 12 to 23.3 grams. The hatchlings as well as juveniles have scattered posterior marginals which smoothens with age.

Reproductive homing –
Tendency to return to the same area

The Olive Ridley sea turtle return to Gahirmatha beaches during successive years for nesting. They return to the same nesting place where they have been hatched, this reproductive homecoming is a common feature of the marine turtles. During the migration generally the males comes to the coastal waters earlier than the females and leaves after mating period is over, but the female remains in sallow water for a longer period for egg laying.

The Olive Ridley sea turtles are sighted by fishermen of Sri Lanka of the coast of Jaffna, which is located in the N-E corner of Sri Lankan Islands, during their northern movement to the Bay of Bengal during the months between September to November. The mass movement of turtles are also sighted off Pondicherry coast. Also mass movement of Olive Ridley sea turtles have been noticed towards Odisha coast in the vicinity of Tamilnadu and Andhra Pradesh. After 2 months from their shifting at Sri Lankan waters the mass nesting takes place generally after two months. The Olive Ridley turtles don't follow any organized migration from breeding areas to foraging areas after breeding. The adult male turtle returns the feeding ground during mid season as most of the females have already been mated.

The ridleys have a strong tendency to return to the same area in every season for mating and egg laying, called reproductive homing. The phenomenon looks strange, why the turtles return to Odisha coast instead of going to Tamilnadu, Andhra Pradesh, or West Bengal. Apparently no conspicuous sea features are identified that attract the sea turtles to the Odisha coast, there are no visual terrains like mountains, streams, etc inside sea, still the turtles come to the Odisha coast. Their reaching the coast itself looks so strange. The Gahirmatha coast on the eastern coast on the Bay of Bengal is dreamland of the sea turtles, the expanse, approximately a 30 km sandy stretch, is from Ekakulanasi muhana at Maipura river mouth and Barunei Muhan at the mouth of Hansua River. The mass nesting of the Olive ridley sea turtles generally occur in the 12 km coast line stretching between Habalighati and Ekakulanasi, the turtles do not go beyond Ekakulanasi. The coast line in other part, towards the Bhadrakh and Balasore district side, are semi-circular and the sea coast is muddy. The other egg laying beaches in the same area are also the islands just near the coast like, the Wheeler Island, Babu Bali, Duduma Bali, etc. The reproductive homing has one most important component which is finding suitable nest site; the soil quality plays a major role, the soil of Gahirmatha rookery with texture quality to hold sufficient moisture and air.

The turbid influence of rivers like Hansua, Gobari, Mahanadi are deflected northwards during the turtles nesting season which influence the colour of water and also determine the degree of its influence. However, the bottom topography of the sea just in front of the mass nesting beach, is partly muddy and partly sandy, which turns completely muddy towards Balasore districts side, creates a transitional zone, a conspicuous mark in the eastern coast, probably it provide clue to the sea turtle to identify this rookery. The reason of the mass arrival to the area is linked to sufficient availability of food, apart from the proper shape. Gahirmatha is located at the southern extremities of the Bhitarkanika mangrove forest, though disjoined, on the coast of Bay of Bengal and the rivers flowing through the mangrove forests discharges detritus, a good feeding material of the varieties of fishes, to sea, enriching the shallow water of Gahirmatha, creating a fertile breeding ground for the planktons, crustaceans and varieties of fishes, all are the feed of the omnivorous Olive Ridley sea turtle. The plentiful phytoplanktons, zooplanktons, small fishes are the food of adult and hatchlings too. The beach, being secluded, due to its location, the Bhitarkanika mangrove forests are hostile for habitation, the beach shallow too, thus an ideal place for turtle egg laying. The mass nesting usually takes place at Ekakulanasi, which is divided into Nasi-I and Nasi-II) Babubali (Long Wheeler's island). Also mass nesting occurs at Pentha, located at the southern end of the Gahirmatha coast.

The Sundarbans and the Godavari basin also have good beaches, still the turtles are not preferring that area; in fact the Sundarbans is not far away still the turtles prefer to the beach of Gahirmatha. The Sundarbans, though quite big, still does not have long sandy beaches; rather it is full with small muddy islands. The turtles, for their nesting, need a particular texture of sand, which is probably not available in Sundarbans. It is a fact that Gahirmatha is the safe haven for the egg laying turtles. It has the right component of sand, provide adequate protection to the marine turtles in water as well as in land too, to attract the turtles for egg laying. On analysis, it was found that the texture of the sand is important for laying of the eggs.

Even though Gahiramatha is the paradise, still stray nesting have been reported at the coast of Tamilnadu, Kerala and Andhra Pradesh. Some Olive ridley turtle population too goes towards Sundarbans, East Asian countries, Indonesia.

In Odisha, the mass nesting sites at Devi river mouth was discovered during 1981, and the third mass nesting site at Rushikulya river mouth was discovered quite late, only during 1994. Sporadic nesting too have been observed in bigger sandy beaches all along the coastline of Odisha. Also nesting sites have been found in sand pits on the left bank of Mahanadi, coastline from Puri to Chilika, beach near Malud on Chilika coast, etc.

The turtle nesting in Devi river mouth has been reduced now, the reason is that around the river mouth, the land is not protected, so it might be the one of the reason for less turtle nesting there. The legal status of the sanctuary has not been extended to Devi river mouth areas and there were a lot of turtle casualties due to trawlers movements, this probably compels the turtle to go to other areas. This nesting site changed significantly, a new mouth has opened after the super cyclone of 1999. In 1999-2000, during mass nesting season approximately 25,000 number of turtles emerged for nesting beyond Gundalva village side, towards mouth of Kadua river, a distributary of Devi river. In Gahirmatha, there are turtle hits due to the trawlers plying there, but the number is significantly less, not alarming to compel turtles to abandon the area.

The mass nesting beach at Rushikulya river mouth, in the district of Ganjam, spreads over six kilometers, one kilometer north of Rushikulya river mouth to beach front of Kantiagad villege. The beach width is 100 meter on an average. During 2000-01 approximately 1.59 lakh turtles emerged for nesting in this beach.

The turtle nesting behaviour and other related phenomenon are complex, many studies were carried out on the turtles of Bhitarkanika. Arribada, the mass arrival is most spectacular. The detail account of the turtle related activities is collected from different sources.

Arribadas

The mass nesting of sea turtles, called "arribada" by scientific community, is a Spanish term, meaning mass arrival, a familiar word to understand turtle behaviour. This mass arrival is probably a mechanism against predation, where the predators are confused over the arrival of such huge population, and even if some are predated upon, sufficient number of sea turtles are still available for reproduction. Gahirmatha is the place where maximum number of mass nesting is found at a particular place in the whole earth, a strange incident. About 90% Olive Ridley sea turtles of India visit the beaches of Odisha, which is again 50% of the total world turtle population of the same turtle. So, the importance of mass nesting in Gahirmatha is well understood, after all the coasts of Odisha is the paradise of the Olive Ridley sea turtles.

Outside Gahirmatha in Odisha, arribadas too occur at Nancite and Ostional beaches of Coast Rica; Chacocente and La Flor beaches in Nicaragua and in Mexico one at Playa Escobilla in Oaxaca.

In the coast of Gahirmatha the random nesting occur throughout the year, the maximum usually continue between December to May. In this period there are 1-2 large arribadas, the first arribada happen between December to Mid February and the second occur between March to mid April. In the large arribadas around 10,000 or more numbers of nests occur in a night for 10 km stretch beach, generally continue for a week and mostly take place around half moon period, but occasionally continues up to the full moon. Few mini arribadas too occur in between for 1-4 days. During the mass nesting season, the average width of the beach remains at maximum, thus providing room to the nesting females and sand temperature remains suitable for egg lying. If the beach is not adequately formed, then the arribada do not occur and turtles return without emerging to the beach. It was recorded that almost half a millions of Olive Ridley sea turtles nest at Gahirmatha between January and May every year.

Moon phase seasonality of arribada:- Moon has a significant effect on arribada. During the first and third quarter of moon, the tidal rise and fall is minimum, the smaller neap tide take place during the seventh day from the full moon, new moon too; during that period the tide starts going up after sun set, thus enabling the turtles to approach the beach with ease. During the mass nesting time usually strong off shore wind blows from land to sea.

Temperature on migration:- The surface temperature of sea water has a lead role to play and is the most possible cause of seasonal migration, and a marginal temperature difference of 1 degree to 2 degree celsius has a marked effect on arribada. At the beginning the temperature of sea water in winter remains at 27 degree celsius during November and at the end of winter it remains at 25 degree celsius during February and the temperature during the early March remains 27 degree celsius. The temperature might be the most possible cause of seasonal migration.

Food:- The turtle remains for a quite long period in the Gahiramtha waters, sufficient nutrient food is a necessity to this large mass, the coastal water support good fishery during the entire period. After the hatching, the peak hatchling period occur between months of March to May, the turtle hatchlings feed on carps, clamps and many small fishes.

Gahiramtha Beach Characteristics:- The low salinity at Gahirmatha coastal waters besides other factors is a major reason for the formation of turtle rookery there. In the Gahiramtha area the low salinity in the waters is caused by the influx of water from large river systems like Brahmani, Baitarani and Dhamra at the northern most end and Mahanadi and its distributaries at the southern most end.

Due to strong monsoon wind blowing from South to North direction, which is from sea face to landward, between July-August the beaches get eroded due to high tidal action. However, the wind direction changes from the months of October-November, the wind blows from North to South, which is from land to sea. The sand gets deposited and the beach area gets rebuilt.

The beach remains ready for nesting from mid December-January onwards. The scientific community believe that the olive ridley sea turtle can sense the chemical change of the rookery.

The turtle nesting sites around the world located at different river mouths, certainly have a low profile. The gradient of the beach is gentle towards sea waters, above high tide mark, free of debris; and generally the turtle nests on relatively flat mid beach zone. The sand in the Gahiramtha beaches contain fine black silica, the degraded rock forms of slates and shells which makes the sand form remain harder after compactation, thus maintains high moisture necessary for incubation of eggs.

In the Gahiramtha beaches, most of the beaches have sand size in the range of 0.5 to 0.2 mm, a thin sand type. The Gahirmatha sand is usually is a mixture of fine black and brown colour silica sands, it has a good capacity to hold water and maintain adequate temperature. The nesting sand is free of coarse sand particles, pebbles too, which are potentially hazardous to the eggs and new hatchlings. The turtle looks for proper nesting site on the beach, removes a layer of sand by thrusting its body or by head, then it evaluates the condition, its throat remains pressed against the freshly exposed sand. The females can follow a temperature gradient from the sea surf to a wet beach zone, then to dry beach zone.

The turtle makes a cavity with depth of 25-50 cm below the beach surface, there is very small fluctuation of temperature, may be between 1-2 degree centigrade where as on the surface the temperature fluctuation is around 20 degree celsius.

Mating:- Usually mating occurs near to the nesting sites, copulating pairs have been reported over 1,000 kilometer away from the nearest beach. Many researches were conducted, the one from Coast Rica reported that copulating pairs observed off the coast couldn't be responsible for fertilization of tens of thousands of gravid female turtles which implies that significant number mating too takes place elsewhere at other time of the year.

Usually the turtles mass around the nesting beaches approximately two months before nesting, but the period vary throughout its ranges all over the world. At the beginning, the turtles come under water from their forage grounds to the breeding grounds, starts coming to sea surface during their mating period in November which sometimes continues up to January. Big mass of copulating pairs are usually found swimming passively in the surface currents. The mating course continue for several hours, many a times for days together; during the mating hours the copulating pairs generally remain indifferent to external obstructions and continue with their act. The mating occur in low waters, very close to the nesting sites, sometimes even at a short distance of around 50 mtrs away from the shore. The mating zone in the Gahirmtha sea is usually extended up to 4-5 km from the beach. During that time they make pairs, float on surface water for prolonged periods, and don't shy away from the intruders – the turtles used to dive as an intruder approaches them. The turtle nesting used to take place approximately after 45-51 days from mating date, and the egg laying usually begins from February. The turtles remain in the sea around Gahirmatha up to April, and return to deep sea after that.

Many a times prominent mating scars have been seen on the marginal laminae of some nesting females, the males during copulation try to strongly grapple the female using its fore flipper resulting in mating scars mostly the central laminae; and sometimes on the neck of the nesting female, which is due to biting by strong males while they attempt to mount on a female in the sea water.

There are following distinct phases of nesting process:

1. Parting from the surf
2. Search for nesting site
3. Body packing
4. Nest cavity digging
5. Egg Laying
6. Nest hole covering
7. Nest Packing
8. Camouflaging
9. Return to the sea

Nesting behaviors:- The sea turtles are choosy about the loction. The nesting females swim parallel to the seashore and come very close before their emergence to the beach. The gravid females approach the beach, thousands and thousands of turtles congregate around the nesting beaches, innumerable heads can be seen in the waters around the beaches of Gahiramatha. Usually the floating turtles lay eggs within next 2-3 days. Many a times the females raise their heads, look at the nesting beach, the turtle prefer a well-formed beach and avoid eroded part.

The mother turtles come during the evening in normal situations. If the sky is overcast and weather is cool then the turtles might come during the day times to lay the eggs in the beach. When they come for laying the eggs during the evening, they don't like biotic interference, mostly return to waters and wait for suitable time. As the tides rise, the turtles come closer, the high tide pushes the gravid females towards the beach. The turtle come in contact with the sandy beach after the tide water goes back. The turtles remains in a stranded position for a short while, the muzzle is pressed to the wet sand, the fore flopper remains in resting position. This is a crucial period; the turtle remain sensitive to disturbances on the sea beach, returns immediately to the sea if any obstructions are caused by humans or animals. Apart from biotic interference, artificial illumination affects the turtle behaviour; it comes towards the lighted portion leaving the nesting beach behind and do not lay eggs. The turtle nesting usually begins from one side of the beach and extends to other parts continuously. The turtles come to the beach during high tide, they crawl to the appropriate spot in the beach, the first turtle nesting generally starts during mid-night.

The turtle has a characteristic reptilian movement. The diagonal limbs move together, they make zigzag course while traveling from high water marks to nesting site but is straight from surf to high water lane. The turtle climb the beach in a series of forward movements using the flippers followed by shorter pauses. During the forward movement the head of the turtle remained low sometimes making furrows on the sand. The gravid female takes between 9-54 minutes to find a nesting site. The turtle doesn't choose washed beaches, avoid hard grounds, the softness of sand is assessed by flippers. The gravid female many a times walk over the other nesting female in search of appropriate nesting ground which usually have low gradient. The nests in Gahirmatha are usually 4-5 mtr away from the high water line.

Body pit and Pit digging:- The mother turtle after coming to the beach dips its nose into the sand, knows the right temperature and humidity, and confirms whether the sand is clean or not whether – small woods are inside or not. Then the turtle tries to find out the best place where the sand is clean, there is no external matter is inside. Finding a suitable place, the turtle makes very shallow body pits between 9-12 cm deep. The turtle stops on its journey, keeps the front flipper together in front of the head, separated from each. The front flippers moves simultaneously and sand is thrown backwards vigorously and the wet sand below gets exposed. The turtle rotates by moving the body left or right using all four flippers and the body pit is formed.

Pit digging is a long phenomenon, in which the rear flippers work alternatively in quick successions. In one cycle a flipper remains firmly pressed into the ground, rotates 2-3 times to loose the sand below, then scope out a handful of sand on to the surface; then the first rear flipper stops. The turtle rests for around 10-15 seconds, then the posterior part moves from one side to the other side of the cavity keeping the digging rear flipper directly over the chamber and other flipper supports the body, and again the other rear flipper performs same job and the total process is repeated many a times. The pit digging time varies between 6-35 minutes. As the egg chamber gets deepened, the turtle raises its frontal portion upward along with front flippers to increase the downward inclination of the lower part so that the back flippers can reach further depth and the pit digging continues till the rear flippers are unable to remove further sand from the cavity. After that the turtle removes sand from the chamber side, makes it very broad at the base, the egg pit resembles a broad flask on its completion, depth is around 31-32 cm. The base permit all the eggs to remain in a particular depth range, develop within a particular range of temperature too.

Once it digs a hole, in case it is dragged to another place, then instead of digging another pit, it would come to the same pit for egg laying. After pit digging the turtle takes rest for a long period, the tail and the cloaca remain at the centre of the egg chamber, the posterior part of carapace completely covers the egg pit. The cloaca is then lowered a little into the chamber and egg extrusion starts, the eggs are laid singly or in groups of 2 or 3 at one time. The total time for egg laying is between 12-36 minutes. During egg laying the hind flipper remains curved and the head and neck are retracted and bends down. During egg laying, the eggs fall in intervals, in one go three eggs fall. Generally the turtles lay between 100 to 130 numbers of eggs, but sometimes they lay less number of eggs, and some times the number shoots to around 180 numbers. During ovi-position, secretion comes from salt glands located at the corner of the eyes, the secretion helps in removing the sand particles from the eyes of the turtle, also the turtle takes heavy breathing. After egg laying the females take brief rest of 2- 3 minutes and then starts covering the eggs using its flippers, at that time the head points down and almost resting on sand, then it packs the chamber by thumping its belly, thumping sound is audible from a distance. Then the turtle fills up the body pits, and the nests are camflouged using both the front flippers. The sands are thrown on to the nest site and pseudo body pits are created. In camflouging it makes a false crawl at some other place. So if somebody tries to find, he will not be able to locate the pit as the turtle has also made marks at other areas. The time taken for the camflouging of the body pit takes between 1-11 minutes and the concealment of nest is between 2-10 minutes.

After camflouging the turtle returns to the sea, the return journey takes between 1-35 minutes, the the turtle stops in between and takes heavy breathing and reaches the water and after 2-3 waves the turtle slowly disappear into the sea. If its direction is changed, still the turtle will turn towards sea side and will enter into the sea waters, it knows the position of the sea by listening the sounds of the wave, seeing a lighter surface. The total time spend by a female olive ridley turtle on the beach for egg laying varies between 55-155 minutes.

Eggs and turtle hatchings:- The egg of the Olive Ridley looks white or pinkish white, is flexible and has leathery shell, the shape resembles a table tennis ball, with the diameter of 3.6-4.76 cm and the weight varies between 23.5- 34.01 gm.

The incubation period for the eggs laid during winter months are more than the eggs laid during the summer months. The average incubation for the egg laid during the months of January, February, March are 64 days, 58days and 50 days respectively. On an average, the eggs are hatched generally after forty five days.

It has also been observed that the temperature at incubation period has direct bearing on sex ratio, for Olive Ridley sea turtle eggs incubated at 31-32^{0}C produces only females, eggs incubated at a temperature 28^{0}C or less produce only males whereas at temperature of 29- 30^{0}C hatchlings of both sexes (40% male and 60% female) are produced.

The turtle young emerge from the egg cell by rupturing the egg cell with their egg-teeth, the baby teeth disappear after few days. The turtle hatchlings takes around 8-24 hrs to come out of the cell, emerge mostly during night, but occasionally during the cool periods of the day like during early dawn or late afternoon. From the same nest, majority of hatchlings come out during the first night followed by small groups in subsequent nights. The emergence success of hatchlings are around 92% and the egg hatching success is around 85-90 per cent.

Visit to the Turtle nesting site-

After getting a fair idea on turtle behaviour I proceeded once to watch the turtle nesting and we started from Gupti, moved in the creeks, the river Mahipura, a distributary of river Brahmani, was widening near the sea. Now the waves were turning bigger, the last village hazed in the horizon, the country boats sailing inside the creek waters vanished in the narrow creeks.

After the brief journey in the waters, we were closing in to turtle nesting site in the northern tip of the Gahirmatha beach on the wheeler island portion, the water was shallow, the movement of the bigger boat was turning to be more and more difficult, so the bigger mechanised boat anchored at closest point to the beach, on neck deep water, difficult to disembark at the depth. So to facilitate the disembarking a wooden ladder was lowered onto the sand and we disembarked using the ladder. The night was closing in, the horizon was getting darker, the white lines of the crashing waves on the beach were getting thinner, the sand was losing the colour and I looked at the beach. I was amazed, the beach was full with innumerable round structures, the dome shaped turtles appear like lotus leaves on the semi-white sands, black circular shapes all around. I looked keenly, one turtle was climbing over the other, and they were fighting to lay their eggs, scrambling for individual space. I looked around, turtles at my left, turtles at my right, turtles at my back, turtles at my front, innumerable turtles all around, the relatively white sand was turning black with the night fall, presence of innumerable turtles too. That beach in the wheeler island portion, as it appears in that dark evening, was almost two kilometers long, width may be 100 meters, not a really big breach. I got pressure on my left foot and looked at a medium sized turtle crossing my feet. I could not count the number, the turtles were coming, with each wave the number was swallowing.

The waves were nearing, many black turtles on the crest, the white surf was covering their body partly, they were swinging with the waves, trying to reach the beach sand. Sometimes the waves were crossing over their backs, next moment they peeped from the waters, hundreds and hundreds of turtles were floating in the shallow waters. A big wave came from the sea, it lifted many struggling turtles, the crest rose and the waterfront rushed towards the dry sand, the black spots went into hiding in the white wave lines, next moment the wave crashed, many turtles reached the shore, pushed further towards the sandy surface. Now many turtles on the last waterline, their body partly on water, heads protruded upwards, front flippers were stretched forward, they were pushing the sand inward to crawl forward, like a very young baby was crawling for the first time. Their movement appeared like the synchronised movements of a modern dance troupe, the dancers all sat on the ground, all moved on their knees, the shield on their back, hiding them protecting them from air attacks, they stopped a little, all looked up, took a breather then pushed forward, a stealth movement of an attacking troop, the turtles were depicting a war game. The turtles were advancing from the waterline, I looked at one turtle, keenly notice each movement of its, now the fore flippers were well stretched, its colour appeared like diamond shaped black spots were organised symmetrically alongside few thick grey lines, the flippers were thin skins, wide and triangular at the end, jointed to a flexible strong limb which connects to the main body near the neck. The look was more like a flag attached to a thick rubber tube. The front flippers, each was around one feet long, the back flippers, a little shorter than the front one, each was around seven inches long. The neck is positioned between the two fore flippers, the neck skin was loose and flexible, light grey in colour on which smaller black-green spots spread out, and the head was embodied into the thick neck muscle. The frontal body was connected to the thick carapace, the view from the front appeared like a curvy bracket with middle elongated upward and face down. The head was small, from top triangular and a parrot like strong curvy beak elongated outward which was needle sharp, irregular olive green polygonal spots with white borders connected to each other centered around a 8-9 armed polygon, appeared all over the head, and between that the black eyes somewhat elongated towards the inner side, popped a little. The small nostrils were located below the eyes, much close to the beak. The turtles were pressing their fore flippers into the sand, gave them inward push, the opposite action balanced their weight and pushed them forward. The action was now more like a swimmer, the hands stretched, the palms and the hands pushed the water backward, the hands too moved backward, now more close to the body, again the hands were brought to the front, the hand pushed the water backward again, the body moved forward.

Slowly and slowly the tide was rising, the wave size was increasing, the water was covering the higher lands, the beach size was shrinking, so also the egg laying space for the turtles. Gradually the sky turned slate dark, no sign of moon, the bright stars were twinkling at the top like glow worms of Bhitarkanika waters in the nights of monsoon, covering the entire length of the sky; I had a strange feeling then, standing in the solitude of nature, no sound of the madding crowd around, the waves of the massive sea in front were infusing strange feelings, own presence in the natural theatre. I felt like standing in a vast expanse of sand, no end, unlimited, not on the small beach of Gahirmatha, surrounded by water all-around; the sea, the sky, the sand all were unlimited, unending. The vastness of the sound of the sea waves was passing through my body, still I looked at the beach in the dim light of the stars, they were faintly visible, their water washed body was shining in the stars, the semi black sand was giving the contrast, and the domes were moving continuously.

I looked at a turtle, it was taking rest a little during its onward movement, the beak and the frontal portion was covered with fine black white sand particles, some sand also covered part of the eyes, the nose was partly covered too, the beak was resting on the sand, fore flippers close to the body, the passive look in the body. Then it moved forward and raised its head. I could watch it more closely, the nose is facing upward, the loosened skin hangs down the neck, just below the beak, the green grayish white skin was shining, it came forward, ignored me, and moved further, then dipped its head a little into the sand. The frontal portion of the beak was dipped into the sand, eyes downward, and the fore flippers expanded fully and then it started further and after a distance stopped, it had found out the proper nesting place, was preparing body pit. It moved, positioned itself, then started removing sand and threw it away with force.

I looked around, not a single inch of space on the beach, crowds of turtles like innumerable human heads in large festival, all the remotest corners were covered too, all places were occupied by egg laying turtles, some were laying eggs, some were digging the nests, some were comflouging.

I looked around, three turtles were laying eggs close to each other. Their heads were touching each other almost, a geometrical shape; the three arms of the equilateral triangle, their sizes were almost similar. The turtles were not big, small sized marine turtles – 2 to 2½ feet long, little oval shaped, the head was coming out from the carapace at one end, the back erupting a little upwards at the middle, and when it walks, it appears more like a stone being carried away from one place to another, a small armoured vehicle moving on the lunar beaches. A nesting turtle was in front of me, its body was partly covered with loose sand, the fore flippers were almost hidden on sand, the neck and the head rest on the sand, the sand too scattered on the head, neck, the body was almost dry after a long exposure on the beach. It was sitting motionlessly on its nest, the appearance was more like a Pakshia, a type of non-foldable palm leaves umbrella used by the villagers during paddy cultivation in Odisha's coastal areas. Alongside, there were many egg laying turtles, all were sitting motionlessly, coming close I looked at the egg pit, it was around 1½ ft deep. Like an earthen pot, narrow at the mouth, wide at the centre and base, a perfect shape for the incubation of the eggs in the absence of the mother. One turtle was laying the eggs; deep breathing followed intermittently; after all the labour pain was there. The sounds of the waves were increasing, it was the high tide time, slowly our standing place was getting submerged. I looked at the breaking waves on the beach, glowing stars all over, to me it appeared as if the stars of the sky descended to the sea filled with the egg laying turtles. The plankton rich water was glowing, the planktons had fluorescence. They can glow in the night and when the waves break, the florescent part was exposed, it was so interesting. The crest line of the wave was glowing, the fairies of the sea were coming to the beach, the waves suddenly broke on the sand, the stars appeared all over the moist sand, the turtle land glowed in the dark night.

I looked at the other side, another mother turtle took a long breath, opened her mouth, the faint star light was reflected from her glowing eyes, pain was there, promise for the new comer was there, she came towards me walked over my legs. It was such a marvellous experience. Some turtles had finished the pit digging and were laying the eggs, no movements of the head; the whole body appeared like a stone, no movement of the hinge flippers too. The whole beach bore the sign of the egg laying turtles, so many transitory rocks on the whit black sand, the little high level land from the sea level, the liquid full with glittering planktons.

The fairy of the sea was chanting the good words for the mothers, *"Let you have the beautiful journey, let you have a beautiful sky, let your world be beautiful, I promise to make your world more beautiful."*

The fairy was promising, the voice was coming from the wave crests, the fairy queen was adorned with the glittering plankton jewels.

The stars of the sky started telling too,

"Your pain, our imagination, our effort go together, let you lay your eggs peacefully, I shall protect it with the greatest zeal. I promise, you will live longer, your new generation will move to the deep sea, establish kingdom there."

Another turtle was packing the pits with its back flipper, pushing the sand in to the egg filled hole, one flipper moved down, the other flipper moved up, the hole was filled up with sand. It moved a little, swung around the central back line, body moved like a pendulum, the left part hit the sand with a thump, then it moved up, the right part then hit the sand with another thump; then again the left part hit the sand with yet another thump and the process continued. Intermittently, she was taking rest. Breathing heavily, she was after all tired after a long egg laying session. I looked at the turtle, its head was laying still on the sand, and the little head was very small in comparison to the huge body, was somewhat circular at the tip which was protruding a little from the shell. The resting, tired turtle looked as a stone, flattened at the middle. The mother turtle would leave the eggs, never see it in future, the eggs need to be properly protected, after all each animal has the survival instinct, each animal has to build a better future for its new born, here the young new turtles would never know about their mother, the mother would never be identified, but the mother was trying her best to give its eggs the best protection. A turtle was returning, it had finished her egg laying, it was inching ahead using its strong flippers. The waves crashed on the sand, the flippers of the returning turtle get wet, but they moved ahead. A big wave came, I could see the surf in that dark night, the black dots disappeared, and the returning water pulled the turtle into the water, the dark protruding back slowly drowned in the water, no sign of the turtle. The mother turtle had finished her egg laying, the mother nature will nurture its eggs, on the golden sand the new turtles will take the first breath, they will find the sea and again the journey to life will take its own turn. Hours passed, the night was thick, the water was rising, the nesting beach was sinking, we retreated.

Threat to survival:- Threat to life occurs in all phases of their life of marine turtle from the eggs in the pit to the eggs, hatchlings, sub-adults and to adults too. Eggs are eaten by various lizards, birds like vultures, crows, etc. and mammals like raccoons, mongooses, feral cats, jackals, dogs, etc.

Few dogs are found in the turtle nesting areas of Gahirmatha, but there is no such residential population of the dogs, as no human habitat is nearby, usually they are not a menace. After 2-3 days of egg laying, the smell vanishes from the beach sand, even the dogs who is having a very good smelling capability can not locate the eggs in the absence of the smell.

The greatest single cause of Olive Ridley egg loss has been resulted from "arribadas" itself, the density of nesting females are so high that previously laid nests are unintentionally dug up many a times are eggs get destroyed.

After emergence from the pit, the hatchlings are predated upon by different crabs like the hermit crabs, different fishes, snakes, lizards, birds such as sea eagle, crows, vultures, frigate birds, etc., and different mammals like mongoose, feral cats and feral dogs. The black and brown head eagles often hunt the hatchlings in the sea while they swim on the water surface.

It is not on the beach, rather the biggest predation of the hatchlings take place after they actually enter into the water. They are eaten by varieties of fishes like barracuda, small sharks, etc. and bigger sea turtles like leather back turtle often predates on this hatchlings. In the deep waters of the sea, different species of shark like tiger shark and killer whales predate upon the juvenile and adult turtles and this predation occur throughout their entire life cycle. The characteristics behaviour pattern of the sea turtles such camflouging of nests, emergence of hatchling during night, production of large number of offsprings, diving of sea turtles into deep water at the shadow on the surface waters are considered as an adoption against predation, safeguarding the population.

The trawlers, while trawling for fish in the shallow waters prove to be biggest culprit for the deaths of egg laying turtles in Gahirmatha waters. During mating, the turtles are most vulnerable, they come to the water top, remain in pairs, do not move, float for long periods, heavy mortality of breeding turtles is due to incidental entanglement in the fishing and trawling nets during a mass nesting. When the trawlers move without proper gear called Turtle Excluder Devise (TED) or don't take adequate peculation, the turtles get caught in the trawler nets and get killed due to suffocation, after all the turtle breathes air, need to come to water surface for air, and can't remain under water for more than 45 minutes.

The changes in land use pattern of coastal areas and sea have direct bearings on the turtle nesting at many places. The casuarinas plantation near the beach, it is a threat, once the casuarinas establish, it changes entire beach topography, by its wide root growth, deposition of litter, thereby restricting the nesting place substantially. Much of nesting habitat around Devi mouth, also near the Chilika mouth have been lost due to lot of casuarinas plantation. The casuarinas should not be planted up to 100-150 meters from the high tide line

There are many conflicts between the protection staff and the fishermen. There are three categories of exclusive areas inside water as per the Odisha Marine Fishing Regulation Act. The water body up to 5 kilometers from off-shore is reserved for the traditional crafts, for mechanised crafts up to 15 meters length the operational area is beyond 5 kilometer off shore and the mechanized crafts over 15 meters length the operational area is beyond 10 km off shore. The Odisha shore is frequented by migrating fishermen from Bengal as well as from Andhra Pradesh where they fish between Bengal border to Dhamara and Andhra border to Puri respectively; Odisha fishermen mostly don't operate in the area.

Early Morning visit to the Beach: Next morning came, before the light falls on the beach we arrived, the golden sun was waiting for us, I never expected in my widest imagination to find a turtle there, the feast of the previous night would only have the signs of their presence. I was dumbfounded, turtle, turtle, turtles all around, where ever the eye goes, the eyes only caught the turtles. At that time, I was standing in the last section of the wheeler island beach, a vast one with darkish golden sand extended towards the south, and vanished at the horizon. On the back, the casuarinas trees are standing like silent observers, to witness the arrival of the distinguished guests on the shore. On the shore line, the marks of movement all over, criss crossing, overlapping, and the marks appeared like the tracks of a tractor, the grooves at the edge, the sand is pressed and at the direction of travel the grove was pressed downward, other side it was lifted a little on the edge and the flat strip remains at the centre of groves at both sides.

The beach was visible clearly, the turtles were in their body pits, no more arrival, the late comers of the night were laying the eggs, many turtles in their body pits, almost the entire body was below the beach sand except for the back, the back portion was more dug into the sand, the head on the other side was dug into the sand too, the eyes were wet, the sand particles were accumulated, except for eyes which were moist, other parts of the body were dry. The reddish and bigger morning sun was emerging from the calm waters of the sea, surprisingly no waves, previous night was full of waves, and the first light of the morning sun fell on the mother turtle; the eyes were closed, the body was still, the front flippers remained at the side, surprisingly the sands were not all over the body, only little on the head which was shining in the orange ray, the eyes opened, the morning sun get reflected from her eyes, the first light gave a reddish tinge to the soft neck, its head too, a great satisfaction in the face.

The sound of continuous loud thumping was coming from the turtle in front of me. In the absence of breaking waves, other disturbances, the sound was more clear. She was packing the egg pit, it took a little rest, then started packing the hole by thumping its lower body on the nest, her body was hitting the sand constantly, she was continuing in her job. I looked at the other side, one turtle was almost hiding in a shallow sand pit, its head was the only visible part, the rest part was covered with sand, thrown away by her while making her pit and by others too while they were digging their pits in the vicinity. I looked at the eggs, those were like table tennis balls, and to my greatest surprise, the eggs were soft, the shell was not hard. I picked up an egg, intentionally dropped one on the sand from three feet height, the egg did not break, rather it jumped like a sponge ball. The Mother Nature was kind; the mechanism was there to protect the eggs from fall. The eggs got hardened after a couple of minutes, after getting exposed to air, I could feel the hardness while touching the same egg after few minutes. I pepped to the nest, the nest was slowly getting filled up with the eggs, round, white pink eggs, one stacked over the other, the black white sand gets filled up in the space, not a single egg was broken or damaged.

The sun was a soft orange ball, the water was orange green, the morning beach was tinged orange too, the turtles also adorned with orange necklaces around their necks, and they were departing, the egg laying process was completed, I followed. The front flippers of the turtle gave deeper mark, the back flippers gave the fainter marks in the middle; sometimes it dips its head on to the sand and creating a deeper mark at intervals, on the front the calm waters and the sky merged to each other. It paused, dipped its beak into the wet sand, eyes looked down, then it looked forward, took a deep breath and moved forward. The sea front was only few feets away, no sign of the turtle mark there, the marks were washed continuously by the waves, the morning sun was getting reflected from the wet sand, the turtle head was now towards the sea, the fore flippers were spread more, the hind flippers also spread a little, the little body was supported by the flippers, on the back the marks, the small pits formed due to the movement was constantly with seeping water, the sign was getting erased, the sun was in direct sight, its figure got hazy, the sun was reflected from its body, its path was illuminated, the sea was illuminated with the light of new sun, the body of the turtle was glowing, the dividing line between the sea and the beach was vanishing, the turtle vanished into the vanishing line.

Another turtle was slowly going towards the sea, its body was covered with sand, the morning orange light was falling on the dusky structures, giving it a hazy glow, the turtle reached the wave line, white surfs spread all over the beach, surrounded the turtle, a crest created around the body, the further sea was full with white surf, the back shore was filled with white surf too and the turtle was advancing. A small wave came, then a big wave, it got washed away, the orange sun got reflected from its wet back, so many suns appeared inside the water, it sank into the waters, the white line of the waves made a contour, the last sign of the departing turtle. I looked at the beach, so many lines, the beach was filled with departure lines and the lines were constantly washed away by the waves.

I looked at the sea, black dots at every crest, floating stones all around, hundreds of turtles had already nested, some are going to nest and some would nest within a couple of days. The reflections were hopping, the sun was moving with the moving stones. A big wave came, the turtles were lifted to the crest, and to me it appeared that they jumped into the sky.

A Gorge Twenty-Two Kilometers Long

That day I remembered the old songs of Akshaya Mohanty, the greatest Odia singer of all times. The songs flew like the ripples in the Mahanadi water, the Kashtandi flowers moved in the sandy beaches with the gentle breeze. The silver fishes jumped with the arrival of the full moon, his song depicted the lives alongside the Mahanadi river. The river is known also as the lifeline of Odisha, I was listening to the faint music coming from the waters of the river.

Odia	English
Jare bhasi basija,	Float my boat
Nauka mor bhasija	Run on the waters of Mahanadi
Mahandira niladheure bhasi bahsi tu bhasija	Dance with the blue waters

The boatman moves with his boat on the Mahanadi waters. It floats on the emotions of the young minds, moves with the blue waves, touches the bathing ghats at different places, the girls are taking bath at different places; the boatman is worried about their youth, he is moved at seeing their loneliness, and asks innocent questions.

The beautiful girl from Sambalpur is taking bath, the red saree was seen and the boatman is amazed. He asks a question,

Oh ! you beautiful girl of Sambalpur, your beauty touched me, still you are unmarried, so unkind is your father, he is yet to find a match."

The girl then replies –

"Oh! Boatman, my family is searching for my groom, father looks for a proposal in a far off land; mother looks for a groom to stay with me in my family."

The boat moves further down, the ripples on the blue waters brings emotions, and the boat reaches Kantilo. The beautiful girl is taking bath below the Nilamadhaba temple wall, her cloud dark hair is flowing in the waters, the boatman looks at the girl, the same question puzzles him and he asks the girl about her marriage, and the girl replies.

"Oh! Dear boatman, my horoscope matches with that of the groom, but unfortunately the groom of Bhubanabandi area calls me a girl with no caste."

The boatman is moved, the boat moves further down with the ripples of Mahanadi and reaches the bathing ghat of Banki. An attractive young girl was sitting alone, gloom shadows her face, on the women's bathing ghat and she draws the immediate attention of the inquisitive boatman. He asks her about the marriage, the girl replies,

“Oh! Dear boatman, who will marry me, the grooms don’t select me, they calls me a dark skinned girl, so unkind.”

Her sorrow creates further ripples on the Mahanadi waters, the boat moves further down and reaches Cuttack city, the ancient capital of Kalinga empire. On the Gadagadia bathing ghat, the beautiful girl from Cuttack is rubbing her golden body, the radiance of her beauty illuminates the ghat; the inquisitive boatman asks the same question again to the girl and the girl replies,

“Oh! Boatman, you are shameless, a small man thinks too big, what makes you to worry about my marriage?”

The girl shows her aversion, the boatman is disturbing her unnecessary with probing questions. The boatman knows, the charming girls of Cuttack are well-known for their get up, look and beauty too. The boat floats further down, towards the sea, and the boat approaches the Talmala area, the lower basins of the river.

The stunning beauty changes her saree on a lonely ghat, the boatman is moved, at the beauty, the ripples on the river moves the boat too, he asks the question and the girl answers

“Oh! Dear boatman, how can I marry? The clerk groom from Bhubaneswar is asking for a motorcycle on dowry.”

The life, molten emotions of the young hearts, the stories move with the ripples of Mahanadi to the unending sea far away. We were sitting alongside the river, on the protruding rocks, the reflections of the mountains were falling on the water, light breeze was blowing through the mountain folds; we both were looking at the green ripples, the water of Mahanadi captured the colours of the green forests. My companion, a young fisherman, 20-21 years of age, a dark complexioned, around five and half feet tall, strongly built with long dark hairs, was wearing a checkered (tartan) lungi folded at the knee and on the body he was wearing half-sleeved shirt, was looking at the green waters.

“Do you love somebody?” I asked him jokingly, naughty laughter on my face.

He smiled, the fisherman of Tikarpada loves the girl of Boudh, his would be wife will come from that area. During the Dusshera and other festivals, the young fishermen used to row their country boats to Boudh on the up waters of the river, beyond the starting point of Satkosia gorge, used to find soul mates there and return to their respective houses with news of the newly found brides. Life is simple, the calm waters of Mahanadi gives them food, the wind from the green hills gives them the energy of the King Cobra, the fisherman of Tikarpada dance merrily during the Danda time in the summer months, sing the songs of the life. Once, I saw them singing and catching fishes from the crocodile filled water of the river.

Dibakar Behera, the unmarried young fisherman, was sitting near me, narrating the lives inside the Satkosia gorge. His village, a habitation of around hundred people, did not have a single living member above forty-five years of age. All died prematurely before they reach forties, the life of a man at Satkosia sets behind the mountains, the burning ash flows into the green waters. The waters of Satkosia is not a place for the old, it is for the young souls. Many roam on the river banks with the twinkling stars; the teenage girls call the young fishermen from the deep waters of the gorge. Most of them died from cerebral malaria, some are victims of crocodiles in the waters, snake bites too.

"Can't you sing a song?" I requested. It was not the time, there was not the usual cloud, the mind was not rebellious, still I requested. The evening breeze was cool, it carried the energy of the mountains, induced the emotion into the heart, he was hesitant in the beginning, soon the breeze removed the hesitation from his voice, and he sang the Nabakeli songs in the quiet banks of the river.

"Jaya Jaya Krishna-----------------, Kale Kalia Manthana"

(Oh! Lord Krishna, you subjugated the great serpent…..)

It was the devotional song of Lord Krishna, about the subjugation of the serpents. The Kalia Manthana, the days with the Gopis, the Mathura days and the description of the Lord was explained in detail, the Nabakeli song was composed by one Baisanada, not known to many, an almost unknown poet. The song gives the fisherman the strength, the snakes of Satkosia need to be remembered, the harmonious relation need to be mentioned. More songs, I was interested, after all listening to the songs at Mahanadi bank had the mesmerising effect. I was interested for the songs he sings for his soul mate, for his beloved.

"You must have sung for your beloved, your dear girl, a young man like you, after your entire village is full with young persons, the gorges of Satkosia must have been reverberated with the songs of your hearts," I requested him. I wished to bring out his youth. The young man did not reply, immediately did not want to open his heart to a stranger; but did not want to avoid the topic altogether. We walked a little, I asked many questions, he listened, our footsteps were synchronised.

After a brief walk he started singing

Oh! Beautiful girl,
You are like blooming lily, nowhere to be seen,
So beautiful girl in the land
I am dying for your love.

He was narrating his heart. The river of Mahanadi was reverberated with his songs, the mountains; the river was thrilled with the songs of the heart.

"Your life is so interesting. So much love is in your heart, respect for the God in your voice, energy of the stream in your arms. How do you get so much?" The question came from my mouth.

He did not reply immediately, his eyes were fixed on the green mountains of the other side, on Manibhadra hills, the kingdom of fearsome serpents. He nodded his head, the serpent; the ruler of the snakes is being worshipped in his society.

"We get the energy from the Lord Shiva, we perform Dandanacha for Him, depict the characters on his praise, the praise of the Lord of the snakes." He was narrating, singing simultaneously. Then he sang the Dandanacha songs

Oh! Lord Shiva, the remover of great danger
This poor man calls you,
Remove the pain, remove the danger

Another devotional song from the fisherman, the song was speaking his life; it was the song of the Dandanacha, the dance drama, description of the acrobatics performed on the honour of Lord Shiva, depicting the life of the ordinary Odia man. The fishermen retreated to the dances during the lean period, to give their body and mind a break, the tradition for a new lease of life. I looked at the man, his eyes were closed. Then he opened his eyes, looked at the river and on my request narrated the festivals of Dandanacha.

Danda Dance

Dandanacha or Danda Jatra, the ritualistic dance festival of Odisha is one of the ancient form of theatrical arts, meant to worship Lord Shiva for the blessings – for a child, fulfillment of ambitions, getting rid of sickness, good harvest alike. The Dandanata commences from the Chita Purnima (falls in early summer) and continues up to the Pana Sankranti (Vishuva Sankranti) day (falls in late summer). The dancers called Bhoktas take 13 pledges, and it continues for 13 days. At the beginning the pitcher called Kamana Ghata is filled with water, first worshipped below a banyan tree, then taken out in procession through the village and kept in a hut, preferable in front of a Shiva temple. Two cane sticks are kept in front, representing Hara and Gauri, which are also worshipped. The sacred fire is kept lighted in front of the hut in an oil lamp, resin powder is thrown to the lamp, it burns with flare and the Bhokta shout "Kala Rudramani Ho Joy".

The Bhoktas lead a very pious life for 21 days, do not eat any non-vegetarian food, nor cohabit during this period. They feed on only one simple meal during the full day, the food too need to be cooked by them. The principal Bhokta, called Pata Bhokta, does not even eat rice and lives on fruit. They are very strict about the piousness; during eating no other person should be present, if any other person comes then they will not eat further for the day, so at some places they keep on beating the drums until the eating is over. The Bhoktas goes from villages to villages, in procession with a band of musicians and perform Danda Dance in front of the houses.

Danda nata has three phases, 1-Dhuli Danda, 2-Pani Danda and 3-Danda Suanga. The Dhuli Danda, also called Bhumi danda is one in which the dancers perform some acrobatics. In the dance sequence a few formations, pyramids are displayed. The common workings in a rustic life like ploughing, cultivation, harvesting, etc. are depicted in art form in acrobatic manner.

Pani Danda, is the dance form in the water, performed either in a pond or in a river where the performers swim and make pyramids in the water. The musicians play Dhol Mahuri, villagers gather around the water mass, the Bhoktas perform their skills in water. After this performance of Pani Danda, the Bhoktas return to their camp, have their only meal of the day and prepare for the night performance.

The third form of Danda Nata Suanga are simple dances in the Jatra form, performed during the night time, the performers enter to an open space surrounded by the spectators and spell out the dialogues of the characters.

The main musical instruments in the performance are Dhol, a double sided drum and the Mahuri, the wind instrument, the Ghanta (Bell metal disc), the Sankha (Conch shell), the Kahali (Clarion), the Jhanja (Brass alloy clappers). The dancers wear ghungura, ghagudi (small and big tinklers), daskathi, ramtali (wooden clappers) khanjani, etc.

The most important character of the Danda Suanga is the Chadheiya, a traditional bird-catcher who lives in the forest, he catches or kills birds, sells those for a living. He enters the arena with a long pole (Danda) in one hand and a noose in the other hand. The Chadheiya goes around in search of birds, finds a peacock on a tree in the premises of a temple and kills it; the act is a great sin; killing of peacock is prohibited in the temple premises. As a result, he is now cursed, a snake bites him and he collapses and dies. His wife, the Chadheiyani enters into the arena, looks for her husband and finds him dead.

She prays to Mother Vanadurga, the Goddess of the Jungle, the deity appears before her and tells her that five types of birds such as Parrot, Mynah, Pigeon, Duck & Peacock are the favourites of Lord Shiva; for killing a peacock the Chadheiya is punished. She is given the hints – deep faith in God will bring her husband back to life.

The Chadheiyani meets a Gunia (witch doctor), a Vaidya (local medicine practitioner in a village) to cure the dead man, but all fail. However, later a Sapua Kela (Snake Charmer) recites spells in the name of God Mahadeva & Goddess Parvati; and the Chadheiya gets back to life.

I knew about the character of Sapua kelas, the snake charmers are known by that name by the local people, his role in Dandanacha gives him much of prominence in the society. In this traditional dance, he has the role to save the Chadheiya's life which is lost in a snakes bite. He knows the snake world well as he is a great devotee of Lord Shiva; and with blessings of Lord Shiva he got the power to cure the patient of snake bites, also he has acquired other powers like stambha (benumbing), mohan (causing delusion), udana (flying) and other black magic. He plays a Nageswara (an wind instrument made out of dried guard) and brings out Sapta-swara (seven sounds). He also plays a Dambru (a small double drum held in hand-the favourite musical instrument of Lord Shiva) and displays snakes, makes them dance to the tune. He sings invocatory songs, the Padmatola songs (song relating to Lord Krishna plucking of Lotus from Kalindi lake) and songs related to places, mountains, rivers, etc.

Snake stories

The evening was descending, the Satkosia gorge was slowly disappearing, the coolness of the river was increasing, and in contrast, the warmth within me was increasing. The mysterious hill of Manibhadra was slowly dipping into darkness, the stars were twinkling, appeared as twinkling jewels on the head of serpents. The myth goes, if a snake lives for a quite long life, shining jewels would appear on its hood.

The darkness of the nearby mountains had lengthened further, the village roads, the fields and the small huts of the fishermen were hiding behind the covers of tree leaves, sneaked in to the was the veils of fear. I, on that evening was sitting on the front place, listening to the stories of fearsome reptiles and of course about the lives of the fishermen. The partially opened terrace was filled with the sweat smell as well as fishes too, a usual odour for fishermen, but offensive to un-habituated persons.

"Satkosia, the kingdom of the snakes," I started the topic, paused a little and looked at the gathering. We were around eight people, some on the verandah and the rest sitting or standing on the ground. The darkness of the jungle was gripping us; the cool wind of the dark mountains instead of cooling the atmosphere was warming the gossip. They nodded their head, little nod, the eyes of each individual went to the darkness, the mountains, the forest were covered in black blanket, its depth of the dark colour symbolised the presence of the ferocious snakes, and the hair roots of the participants were swelling.

Once Dhaneswar Nayak, a forest watcher from the village, was walking towards the crocodile research centre, adjacent to the guest house, in front of the most frequented picnic spot of the area, located on the left banks of Mahanadi river, which was and half a kilometer away from the village, during the evening. At that time, the full moon had come to the mid sky, but there was no respite from boiling heat of the summer, sweat was coming out continuously on his face. He was walking slowly, alone; other persons of the village had gone for as usual early sleep. A strange long hissing sound came, he stopped immediately, and looked around, on the left, the small cemented Shiva temple was shinning in the moonlight; the whiteness was apparent with the dark background. He could not find anything unusual, so he switched on his torch, a flood of light washed the temple wall; his eye lids couldn't drop, a big snake, a very long one with faint white broad band over the black body, was passing in front, its scales was shining, his legs stopped, hands got immobilised. The snake slowly descended from the white wall of the Shiva temple, its shining black body appeared like a thick rope, slowly it came to the road around twenty feet away; the snake was hissing continuously, the sound, to him appeared like whistle of the electric kettle. He could not switch off the light, he was not frightened, knew, a little movement would attract immediate attention of the fearsome reptile. Instead of going forward he waited for the snake to pass the roads. The snake moved, its shape was better visible, head flatter, appeared like that of a very fat rat snake, but the sheer size of the present snake spoke about its ferocity. The snake remained for some time on the road, and then it slowly went backwards, when the distance was around fifty feet, he threw a stone to scare it away; the snake roared, lifted its hood to almost five feet and angry hissing sound came continuously. He was sure; he encountered the king of the snakes, the King Cobra, the most feared of the Indian snakes. He ran for cover, ran almost 300 meter backward and came close to the village. The snake was not chasing him, after an angry moment it slowly descended down, the hissing sound was coming continuously from its mouth then it reached the water. Later after seeing the marks of the snake on the sand deposits he confirmed that the snake had crossed mighty Mahanadi, a 300-400 meters wide water channel at Tikarpada side at that time. He returned and tried to calculate the length of the snake, its whole body was covering the road and extended up to the palm tree on the other side; the forest watcher kept two stones, one at the wall and other at the palm tree, the length need to be measured with measuring tape later. He returned in the next morning, aatandi creeper was cut and marks were done on the creeper, and later was measured with the measuring tape, the snake was 18 ft long, much bigger than other snakes of the area.

"Is he here?" I asked the question and enquired about the person. They looked around, and as a character of a drama, in came a lean and thin person, dark complexioned, fear in his eyes; everybody looked at him, he was puzzled, did not know that the discussion was about his encounter with King Cobra, he was briefed and he understood.

"How did you know it was the same snake that crossed Mahanadi later?" I asked him.

"I knew the direction of the movement of the snake, during the previous night, and the mark of the snake confirmed that the same snake had crossed the river on to the other side of the river," He explained. I asked about the behaviour of the snake, which he explained.

"The snake eater, the King Cobra, mainly feeds on rat snakes and occasionally on other poisonous snakes like Krait. It catches the prey by its head and rotates it very fast so that the pray snake can't coil around the King Cobra. Within a short time the body of the pray snake gets straightened and the King Cobra easily swallows the other snake," He was narrating the behaviour of the big snake.

The night was getting thicker and thicker, the wind was blowing through the thick forest on the back producing strange sounds, and to me it appeared like hissing sounds of the snakes of Satkosia. Earlier, I knew about the Satkosia gorges, the deeper part of the Mahanadi river, it starts at Boudh and extends down up to Athagarh, is around seven kosh, approximately twenty-two kilometers long. Because of its expanse to seven kosh, the gorge is better known as Satkosia gorge. The river is bottomless here, reaching up to 80-90 ft) at specific points and mostly the river is around 40 ft deep even during the summer. The mountain ranges run parallel to the river on both sides, appeared to touch the sky from the river bed, and are ideal habitats for the rarest of the rare snakes; snakes of all sizes and shapes are found in the forest around the Satkosia gorge. The white sand dunes in small patches scattered along the whole length, are the right places for the resting crocodiles; the riverside forests up to the banks are the best nesting place of the sweet water crocodiles.

Our discussion was interesting; the forester of the area, an old man, an experienced person in wildlife, posted in the Wildlife Range for last 25 years and worked in Baghamunda beat under Purunakot Range started telling about his experience.

On an eventful day, when he was much younger, he went to Pampasar Range for some work, a place far away from his working place, by foot. He reached the range headquarter in the late afternoon and couldn't dare to return to his working place and took shelter in the range office itself. All the forest guards and foresters have the common habit, to go to forest to attend the nature call. At the back of the range office the bamboo forest was standing, there, many Sal trees were covered with broad leaved atandi creeper, the storm broken trees were scattered throughout, an ideal living place for the snakes of Satkosia, a fast flowing rivulet was also located in the area. He went to the embankment of the rivulet near the range office to attend the natures call, and there he saw the snakes, a big one and a small one, both in locked position; the bigger snake was trying to swallow the smaller one, and the smaller one instead of giving up, caught the bigger snake at its jaw and the bigger snake was started biting the smaller snake on its head. The bigger snake was around 18-20 ft long, with faint white bands on the black body, and the smaller one, much darker, deep maroon in colour, was around six ft long, probably a rat snake. The rat snake was partly in water, but was not giving up the fight; the King Cobra was trying hard, was rotating. Slowly and slowly the rat snake lost strength, the poison entered into its body. The forester called the other persons, to witness the snake fights, people ran at the bund, they recognised the bigger snake, it was King Cobra and the smaller one was a rat snake. The King Cobra rotated the smaller snake, its body slowly straightened and its jaw opened. The King Cobra then started swallowing the rat snake; and the rat snake, poisoned through Cobra bite, unconscious by that time, was dying.

I was listening to the story in the cold embrace of the hills of Satkosia forests, the warmth of the room had reduced with the hissing of the fearful snakes. The jackals started howling in the forest on the back side, the sound was getting louder, they were coming towards us, and the night owls arrived at the trees in front. The mosquitoes, infamous for causing malaria, were singing and biting us occasionally. I was apprehensive, frightened too. Satkosia area is the store house of mosquitoes proliferating brain malaria.

"Whether, King Cobra ever chased?" I asked. Fear of Tikarpada dropped to his eyes and his words turned incoherent.

"They do" was the reply, "I heard it from others, but never encountered, but the Domas were chased by the furious King Cobra." Then he narrated the chasing incident.

"Once, I was patrolling in Pompasar Range, then I saw the panting Domas, a group of low caste people; they were running down the slope hill like mad men, as if they were chased by a rogue elephant. I did not hear the trumpet of the elephants, but the human figures ran towards me, no body looked back, but there was no elephant, no tiger. I was around 500 meters away from them, standing in front of a game tank inside the thick forest. The Domas, right holders of forest produce for their livelihood purpose, used to go to forest to collect bamboos. They reached the game tank, paused and looked back at the forest with frightened eyes; I was watching them from a distance. They were trembling when they saw me there, ran towards me and sat under a tree; I offered them water, then they narrated. That day, the Damos were collecting bamboo in that area, suddenly, they listened the loud hissing sound, and saw a big snake raising its dark broad hood to almost five and half feet. It chased the bamboo collectors, they threw away the bamboo and ran for their life; the big snake was charging at full speed. They escaped somehow, and the big snake after a brief chase vanished into the forest; they thanked God for saving their life, did not return to the spot again. We contacted the people from nearby areas and all were afraid to enter into the forest. The big snake had laid its eggs there and out of fear it had chased the Domas." He told the story.

It was a strange story to me, he looked at the twinkling stars, and the snakes of the forests were watching him. Then he narrated another story.

Once Sarberwar Majhi, a man in his 50's, of Tuluka Range enthusiastically entered into the forest along with other staffs, and they saw a big log with white marks, there were so many logs around. He stood on a log, surprisingly the log moved; so he jumped on the ground; the log turned out to be a huge python; it was laying still there after a good meal, a big bulge at the belly, the python would remain idle for a couple of days, may be for a week. The snake did not catch Majhibabu. It was such an interesting story, but I was much eager, the stories were hypnotic.

I recollected a small film, the python was swallowing a chital, a huge python, the mouth expanded like a big bag, it was swallowing the big spotted deer; in fact unless watching it with my own eyes, I would never have believed that a snake could sallow such a big animal. The chital was dead by that time, the huge snake had curled over the entire body, was swallowing the animal from the head side, its huge mouth was moving, also the coils on the body was moving, the huge serpent swallowed a little, its upper body curled forward, the black grey and white skin was taking curves, the white liner pattern were taking curves, a huge and heavy coil on the mid body of the dead deer was rolling continuously, another curl was towards the back body; the deer's front legs were now pressed backwards due to pressure of the snakes mouth on the leg joints near the neck, facilitating the swallowing process. The mouth of the snake appeared huge, long triangular shaped upper head was strongly pressed over the body, the side skin of the jaws were expanded as per the size of the deer, when there was any difficulty in swallowing, the coils outside the body was pressing the dead deer, aligning it nicely for the swallowing. The eyes of the apex hunter were glowing, the top head was appearing like the symbol of death, a huge head, burning eyes towards the side, a dark band going over the eyes making it more fearful, a straight white line on the forehead like a white tilak, the huge nostril was open, the open mouth was curved at the centre, the appearance of the python was terrifying. Slowly and slowly it swallowed up to the shoulder portion of the dead animal, the massive black and white trunk of the snake was covering more and more part of the deer's body, the coils on the body was moving continuously. Huge pressure of the trunk was breaking the bones, thus helping the swallowing process, the bulge on the snake's body was increasing, here the size of the deer's body in open was decreasing. Slowly and slowly the python swallowed the entire body, a huge bulge appeared at the central portion of the trunk, the huge head now took a small size, and slowly the huge python moved ahead into the thick grasses, on the side a mosses covered big stone remained as the silent spectator. The huge body slowly crawled; like an insect, little movement little rest, the skins were compressed and elongated continuously.

The memory of that huge python was creating a chill, but more dreadful was the King Cobra of the dense forests, I came out; the young fisher man was walking with me with the cold wind of the Satkosia.

"Ever seen a King Cobra?" I asked the man, he nodded his head in the faint light. I saw a shadow moving his head, and then he started describing the snake.

"Many a times, it is the longest snake, no other snake could match its size, the length about four times my size, it is venomous, the venom can kill a full grown elephant in three hours." Then he narrated about the big serpent.

"The food habit is interesting, it feeds on snakes exclusively, all snakes, venomous, non-venomous snakes alike constitute its feed base. It swallows the other snakes, its toxin starts digesting its struggling victim in the process. This snake usually preys during the daytime, not during night, quite unusual for a snake, after all the King Cobra is so different, so deadly, so fearsome. The King Cobra can rise taller than a man. All snakes lift their body to one-third of their length or a little more, the King Cobra, due its sheer size lifts its hood to more than six feet; and if you see this fearsome snake in its real habitat in a rising position, then you are mesmerised, it symbolises sure death." He was trying to increase my interest in the most fearsome snake of the region. He continued with the description.

"Satkosia the choicest habitat of the King Cobra, was dotted with streams, rivers and rivulets and water masses, and the abundant bamboo forest around with rock bodies scattered all over this area; it creates one of the best habitat of the king." He was narrating.

"Do you know why it charged the Domas so ferociously?" He asked me. The story of the ferocious attack on the Domas was known to everybody.

I didn't reply. Though heard a lot about the ferocity of the snake, I actually had little knowledge about the snake.

"This snake makes nests and lay eggs, unlike other snakes who don't make nests. A nest is constructed by the female characteristically from rotten leaves and vegetations; it loops her coils over loose debris and drag the material to create her nest; the nest is just a simple pile of leaves mounded above the ground where she lays between 40 and 60 eggs. The King Cobra eggs incubate after 65 to 80 days and a baby is born measuring 18 inches in length on an average. The snake is deadly from first day. Over the body of the baby King Cobras, there are a lot white and black bands which slowly disappear as they grow into adults. Both male and female guard the eggs and it must be that time the Domas were closer to their nest. The mother must have charged at them," he was correlating the events to his knowledge, relating it to the life of the snake.

"Do you know, the snake judges the movement of the prey by its tongue? This snake has superb eyesight, could detect any movement almost hundred meters away, and is very sensitive to vibration." The man was explaining, I was praising his knowledge, the extent he knows about the snake.

"What happened to the mongoose snake fight?" I asked, there is eternal enmity between the mongoose and the snake, I was testing the knowledge. The mongoose, the agile attacker always defeats the snakes and what happens to the fight, the query was in my mind.

"If King Cobra encounters a mongoose, it starts to flee, after the entire king loves his life too. But if cornered, it will flatten its upper ribs, forming the prototypical Cobra hood about its neck, the high pitched hissing sound then comes from its mouth, to frighten the mongoose and sometimes it charges at the mongoose with feigned closed mouth strikes." He continued.

"But, the winner is the mongoose. Generally, seeing the sheer size of the King Cobra, the mongoose tries to avoid the fight." The words of respect for the King Cobra came from the mouth of the speaker.

"I know, the King Cobra venom could kill a full grown elephant within 3 hours, the venom attacks the nervous system, sever pain, blurred vision resulted, followed by drowsiness and finally cardio vascular failure" the session was quite educative to me."

"We worship the snakes, don't you see the symbols of snakes every where? The praise for the Shiva, the Dandanacha has one clear angle, respect the snakes of Satkosia, and respect the snakes of Manibhadra hills." He expressed his belief.

I closed my eyes, and visualised the snake. A white stripped black snake was standing taller than a man, its hood appeared to be bigger than the human head, was hissing loudly, forked tongues was coming out like flashes, eyes were burning like burning charcoal and was charging like a wild horse. The snake, with narrow head at the top, burning static eyes at extremities, blackish yellow belly, red forked tongues coming through the small mouth opening like the tongues of the fearsome dragon and the deadly fangs of the mouth was visible occasionally, it appeared like the serpent of the devil king, anger at every inch of the body.

The night was getting thicker and thicker, we were walking. I looked at the Manibhadra hills, the serpents with burning jewels on their head were playing in the sky, the most powerful one was shining just over the tallest peak of the Satkosia ranges. In the night I recollected my knowledge on some important snakes of Indian forests.

Description of some important Snakes

Python

Python is a very big and heavy snake which sometime grows up to 20 feet, weigh up to 50-60 kg, but on an average the fully grown snake is around 40 kg in weight. The adult pythons are whitish or light yellow in colour with asymmetrical dark brown, black edged blotches, and the body from a distance, inside the forest, looks like a log with mushrooms. This snake is highly lethargic, it moves in a linear fashion, body moving in a straight line, this movement is absent in most of the snakes. The snake is a good swimmer.

They eat all types of animals, mammals, birds and reptiles all, but usually prefer mammals. When the prey comes within the striking range, it lunges with open mouth and the prey is caught; the live prey is then constricted, one or two coils are thrown around the prey, holding it in a tight grip; and the prey finds it increasingly difficult to breathe, succumbs and gets killed. The head is swallowed first, and prior to swallowing, the snake smells the prey with the tongue to know the head portion. The snake does not move after a heavy meal, the meal inside might damage its body. A python may go without food for weeks.

Cobra

The Cobra is a poisonous snake, has a characteristic spectacle mark on the hood, scale is smooth and glossy, head is broad. It mostly feeds on rodents, so the Cobras are mostly found near the human habitats. The snake feeds on rodents, toads, frogs, birds. This snake is active during the day, also during the night. They nest below the ground, often in rat holes or termite mounds. The Cobra is used to be around six feet long, though deaf to the snake charmer's pipe, dances to the tune as it follows the visual cue of the moving pipe of the snake charmer, and it can sense the ground vibration from snake charmer's tapping feet. If alarmed, this snake may raise almost half of its body and spread the hood, and if further disturbed it will hiss and strike.

It is one of the four most dangerous poisonous snakes of India. The venom acts on the nerves, paralyses the muscles leading to the respiratory failure.

Krait

Krait is a much smaller snake, not that feared but highly deadly, having yellow black band on the body for the banded Krait, black white body for the common Krait, is around 4 feet long. The bands helps the snake to camouflage in its habitat. This snake also eats other snakes, including venomous ones and sometimes eats its own brethrens. Sometimes it eats lizards, rodents and frogs. This snake is active mostly during night, thus encounters with human beings are rare. During day time it takes rest in rodent burrows, under rubbles, often found in farms and gardens near water.

Its venom is extremely powerful and quickly induces muscle paralysis which is many times more potent than Cobra venom. The bite will not give much pain however later the victim complains of severe abdominal cramps accompanied by progressive muscular paralysis, frequently starting with ptosis. Even today, the Krait anti-venom is often ineffective; as a result, mortality rate is high even with treatment. If somehow the man is able to breathe through mechanical ventilation, generally available at hospitals, then only the venom is metabolised, and the victim can survive. Otherwise the death occurs due to respiratory failure because of complete paralysis of muscles controlling the ribcage.

Russell's Viper

Russel's Viper, another deadly snake of the area, again around 4 to 5 feet long, body is stout, scales is strongly keeled, the head is triangular, and the colour is deep yellow, tan or brown, ground colour, with series of dark brown spots which run the total length of its body. Each of these spots has a black ring around it; the outer border of the ring is intensified with a rim of white or yellow. This snake is usually nocturnal. They prefer open, grassy or bushy areas, and are also found in scrub forest and farmlands. This snake is often found near villages, the main attraction being the rodents, but it can feed on rats, mice shrews, squirrels, etc. The young prefer lizards. When disturbed, they produce loud hissing sound, similar to the sound of pressure cooker. This snake is usually slow, but is capable of incredibly fast strike.

The pain starts immediately at site of the bite, followed by swelling of the affected portion and bleeding is the common symptom; the gums may swell, sputum may show signs of blood within no time, the blood pressure drops and the heart rate falls. One may get blistering at the site of the bite, with vomiting and facial swelling not uncommon in many cases. Severe pain may continue for almost a month, and local swellings may continue for three days.

Saw Scaled Viper

The Saw Scaled Viper is a poisonous snake, considerable smaller, usually less than three feet in length, the body is short and stout, scales strongly keeled, rough in appearance. The head is broader than the neck, eyes are large. The scale is light, dark brown, brick red, grey or sand coloured with zigzag pattern. The snake's head top has a whitish cruciform or trident pattern.

It is generally found in the open dry, sandy or rocky terrain, often found hiding under loose rocks, inside deep mammal burrows, rock fissures and fallen rotten logs. This snake is mostly nocturnal, hides during the day time. This snake is not lethargic, is alarmingly quick, move sidewise and can climb bushes and shrubs. They feed on rodents and lizards, frogs, scorpions.

The venom induces swelling and pain, which appear within minutes of a bite, and in cases the swelling may extend up the entire affected limb within 12-24 hours and blisters appear on the skin, hemorrhage may occur, followed by kidney failure, and there may be renal failure.

Some general information on Snakes

Most of the snakes are short sighted except for King Cobra, rat snakes and tree snakes, see the world mostly in black and white. Snakes have heat sensitive pits between the nostrils and the eyes can detect warm blooded animals. The Pit Vipers can detect temperature variation as low as 0.003^0C. The snakes can hear low frequency sounds in the range 200 to 500 Hz, can't hear our talk, but are sensitive to vibration on the ground. The snakes use their sensitive forked tongues and an organ on the roof of the mouth to pick up odour.

The snakes hunt the prey mainly by secrecy and ambush; some of course pursue the prey. The Cobras, rat snakes, etc. like rodents, tree snakes go for lizards, birds and frogs. Also snakes eat eggs, snails, and some snakes are snake eaters too like the King Cobra. The venomous snakes have toxins as well as digestive enzymes for killing the prey. Many non-venomous snakes have some toxic saliva which controls the prey. The pythons suffocate the prey by constriction. All the snakes have backward curved teeth to prevent prey from escaping.

The fang of a venomous snakes is a hallow tooth which works like an injection system to inject venom; the amount of venom to be delivered can be controlled by the snake during a bite. The snakes like Krait and sea snakes have very small fangs measuring around 2-4 mm, but for Cobra the fangs are much longer at 5-10 mm. The snake used to bite the prey and chew for sometime till sufficient venom is injected. But for the Vipers, when it strikes the venom is instantly injected and then withdraws immediately from the prey. Sometimes the fangs are used to spray venom from a distance as in case of Spitting Cobra of Africa. Its venom can be sprayed up to a distance of around 2.5 meter. None of the Indian Cobras are capable of spitting the venom. The venom of the snake are either neuro-toxic (affect the nervous system) or haemotoxic (affect the circulatory system), in some cases the venom may be combination of both. The baby snakes have fully functional venom organs.

For all the snakes, teeth and fangs used to shed off and new teeth and fangs come up after some time, the fangs shading cycle are between 10-70 days depending on the snake species.

In India, around 5 lakh people are bitten by snake each year out of which around 10,000-50,000 people die. The most of the snake bite are attributed mainly to four snakes viz. Cobra, Common Krait, Russell's Viper and Saw Scaled Viper. It appears that most of the causalities in snake bite occur due to bite of Russell's Viper snake.

The venom of the Vipers damages blood vessel walls and disturbs the normal blood clotting mechanism. For Cobra and Krait, the venom is neurotoxic, block the nerve impulses resulting in progressive paralysis. The Viper bite causes severe pain at the site, rapid swelling, non-clotting of blood, shock and kidney failure results. The Cobra bites are also painful, causes swelling. The Krait bites are not much noticeable. The Cobra and Krait bite results in progressive paralysis, the symptom of which are drooping eyelids, double vision and difficulty in swallowing.

In India around 75% of all snake bites occur below the knee, mostly occur while people are walking at night. The snakes generally flee when a person approaches, but sometimes bite out of fear in self defence. Most of the snake bites are by non-venomous snakes and majority of snake bite, 85-90%, are not life threatening as snake does not inject sufficient venom or in many cases no venom is injected.

SNAKE BITE FIRST AID:

* Keep calm – Fear and panic raises the blood pressure, thus venom spreads faster.

* Immobilize the bitten portion without compression: The compression results in localization of venom for a longer period resulting in serious local damage at the bite site.
* Take medical help immediately.
* Check for the following symptoms –
  - Continuous bleeding from the wound
  - Progressive swelling
  - Difficulty in breathing
  - Drooping of eyelids
  - Difficulty in speaking
  - Bleeding of gums
  - Drowsiness

Anti Venom and Snake Bite Remedies:

Anti venom serum is available for mainly four snakes like 1-Common Krait, 2-Russell's Viper, 3-Saw Scaled Viper and 4-Cobra. The dry serum lasts for five years at room temperature and is good for the above four species. Anti venom is not available in India for Branded Krait and other Kraits, King Cobra, Sea snakes, Pit Viper. Simple mouth to mouth or mouth to nose ventilation can save one's life when breathing muscles are paralyzed. The respirator (artificial respiration against paralysis of longs muscles) and dialysis (to prevent kidney failure) can save a life.

Morning in the Forest

The next morning came with the chirpings of the birds at my window, the dew drops were falling on the tin roof top from tree leaves; and I proceeded for the Mahanadi bank to the place where the fishermen used to keep their boats for fishing with my companion, a fisherman of the Satkosia. The forest was covered with thorny bamboos, not very tall, appeared to be strong with sharp thorns at nodes, and the bamboo clumps were dense. The bamboo branches were coming to the road, bamboo thorns were scattered all over; the thick carpet of yellowish white bamboo leaves spread over the road, venation of the which were prominent due to decay. On the back, the tall trees were going upward, covering the sky, and in front few small swamps, around 2-3 meters wide, were found at intervals, water plants were coming profusely in those areas. Sometimes other trees were coming on the way, and there was little light in the morning due to heavy canopy, the forest along the road side appeared to be much darker. The forest road was around four-five feet wide, constructed by selective cleaning of forest, light leveling of the uneven land and constructing small log bridges on minor streams. There were many small streams, the beds were rocky, large boulders, some as big as a size of the living room, remained scattered, many trees were coming up well between the rocks, were going straight. On the stream, through the gaps between the massive boulders and stones, the clear water was flowing with mild sound, the chirping of the birds mixed with that sound was creating an amazing symphony. The streaks of morning sun rays were falling on the black stones, giving the dark stone a little orange tinge at the darker background of the forests behind. A sound came from the tall trees on the right, and I found a giant squirrel, reddish brown in colour with thick hairy tail, a beautiful animal; it jumped from one branch to the other branch, around fifteen feet away. To me, its jump appeared like a flying, smooth sailing in the air, bodies straight, tail straight, the rear and hind legs spread out, head coming out in front. It was such a beautiful creature, the forest of Satkosia was live with its colour, the birds chirpings, the sound of the dew drops falling on the leaves on the ground was giving the background music. In that beautiful morning we were going towards the river.

After a brief walk we entered into a thick bamboo area, then to the swampy land and walked on the bamboo bridge in low lying area, the bridge not exactly connected to two high points, and below it the water from the stream was flowing. The patch was marshy, around 100 meters in length, with width of 70 meters, the water passes from the higher side, formed a swamp there. The make shift passage, and the bridge was made of bamboo mats on the top, below which wood logs, thick tree branches were kept in parallel positions, to give required support on the marshy land. The bamboo mat road was covered with little sand on the top, the sides of the mat were attached to wooden poles dug into the ground, and the mats were interwoven to each other by spitted bamboos at small intervals. In fact, due to its support underneath, and the light weight of the used materials, the makeshift bamboo road was probably the best alternative to an expensive all weather bridge. The water of the marshy area was drained to a deep channel dug parallel to the road, and later was collected in a small pond, just adjacent the road. The accumulated water was finally channeled out of the area through a deep drain over which again a small makeshift bamboo bridge was constructed. The bridge was small, around four feet in length, constructed over much thicker logs tightly knitted to each other by canes, and on the top the bamboo mats were kept to give the bridge a better smoother surface for the passing vehicles. The forest roads are always easier alternatives to the expensive permanent roads that are ecologically unsuitable in sensitive environments.

We climbed to the river bank, in our front a big river was flowing with greenish-blue water, around half a kilometer wide, no waves, very small ripples, the morning calmness had calmed the flow of the mighty Mahanadi. The morning light had illuminated the waters, the fishermen had come to the waters, one small narrow boat with two sailors were moving slowly on the waters, the boat was very narrow. From the bank of the river it appeared like a big floating log, both the ends were raised a little from the water surface, on opposite ends the two persons, one in blue shirt and the other man with red shirts were sitting and their eyes were glued to the waters. I looked at the other side, Baisapalli Wildlife Sanctuary side in Nayagarh district, the forests were illuminated with first light of the day, and light orange tinges washed the green forest. A narrow white line was touching the green waters of the river, the exposed part of the soil with very narrow sand deposit was shining with green waters in front. On the back big green hill ranges were touching the sky, the big hills started just from the waterline with steep slopes. On our side, the forest was still dark, the big hill on our back had delayed the morning, the dew drops were still falling on us continuously, the morning moisture was wetting our eyes. I looked at the trees around, many massive trees raising their heads, the canopy was closed with the leaves, and the light streaks were dripping with orange tinge, creating a mesmerising atmosphere. On the branch of the big tree were the orchid flowers. These are characteristic beautiful coloured flowers growing. On tree barks at a higher height, mostly saprophytic, some of course parasitic.

I looked at the orchid plants, these orchids, to me appeared like saprophytic, were small and had no woody branches; the leaves were thick and fleshy, light green to yellow in colour, narrow, elongated and ends in broad circular edge. The ash coloured thick aerial roots, exposed at lower portion, passes over each other, like the thin jute ropes, more like the hair of an African lady, hung to 2-3 feet down; some roots passed over the fissured bark of the host tree, holds the bark tightly, appeared like swelled nerves on the hand of a hard working farmer, it gives strength to the orchid pant. I looked at the plant more keenly, long narrow thick linear leaves moved from the pseudo-bulbs of the plant continuously; towards the top end a long light yellow inflorescence, like a long straw moved upward. From the mini inflorescence, six smaller connecting inflorescence emerged from the nodes, and on smaller inflorescence the light pinkish-white orchid flowers were hanging, the flower shape was much different from the other flowers in the area, the bright colour was charming too. Thick individual long pink white petals with irregular small white spots moved away from the base with wide space between each florets; the orchid cup, the characteristics of the orchid flower, was small, light violet-pink in colour; and the flower with dark back ground was shining in the diffused morning light. I looked around, many orchid flowers on many trees, the beautiful flowers blossom in low light, under the main foliage, giving the dark forests a beautiful robe, increases the beauty of the dark forest; and here at the backdrop of green mountains on the other side, green-blue waters, the orchids were giving the forests the best outfits possible.

Mahanadi in the morning

I looked at the green water of the river from the bank, from a height of around 20 from water level; the slope of the bank was very steep; the small passage to the water body was on the loose soil and sand. The area near to the water was covered with thick, long grasses, giving the bank good stabilisation, and the rest of the areas were covered with taller trees towards the upper side, some of them were hanging, branches touched the water; an ideal habitat of the water birds, because of its proximity to water. One boat was seen inside the water, two boatmen were downing their fishing lines into the river water in the middle of the river, and they looked like small toys in view of distance from the bank. At the edge of the waterline few narrow boats were dancing with the water flow and just on the edge of the waterline few men were sitting and chatting. We went down, the fisherman who accompanied me from the start had promised to take me to the Mahanadi waters, he saw the group of below, whistled, the other people reciprocated, with whistles.

"*Rasarkeli, Aailu,*" they screamed.

("Oh! Dear friend you have come.")

He laughed, ran towards them and the whole group turned jovial; I could not follow him even though I was a good walker, in that unknown steep slope passing through the big rocks I was apprehensive and got down cautiously. The fishermen were standing on the rocks, some of which were very big; over the flattened surfaces of the rocks they had kept their fishing lines and floaters. Some of the rocks had smooth surfaces like walls, and some had protruding ends, but none had sharp edges, sharpness blunted by regular water action. I looked at the water, their boats, four in number, were kept side by side in the water, one was bound to a tree grown on the water line just next to the small sandy beach.

The whole group gathered, two sat on the black granite stones, and rest stood on the rocks. The bank on the back was around forty feet from the water body, was almost over their head, that portion was covered with thick riverside forest; the dark green leaves reached up to the rocks. The fishermen were in their tartan (checkered) lungis, double folded at the knee and wrapped around the waists; four persons were in their sleeveless banyans, rest two in were with shirts. A small boy, around 10 years old, with loose red shirt on the body probably his father's shirt, brought rice in a blue coloured plastic plate and scattered it over the soil mix. His father, a man in his late thirties, was in white half-sleeved banyan, was sitting just on the waterline, his legs were touching the green water of the river. The man was busy in preparing the bait mix. The boy brought fistful of rice and dropped it on the soil mix, after then he mixed the same thoroughly with mud, sometimes adding little river water, prepared the right concentrate, the father-son duo was preparing the bait mix for the group. The father, a jovial man, I saw him being cheered at his arrival, was singing continuously and the son was smiling at others, occasionally bringing more water and other mix for the bait preparation. On the water the country boats were dancing with the breeze, with the small ripples of the river. The group was busy in gossiping, the matter – Danda dance, the wild animals, rain and of course the fish catch, crocodile was rarely mentioned in their talk. The crocodiles, though fearsome in the gorges of Satkosia, not that feared by the fishermen living on the waters of the gorge.

Wind of Satkosia touches the body
Eases pain, sufferings
Green mountains give water
Fishes swim, grow bigger
Our boats go into the river
Big rohu eats my bait
Sola dances
My children will be happy

I looked at the water, the morning sun was shining brightly in the clear sky, the foggy mountains were getting clearer, and the moist leaves of the previous night were shining. The fisherman boy merrily went into the water, sat on his boat, his father was busy in preparing the bait and was singing the songs of Satkosia; he did not prevent the youngster to go into the water alone. The child pushed the boat a little by a long bamboo (KATA) stick, the boat moved to more deep water, the eyes of the boy shined like bright stars. He took the rowing oar and sat at the rear end of the boat, the little hands pushed the water using the oar and the boat entered into the deeper water. The sun was yet to raise its full head from the hills, streaks of morning light were falling on his sweet face, his wet dark face was glowing, the energy of Satkosia had entering into his blood. I looked at his boat, small bamboo sticks were kept in bundles at the middle, a long bamboo oar was kept at the side; a small plastic pot was kept to remove excess water from the boat. Slowly he entered into deeper water; his face was still towards our side, not to the other side, though he was rowing into the deeper water. The boat was coming from the shade of the trees at the bank, to more open waters; the dancing ripples were shining on more illuminated portion of the water, giving a darker appearance to the boy with the sail. I looked at the other side, the forest on that side of the river was equally thick, faint near to water, the faintness increased with distance, the farthest forest was covered with fog; the green colour was hazed. There were a lot of sand deposits on the other side of the river, and in this side, the river bank had many protruding rocks, the river was much deeper in this side, so an ideal place for the fishes. I looked at the boy, he was rowing, moved a little into the water, took a round and slowly returned to the bank and tied it to the tree and went to his father, his father smiled, he had been watching him since the son was inside water, his muddy hand didn't tremble, but heart definitely. The boy laughed, everybody at the bank smiled, the new generation was coming into the waters of Mahanadi.

I looked at the other side of the same bank, the Sola (a type of very light reed of marshy land) floaters were hanging from a hanging bamboo by separate individual hooks. The floaters, essentially needed for this type of fish catching in the river, were a group of individual cut pieces of Sola, each individual member of the floater were around one foot long, 4-5 members are grouped together, tied at both ends and loose at the centre, floats easily in waters; once the fisherman descends into the water, his boat should be filled with these floaters. I looked at the people, bait preparation was about to end, the group was enjoying the morning sun of the January at the river bank. The cool breeze was blowing from the Manaibhadra hill, the fog was getting clearer, the fishermen were laughing with the increasing warmth. One person brought out some tobacco, shared it with the all members, a little was offered to the man making the bait. The fishermen were all young individuals, but experienced, to me except for the man with bait, all looked less than twenty-five years of age; I asked them, everyone had spent more than two decades in the Mahanadi waters. They were busy in preparing the mix, were gossiping, suddenly a noise came from the river, the descending branches onto the river water were parted; in came the hazed shadow of a new fisherman in a boat, he was asking for a little share of tobacco, his bare tanned black body was illuminated, he was smiling, was greeting the group, on his boat his left hand was almost touching the water as he was rowing with great force, on his right hand he was wearing a Deonria, and on the neck, he was wearing the religious tulsi threads. Here, the fishermen were quite religious, believe in god, and for every happenings, remember god, after all. They also perform Danda, the typical dance performed during the summer season. The boat, around 20 feet long and 3 feet wide, was having joints in between, over which a bamboo mat was kept, to keep the fish, to have more plain portion for food inside the water, plastic bags containing bait materials were kept in the middle, the food for the day was kept in a aluminum can, and a long bamboo was kept on the boat on his right. The boat slowly came to the light, he pushed the other boats for space and the boatman jumped on to the soil, pulled his boat, tied it to the branch of a tree by nylon rope. The other members greeted him, the old friend shared his feelings, and he smiled after a good tobacco bite, the Mahandai waters smiled.

The life of the fisherman starts with the first call of the birds and they enter into water with the rising sun at the mountain top and return with their catch with the first blinking star on the other side of the gorge, the Mahanadi river is full with fishes, both scale less, scaled fishes of all sizes. No net fishing takes place, all fishing are done by line fishing with Sola floaters, fishing hook jointed at the down end, the fishing is permitted only for the scaled fishes like Rohu, Katla, not the un-scaled fishes which are the pray base of the crocodiles. The crocodiles and the fisherman live side by side, harmoniously, without disturbing the pray base of each other in the same territory. Here, the fishing bait is unique – Pan masala, gudakhu, tezpatta, rice husk, tobacco and soil, all mixed thoroughly, are rolled together, balls are made, and the small hooks are kept inside the ball to catch the scaled fishes. The balls are then lowered into the deep waters of the river by attaching stones to the lines, no lead or iron is used, the lower end of the line touches the soil down below and on the top the Sola floats and dances on the water with the ripples. The lines are drawn across the river, and the fisherman waits at the river bank for the fish to eat the bait. The fish eats, the hook pierces into the mouth, the fish swims with the line, the Sola (floater) moves and the fisherman rushes to that particular Sola. Fishes weighing up to fifteen kg are caught regularly, the record catch was a twenty-five kg fish. In the deep waters of the gorge, catching a big fish with line and bringing it to a narrow country boat, is always a challenge; the big fish used to pull, the fisherman used to loosen the line, then pull again, loose and then pull the line and the process continues for some time. The fish finally gets tired, comes to the top, and the fisherman rushes at it, and catches the fish with an implement called Kinei made up of nylon nets. Then the fish is pulled up and kept in the boat.

"What kinds of fishes are there?" I asked

Kanabunga, Jalanga, the non-scaled fish weighs sometimes up to 50 kg, the scaled fishes like Bhakur, Kalabainsi are usually smaller than the non-scaled fishes, weighing around 15-20 kgs. One has to be very careful, the big fish can pull the boat very fast.

River crocodiles

"What about the crocodiles in the waters?" I asked

"The crocodiles swim across the river, many a time are found on the sandy beaches, but never attack a boat. The crocodiles and the boat have elder brother-in-law and younger sister-in-law relation, the crocodile is the sister-in-law and the boat is the elder brother-in-law." The sister-in-law can't touch the elder brother-in-law. In the tradition of fisherman elder brother-in-law is a person revered, not to be touched and the crocodile obeys the law most religiously, they never ever touch a boat. But unfortunately, the tradition is dying fast, sometimes the crocodiles are forgetting their vows and are coming closer to the boats, sometimes they touch the boats by their tails." Some kind of disbelief was seeping into his thoughts embedded deep inside, and the hollowness is formed.

Then he started telling about the crocodiles of the Mahanadi river.

"The crocodiles lays around 30-40 number of eggs during the rainy season, on the high land, in smallpit on the sandy beaches of the river. The mother remains in the water, ensures her eggs are well protected. The eggs are then hatched, the young ones are like big lizard (Endua in Odia language), and they used to run towards the water. If all the young grow, then the whole river will be filled with crocodiles, and they would eat all the cattle, cows and bullocks alike. The crocodile mother watches them from the bank, allows the young to move to the water, then the crocodile mother moves fast, catches the fastest and eats it. Like this she will kill most of her children, only 3-4 will survive. That is the rule within the crocodile family." He was narrating the strange behaviour of the mother crocodile as he knew, it was not actually true, the crocodile hatchlings are preyed on by fishes even. But I wanted to listen from his mouth.

"But why?" I asked. I was totally surprised.

"The mother thinks – Now the child is so young, still it beats me in speed, if it would grow to its full size, it would beat me, would kill me. Thinking this it then kills the fastest, the fittest one" The man replied.

"In the water, there are Gharial, or *Thantia Kumbhir*; and Mugger or *Gomuha Kumbhir*. The Gharial has the Ghadi on its snout, by nature the *Thantia Kumbhir* is not that aggressive, but the *Gomuha* is aggressive, but it never attacks the boat; the relationship is like between elder brother-in-law and younger sister-in-law" he explained about the behaviour of the crocodile.

Gharial

I recounted my knowledge on the crocodiles of Mahanadi at Satkosia for better understanding of the location, myths and beliefs associated with the gorge. The sweet water crocodiles, the Gharials are usually found in the different river systems like the Indus, the Brahmaputra, the Ganges, and the Mahanadi in India, and in small numbers in the Irrawaddy River in Myanmar. This crocodile is best adapted to the deep calmer areas of fast moving rivers. The physical characteristics of the Gharial are not suited for moving on land. The Gharial leaves the water either to bask in the sun or to nest on the sandbanks of the river.

This crocodile has a characteristic elongated, narrow snout, the bulbous growth on the tip of the male's snout is called a 'ghara' (meaning 'pot') The shape of the snout varies with the age and becomes progressively thinner with older Gharials. The ghara is used to produce a resonant hum during vocalisation; the appearance is a visual tool to attract females; the air bubbles are created by the ghara during the mating rituals of the species.

The young Gharials eat insects, small frogs, where as the adults feed solely on fish, some individuals may scavenge on dead animals. Their long, narrow snout is well suited to catch fish in water during swimming, and numerous needle-like teeth are ideal for holding on to the struggling fish.

The Gharial is not a man-eater; its thin jaws make it physically incapable to consume a large animal.

The mating season of the Gharials occurs during winter between November to January and the nesting and laying of eggs take place during the dry summer season of March, April, and May when the rivers shrink and the sandy river banks are available for nesting. The female Gharial lays between 30 and 50 numbers of eggs in the dug up, after egg laying the hole is covered. The juvenile emerge after about 90 days, and they themselves go into the water after they hatch, unlike other crocodiles who used to carry their young to water; probably because their jaws are not suited for carrying the young due to the presence of needle like teeth. The mother however, protects the young in the water for few days.

He gave me some interesting formulas to calculate the body size of the Gharial crocodiles.

a) If the entire body is seen, the approximate total length based on eye-estimation is mentioned.

b) If only the head is seen, body length = 7.0 x head length (from snout tip to post-occiput).

c) If snout-tip to hind leg visible, body length = 2 x (snout-vent length).

d) If tail tip to hind leg is visible, body length = 2 x tail length.

It gives so much interesting facts, I really appreciated his knowledge.

Mugger crocodile

The Mugger crocodiles can measure up to 12-14 feet long, but on an average around 10 feet long, and the female is around 7-8 feet long. The big individual males can weigh upto 450 kg. For a short distance, on a short pursuit of prey, this crocodile can achieve speed of around 12 Kmph on land, however it can swim much faster at around 15 to 18 Kmph for short distances, but generally swim at a speed of about 1.5 to 3 Kmph.

These crocodiles are generally found all over in India, Bangladesh, Nepal, Sri Lanka, Pakistan. It is the most common and widespread of the three species of crocodiles in India.

This fresh water crocodile is found in lakes, rivers and marshes. It prefers slow-moving, shallow water bodies, not fast-flowing waters or deep areas. Though it prefers freshwater, but it has little tolerance towards saltwater, therefore is occasionally found in saltwater lagoons. This crocodile is more mobile on land, can move considerable distances over land in search of a better living area. This crocodile can chase prey for short distances on land. They dig burrows as shelters during the dry seasons.

The Mugger crocodile eats fish, other reptiles and small mammals. This crocodile catches the prey at the water point, drags the animal into the water, then drowns it and eats at suitable time. Big adults sometimes prey on large mammals such as sambar deer, and even domestic buffalo. Sometimes, at night they hunt on land, wait to ambush near forest trails. The Mugger crocodiles are capable of high walk, only tail touching the soil.

Body length

a) If entire body is seen, the length is calculated on eye estimation.

b) If only the front part of the body is visible, upto the beginning of the tail, then: Body length = 2 times the length visible.

c) If only the head part of the body is visible, up to the post occipital scute then: Body length = 7 times the length visible.

d) When a crocodile basks on land, then due to movement of its tail parallel lines are created. Body length = 65 times the maximum distance between the two lines.

By measuring the hind paw length, without claw length, the total length of the crocodile can be found out.

For Mugger – Total body length = 14 times of hind paw length.

For Gharial – Total body length = 12 times of hind paw length.

Locating crocodiles

Many a times crocodiles are not sighted directly, it is necessary to look for the different indirect signs.

Signs for tunnels: Mugger crocodiles avoid extreme temperatures by entering into tunnels dug by them. These tunnels open into water and have narrow mouth. Height of the mouth may be about 30-60 cm. These may be up to 5 meters deep.

Body spoor: When a crocodile comes out for basking on sand or mud, and returns back to water it will leave the marks of its body, tail and paws on the ground.

Distinguishing the spoor of Gharial and Mugger crocodiles

Gharial – If the body spoor is without sign on a dragging trail, then the mark is of Gharial as the Gharial crocodile is not capable of high walk.

Mugger – If there is presence of sign of tail with paw marks on its sides; then the mark is that of Mugger. This crocodile is capable of high walk.

"Now only the crocodile number has increased, earlier people used to hunt the crocodiles for skin, my grandfather used to tell about the stories of those crocodile catching." He increased the interest in me, I was also keen to listen more on the crocodiles. I looked at the small sandy beach, the golden sand was appearing like molten gold in the early morning sun. I looked at it, one log was lying on the sand, it resembled a crocodile. The high banks were starting just beyond the sandy beach, and then continued the tall hillocks. In this area, catching the crocodiles must be difficult, deep water in the river, and high impregnable forest at the background, how the people could catch the river monster. Then he started narrating the events which he listened from his grandfather.

Catching of crocodiles

Earlier, people from Cuttack and other far off areas used to flock in Satkosia gorge for crocodile hunting. They came in their boats, carry goats, and chicken with them. These animals would be used as bet to attract the crocodiles of the river. They take the bait, throw it into the water, the strong lines are connected to the boat, the chicken floats on the water and flaps its wings, the river crocodile seeing the disturbance and sighting the prey attacks the prey and tries to swallow it. The sharp hook then enters into the throat of the crocodile and the crocodile has no chance to escape, it tries to escape, swims fast, the strong lines move with it, then the boat gets pulled in the course; and the crocodile seeing the futility of its escape and also the boat nearby, tries to attack the boat. On the boat the people are ready with long pointed spears with hook, at the other end of which again the lines are attached, as the angry crocodile comes near and tries to attack, the spearmen throw the spears at it. The body of the crocodile is now nailed with the spears, the animal is now deeply hurt, it tries to swim away from the boat, with so many lines it can't escape, it gets tired, the hunters then kill the crocodile by attacking it with sharp long spears, then they remove the skin. The story reminded me of the famous classic *Mobydick,* the whale was harpooned for its fat, the big whale was raising its massive head from the waters, the people on the hunting ship were throwing harpoons with lines, the animal could not take so many harpoons, it tried to flee, the long lines reduced its speed, the massive animal lose strength and were finally killed.

I looked at the boats, all were dancing in the green water of the river, the sun was getting brighter, I requested them to take me into the waters. One fisherman took me into the deep waters of the river, the other boatmen smiled, I too smiled; after all I wanted to take a look at the Mahanadi from its waters.

We entered into deeper water, small ripples were constantly touching us, and the sounds of rowing, ripple too were creating a symphony. The peace of the mountains was touching me, the colours of the mountains was colouring the watersand the sky appeared to be washed with morning fog. I looked ahead, mountains, mountains, innumerable mountains, each appears to came out of the waters, then took a detour, went backwards, climbed to the sky, vanished in the fog. Slowly mountain folds turned hazy, the green mountains were hazed in fog, and we entered further deep into the water. On our side, the sun was coming from the mountain top, the forest was slowly illuminated, the green colour of the trees were more apparent, less illuminated portions of the forest were looking darker. The mixture of dark, darker and darkest, the forest of Satkosia gorge was looking terrific, the forest colours has its say in the landscaping. The shades were hypnotizing, it was mesmerising my thoughts. Few boats appeared from the dark and came to light; they were silhouetted against the backdrop of the morning mountains.

I looked at my boatman, he was in his early twenties, was short, wearing a mild pink coloured half shirt, behind him another fisherman boy in his late teens, was helping him. The man was having thick beard on his face, local gamochha adorned his body, on the hand he was wearing a Deonria (a small silver or copper tube, inside which some medicine or ritual materials are kept; a remedy against bad omen), the tanned, dark body of the fisherman was shining in the bright sunlight.

I looked at the waters of Mahanadi, the ripples were touching the boat top, the small boat was dancing, and with it danced the vocal cord of the fisherman. The man, short, chest open, sun tanned, dark, the body without much bulging hills, muscles, but the tone had the vibrations of the river. He was rowing, the sun was on the back, his figure silhouetted against the backdrop of the mountains and he was narrating the stories on my request. The sounds of the rows were coming, a sweet sound, the boat was going ahead into the deeper waters of the river, the myths, the snakes of the Manibhadra are hidden behind the green veils of the mountains. The sun was shining in the right, the ripples were dancing and the water droplets were glittering like molten silver; no sound, except for the music of the waters.

The storm removes dust from the body,
Witch doctor repels the witch,
God removes the sin, removes the sin

A devotional song, the fisherman sang the song for his god, the sound of the rows was the background music.

River Mahanadi

I recounted my knowledge about Mahanadi, the river Mahanadi enters into the fold of continuously close mountains at Binkei temple towards upside and leaves the folds at Baliput at the downside, during the rainy season river Mahanadi swells, devastates the plain lands. The mighty river, due to its heavy size creates a deep gorge for the entire length; of course some sandy beaches are found at intervals. The gorge forests are mostly on mountain ranges and small narrow valleys formed in between the ranges, the area of the forested is around 964 square kilometer, comprising of two wildlife sanctuaries – the Satkosia gorge sanctuary on the Anugul side and the Baisipalli sanctuary in the Nayagarh side and the forest areas are spread into four districts namely Boudh, Anugul, Nayagarh and Cuttack. Satkosia area is the meeting point of two bio geographic regions of India, the Deccan Peninsula and the Eastern Ghats, thus holds immense biodiversity. There are over 400 plant species, out of which 126 are trees, 98 are shrubs and 51 are climbers; the main trees are Sal, Jamun, Bija, Sisoo, Arjun, Asan, Dhaura, Siris, Gamhar, Bahada, Harida, Amla, Siddha, Char, Kasi, Kendu, Phasi, etc. apart from Salia and Daba bamboos and extensive teak plantations.

In the forested areas around the gorge have 38 species of mammals, 27 species of reptiles and 4 species of amphibians; also 183 species of fishes are found in the gorge and rivulets. In the dense jungle tigers, elephants, spotted deer, sambar, chowsingha, barking deer, bison, wild dog, sloth bear, jackal, giant squirrel, porcupine, etc. are found in good numbers. In the gorge waters two species of crocodiles, the mugger and the Gharial live in; the turtles, terrapins, crabs, mollusces are too found in the water.

The landscape is mostly hilly, the slope of the hills is from moderate to steep, the average elevation of the hills is around 350 meter, the highest peak is Sunakhania with a height of 933 meters, say 3000 feet. The gorge is deep all over, is around 51 meters, say 165 feet deep near Tikarpada.

I looked at the green waters of Mahanadi, the ripples were making waves in my heart, the boat was silent; I was lost; opened my eyes, and then looked at the same fisherman who accompanied us so far. The boat was moving with the river currents for some time so that we could have a better look of the riverside, the water was not turbulent always.

"How deep is the water here?" I asked

"An eight storey building can be drowned here," he replied, so deep is Mahanadi here in Satkosia. This place is the play house of the big fishes. The gorge continues from Binikei to Badamuha, at Binikei, there is a Goddess, a festival is organized in his honour we respect Mother Mahanadi there. The other animals, snakes were also respected," the man replied.

We were close to a sand bank at that time, the quartz in the sand particles were dazzling like diamonds, the Maninag of Manibhadra hills descended down from its abode to drink the water of Mahandi.

Forests on the right bank side

On another day, to know about the mysterious snakes of Manibhadra hills, I entered into the Baisipalli wildlife sanctuary forests in the Nayagarh side. The Manibhadra hill is located near to Brutanga river and listened some unbelievable stories, history, mythology associated to the forests. We moved deep into the forest, strange settings, strange trees, the forests were full of unimaginable designs.

Sapua Stone (Snake stone)

I listened to a strange story amidst the thick forests, on the forest floor, the dry leaves formed a brown carpet, the Moi tree alongside the long tapering rock mass was full with new leaves, all other trees were full with new budding leaves, and the forest was changing the costume. I imagined of a big serpent, a huge one, around hundred meterslong, its tail lies between the bamboo bushes, Sal trees and ferns; the upper body went up, the serpent was raising its hood, white flowers of Sal trees were scattered on the ground, a small spring was flowing nearby. It was staring at the intruder to its space, hissing slowly, the wind when passed through the hills was generating a low hissing sound; a true habitat of the large reptile, the stone was getting life. Then I looked at the solid mass of rock, the local myth revolved around it, the smooth granite rock curled as a snake, diameter around 6-8 meter, widened from the tail upwards, took almost the shape a huge serpent, the body portion also curved, smoothened like snake, this huge stone snake took the first curl at around thirty meter, raised his rest of the body further upward, and ends at neck. The snake didn't have a head, head had been chopped off by a Kondh man.

THE STORY

In the olden times when the forests were black, shadow of a tree didn't fall on the ground, the canopy was closed, undergrowth was thick too; that time a Kondh tribal family consisting of husband, wife and a son was staying in the deep forests of Satkosia gorge area in Daspalla portion, now known as Baisapalli Wildlife Sanctuary. No other house was nearby; the nearest hamlet was far away, the tribe man stayed happily in the deep forest amidst fearsome tigers, enormous elephants and the scary snakes. The snakes of Satkosia area always reaches imagination, hundreds of feet long, thick as the bole of the largest Sal tree available in the forest. The man, as any other Kondh tribe man, loved to stay inside the deep forest, and he once went to further deep forest for hunting. He lived on fruits, hunted animals, and some cultivation, drank water from the clean springs. As usual, both husband and wife went away from the hut in search of food and other household materials, their child remained unattended, the mother went little away in search of firewood. Both returned at same time, they were shocked to see a huge serpent, the snake was raising its massive hood, the child was deep asleep under the hood. The parents were at their wits end, the huge snake could swallow the child in any moment, and they waited to see the next move of the serpent. The snake didn't leave its place, remained in raised condition, when it lowered its hood towards the sleeping child, the man fearing for the life of his son gave a heavy blow on the snake's neck by his sharp axe. Instantly the body of the snake was cut into pieces, the head flew to a place called Ranpur under Nayagarh district; and there the head has been worshipped as the Goddess Maninag, and here the massive body of the snake remained in the dense forest, turned to a granite stone.

I looked around, cool evening was approaching, thick and impregnable bamboo bushes were spread all around the area, a stream flows in a serpentine fashion through the bamboo forests and created a small waterfall at the tail of rock snake. The Sal trees were covered with white flowers, the rocks too were covered with white fallen Sal flowers, the rock was light dark grey at patches, dark bright grey at some other places, the shades of dark were creating almost parallel bands. Few ferns were standing alongside the snake rock, the appearance of the fern trees were like big upturned umbrellas. The thick hand sticks were embedded into the soil, the green clothes were attached to the body by green spikes, and many such trees dotted the course of the snake. Climbers, their trunks were as thick as large python, many much bigger than the size of the pythons too, curled around live trees, the thick climbers were strangulating the trees like a python curl around its prey and strangulate it. Many too went straight up to the highest canopy, as if big serpents hung from the branches of mighty trees, waiting for the victims to come near and then the snake would jump at the prey, strangulate it using its mighty curl, the forest to me, at that time came to life with the hissing sound of the snakes. I entered into the forest towards the tail of the rock snake, snakes everywhere, innumerable climbers, entwined, straight, curled, all imaginary arc shapes. The climbers of Satkosia were exhibiting geometrical designs of a curve, and there was no space to go further; you can't avoid the snakes of the forest. The bamboo forests were standing thick, impregnable, the forest floor was covered with golden white dry leaves of bamboo, the water was flowing between the bushes, and the true habitat of the serpent of Satkosia was created.

Nearby, so many big rock floors, none was as big as the snake rock, on the road there were few cactus trees, the branches were coming from the main trunk, almost leafless, the thorns were prominently visible. On the foot track the spikes of porcupines were found, the length of each spike was around a feet, thickness as a small pencil, the spikes were hallow, banded black and white, darkened towards tip and are very sharp; the strange animal is covered with thorny defence, the tiger can't put its paws on the animal, the spikes would protect it. In the habitat of the snakes one should be careful of thorns, thorny bamboo, thorny bushes, thorny cactus and thorny spikes of the porcupine.

We halted at a big rock floor, a huge one, length was around two hundred feet, and width around one hundred feet, surrounded by thick forest all around; over it around four hundred people can sit comfortably, lightly graded, but not very smooth mostly, the portions where water flew were smoothened, deep forests surrounded the rock, low hillocks with thick forest started almost a kilometer away. I couldn't believe when they told me about the stone; it bears the imprint of a mutiny, the warriors once revolted against the Britishers, the tyrant political agent Budglegate was killed by the agitators and the mutiny was planned here. A little detail sketch of the event was collected.

The militant mass struggle directed against reactionary ruler of the Ranpur state began when Prajamandal was formed towards later part of 1938. The uprising against the oppressor of Ranpur estate was planned here which led to the murder of Major Bud legate; the British political agent was a tyrant too, used to torture people for taxes. They gathered on the Bichara pathar, planned for the uprising, one eventful day when Major Bud legate went to Ranpur to collect taxes, the mutineers blocked the road by felling trees and keeping carts, the man was beaten by bamboos and lathis (sticks) to his death, the police couldn't come for his rescue.

I looked around, just at the foot of the huge rock floor, a white plant was flowering, beautiful radiating flowers, the small herbal plant without woody stems emerged from the ground, the long thick, narrow and tapering leaves were moving away from the base on the ground; a long thick stick (pedicel) emerged from the base, overtook the leaves and beautiful flowers were exhibited at the end. I looked at the flower keenly, what a soothing white colour, five long petals from the flower base over which a beautiful curved base with small spike like design, the longer individual petals were curved after a distance. The white stamen was going upwards, the golden anther were placed on the top, the anther somewhat converged and a folded hand formation came out. The flower was smiling, the sanctuary paid floral tribute to the unknown heroes beyond the eyes of the common people.

I looked at the beauty of the forests, I was seeing so many shades, so many colours, so many unthinkable mechanical designs, forest is the store house of knowledge, the unimaginable structural designs are created in a forest, the way the branches hung from a big tree on a steep slope, a structural design is there to understand the cantilever theory, also to understand the principle of balance, the structural designs of big cities were displayed in the forest. Also how the rocks are embedded, otherwise how a big tree is dwarfed – the trees come up within little space between the rocks with littlest nutrients, the concept of Bonsai was displayed in nature. The building configuration, the drainage pattern, use of bio degradable material, the concepts of so many branches of science was gathered in the forest, the self-cleaning mechanism of the lotus leaves created the modern non-stained paints, the examples are so many, forest is the laboratory for physics, chemistry, and so many branches of science.

A Village, No Bulls Ever Visited

After a while we arrived at a small village surrounded by forests all around, the cultivation fields started just at the edge of the house clusters, the villagers here in Gadajat have house clusters, the villagers don't stay in individual houses in individual fields, the house cluster gives the village the size, creates a protection wall for the village.

"This village is called Makar Prasad, and most strangely no bull ever visited the village. Any bull if unknowingly visits the village it would die. The cows, when hot, go to the forests around the brass Mahadeva temple, where they used get impregnated strangely." He started telling about unusual event, it was unbelievable, how it could be possible. I was perplexed, I disbelieved him; he was telling strange things just to attract my attention.

"You may disbelieve, the news came in the TV the veterinary authorities visited the area, but they couldn't get any plausible reason of such cow impregnation event." He wished to remove the disbeliefs in my thoughts.

"When a bull comes to the village limit and roars for two three times, strangely next moment it would fall sick and subsequently would die, it would never mount on a cow. The villagers, the people couldn't find any reason for such death. The cow, during its heat period used to go to the forest, the owner doesn't arrange for a bull, the cow comes impregnated and bears a calf. The villagers had not seen a bull inside the forest; they are still unable to solve the mystery." He explained.

I looked at the hill in front of me, beyond the cultivation fields, the hill shape was like a sitting bull, green forest covered all over, the top portion was flat like the back of a bull, the hump of the bull was near the exposed rocks which were raised a little from the flatter shape, then curved inwards, and the head portion started. The hill actually resembles a bull to some extent, but actually did not look like a bull, but the local belief created the shape and they believed the bull God resides there. Many stories evolved, the village priest used to go to the hill to worship the Bull God, the travel to the hill was difficult, seeing the daily struggle, the Bull God threw the brass pot towards the village and it felled near a Sahada tree, there the priest established the God.

Our travel inside the forests continued, we came to Padmatola portion of the continuous forests, a thick forest, the trees were little bigger, impregnable as usual. The day was dark high canopy covered the sky. My eyes were searching for the lives, all the shades were increasing my interest, in the jungle, the sensory organs need to be alert, to understand the lives around; breaking of twigs may be caused by the cautious tigers, the yellow dark shadow may be the sign of the leopard, a little pressure on your body may be due to the presence of the Krait on your side, the foul smell draws you to a tiger kill nearby.

"Do you know the ancient kingdom of Kalinga was famous for its elephant troop?" he opened a new chapter. I knew about the Mahabharata epics, the mighty king of the Kalingas, accompanied by a large army with 10,000 elephants and the Nishada army fought in the Mahabharat battle. Then he narrated the way the elephants were caught from the Padmatola forests.

The Hatikheda

The mighty kingdom of Kalinga was once famous for its warrior elephants, the kings used to capture powerful elephants from the forests of Satkosia gorges, around Padmatola hillocks. An area of around four acres would be demarcated, inside the area trees like banana, bamboo, etc would be planted, and around the periphery strong tall strong Sal pillars would be posted. On the top of the pillar sharp iron rods would be attached, and the logs would be connected to each other; and there would be a strong gate at the entrance. The structures would be camouflaged with the jungle landscape. The elephant while searching for food unknowingly enter into the trap, it merrily eats the plentiful of banana plants, then the gate would be closed. The elephant after getting sufficient food and water forgets about the outside jungle, then the food gets finished, now the elephant has no route to escape, it remained in hunger for a long period, around 1-2 months. When the wild elephant is sufficiently weak to retaliate, the trained eiephant would be brought, it chains the captured one, and the roaming elephant would thus be chained for the rest of its life, and remains at the service of the king.

We moved forward, my companion started telling about the importance of the forest, the myths and history embedded in the land, unknown to many. On the way, we crossed a river, they called the river as Brutanga river. I was surprised, the name appeared somewhat Burmese, and no history ever mentioned about Burmese influence over the area, never any one from Mongoloid race ever came or never a lady of that area married a man from this place, and Brutanga is the name of the tributary of Mahanadi which flows through Nayagarh district , discharges huge volume of water from the catchment areas in Phulbani and Nayagarh into the Mahanadi river at a place a few kilometers away from Manibhadra hills. The river, though discharges a huge volume of water during the monsoon, remains dry during the dry season, the local believes it to be Gupta Ganga, the reason – if small pit is dug on the river bed, water oozes out and fills up the pit, where as in the Mahanadi river bed in the dry season water doesn't come out. It was a strange phenomenon for the locals, the river Brutanga holds immense water in its fold, they in fact named the river as Gupta Ganga, which over the period of time lost its original name and presently is known as Brutanga.

They told me about the mythology associated with the river, why it in fact was called as Gupta Ganga. Once Arjuna, the famous character of epic Mahabharata, took Agyantabasa (living in unknown land), in the deep forests of Manibhadra, alongside the blue course of river Mahanadi and Sreekrishna showed himself to Arjuna in his Nabagunjara shape in the forests of Manibhadra. In lived a demon there, infamous for his arrogance and torture, in the dense jungle of the Mahanadi River, named Gosingha and Goddess Narayani was his deity. He stole Satyabhama, the queen of Krishna, and took her to his fortress in Gosinghagada, after sending Balarama and Krishna to the Yagna for sacrifice. Arjuna, listening to the cry of the woman, fought with the demon; in course of heavy fight Gosingha was killed, and queen Satyabhama was freed. The lady wanted to take bath, the demon had touched her, Arjuna shoot an arrow into the dry river bed and the water came out and the charming lady of Sreekrishna took bath in river, inside the deep forests of the Manaibhadra and other hills. Since the river holds so much of water underneath, then onwards the river was known as Gupta ganga, now called Brutanga. Today, the epic events in the laps of Mahanadi are hardly known; the remains of the fortress lies hidden in the Baisipalli Sanctuary, the remains of the bones of the demon are gathered at Asurakhola inside the forests.

Maninag and other snakes of Manibhadra hill

In one afternoon, I looked at the green hills in front of me, it was Manibhadra hill. They didn't appear that dreaded, the hill started after the village limit, not very thick forests now, but the hill holds so much of stories, so much of beliefs.

In the following evening I was not alone, the old man in front of me had crossed his age many years ago, the old frame was frail and fragile, many curves on the tiny black body, the eyes lowered too, and the muscles didn't bulge any more, voice was shattered, no more deep and strong. I found it difficult to understand how there was so much adventure inside. He looked at the darkest corner, the candle light was dancing on his frail body, changing him to a shadow, when he spoke his shadow spoke too, the shadow grew bigger and bigger, fearsome, the reflected voice was deep, full with the hisses of Maninag hills. When he talked, his companions listened in silence, except for the movement of heads no other movement was noticed, they were recollecting those golden days, the myths associated with the Maninag serpent.

The Maninag snake, the king of the snakes, used to descend from the hills riding a King Cobra in the dead of the night. I quoted his description, many were unbelievable, the snake was not big or long, of around three inch diameter, the snake swells if it sees a human, the girth can go up to five to seven feet. A shining jewel, called *Nagamani*, is placed between the eyes. From a distance it appeared like glow worm, if the light from that mani fall on any man or animal it gets burnt, even the grasses, leaves on the way gets burnt, and most strangely the highly educated mass in that area too believe in the existence of Maninag today. For them the jewel is in existence and many myths are associated with this snake. Once a *Sapuakela*, a group of people who perform snake charming and are adept in handling snakes, came to the Manibhadra hill area, and to capture snakes he started reciting the Padmatola, the mantras to control furious snakes. The *Sapuakela* in fact dared to recite the Padmatola mantra at the closest vicinity of the Manibhadra hills, the mantra has an effect. If the *Sapuakela* recites the mantra and spreads sand around a snake, the snake would never escape from the boundary till the *Sapuakela* frees the snake from the effect. The snakes there lived on the trees, inside the caves, in fractures of the stones; strangely some mighty snakes live on atop the big trees.

The eyes of the old man gloomed in fear, he recounted one such nest of a mighty snake atop a big Sal tree, the circumference of the tree must be more than twenty feet, the nest was on the top, big logs – the girth around three feet were crossed together, sized and nest was formed. He himself couldn't believe the might of the snake, whether the snake really could carry such big logs to the top of the trees and could form a nest there, but he had seen one, he was convinced of the size of the snakes of Manibhadra of the olden time.

He recounted another story, a huge snake returned late from Mahanadi, the recent time story, the early morning Government Bus encountered the snake, it hissed loudly, the driver stopped the engine, everybody closed the window, the bus came to standstill. The bus driver couldn't dare to run over the huge snake, it raised its hood, all the people panicked, froze themselves, the snake looked at, hissed loudly, here the passengers shivered in fear, but finally the snake left; such are the size of huge snakes of Manibhadra.

Here, the snake man recited the Padmatola mantra, played the *Saptaswara* and beat the Damru. The sound reverberated from the forests, the hills, other snakes came, any snake who listened the mantra came to the *Sapuakela*, so came the Maninaga, the king of the snakes riding a King Cobra. It saw the *Sapuakela*, its size swelled, the *Sapuakela* recited the mantra, the Maninaga was not hypnotised, its size swelled further. The *Sapuakela* was unable to control the snake which so wanted to flee, but the mighty snake sucked the *Sapuakela* into its mouth, the man wrongly challenged the power of the Snake emperor, and met his final fate. No man ever caught a snake at Manibhadra hills.

Earlier I listened about the Padmatola Mantra, it was strange. I looked at the man, what would be the effect of the mantra on the snakes. The old man looked at me, his eyes glowed, then he told,

"Padmatola is the verses to capture a snake, the Gunia (man perfect in the mantra) can recite the mantra. The Gunia when finds a snake, takes little sand or dust from the ground, then recites the mantra, and throws at the moving snake; whatever powerful the snake might be, but it can't leave the place, it is imprisoned by the mantra, remains within the periphery over which the sand or the dust falls. Unless the Gunia recites the other mantra to free the snake, the snake can't leave the area," he was describing the power of the mantra. I looked perplexed, if the mantra is so powerful, then how the Maninaga was not captured. He understood my confusion, then explained,

"Padmatola is the most potent weapon, a Gunia can have, but the recitation has to be perfect, again your internal power matters, the Maninaga was the most powerful snake. The Padmatola of the Gunia was not that clear and strong, so the snake broke that mantra barrier, could overpower the Gunia," the answer was strange, to his satisfaction, in me still confusion and fear roamed.

The ferocity of the snake of Manibhadra almost paralysed our thoughts; we couldn't utter a word for some time. I looked at the flame, a blue one, I could see the ferocious snake there the serpent was looking at us, burning fire in its mesmerising eyes; the flamer moved with the light wind, the serpents descended from the hill into the room, dark shadows danced on the wall, from all dark corner the snakes peeped their heads to listen about the Maninaga. Outside, the dark night was filled with innumerable stars, they gathered around the dark hills, the Manibhadra hill was coming to life.

The old man took a long breath, faint light was falling on the man, a very old man, may be in his eighties or nineties, the dark face was covered with white beards, the eyebrows had even turned white, the skin was loose like the scale of a snake, the uncombed hair on the head were rising like the small snakes. He understood my feelings, I was interested to listen to the snake stories of the hill, he continued about the stories of recent times.

Snake Encounters

It was the month of Baisakha, the summer was in peak, few villagers went to Mahanadi early in the morning before sun rise to take bath, the days was Panasankranti, that day the Odia households make Pana – a type of non-alcoholic nutritious drink in which a lot of ingredients like coconut, bel, chattua, gud, etc. are added and a drink is prepared which is offered to the deity, also the people drink; they took Shiva Paita (sacred thread) on Mahanadi waters and were returning after crossing long sandy beach when they witnessed two large snakes in their mating ritual dance in the fields, just at the outskirts of their village. Seeing the large snakes they didn't go further, the snakes during their mating ritual dance turns to be more aggressive, the snakes curls to each other, raises their heeds, move their bodies in synchronised fashion, a treat to watch the dance in open. The snakes were unaware of the humans; and the red-brown village dogs were close. Suddenly seeing the snakes in the vicinity, also seeing their master close by, the dogs garnered courage and charged at the mating snakes, barking at them regularly. The unwarranted presence of the dogs broke their mating dance, the smaller snake went to a bush and the larger snake charged at the dogs with long hissing, the head was raised almost five feet, with lightning speed, it came to more open areas. Now the snake was vulnerable to counter attack from all sides, the jungle was around two hundred feet away. Instantly the dogs retreated, but didn't gave up, and charged at the snake as it took the turn and tried to go back to forest. The snake was angry, the snake turned once again, and charged at the dogs, they retreated, but their courage increased, the snake could not leave the place, as soon as the snake turned the dogs went to the tail side and barked at it, but they never came to the striking distance. Two more dogs joined the group; four dogs now charged at the snake from all sides.

The villagers seeing the snake-dog fight gathered around, now around two hundred people, they were surprised to the see the size of the snake, it would kill human and cattle at any moment if it stays near the village, so they all threw stones at the mighty snake, the dogs were charging from the other side.

Many stones were hitting the snake, the stones were returning as if it had hit a spring, a rubber. The snake was very angry now, its hissing increased, the people retreated a little, but the dogs were relentlessly charging at the snake, the people again started pelting more and more stones, and the snake couldn't escape, a big stone hit its head, the snake fell onto the ground, continuous stone pelting took its life, a sorry end for the large snake of Satkosia.

Listening about the ferocity of the snakes, the power of the snake king, my mind went to the Gunias, the man who catches the snake in the hinterlands of Odisha, the man in front of me was the store house of the traditional knowledge.

"How could the Gunias catch the snake." I asked him.

"It is not Gunia, but the *Sapuakela* catches the snake. The *Sapuakela* comes to the place where the snake resides, then plays music in his *Saptaswara* instrument, also plays Dambaru. The snake, if the saptaswar is played, can't remain in its hiding and would come out. The *Sapuakela* then tries to catch the snake, he is an adept snake catcher, still some times the snake bites him; the man beforehand has to take Gada (a type of mysterious root), or keep the Gada in the mouth and suck it, the snake poison will not harm him. In case the snake poison is more than the potency of the Gada, then the accompanying man will administer further Gada to him, the man will survive and catch the snake. The poison teeth of the snake then will be broken and the snake will be kept in a bamboo basket," the old man was explaining the ways to capture the snakes.

"Saptaswra, *Dambaru, Padmatola mantra*, still are insufficient to control the snakes of Manibhadra hills. The snakes of the Manibhadra hills are more powerful than the power of all three put together, so the *Sapuakela* never catches a snake from the Manibhadra hills," He elaborated the details, also tried to remove my confusion.

"Can you recite the *Padmatoala mantras*?" I asked him.

He looked at me, a smile, then deep lines surfaced on his forehead, the man was trying to remember the Padmatola mantra, the most potent mantra to pacify the big serpents, I initially thought it to be a strange recitation.

Odia	*Translation*
Kansara Ghrani, Padmavati Rani Perform Dhanitiri puja Lakhe bhra padma debure kahniai Tanhi Pakhuda Nathiba Misha ki	Padmavti, the queen of Kansa perform the Dhanitiri puja Kahnai, bring one lakh loads of lotus The petals should not mix with lotus

i)	Govinda Hare Kalindi Jalare Kalinag thila Bishara jwalare Hradara jalare Sri krushna padile dhalike Gobinda hare	Govindaa Hare The black sepent was in the Kalindi waters Lake water was poisoned Sri Krishna fell down Govinda Hare
	Garuda sumarante aanila amruta toliki Govinda Hare	Garuda remembered, he plucked Amrit Govinda Hare
ii)	Jasoda khuchhnti Shunare Kahnai Se nuhein Klindi hrada, prninkara kala Maha Maha rushimane bhasile agrala Dhana naja phula toil Kali nagunin dansib payare tohari.	Jashoda is telling, "Listen Krushna Kalindi Lake is the death water Big Rishis fell victim Dear son don't go for plucking The black serpent would bite you."
	Krushna Blarama dui bhai gale phula toil Phula tolila bele dansana karila pade kali Dhli pdile banmali Prasu kedara gada Kara sumara pad Amruta kunda pani Nayane chhatile ni Tebe uthile banamli.	Krushna Balarama went to pluck flowers The black serpent bit on foot Sri Krishna fell down. Let eat Kedara gada Recite the words The water from the Amrita pot Splashed on the face Sri Krishna got up.

These songs are simple songs, on the occasion of Kaliya Manthana – the subjugation of black serpent of Kaliya lake, not complex recitation, the audience can understand the spell well. Then how did the snake charmer manage the show; the snake charmer sings the song for the audiences, his hand and body movement attracts the snake.

As a young kid, I listened to the power of the Gada to cure a snake bite, but I didn't know what material it was, I asked the question to the old man, he also nodded his head, no confirmation, he didn't recognize the root, he only knew the root is available from the forest, but was unsure of the exact origin, exact herb.

The evening was getting thicker, mystery clouded hill was looking bigger with increasing darkness, in the sky only faint star light, the depth of the mysterious nights were deepening. The cool breeze was coming from the hills, as if the untold stories were carried towards us. I asked about the myths of the hill, not snakes alone for which the hill was known, but also the extraordinary events associated with the hill.

Rishi Gumpha (The Cave of Rishis)

The shadow then started telling about the caves in the Manibhadra hills, the snake caves, the wild boar caves, the porcupine caves. The snake cave is wide, fifteen to twenty people can easily stay there; the wild boar cave is a cave in the shape of a hole on a big stone and the porcupine caves are small caves in the stone faces. The Rishi Cave is located above these caves, a huge cave, people couldn't enter beyond hundred to two hundred feet. They believed that a golden platform exists inside the Rishi cave, many men tried to enter into the cave, but could not enter into the cave fully.

That time, more than half a century back, Laxman Behera was in his prime youth, he heard from his friends, his folks, that his forefathers had been talking about the Rishi, the riches of the Math atop Manibhadra hills, at the dead of the night people used to listen devotional songs, at the deepest silent hours used to come the sound of Khola and Kartal, Sankirtan music, bright light used to move at the hill clouded with myths and beliefs, it was the abode of the large snakes too. The Maninaga and other snakes stay in their caves in the Manibhadra hills and above their caves the cave of the Rishi was located, many people wanted to enter, they heard about the golden altar of that cave. He was motivated by the adventure of some of his villagers. In that olden times Mangalu from his village entered into the cave for the first time, came back after one and half days, narrated his experience to the village the cave was a deep cave, the entrance was very narrow, around two feet at the beginning. He had to crawl at the beginning for some distance, he crawled like a snake, the cave mouth widened after some time, he could move by his knees, and after some time the height and width increased. He could stand in a bending condition and moved forward, he reached a spacious place but couldn't venture further, so returned.

Getting initial clue from the first explorer, Laxman entered into the cave, initial entry was difficult. After some time he came to a relatively broad area, found many routes, ways leading to all direction, in the dark cave if the direction is lost, one will be lost forever, and these explorer were not equipped with modern gadgets, and in the rustic setting they ventured into the place with whatever implements they could gather their hand. Laxman crawled for almost one hundred feet in that dark, and arrived at a hall which can accommodate two to three hundred people, the walls were smooth as the wall of the house, and the height was around twenty feet. A well was there, and inside the well there were a lot of bats. There were three paths, the width were around six inches, he couldn't venture further, the width was too narrow. He recollected, the place must had housed the sage once, such a wide hall, the walls were so smooth, the well was so smooth and deep. Must be the sage was living there, his throne must be golden; he couldn't get any items from that place, couldn't get the sign of life there except for the bats. He recounted, many people who were fortunate got many implements of the sage, many got food too. Now the people were impure, the sage had hidden himself from the eyes of the people. Still, they listen even today, at the dead of the nights of the auspicious days, the sounds of Khola, tala, kirtan for a few seconds from the hill top of Manibhadra, the saints are taking name of God in the auspicious days.

I was carried to the world of myths, in the deep forests of the Satkosia gorge, so much adventure was stored, the men dared to come out of disbeliefs and could do some daring works, the task was not easy for the men. Their world was so small, so many Gods, Goddesses, demigods, snakes and stories of human limitations; so much of distress around, still the man could dare, to me it was a story of a traveller crossing insurmountable. My eyes were closed in disbelief, in the land of beliefs and disbeliefs; I too was carried away with the disbeliefs, strength within me waned. He smiled, he could gauge conflicts within me, and the myths should have discouraged the man, but getting courage was strange. Then he revealed the source of inspirations, the land holds the story of the epic Mahabharata, the man in the deep forest derives strength from the beliefs within, the god fearing man sees the inspiration in the characters, creates the will.

Next day morning I came to the end of the long gorge. The hills now parted away, took turn at both banks, they were no more coming closer, the river slowly turned wide with long and wide sandy beaches. I looked at the back, Mahanadi water was calm as that of a village pond, no ripples, no waves, and absolute calmness. On both banks green mountains towering into the morning sky, the skyline was hazed, so many wavy lines descended into the waterline; reflections of the green mountains were creating shadows on the river water, thus reducing the bright water, the river was further narrowed. I looked front, the long bright green white line widened, brownish white sand deposits increased. A fisherman was coming towards us in his traditional country boat, a narrow one as described earlier, the red gamochha (towel) was falling on his shoulder, a lenguti around the waist, he was looking at the deep gorge at my back, the oar on his hand moved quickly, the man was moving forward in the calm water. Alongside the sandy beaches, an old fisherman, and a boy, the grandfather and the grandson, both semi-naked with open chests, were sitting in their boat, the old man was raising the nylon net, the boy was collecting the fishes from the net, the boat was on the sand, they put their legs on the water, low ripples were wetting them; the children of Mahanadi were busy in their daily cord, the traditional knowledge was passed from the generation to generation.

A herd of cattle was descending to waters of a nallahs alongside the bank, they first drank water, the reflections on the water changed, green was now replaced with red, white, black. Slowly they entered into the water of the tributary, and then they swam, their heads were raised, the tails were raised too, the ears were almost perpendicular to the water. They swam for around 100 meter and reached the other side. A group of women were taking bath, they were cleaning their teeth using the sahara stick (a type of tree), their bright skins were glowing in the morning sun.

I looked at the long sand deposit near me, low water around it, Mahanadi was calm, the – Tintian birds (Lapwing birds), a small dark brown coloured bird with dark head and beak, as well as black feathers at back, were standing on the golden brown coarse sand and enjoying the morning sun, they were passively watching the events around. A little away one bird was sitting alone, alongside a small log, its belly was placed on the golden sand, the dark eyes were watching the flowing waters, Mahanadi was leaving the land of uncertainty, beliefs and disbeliefs.

The Kaliani Wind

"Many are not aware that the present day direct air link between Delhi and Bhubaneswar, owes its very existence to this gracious animal."

The sentences brought immediate attention, I was reading the article "Tigers of Odisha" written by Mr. A.N. Tiwari, Former Secretary Tourism and Chief Editor of "Reference Odisha", I simply paused at a line, which read like above.

I read further, earlier, the air travel to Delhi from Bhubanesawr was via Calcutta, and a tigress impressed the Union Minister, he was hypnotised by the imperial tigress, and presented a gift to people of Odisha who reared the wild tigress with parental love.

Mr. Gangadhr Mohapatra, Minister of Tourism, Govt. of Odisha raised the issue of direct air connectivity between Delhi and Bhubaneswar with the Union Minister of Tourism Mr. Raj Bahadur at Delhi, and in the course of discussion informed about the royal princess of Similipal forest, the tigress Khairi; the Union Minister was immediately impressed at the news of uncommon and decided to pay a visit to Khairi.

Khairi was brought from Jashipur, she waited at the adjacent room for the arrival of the minister, the minister would be given a surprise. The Union minister arrived with his full team, sat on the chair, the Minister of the state sat in front along with other officials, The connecting door was opened and Khairi stepped in, in her step the arrogance of the princess was there, all noise fall silent, a pin drop silence. The Union Minister and his troupe was face to face with a live tigress in a closed room, they simply froze. Khairi moved gracefully, stood in front of the main chair in which the Union Minister was sitting, and sprayed urine on the wall, nobody could utter a word in front of the grace of the majestic tigress. Khairi looked at the people, slowly stepped back and returned to her place at the adjacent chamber; her mere presence casted a magic spell on the insiders, the Union Minister was bowled over by the mere look of the tigress.

I looked at the photograph published on that book. The Union Minister in his Neheruvian attire with long coat on the body and Gandhi cap on the head, was sitting on the chair, his hands were on the big office table in front, his head was moved in the direction of Khairi, and Khairi, the big loving tigress was standing at around two three feet away from the minister, his face was moved towards the camera as if the princess was giving a pose for the photo shot.

The Union minister was spell bound. His eyes behind the thick glasses were glued to the tigress.

Mr. Raj Bahadur, the Union Minister returned to Delhi, and made the announcement of direct flight from Delhi to Bhubaneswar and from that day Bhubaneswar is connected to Delhi directly. Owe it to the graceful appearance of Khairi; an unknown chapter of Khairi's life, an acknowledged contribution of Khairi for the development of the state.

In a Kharia village

After reading the article I was interested to come to the motherland of Khairi, she was instrumental in developing Odisha, I still couldn't believe it, so I entered into the deep forests of Similipal, came to a Kharia village of Astkuwanara, the Kharias were the people who collected the tiger cub from the deep forests, alter the same cub turned famous as Khairi. I was looking at the Kharia boy; his extraordinary climbing skill was creating so much of anxiety in me.

That day, the Kharia boy was climbing a straight tree in the forests of Similipal, I couldn't believe my eyes, a straight trunk runs up for minimum thirty feet, the boy put his right leg on a fissure, the figures were pressed hard into the gap, the left leg was on another fissure, both hands were holding whatever fissures, barks that had come out, eyes were fixed on the trunk; the boy took the first step in his climb on the straight tree. Next moment his right leg pressed whatever gap available on the bark. The left leg lifted to the waist height, body half bowed, the hands were at the waist level, eyes were on the hand and his small axe was hanging on his left shoulder without any support. The boy climbed for some fifteen feet, the tree was now straight, no fissure, gaps or branches, the tree bark now turned smooth; the boy halted a little, both of his legs were in parallel position. The left hand was holding the tree trunk firmly. He looked up, some hallow need to be created for further climb; he freed his right hand, brought the axe on his right hand, hold the axe at the base, and started hitting the bark, some small split wood came out, one small hallow was created, he took the axe on his left shoulder again and started climbing the big tree with ease; he reached a branch, stopped for few seconds, looked down at the ground, a smile came out from the mouth. The population adept in climbing was displaying the special qualities without aid of modern climbing equipments and safety tools. The Khadia tribe of Similipal were proficient in climbing for centuries, far away from the eyes of modern civilization, they have been collecting honey from tall trees, steep mountains, vertical cliffs, no place could remain untouched. The Khadia can reach the height to collect the honey, they are still food gatherers, collect honey, Jhunas (Sal resin) from trees, Mandei tuber, Pitalu tuber, Baian tuber, Palua (arrow root), etc. from the forest floor, still far away from settled agriculture. In the forests, both husband and the wife move together. The best company is the wife, she stays together. The man climbs the trees, descends on the cliffs, the wife looks at the husband and assists him in his daring daily mission.

I looked at the man standing next to me. Kharias were a strange tribe, surprisingly an Odia tribe, lives deep inside the forests of Similipal, their language pure Odia, not like many other tribes whose languages are difficult to understand, the other Odia speaking tribe like Bathudi, Mankadia, Sauntia live in and around the forests of Similipal. The Bathudia and Sauntias live in the outskirts of the deep forests, the Khadias and Mankadias live deep interior. Kolhas, also Santhals are the other major tribe found in deep interior. They are not the original tribe, they colonized the flatter valleys of Similipal, were brought from erstwhile Bihar state, now Jharkhand areas, to assist the kings of Mayurbhanj in his Pariidhi (hunting of wild animals) in the forests. The local people were averse to the killing sprec of the kings in the peaceful lands of the Similipal; there was a myth too, the Kharias and Mayurbhanj kings descended from same lineage. According to a common myth, both the Bhanja kings of Mayurbhanj and the Kharia were born out of a pea-fowl's egg. The king was born out of the yoke of the egg, the Purans (another community) out of the white part and the Kharias out of the shell. The Kharias, being from the same lineage can't perform such duties which are against their principle, can't be a part of the senseless killings. It is also very strange, the Kharias don't perform mass Shikar (hunting) which is prevalent in other tribal societies, the link to the past prevents them from doing so.

I couldn't believe when I listened for the first time, never thought that those slender creatures are capable of doing so many astounding feats; collection of honey from the cliffs of Jorands falls in the dead of the night; they call the cliffs as 'Bhandara' (literally meaning-store house), I learnt so much about the fall, so much mystery is surrounded, the seven sister witches, the powerful strange lights, and fearsome animals; still the Kharia man dares to descend to such depth in the dead of the night.

I recollected my memory; surrounded by total greenery a huge waterfall spews massive volumes of water down, straight down, the Khadia man drops down the cliffs of the straight fall, the 19th tallest waterfall of the country, to collect honeycombs hanging on the vertical inaccessible cliffs of the hill, he descends at the dead of the night on a swinging Siali creeper ladder – a ladder made using the fibres of Siali (Bahunia valhii) creepers, in between short sticks were attached to both creepers at regular interval with the torch created by burning chipped wood of sisoo tree, to collect honey.

Many precautions are taken in the forests, the collector or his companions don't utter the name of the elephant in the forest, as they believe; elephant has the power to know it and it may cause chase them in the forest. The wife shouldn't enter into the forest with red cloth or red saree; the deities of the hills, streams and rivers are believed to be decorated with red sarees, they will feel offended and cast evil eye on the concerned persons. There shouldn't be any auspicious sign or bad omen during the starting of the journey; no empty pitcher is sighted which is a sign of unsuccessful endeavour, the dogs shouldn't bark when the team leaves for the forest journey, the barking also is inauspicious.

The man climbs up to the cliff, as near as possible to the Bhandara with one or two companion, may be his wife, or his brother-in-law, or father-in-law, the trust on the person is extremely important, the collection process is extremely dangerous. The collector then secures one end of the rope to a nearby tree which they call a '*Khuntuni Munda*' and the rope is then thrown down to the bee hives below the cliff from this tree, the ropeis further divided into two parallel strings to make a loop called 'Hala' (or pair) and to this pair, small sticks are tied to make a ladder. The honey collector then descends down using this ladder in pitch darkness for the collection of honey; they avoid moonlit night which enables the honey bees to see the collector and furious attack then results. The honey bees are unable to see in the dark night, the collector smoke the bees out of the hive.

The collector makes arrangement for smoke, the chipped sisso wood pieces are allowed to burn with green leaves to form a smoke producing torch which is hung from rope, this smoke torch with rope is called Barehi which is thrown down and allowed to hang below the hive; the Barehi produces a lot of smoke which suffocate the bees and drives them away from their hive.

When the collector descends down, he is in an extremely dangerous situation; any damage to the rope means fatal accident and sure death due to fall from such great height, so the most trusted people like the son-in-laws or brother-in-laws, or wives watch the rope. The man then descends down, the axe hangs on the shoulder, a bamboo basket hangs on his waist by ropes; with little wind the man swings in air, the water drops of the mighty fall falls on his face, the endless ground remain hidden below in total darkness, the sound of the water deafens the ears, the white lines of the water surf shines in the starry night at some distnces; and the Khadia man drops further down. Smoke of the Barehi engulfs the bee hive, the ferocious Baghua honeybees (ferocious rock honeybee with poison stings) flee from the comb. Day time it would be impossible to collect honey from cliffs, the honeybees would attack; the bees flow away at the smell of the smoke, the Khadia man then removes the comb from the cliff using a knife like flattened wooden stick from the stone surface.

Before the honey collection, the collector prays to the concerned Goddesses of the hill, as per the belief each hill or forest is controlled by a specific deity called Basuki; he then prays to the Sun God, Village-Goddess, Badam (the principal deity of Similipal as per the belief). The collector offers honey after the collection is over to the Gods and Goddesses. A part of the first collected hive (the part containing only the larva of honey bees) is thrown down in the name of the hill goddess or Basuki; they believe, Basuki takes the offerings in the form of a tiger.

After collection, the collector climbs up with the honey combs, reaches the cliff, goes to his companion or his wife, the woman smiles, the wife is the protector, the seven sister witches will not come – a glimpse of theirs will bring sure death, the moving light of the deity of Joranda will not come, she remains at the top with the tied rope, the Khadia can't believe any one, she or her in-laws are the true companions, other might not notice the rope that keenly, little inattention would result sure death; most strangely no Khadia ever died from fall from a cliff, from tree heights, during rock climbing too.

I looked at the Khadia man standing next to me in the village of Astakuwanar. The small village was located after a beautiful valley of Nawana which is inhabited by the Kolhas, the language of the Kolhas are different; a lean and thin man of medium height, hands were hanging loosely from the shoulders, I couldn't see bulging muscles anywhere, a thin body like a teenager boy, the legs were not heavy too, the body was made for swift walking and easy climbing, no fat or unnecessary weight which could hamper the tough climbing. No fear in the eyes, no anger or arrogance, in the unpolluted atmosphere of the Similipal, the man was unpolluted, uncomplicated; the light dark body, flowing black hair and glowing complexion was reflecting innocence of his heart.

I peeped into the house, an extraordinarily simple one-roomed house with earthen walls over which red soil paste was applied and polished. As a result a beautiful reddish glow was coming out of the walls; the floor was brownish and well polished too. Wooden poles were raised from the ground to support alongside the wall. The cooking place was at one corner, some wood were gathered at the side of the earthen Chullah, some ashes were still gathered inside the Chullah. Two three aluminum utensils were placed alongside the burning area. Just over the Chullah one Kullah was hung from the wall, little above it maize corns were hung in a bunch, blackened due to constant smoking, the wall too was blackened above the Chullah. On one wall a rope was drawn between the wooden pole at the centre of the wall and the wooden pole at another corner of the wall; over the rope some clothes were gathered, a bag was too was hung on the wooden pole. I looked at the persons inside – a child was sleeping on the floor over a cotton cloth, a young Khadia man with bare body and a lungi around the waist was sitting on the floor, eating watered rice from an aluminum utensil, no other vegetable, only some salt was placed at his side. A child was eating from the same utensil, the child looked so cute; she came to the door, naked body, a white thick cotton thread was wrapped around the waist, another thick cotton thread was hung from the neck with a wooden Deonria. On her dark hands she was wearing a pair of white bangles and she looked at us, a sweet smile moved on her lips, not very thick lips, eyes were big and dark, long ears, straight flowing hair was covering her forehead, coming to the eyes, smooth baby skin was shining, face looked so simple, the childhood innocence was not adultered in the deep forests, the deep forests rather preserved the childhood innocence.

I came out, looked at the house, the mud house was almost hidden from the eyes with tall maize plants on the front and looked at the climber, he was sitting comfortably on the ground, no sign of arrogance and pride, a simple man with extraordinary skill, I was confused at their skill, at their belief. He explained,

"We prayed to the God, Oh! Great Basumata, Dharam Devata, Goddess Gramashree, Kalamuhin Chandi, Kulari Chandi…, we kneel down before the Gods, apply vermillion on them; offer ganja to our God as offering, the Ganja is put over a tender Sal leave, then the leaf is rolled along with the ganja in the form of bidi and the bidi is offered to the God," the man with innocence talked to me in the laps of nature, his face was shining in belief on the nature, God inhabits every corner of the forests.

"We believed in God, if your offerings are satisfactory, nobody can harm you, the case of Jenabil in which one of our man was eaten by the tiger was due to wrong prayer before the God, before starting for forests, we prayed," he was showing confidence in his belief, the aberrations were due to wrong performance in the worship, your heart should be clear during the process, there shouldn't be any doubt." He was explaining his deep belief in clear words.

Barchipani Waterfall and Nearby Areas

We returned, on the way looked at an extraordinary flower, a green flower appeared like snake with a raised hood, the wide top portion was curved like the hood of a snake, almost perpendicular to the main stem. It was coming out of the ground from a small green herb. Ginger type herb plants, leaves resembling with ginger plants with beautiful bunch of little bigger white flowers with pink violet tinge at the outer border of the petals, on a single inflorescence, appeared frequently on the forest floor. A beautiful creeper with big leaves as big as Sal leaves, with funnel shaped big violet flower with deep violet venations, were covering some smaller plants along the roadside. I knelt down on the road, at the side, under small bushes a group of bright yellow coloured mushroom emerged from the soil. What a brilliant colour, the shape of the group of flowers was much more beautiful than any individual flower. As a group they looked more attractive than the dazzling colourful orchids; from the dark nutrient rich soil the florets were emerging with pride and confidence at their beauty. The soft but bright hue was filling the mind, at the splendor look of the small yellow mushroom I was losing my thoughts, just immersed in the bright colour like a bee on a blooming flower. After a while my inquisitive eyes searched for something uncommon in the forest floors – so many mushrooms of so many varieties, mushrooms to me were the flowers of the soil. A red coloured button type mushroom with, size as big as a lemon attached to a very thick stem with almost round cap, was emerging from a small hallow on the slope. The edible cock mushroom was very interesting, this predominantly white thick mushroom with some red and maroon patches is called cock mushroom by the tribals because of its mixed beautiful colour. Another white mushroom with some scales on the convex top looked like a white umbrella made up of loose clothes. Another white mushroom with so many curves at lower belly appeared like Chhatri of a king, thick and beautiful from the lower side and flat on the top.

I was searching for the mushrooms on the forest floor. Suddenly the sound of the Barehipani waterfall came gushing with a strong wind. I looked ahead, the second tallest waterfall of India was displaying its magnificence, only Kunchikal water fall on Varahi river, a tiered waterfall at 455 meter (1493 feet) in the Shimoga district of Karnataka (it is the second highest in Asia) is loftier, and this magnificent two tired water fall at height of 399 metres (1,309 ft) stands tall, the other major waterfall Joranda, the 19th tallest in the country, in the same forest, a throwing type waterfalls with single drop stands at 157 meters (515 ft).

I looked ahead, on my front on the opposite hill this magnificent waterfall was exhibiting its splendor in the afternoon light. The illuminated mountains were brilliant green in colour, there the green forests extended to the horizon, the green colorations at the right, at the front, at the left, also below a large cliff. The water from wide catchment was flowing through the upper hills, a wide brown line was displaying the course, the water channels were spreading little on the rock floor at the top, then merged just above the mouth of the fall, the waterlines then fell deep down, a bigger wide band at the left side and a smaller group of lines at the right. A narrow brown rock band separated both the lines; huge volume of water was falling on base with great force. On our side of mountain a young Kolha couple were returning, the young man was carrying a load on his shoulder, a green bamboo was placed on the left shoulder, at the end of the bamboo stick a bag was hung on the front side, on the backside the bamboo shoots were hung, bamboo shoots are a delicacy for the tribal inside the forests. The girl was displaying the youthfulness of the forest, the energy of the mountains wind on her legs, the pride of the glorious forests on her body, the life of the tall waterfalls on her face, she was looking magnificent in that afternoon. A load of bamboo leaves was placed on her head, she was looking at us with soft eyes, the glamour, texture of the skin, the youthful radiance in the natural environment was unparallel, the girl without makeup was looking awesome, her walk was graceful, her smile was innocent, her eyes were laced with simplicity, her figure was depicting the brilliance of Similipal, untouched and unparallel.

A wind came through the opening of the trees in my front, from the waterfall side, a cold one laced with drops of water from such a far distance; I looked at the fuming waterfall, the water mists were raising, the young couple had vanished in the deep forests long back. Like me, my friend's eyes were fixed on the water vapors.

"The deities, you may also call them witches, they stay in the waters of Barehipani," he was revealing some mystery confined within the borders of Similipal.

I was surprised, the unparallel natural beauty was creating so much of interest in me, the colour of green and white was creating ripples in my mind, under those circumstances he was revealing some strange world, I was astonished, the forests of Similipal must be full with natural forces, call them witches, call them Goddesses.

"They were extremely beautiful, the young unmarried man when goes into the water, they appear and then takes the man deep into the waters, the man can't return alive, they are fond of lives of young men."

Some moments earlier I had seen beauty unparallel. The radiant black figure was mysterious, a strong magnetic force was emanating from the figure, a weird attraction, a strange feeling, such was the appeal, that beauty created a feeling of love, feeling of attachment, to leave the far away land and to remain with her, move with her in the deep forests, her company always, day and night together.

The young unmarried man, if bathes in those lonely waters, the girls from the water rise, invite to their land; if not, the boy returns to his house, in the nights they appear frequently in their dreams in white saris, in the dream beautiful girls take the boy in their arms, he makes love, they cover his thought, now except for them the boy can't think of any other things, slowly he stops his food, body shrinks, strange symptoms appear in the body, and the boy dies after some days; the seven sisters take the boy into their arms forever.

There are some remedies – the seven sisters need to be pacified, some offerings need to be given, some puja need to be performed, seven green leaves with petiole need to be plucked over which alta, methi, vermillion, kajal, turmeric, gandha, amla, etc. need to be put, to be kept outside, the seven sisters will be satisfied with the offerings, the boy will be freed from their holding.

No word could come out of my mouth, disbelief definitely, but in the deep forests, cut off from all kind of modern amenities and medical facilities, the man here believes in the powers of natural forces, belief itself creates miracles, the healing power improves, may be the puzzling performances has some true effect, the mysteries are still hunting the innocent people here.

We returned, evening was descending on the flat cultivation lands of the Barehipani area. There are many such flat areas like in Nawana area, Barehipani area where the tribals, mostly Kolhas had some settled agriculture. Barehipani was a long flat land surrounded by green hills, the light green cultivation fields were looking beautiful in the dim light, the afternoon sun has sunk behind the hills, only the orange tinge was left. I looked at the fields in front of me, a small naked boy was standing over a stump of a tree, part of the stump had rotted, creating some hollows, his legs were inside the stump, a red thick thread was wrapped around the waist to wade off the witches, at the backdrop the green field with flowing water, at the right, the white cattle group was returning, the new born of the Similipal was looking for a prosperous world.

On the front, the world looked mysterious, with light dimming the puzzling beauty of Similipal was displaying the grand splendor; a big mountain was raising its head, arms fully stretched, in front of it another smaller hill was spreading its hands too. The head at the centre, a series of such spreading hills in front of the taller hill and just between each fold white clouds were nestled, all disjointed from the other. Below the dark smaller hills still darker tree line of the lower hills were formed in curved fashion, thin clouds as a band covered the tree tops for a large distance, and below couple of houses, hazed with the descend of the clouds were adding mystery to the setting, in those houses the mysteries of Similipal take shelter. The flat lands with green rice fields spread in front of the house, the water streams carries the message of fear and uncertainties, the trees in the field were now darkened, lost colour at the settings, couple of dry branches were twisted outwards like horns of massive strange animals, uncertainties only rise from the dark trees, the witches of Similipal were watching us keenly.

Witch stories

I returned to the dak Bungalows of Chahala, the erstwhile king created this magnificent bungalow as a hunting house, now some say the bungalow had been hunted. I read it elsewhere, the bungalow now gets filled with the sound of Paunji, the anklets which produce sound on walking, during the full moon, or in the dark nights, some mystery descends to the floor of the bungalow. A candle was lighted that night, long shadows were created on the walls, the night turned deep very quickly in the mountain folds. I listened the puzzling creature, the witches of the forests, they move in the forests like deer.

Earlier I read about witches from the accounts of John Beams, an Englishman who worked as political agent in Odisha during the British period. As per his accounts, the witches have power to leave their bodies and go invisible, but if one keeps a pan leaf (the betel leaf) on the right ear, then one can see the invisible witches. The witches gather under a banyan tree or pipal tree which generally grows at the margins of village pond or any water source, mostly on Saturday or Tuesday, the days in which the witches become immensely powerful; in those long past days Odisha was in semi darkness) witches had been haunting the countryside.

Here, the witches of Shimlipal remain in the villages, they in fact are simple women of the villages, but turns to blood suckers in the night; whoever has seen the witches has faced bad times; evil always has casted its eyes on him. Many have seen the witches on buffalo back, sucking the blood from the tail of the animal.

I feared to imagine the blood sucking witches in the dead of the night in a probably hunted house, with so many long shadows on the walls, cold wind was blowing, the night calls of the birds were piercing the ears, the dying call of animals were freezing the blood, the bats were flooding the night sky.

The witches perform many ritualistic dances, but they need to get siddhi, the mantra was not difficult, only 2½ words, but recitation need to be performed with great devotion and austerity as per witchcraft traditions. She has to go fully naked, the hairs should be open, nobody should notice her, to the pre-designated palaces, strange light comes from the tip of the small figure of left hand. Like a torch it shows the direction, the gin of the mantra shows the way, they run faster than a deer, can also fly. The group of witches gathers at the burial place, then they start ritual dance, one witch takes the shape of a tiger, other dance around it, nobody should witness, death is inevitable for the witness. The siddhi is difficult, to become a perfect witch one has to kill the eldest son of a person through mantra, only then supernatural power will come to the practiced woman; the look and evil spells are sufficient to kill the healthy child. The witch is capable of seeing the inner parts of the body, can see the liver, can harm people, invite wild animals to harm the people – tiger can jump from dark corner, the elephant can trample, the beer can tear the man, the man will die from fall from the cliffs or tree and also strange ailments will appear and the man will die; the witches are feared weird creature of the green forests.

Time passed, the blood thirsty wild animals came to the discussion, the black tigers, and man eaters came to the dancing walls of the dark bungalow.

Black tiger

More than a decade back, it was the afternoon of the dry month, the forester was returning from his duty at Dhuduruchampa, was nearing Sharda village, the forest area, no clear road. The footpath was also covered with bashes at some places, branches were coming frequently over the road. The time was getting late, the forester was in hurry, nights were difficult time, he had to go long way; he pedaled his cycle faster. One Sal tree was almost uprooted, the main trunk had come onto the road, the path passes below it and the man looked up. A black tiger was sitting on the angled trunk, he was only few feet away from the black tiger, till that time he only listened about the black tiger, never saw it in his eyes. He was at his wits end, long experience in Similipal gave him enough confidence to handle difficult situations. He stopped the cycle, got down from the cycle and looked at the tiger. The black tiger, same size of the Royal Bengal tiger, was looking at him with burning eyes, though fear in his mind, he mustered courage and looked at the tiger. The large beast looked at the daring man for some time, the forester was holding an axe. He was determined, if the tiger would pounce, he would use the axe. The animal glanced at the fearless man at that time, and continued to stare at him for some time, then turned back and descended from the tree and moved into the bushes. The man wilted for some time, the tiger in fact vanished, prayed to God, and came to the village. He sat on the earth, asked for some water, the villagers were curious to know about the events, he narrated. The older people told that they had been seeing the tiger on that tree for quite some time, till that date it had not harmed any one, still one should be careful.

I remembered the reporting of Black tigers during June 2007 in *The Hindu,* three black tigers were sighted during a tiger census; the cameras trapped the images of three different melanistic tigers, known as black tigers near Upper Barakamuda and Devasthali regions in the core area of Tiger Reserve; so the black tigers were available in good numbers in the area. The black tiger sighting have been reported at different periods, at different places like on the road leading to Matughar meadow; Baladaghar, near Bachhurichara between Patabil and Devasthali.

I looked at the man, the medium built man was more than fifty-seven years of age, was due to retire within another two months, spent more than thirty-five years in the forests of Similipal, still looked to be full of energy, enthusiasm in his talk, hairs on the head were yet to be discoloured, glaze was still left on the skin, the Similipal forests was the source of eternal youth; he looked at the dark night, went out of the closed room, cold wind entered, the flame shivered as if in fear. He returned after few minutes, looked at the flame, a smile roamed on his face, the memory of the past had a happy ending, but he started with the killing of Khadia man, the end was however satisfying, then started narrating about the man eater of Similipal.

Long back, Shriram Khadia of Jenabil village, on that day went into forest with others to collect Jhuna, their daily chore, they were eight to ten in number, entered silently, strangely the forest was silent, they didn't notice that. They were moving on a narrow path deep inside, Shriram was few steps at the back, other were ahead and suddenly a tiger jumped at the Khadia man from a dense bush. As he caught the man, the man shouted for help, but the other Khadias were panicky at the roar of the tiger and shirk of the most powerful Khadia in the group. They ran for cover, the tiger killed the man in no time and ate almost the entire body, by the time the Khadias returned only the clothes were found.

In another incident one wood cutter was going to the forests, near to the reserve line, people of the village requested him not to go to the forests in view of man eater in the vicinity, but he ignored the warning and went alone. While he was returning with the wood on his head the tiger pounced on him and killed him instantly.

Many attacks took place, sometimes the victims also resisted. In one incident the tiger jumped at a wood cutter, the man was holding an axe, he whirled the axe with full force and hit the animal on the face, injured the jaw. Few teeth were also broken, but the charged animal killed the man instantly and almost ate the entire body; by the time the rescue team arrived, hardly there was any part left.

Everyone were now afraid of the roaming man-eater, but the tribal people can't live without going into the forests. In one incident the girls and village women went into the forests to collect Pitalu tuber, they were almost twenty in number. The man eater was nearby, they didn't notice, one girl came close to the bush in which the tiger was hiding, it jumped at the teenage girl and killed her at once. The women folk screamed and fled, later the men folk gathered and the whole tribal village came to the spot. Seeing so many people the tiger fled, the tiger could eat only a little part of the body. The forest officials were immediately informed. The DFO decided to trap the tiger, so a tiger cage was made, a hide was placed at a safe height on a nearby tree branch, the forest officials sat on the hide with tranquilizer gun. The dead body of the girl was kept at the open. The tiger came, it didn't enter into the cage, went near to the dead body, but didn't touch it, tried to return, the tranquilizing party fired at the tiger, but the tiger was not harmed and it escaped.

The tribal people were very angry. The presence of the tiger in the vicinity of the village was life threatening, they had spent nights without food. They put traps, poisoned arrow was put on the bow and the bow was given the full tension and joined to a trigger mechanism, a string was drawn on the road, in case the tiger passed through that road, mere touch on the trigger mechanism would release the arrow, and it would pierce the heart of the tiger. But that effort didn't yield any result, the tiger roamed freely in the forests.

In the final incident the animal killed a buffalo, the message was passed, the forest department requested a royal of erstwhile king of Anugul to hunt the animal. The man came and made a hide on a neem tree, around fifteen feet above the ground. The tiger came, tried to eat the corpse, the man on the hide fired tranquilizer shot at the tiger, it hit the tiger, the animal roared and jumped at the hide but missed the hide at a whisker. The hunter fired second shot of tranquilizer in self-defence. The tiger fell down after some time, but never regained consciousness, died due to over dose of tranquilizer.

Night was deep, the figures on the wall was not moving, people were getting tired. Time to return to the bed, the nights in deep forest gets deeper in no time, the evening star was shining brightly. I came out of the room, they informed about the presence of group of deer outside, I switched on the torch, pairs of bright eyes appeared at many places, the deer were grazing, they informed the deer came right up to the footsteps of the bungalow. I retreated, I was the lone occupant in that hunting bungalow. My room was next to the open fields, I opened the window and slept. I awake in the night, strange sound was coming from the room, probably the rats, I tried to figure out the sound, not that of rat. I switched on the torch, a flood of light swept the room, no sign of rat, the sound stopped. As I closed the eyes, the sound came once again, definitely not from outside, but from the house itself, again I switched on the light, but no sign of life, the sound continued as the torch was switched off and this sound continued almost for the entire night.

Morning came, birds started calling from the tree hides, I looked at the morning forests, husky figures appeared from the forests on the open land in front of the bungalow. The forest department had created a salt lick, and grass land, the animals used to come to the place for licking salt, also to eat the grasses. The evening haze had descended into the forest floor, a hazed wide band covered the entire grass land, and the haze reduced from the ground towards the tree top, the morning light was touching the tree tops. Dark figures appeared in the morning haze, group of deer on the ground, their body was hazed in the mist, and only dark lines could be visible. The neck slightly stretched, tail shrunk to the body, they were feeling cold in the morning in open. The eastern sky was opening up, the morning sun was yet to appear, the husky figures were busy in grazing, our presence almost two hundred feet was not disturbing them, we refrained from going close, watched them from safe distance and time passed. I turned my eyes, thousands of dragon flies covered the sky, so many dragon flies at one place, I never expected so many of them at one place, they moved quickly. I looked at them, a sense of satisfaction passed over my body, the morning breeze, the morning life was rejuvenating.

Meghasani Hills

On another day, leaving behind the rainy days far behind, I once traveled to Meghasani hill in the winter months. That day I was standing on the Meghasani hills, cool strong wind was blowing from north, remembered the word of my little daughter, Thanda Thanda cool cool, those sweet words are echoing in my ears. Hill ranges, hill ranges, hill ranges, so many hill ranges, on may back, in front of me, along both sides, where ever I looked, I only find the green hill ranges. I remembered about the Saranda forest view from Meghatuburu guest house of SAIL, Saranda means the land of seven hundred hills. From the top of the Meghatuburu hills we saw greenery, hills all around, and here in Meghasani I saw hills, we were standing on the cliffs of the Meghasani hills. Where my eyes went, I only find the hill range, green, untouched, serene. Two black kites were flying from one hill on the right to the hill on the left, they were floating in the air with grace, sometimes coming down, next moment rising up, and then dive long, they moved like rocket, downward, but before touching the ground, before touching the green line of the forest down below, they suddenly changed the direction, moved up, then they started floating. My eyes went to the hills, many, so many curves, so many ridges, slowly the horizon was getting fogged, the dark lines were getting fainter and fainter. The feeling, as if I was on the top of the sky. I was standing on the cliff, very steep, we were unable to stand; strong wind was blowing from the back, could not see below even on lying on the ground. Behind thick dark curve, behind light wide curve, and on the sky dark clouds were moving, the sky and the forests were meeting, a fluid situation, no division was seen, as if the green world was meeting the ocean, here instead of blue horizon, and the green horizon was meeting the faint sky.

Clouds after clouds invaded the white sky, so many long irregular lines, irregular curves as if a small boy had painted the white canvass for the first time. He didn't know painting, tried to draw lines as per his wish, didn't know how to catch the brush, with each movement of his brush, the sky was getting painted, I couldn't find the words. The painter was filling the sky, so many shades of black and white; I couldn't imagine so many shades of black. I looked below, a green carpet; the top of the untouched forest took the form of green carpet, was rolled for our welcome, the small hill ranges in between, appeared like chairs, and the cliff in which I was standing, to me, turned to be throne. I bowed my head, could not see the vastness, bowed my head before the nature, so much green was gathered at a place. The expanse of forest, as seen from the Meghasani hills was unseen by me earlier, and I lost myself in that green expanse. I stood silently, closed my eyes, the cold wind was touching my heart, my hairs were flying, the sound of the mountain God was ringing at my ears. Such was the feeling, such was the experience, there were insufficient words to explain the details of the Meghasani hills.

I looked at the rocks below my feet, exposed rocks, lichens had come up, creating some strange shapes, to me some of them appeared like the face of the tigers. In the Similipal tiger reserve, the tigers are not only hiding behind the trees, they are looking at you at the Meghasani hills, from every hill top. Their souls have been hiding behind the rocks, their faces have been recreated by the lichens. The jungle had come alive with the shapes given by the lichens, the deers, the elephants, the sambars, the bison, the hares, the birds, the tigers all were depicted by the lichens on the black rocks. Such was the creation, such was the feeling, the sculpture had recreated the shapes at the Meghasani hills. The soul of the forest was taking rest at Meghasani hills, their sound was being echoed in the strong wind, their voices, if one can hear, all was there, the howling of the jackals, the roar of the tigers, the call of the deers, the trumpet of the elephants, the sound of the water falls, the call of the morning birds, the sound of the night birds, the stress call of the dying animals, the roar of the winners, the call of the new born, all were there in the breeze. I couldn't hear so many sounds, my ear was getting heavier, and my eyes were filled with the call of the green expanse; Similipal, I saw it for the first time, was creating a new world for the animals. The sun was not hurting, the little warmth was giving life, sweet, colourful, enchanting, filled with pleasant experiences. I stood silently on the top of the Meghasani hill, surrounded by the souls of the forest, watched by the animals in the forest, covered by the lives of the hills, encircled by the green expanse, caressed by the thoughts of unknown.

Musics at Upper Barakamuda

The lyrical songs suddenly started reverberating in my ears, Devastali was still some distance away, we were at Upper Barakamuda, the unpolluted Kharia tribe men still live there, the sweet voices echoed from all sides.

Oh! Dear, Will you accompany?
Will you accompany?
Don't tell that I have left you
Don't tell that I have left you

The beautiful songs of the young hearts reverberated from all corners of the open land, I looked at the beautiful faces, so sweet, softness, no anxiety, no sorrow, cute eyes were looking at others.

It was strange, I could understand the entire stanza, the lyric looked so familiar, and they are after all the descendents of the warriors who migrated to deep forests of Similipal in olden times for unknown reasons, forgot the civilization and development with time, but didn't forget the language, the lyric.

The sun was moving towards hilltop at the west at Upper Barakamuda, I was listening to the songs of young hearts, the Khadia girls again started singing –

Dear your eyes
My mirror is your eyes
The thread makes the Paita
My mirror is your eyes

They continued singing, the beautiful rhythmic song was reaching far hill, the eco came from every corner, the golden sunlight was touching the field, the green mountains were turning golden, and the mountain God with the new crown looked marvelous. I can't look at the beauty, closed my eyes and started taking the sound into my heart,

The Bella fruit rolls down,
The Rai fruit rolls down
Oh! Dear friend
I shall follow you
I shall follow you.

I looked at the girls, those beautiful girls were standing in an open field, all young, sweet faces, strange attraction in their voices, and they looked like the fairies of the green mountains with simplest attire, descended from the green mountains to the golden field to recite the songs of life, to spread the message of love, serenity, no lust but divinity alone. Only if we can understand, see their inner beauty, their simplicity, their immortality; these fairies are immortal beyond our vision.

ELEPHANTS ON THE WAY

While we are coming back from Meghasani hills towards Devasthali, and after crossing the tropical pine forests, came across the elephants, they were hidden in the forest, it was almost impossible for a first timer to notice them; the driver, an experienced person in the forest could see the elephants, one a big female and another a smaller one, were breaking the twigs inside the forest, just on the border of Devasthali, on the other side of the river, other side of the jeepable road. We halted, they probably did not see us disembarking, they were busy in collecting the branches, my first encounter with wild elephants in the true forest scenario froze in my mind, the elephants, both had their trunks down, small eyes were looking at the trees in front, their ears parallel to their body, one leg, each of them incidentally lifted the front legs at the same time, were collecting the food. The later afternoon light was falling on their dusky appearance, was giving a grayish tinge to their dark structure. The smaller one was in more open, the other one, probably its mother was massive, looked almost double the size of the young one, was mostly hidden. The young one was moving faster, moving here and there, and on the other part of the small river, we were watching them from the safety of the other bank of the river. The Sal trees were covering them partially, and they started moving on their path to our side passing through the river, which ran towards the salt lick of Devasthali, they approached the river and we left silently from our watching spot.

Devasthali

We reached Devasthali, I was surprised, never thought to see such a big grass land, vast and green, tall grasses were rising almost to the height of a small man, an ideal place for the hunters, sufficient food for the preys as well, the area was surrounded by green forest and green mountains. Small rivulets were passing, cutting the grass land into several parts, plenty of water was available for drinking. This grass land was giving me the idea of an alpine pasture. There the grasses are small, blue mountains on the back, deep green pine forest all around, flowering trees below, and the herd of sheep, and here instead of blue mountain we were getting the green mountains, the backdrop was almost the same. I never thought Similipal would ever have a grassland of such magnitude, could be so majestic. The terrain was almost flat with little gradient, water was not forming swamps, but slowly drained down due to light slope. The grasses in comparison to short alpine meadows, here were little broader and harsh. On our left the grass land was expanding for more than a kilometer right up to the edge of the river, and after that Sal forest, pure one, started, it also gives alpine look from a distance, as the trees were of same shape. On our right, the grassland ran up to a small hill, the forest guard later told that this hill was the meeting place of the magnificent elephants of the Similipal. The hill was small, full with medium sized Sal crop, the Sal was not reaching its peak height due to frost bite, and the Sal mortality rate was higher here.

Behind it the higher, open hills started, we looked closely at the hills on the back, a steep one with vertical cliff. On the top there was green forest, the sides were exposed, white, it was the living place of ferocious honey bees. The upper hill ranges, the hills where the honey combs were hanging, is the hunting place of the Khadia tribes, they descend down using the rope ladder, cut the honey combs and collect the honey. Closely I looked at the vertical cliff, rocks, open and vertical, shapes, to me appeared like elongated faces of the angry tribal, like that of red Indians, as the rock was rather white, to see the shapes in the forest, one need to expand the thought, create new shapes to get the similarity, the shapes and sizes are created by nature, only one has to see through the inner eyes.

With dusk approaching the grass lands of Devasthali, he showed me the hills around, I looked at, the night stars were twinkling in the western sky, he spoke about the mystery, unbelievable, but probably some facts were hidden in it. I listened about the roaming lights from so many persons, many witness it.

Strange Lights

The forester was posted to Devasthali, earlier people told him about the strong round shaped light in the Devasthali area, he never believed, the Khadias told that the lights used to appear during the full moon or new moon nights, at dead hours, the Gods of Devasthali used to move in their territory. He wished to see by himself, on one new moon night he was performing his duty at the Devastahli watch tower. The time was midnight, the night birds were even silent, the stars were shining brightly, cool breeze was blowing, and he was feeling sleepy. Suddenly a bright light appeared in the Ganpati hill, at that dead hour no human could dare to visit that steep hill range. He looked at the light, a bright round shaped light, it was moving slowly on the hill top, alongside the cliff, he continued to watch the light, the light moved slowly from one end of the cliff to the other end and finally vanished behind the woods at far off distance. He simply couldn't believe the phenomenon, was it the deities of Devasthali, or was it the king cobra from whose head the bright light was coming out. To them, the place Devaasthli is the abode of the Gods of Similipal, the protector of people living in deep forests, everyone bows their head before the God of Devasthali.

These strange lights appeared at different places the reference of which have been given in many books. The forests sometimes posses the strange lights, the origin nobody could explain satisfactory, some say the light is from the snake, science says that the snakes can't generate light; some say divinity moves in the forests in the dead of night, but no is sure till date.

The strange lights appeared in the book *"The temple tiger and other man eaters of Kumaon"* a famous book written by notable hunter and conservationist of British period, Mr. Jim Corbett, in the chapter "The Man Eaters of Talladesh". Jim Corbett saw the strange lights on the opposite banks of Sharada River, on the hills; the place was around sixteen miles from Tanakpur. The strange lights appeared continuously on the very steep slopes where group of men can't move, there was no smoke, and the flames were not moving, most importantly those lights were not due to forest fire; the details of the light as given by him is as follows

a) The lights didn't burn at one time.

b) The sizes of the lights were the same, radius around two feet.

c) The flames were not moving as happened in case of fire or Mashal.

d) The lights can move from one place to other.

Mr. Corbett couldn't get the answer to the origin of those lights, he finally believed on a local myth. A Sanyasi was punished by the deity of the Purnagiri because he tried to climb higher than the height of her seat; so the Sanyasi tried to pacify the Goddess by offering puja by burning marshals on a particular night. Strangely only the luckiest few can watch those lights in their human eyes.

In his book *Karanjia Diary* famous Odia writer Shri Shantanu Kumar Acharya mentioned about the strange lights just in the periphery of deep forests. Once Bishubabu, the MLA of the area saw the strange light in a night in the Rashi fields of a Gond man. In one night they were in that area for hunting. First the porcupines came, the hunters didn't shoot, waited for the deer to come. Suddenly they saw a bright light, like a petromax lamp light, the trees were brightly illuminated. Slowly the light dimmed, reddened, and darkness came; again the light came after a short distance, equally bright, then it moved came towards the Rashi field. Once again the light dimmed, reddened and extinguished; only to reappear at a further shorter distance. The hunters were terrified; they fled from the area and reached the village and narrated the incident. The whole village gathered, the old people were totally taken aback; the Goddesses came in such fashion, may be once or twice in a hundred year. Next day they went to the Rashi field, saw foot prints, around ten inch long; it went towards the forests, crossed few hills and finally vanished in the thickets of the Similipal National Park.

We looked at the salt lick, an Indian Gaur was coming to the place, another joined, the Indian Gaurs used to come from the forest all around, from Surmundi, from Sarudala, from Mahabirsal, Brahmunidia nallah, from Bachhrichara – all sides, they used to come in good numbers during the rains.

Many sambars used to come, deers come in plenty, at some time even two to three hundred deer flock the place. They informed, the number of deer have been increasing constantly. The elephant families, the number sometimes swells even to thirty, members are of all sizes, mother child, young and old used to be the regular visitors, on that day we couldn't witness the elephants. The wild boars also used to visit the area in big groups, all kind of herbivorous animals flock the grass land. In search of prey, the tiger sometimes come during night, roars, watchers could not see, but the roar freezes the blood.

The crocodile of Khairi river

We were returning the next day, the forest and river appeared to be not different from the other areas of Similipal, but unless I saw it in my own eyes, I would not have believed it. Similipal could be the habitat of such massive crocodiles, we found the crocodile in a river near Devasthali; it was lying idle on the small open land, just on the edge of the river, strangely during the afternoon. In the morning, it is a common sight to see the crocodiles basking on flat lands adjacent to water body, to warm their bodies. But this time, unusually of course, we could see the crocodile, it was light grey in colour, around 12 feet long, jaws were closed, eyes were closed, was lying like a washed log, alongside the river, on a small open land, below a forked branch of a small tree with small branches and small leaves. The resting place was around 4 feet higher than the river water; a small portion of that land was eroded towards the water side implying it to be regular movement area of the crocodile.

The river below, unless the description is given, one will not get the picture of the crocodile habitat in the Similipal; the river water was crystal clear, absolutely no turbidity, calm like morning water of a big pond, mist around, wetness on the ground. The banks, mostly of soil, rocks in between, were covered with thick vegetation, and many of the trees were leaning towards the water, to draw maximum sunlight, their main branches were making beautiful curves to balance the weight, and some of the branches were touching the water. The reflection of the trees on the water was giving the impression of another tree world inside water, such was the clear water, such was the calmness, and such was the reflection. Small grasses were covering every inch of the open land, giving the bank a velvet look, soft, silky and shining green, in the reflection, the bright hallows were giving the telescopic view of the sky above.

In Similipal, the mugger crocodiles are also only found. These crocodiles have the habit of digging tunnels to take shelter during severe winter; these tunnels open into the water front, have narrow mouth, the height may be about 30-60 cm and depth of the tunnel may be around 5, in meters. In Similipal, minimum temperature sometimes goes below 20 celsius in December during winter, so the Magar crocodiles during extreme temperature, enters into the tunnel dug by them. These tunnels open into the water and have narrow mouth, the height may be about 30-60 cm and depth of the tunnel may be around 5 meters.

In the Khairibandhan river a lot of fishes are available, mainly rohu (Lebo rohita), bhakur (Catle catla), kalibainsi, silua, chenga (Ophiocaphalus gachua), magur (Clarias batrachus), etc. There are many gorges in the river, the length used to be between 200-300 feet, sometimes even half kilometer and average depth is between 20-30 feet, even in peak winter the depth of water remains between 15-20 feet in the gorges. At Kabat ghai gorge, fishes weighing 15-20 kilograms are even available, at that gorge, the rock protrudes from the back to middle of the river, just like a door, and the place is very good living place for the big fishes.

Apart from fearsome crocodiles, the boda snake also remains inside water, this snake is a big snake, around 12-14 feet long, girth may be around 2 feet, remains inside water and wait for the prey.

The Mahasal tree

We were returning, suddenly the vehicle stopped at a magnificent tree, the Maha Sal tree was standing tall on the landscape, on the way from Jashipur to Gudugudia Forest Rest House, a huge tree, the huge bole went straight into the sky without any branching, the canopy only at the top like an umbrella, long narrow fissure lines on the bark went parallel to each other. The brown barks with darker shade with white intermittent tinges looked different from other trees, little buttresses developed at the lower bole towards the lower slope side; the Maha Sal tree was standing gorgeously on light undulating land. The mighty tree was surrounded by numerous number of big Sal trees, but their boles were thinner, they looked like minnows before this astounding trees, they were touching the upper canopy, but little lower than the massive tree, the emperor of the Similipal forests was sitting with its counselors. On the forest floor numerous black rocks emerged from the soil covered with tree leaves; green lichens covered the rocks mostly in the moist atmosphere.

I was not alone on that day in that Sal forest, to understand the spirits of forests I need to be with somebody who knows a little about the area, that day my companion was a man in his late twenties. He looked at the horizon, the colour contrast in light and shade increased there. Similipal forest was watching him keenly, the sounds of the breeze, the flowing water were filling our ears, he was unveiling the spirit of the forest. The songs of the Sal forest were filling the air, from every corner the songs were coming to my ears. He closed his eyes for some moment, then looked at the Maha Sal tree in front, I at that time closed my eyes too, was trying to grasp the spirit of the Sal forests.

"The enormous Maha Sal, the deity of Similipal reside there, everybody believes so, and the story starts from there?" he paused, the intensity of streaks of lights increased, the deity of Similipal was glowing, the diamond studded crown was portraying His power, His supremacy.

"The tribal people don't cut the Sal trees, it is a heavenly territory, God's abode, the village deities reside in Sal forests, one could find so many mud idols, horses, many other structure in Jaher, the unbreakable bond of human and nature is depicted there, not on stone, but on imagination, on belief of the innocent," his style of speaking, the words were so spontaneous, I was amazed.

I didn't know why he spoke so, I was praising the massive tree. I have to admit, sometimes I was evaluating the price of the tree, how much wood would come out of it, the tree was so mature, the timber would be valued like gold.

"There were two wood cutters, they used to cut trees in forest, sell the wood, timber to the merchants, earlier they used to cut the dead trees, but that day they thought of cutting a big tree, and climbed the hill. The forest was full of trees, big, small, all kind, but they wanted to get the biggest tree, they want to get rich in a day, wanted to violate the sacred code of their society, not to cut living trees for greed. Then they found the Maha Sal, the biggest Sal tree of the forest, the spirit of Similipal. They fixed their saw, tried to cut the tree, then they put the saw over the massive trunk." He paused a little. The light intensity suddenly decreased, by that time, the wind blew strong, the spirits of Similipal was bringing the message.

"Next day the villagers found them, the wood cutters were dead, their saw was embedded into the Maha Sal tree, the God's anger had fallen, and they vomited blood on the ground." He took a long breath.

I was surprised at the story, so much respect for the Sal forests, and so much love for the living trees. We moved out of the area, leaving the massive tree at its place, the deities of the Similipal rested without disturbance.

The wind of Kaliani

We returned, alongside the river tall mountains raised their head with full green robe on the body, the robes were fluttering in the wind, the evening descended early into the dark forests of Similipal, the Kaliani Pavan, the chilling cold wind of Similipal, they called it the heart beat of the Similipal forests, not the breeze from the river Khairi-Bandhan flowing below which I thought initially, but the breeze from the core of Similipal, was blowing fast. We were shivering when at that time the rest of the part of Odisha was still under heat wave. They believe, the wind of the Similipal, the Kaliani Pavan starts the journey from a cave deep interior, blow over the river, between the folds of green mountains, to Jashipur and nearby areas, chilling the air almost to freezing point. I was chilling, there in that evening a ray of light from the room was increasing the depth of the dark night; the sound of the night was chilling the spine too. In that darkness, I started recollecting my experiences, was refreshing my memory, didn't know why the massive tigers came to mind often, they surfaced in the black sky, the king of the Similipal forests peeped from every dark corner, the roar of the angry king filled the room as if.

Stories about the tiger

Once I watched the short story of the burning eyes, a huge grassland, tall grasses, almost a meter height, covered the flat land. From the elephant back the grassland looked like a paddy field, the people were relaxed, the elephants were also relaxed, no sign of life on the grassland, a little wind, the grass leaves moved with sweet sound. Suddenly there was movement of the grasses, all looked at the grasses, no sign of animal, suddenly a tiger appeared from the grassland. Its upper body was only visible, a pale brown tinge over the green grassland. The tiger was charging at the huge elephants, its size looked so small from the height, the minnow was charging the massive, the tiger was taking long jumps, the huge head was visible, and mouth was wide open, the black bands on the tiger body were visible more prominently. The elephant had moved its head towards the tiger, the mahout was shouting, but the tiger continued with its charge. The angry tiger came closer, and leaped at the people on the top of the elephants, the left leg of the tiger pressed the ground hard, the long tails were straight and touching the grassland, the front leg was extended forward. The huge mouth was looking fearsome with open teeth, the flight of the tiger from the ground to the elephant head was terrifying, huge mouth was now wide open, the white furs on the neck were fully raised increasing the size of the head, yellow teeth were clearly visible, the huge front left paw was stretched forward with open sharp nails. The angry tiger moved its huge paw which appeared to be thicker than the legs of a young boy, with great force, the right paw was now also extended fully, the head was raised, it easily crossed the head of the elephant, such big was the leap; the huge chest was at the same level of the elephant, the back legs were stretched backward, and the tail was raised fully up, the tiger was taking the shape of death. The tiger leaped to that height with ease with a big roar, the others screamed with fear of death, the huge elephants were not a match to the roaring tiger.

The morning came, I was spell-bounded at the thought of the events associated tiger. The fury of the tiger was awesome, and on another day I entered into the deep forests of Similipal, and there I came across the man eaters, the black tigers, I looked at the room, two laminated photographs were displayed at a corner, a spectacled man was holding a tigress very close to his face, in another photograph the same tigress was sleeping gracefully in a Sal forest. I looked closely at the photograph, the man was holding the tigress in his left hand, his chin was pressed against the nose of the tigress, his eyes were fixed on the animal, the eyes of the tigress were hidden behind, the long white whiskers from the face were hung like the thin white bread of a Chinese scholar. The tigress appeared to be fully contended in the close embrace, it appeared as if the tigress was deep asleep on the embrace of a loving father and the caring father was fully satisfied by holding dear daughter at a close embrace, trying the best not disturb the sleep of the dear child.

I looked at the photograph, a fully grown magnificent tigress, in her full youth was lying gracefully in the Sal forest, her colour matched with white, pale brown and red coloured dry leaves falling on the ground, tall trees started from her side. Her eyes were bright yellow, glowing, but there was no anger or arrogance, but full of energy to play; the ears were raised upwards, aligned towards front, she was the joy of Jashipur, Khairi was looking graceful in her belly lying position.

I came out of the room, looked at the forest rest house, Khairi's place has now been converted to a guest house, the touch of Khairi was still there, it was just adjacent to the NH, big Sal trees dotted the compound, office, rest house and few other structures exist side by side. The rest house was medium-sized house, with a long verandah opening towards the front side. The rooms were located alongside the verandah like class rooms, all rooms open to the verandah and a the sitting room was located towards the other side, opposite to the rooms, towards the roadside. Behind, tall Sal trees cover the background, big mango trees on the side, except for the front side, all the sides are covered with tall trees, in the front small garden was maintained, surprisingly small cemented structure was constructed on the front side. I came close, looked at it, on the red cement floor name of Khairi was written, a beautiful tigress was laid to rest there, she makes the atmosphere live between the period 05.10.1974 to 28.03.1981; my heart turned heavy.

I went into the sitting room, a medium one with netted windows all around, saw me an old sofa, some deep scratch marks, he told it was created by the tigress, she passed away in 1981 but the sofa still carries the memory of the intelligent wild animal even after three decades. Khairi used to jump, move and sit on different items on the sitting room.

I came to the bed room, Khairi had been sleeping with the parents in that room for four long years, and she had grown from her childhood to her prime youth in a small 15 feet by 12 feet old type room, two narrow cots were placed next to opposite walls separately, some open spaces between the cots, Khairi was sleeping between the parents, Mrs and Mr. Choudhury were sleeping on the cots, she was sharing their love, even was using their toilet. Outside, a simple forest guest house with open corridor, I never imagined a full grown tigress could roam freely in an open house, the small house, the small garden, the big mango trees, all bore the symbol of the majestic beast.

Again I returned to the sitting room, and again looked at the photograph of Khairi with her human father, no anger, but a satisfaction, confidence on the face of Khairi, she was a happy daughter, and the father looked contended in his small stature, the spectacle on the face was adding fulfillment, knowledge and belief in his endeavour. Looking at the photograph, in the same room where once Khairi was roaming freely, the snakes were coiling happily, the hyena was laughing jokingly, the deer was jumping joyfully, I never imagined, mere reading of a book will take me to a different plane, earlier I described about the fury of the tiger, here it was the understanding and intelligence.

I opened the book, started reading the story of Khairi, the tigress won the heart of many, instrumental in taking the wildlife preservation to a higher range, brought changes in the policies of the government; the book *Khairi, the beloved tigress* written by Late Saroj Raj Choudhury, was unfolding a new chapter of life, co-existence of a tigress with human beings in open.

She was a tender two month old tiger cub of the Similipal hills of Mayurbhanj district of Odisha, weighing only 6.2 kg and measuring 88 cm long from tip of her nose to the tip of her tail along her spine; was stolen from her mother by 12 Kharia tribe men of village Jenabil of in the central Similipal area on October 3, 1974. The Kharias on that day went to the forest to collect forest produce like raisin, honey, wax and tubers; the daily chord of food gatherers like them, to the upper reaches of the river Khairi. While collecting the materials from forest they came across a big tigress lying before a cave with three little cubs snuggled to her belly. The Kharias, encountering the tigress; her cub Khairi 6 years later was weighing nearly 200 kg measuring 273 cm long from her spine and stands 91 cm at the shoulder, at so close, were terrified but shouted at their full voice. The tigress was surprised at the strange congregation and the loud noise walked away from the cave living her baby at the cave. The little cub tried to escape into the darkness of the cave but the Kharias gathered courage at the retreat of the tigress, caught the little cub at the mouth of the cave and wrapped it in a cloth. She was frightened at the sudden turn of events, could not cry, had she cried the tigress would have charged at the Kharias and so many stories on the Khari couldn't have materialised at all, the cub was stolen from the lap of the mother. The Kharias brought the little tiger cub to their hamlet wrapping it on a cloth and then putting it in a secure resin basket. Next day morning they moved with the same basket, keeping the cub as comfortable as possible, for Jashipur town on NH 6, around 40-50 km from their village and met the Range Officer in the afternoon and handed over the basket.

The little cub was later brought to the forest guest house and placed before Shri Saroj Raj Choudhury, Conservator of Forests; and a new life began for the little cub then after, she got into fame with time. Shri Choudhury looked at the cub, she was chained round her neck and shoulder, thick rope were rounded over the entire length of her body, only her forelimbs were free, and she was lying on her belly, totally shocked at the turn of events. She looked at the onlookers when the lid of the basket was opened, bared her half grown milk fangs, snarling in defence – the natural defence mechanism of a cat. Shri Choudhury was an expert on tiger, had good knowledge on the behaviour of the tiger; he imitated the vocal greetings of tiger, the sounds was much similar to a soft clearing of throat; and the cub was suddenly pacified, the sound was carrying the messages of love and care of her mother. She got calmed, raised her face and looked into the eyes of the man and responded with a soft unh-unh-unh sound, she was reciprocating the greetings in her words. Shri Choudhury again greeted her, communicated the affection, he removed the chain and rope from the body of the cub and lifted her to his lap. He put her on his shoulder, rested her lips under his chin, it was an intimate association which continued till the death of the tigress and she was inducted into the family, the new tiger daughter got the affection of a father. They looked at each other, the tiger cub was relaxed, she had confidence on the father, talked to the man in the language of the tiger. From that minute onwards she turned to be a playful child, roaming freely in the father's house.

Mrs Chaudhury put the cub on her lap and moved her hand over the tiger cub, an intimate sense of security, the cub closed her eyes and went to sleep. Her soft snore filled the room, she got a home after 50 hours from her original home in the Similipal. She woke up after two hours, called in a gentle tiger voice, stood up and prustened, the human mother hogged her and moved her figure on the fur, the tiger daughter then rolled out of the mother's lap and rested on the floor with belly up; in full grown tigers it is the gesture of acceptance of dominance generally displayed by female to a male. After a while she moved from room to room, sat on the chairs and tables and played hide and seek with the new mother. The cub was hungry did not have food for more than two days; she was not accepting milk from a spoon, not from the feeding bottle even, so the human parents opened her mouth and poured some milk into her throat, she swallowed little but spilled more, some milk went into her stomach. Mrs. Choudhury folded her sari and put it below her bed; the cub came from the corner and slept over the sari and the light was switched off. In the night the cub woke up and scratched the bed, Shri Choudhury switched on the light and found the cub standing near the bed of her human mother but could not go inside because of the mosquito net; so he opened the net a little, the cub slipped into the bed and pushed herself into the laps of the human mother and both of them slept hugging each other.

I went on reading the book *Khairi,* Khairi grew up with a lot of affection of her human parents, she liked to play every time, as any little daughter she loved to play with the small dogs, other small animals. Many small and large animals joined the family at different times. Bagha-the puppy who grew up with the Khairi, Chhabi-the female python, Jambo-the male sloth bear, Bhaina-the mail blind hyena, Mainka-the fore-horned antelope, Pukul-the jungle cat, Jhuna-the mangoose, Beda-the wild Boar, Ti-the small Indian civet, Chumki-the leopard cat. The tiger girl was kind, once Bhiana-the mail hyena gets a beating from Mr. Choudhury for being naughty; Khairi always was concerned about his pain and surprisingly she licked the animal, to console. The hyena pup was blind in his both eyes but his ears and nose were ultra-sensitive, it could recognise his fellow family members through their distinct foot steps or smell, sometimes the little animal did not allow the full grown tigress to enter into the room and Khairi never forced her entry into the room. The male bear cub Jambo was the naughtiest one, sometimes he used to fight or make scars on the body by his sharp nail, so sometimes it used to get a beating. The animal children grew up together under appropriate discipline and love and they had good fellow feeling. Jambo was lovable of all, when Khairi beat him up, then Jambo used to stand up on his hind legs and put his furry arms around her neck and give some good hug to her. The tigress learnt different living techniques under the sharp eyes of her human father but always under full protection. The friendship of Manika and Khairi, between the prey and its actual haunter was puzzling, Khairi was always very careful, she was beaten for her arrogance sometimes but she remained playful with Manika.

Time passed at Jashipur, the animal children slowly grew, Khairi turned to a full grown tigress. Many interesting events took place in the family, some of course not narrated in the book but quoted by others. Once Khairi moved out of the family, went into the forest, but didn't return for three days, Mr. Choudhury was highly disturbed, Khairi never stayed so long outside. She might had fallen to the bullets of the poachers. On the third night the Minister of Forests of the State visited Similipal, he was due to stay in a remote guest house, other officials were also present. Their vehicle was moving in the forest road slowly, time was around 2 a.m in the night, the dead hours of the forests, the team saw a huge tiger lying on the narrow forest road, its body covered the entire width of the road, and everybody was apprehensive, encounter with a tiger at that odd hour would be highly unpleasant. The vehicle stopped on the road, the tiger was not leaving the road, one forest official accompanying the team thought it could be the tigress Khairi, any other normal tiger would not stay so long on the road for no reason, he slowly called Khairi, the tiger stood up, and slowly came towards the jeep, sniffed the jeep and jumped onto the front seat, all the occupants at the tips of the accompanying forest officer had vacated the front sat much earlier. The tigress sat there, the driver couldn't muster courage to drive with a tigress sitting on the front seat, next to him, other occupants were feeling uncomfortable too. Message was passed to Mr. Choudhury, he came immediately in that odd hour, the tigress saw her father, jumped from the front seat and leaped on the father and embraced him closely in the dead of the night, in the open forests of Similipal.

On February 12, 1981 Khairi was ill, vomited undigested meat and slept most of the times, and was even unable to get up, so different medicines were administered. Incidentally on that day a stray dog entered into the Khairi's compound through a hole in the net to steal the meat of the ailing tigress; and Khairi in a fit of rage jumped over the dog, killed it with a single bite on the neck, then she returned leaking the dog's blood. No antibiotic or injection was given, the dog did not bite the tigress, but the tigress killed the dog. Unfortunately like any other tigress Khairi had a sharp burbled tongue and when she rolled the tongue and licked her lips hard, then the saliva contaminated with dog's blood entered through scratches into her body. In the beginning, she was lively as usual but the rabies virus entered into her body, into her brain; before the symptoms appeared and her falling to death, the tigress played with Jambo in the morning for a long period and later on that day she did not take any food. The symptoms of rabies followed, she bit dry bush, jeep tyre, etc. In between she ate some food, slept and started nibbling at the root of her tail. Later Khairi bit her animal playmates and few persons looking after her. The rabies could not be controlled, she finally passed away on March 28, 1981, six and half years after she was brought to Shri Choudhury at Jashipur.

Khairi was the tigress living with a human being for more than six years, her close proximity brought out many research findings and understanding of tiger behaviour. I read the book with interest; some interesting facts are produced below.

The tiger has a strong sense of smell, in case of Khairi, it could distinguish the smell of different meats. The tiger used to hide the meat/kill behind the bushes and keeps a track of it.

The tiger has a strong capacity to identify its habitation in the jungle, even in the darkness it can easily identify the areas.

The tiger can identify the sound it has listened earlier.

The tiger has a very powerful eye, any movement attracts immediate attention. The tiger sometimes sits still, camouflaged behind the bush but gently waves the tip of the tail. The prey animal align its face towards the waving tip of the tiger tail exposing the neck to some extent ; a little different alignment ensures that the defensive mechanism of the prey like horns, antlers, hooves, canine teeth do not come on the way of attack.

The tiger's pattern of search on a known territory is usually in expanding loops over the surrounding. Distance probes are usually lineal – to and from the same trail.

The smell of the tiger is known from a distance, the elephants or prey animals flee out of the area where the smell is present. The prey animals are alarmed by the body smell, not by the pheromone of the tiger markings. So the tiger takes some illusive steps to avoid detection, try to approach the prey from opposite side of the wind so that the smell can't reach the prey animal.

The tiger's nose is much less sensitive than its ears and eyes. The comparative rating of sensitivity of ear: eye: nose is 7:5:3. The nose is least sensitive of the three; in any situation of confusion the tiger usually presses its nose for confirmation of smell.

The nose can differentiate smell of different items. The tiger, from the air borne smell, can judge how near the object is and from the residual smell can judge how long it has been there.

The tiger used to urinate at particular spots in its den, squirt its scent markings in postero-dersal jets, spreads the scent over a large area. The tiger marks its territory regularly. The research reveals the presence of two volatile amines – the amines are highly volatile pheromones soluble in aqueous urine. The markings are generally at the nose height and little above, marked along the most frequent trails used by the tiger. The tigress Khairi can even smell the presence of a male tiger 7 km away. Some animals and moths have strong sense of smell; the emperor moth can smell a specific female from nearly a mile away and a male silk worm moth needs only 200 molecules of the female sex attractants whereas our nose, a dull one, needs a at least 107 molecules/cc to confirm.

The tiger's eyes are very sensitive to movements, the retinal sensors are highly sensitive and believed to be 1000 times more photosensitive of diurnal birds. The irises can dilate and almost fill of the wide open eyes to take the maximum available light in the dark. The tiger eyes also function equally well in the day time; in the strong day light the iris contracts to an oval shape and in very strong light the pupil narrows to a vertical eclipse about 3 times of the width.

The tiger is colour conscious and is not like many other mammals whose world are all black and white, the tiger can see the world in colour.

The ears of the tiger can pick up faintest sound, without moving the head the ear can be oriented towards the direction of the sound, can even pick up gentlest rustle of a skink.

Khairi was attracted by the perfumes, scented powers, creams and soaps; she used to rubs her neck on the visitors who applied perfumes on their clothes.

This tigress likes soft music and soft soothing tones; Khairi was averse to harsh tones.

When the tiger sleeps, the eyes sleeps completely, the nose is partially awake and ear is fully alert.

The tiger always avoids the snakes and keeps a safe distance.

Always the tiger keeps itself clean, it does a ritual cleaning immediately after the food, licks the limbs, paws, and chest and lips absolutely clean.

The tiger drops its faeces where the smell can be completely sealed like in water or muffled (in pits, crevices, bolder gaps and thick leaf liter). Sometimes the tiger defecates on dung heaps; the fresh smell of the faeces gets mixed up and loses the identity.

Further information on Tiger

The information on tiger was so revealing I refreshed my ideas on the magnificent animal, I rolled the pages of information on the tigers; the amazing creature draws so much of attraction world over.

The tiger (Panthera tigris), voted as the world's favourite animal, is the largest of the four "big cats", the other three are lion, jaguar, and leopard; these big cats are only capable of roar. However in a more expansive definition of the big cats, other bigger cats like cheetah, snow leopard, clouded leopard, and cougar are also capable of roar.

The tiger is a large carnivorous animal, its body length can reach up to 11 ft including the length of tail, weigh up to 300 kilograms and can have canines up to 4 inches long which are used to make the killing bite. The female are smaller than the males, the males weigh up to 1.7 times more than the females; and the male tigers have wider forepaw pads than females. The most recognisable feature of the tiger is the pattern of dark vertical stripes that is superimposed over near-white to reddish-orange fur with lighter under parts.

Tigers live up to 10–15 years in the wild; can live longer than 20 years in captive condition. They are highly adaptable animals, are widely found in areas from the Siberian taiga to open grasslands to tropical mangrove swamps of the India and Bangladesh. The tiger prefer habitat with sufficient tree cover, usually remain close to water sources and in its habitat sufficient prey should be available. The tiger is a good swimmer in the big cats group, exception is the Jaguar who is also a good swimmer; the tigers are often found taking bath in ponds, lakes, and rivers and during the extreme summer, the tiger cools off in small water bodies.

The tiger's vocal communications are roars, moans, hisses, growls and chuffs.

Physical characteristics

The tigers have typical stripes that vary from brown or gray to pure black over rusty-reddish to rusty-brown coats, the stripes on the body help them to camouflage in the jungle shades and in long grasses as they stalk their prey. Interestingly, the pattern of stripes is different for each tiger, like fingerprints in human. The pupil of the tiger is round and the irises are yellow.

White Tiger – The white tiger is not a separate sub-species, is produced from Royal Bengal tiger when both parents carry the rare gene found in white tigers; which is likely to occur in one in every 10,000 births.

Black tiger – The black tiger is a rare color variant of the normal tiger and is not a different species or geographic subspecies. The black skin is due to pseudo-melanism where thick stripes remain so close to each other that the yellow part of the skin is almost covered. It is felt that such tigers are produced due to inbreeding, are said to be smaller than normal tigers.

Territorial behaviour

Compared to lions, the tigers are solitary and territorial animals, the size of a tiger's territory depends on prey abundance, on season; and for males closeness to female tiger territory. The males may have territories over an area of 60–100 km^2, the territories of females are much less, around 20 square kilometres, and the range of a male generally overlap those of several females.

At the beginning, the young female tigers establish a territory very close to her mother's area, often overlapping with mother's territory but these overlapping territories finally discontinues with time, resulting in two different independent territories. For the male tiger, it leaves the mother at a younger age to mark out its own territory; it either establishes a territory where no residential male tiger lives or remains as a subordinate in a superior resident male's territory until he is old and strong enough to challenge the original occupier.

In the jungle, the tigers usually avoid each other, however both male and female tigers sometimes share the kills; the tigers seem to behave relatively amicably when sharing kills, even unrelated tigers have also been observed feeding on prey together.

The tiger has the habit of marking the territory, the territory marking is done by spraying the urine and anal gland secretions, as well as marking trails with scat; trees scratching have also been made.

The scent glands are found around the tail and between the toes which helps the tigers to recognise each other.

The male tiger do not tolerate other males within its territory in general. The territorial disputes are usually resolved by intimidation displays and actual aggression is rare; the subordinate tiger concedes defeat by rolling onto its back, shows its belly in a submissive posture. Once the dominance is established, a male usually tolerate a subordinate within its territory, but they don't live in too close to each other. When a female in oestrus is around, sometimes violent fights occur between two males, and in rare cases even result in the death of one of the males.

A tiger has one or more lairs within its area which is generally located in cool shaded areas such as a cave, a cavity below a fallen tree, when it needs rest, the tiger goes to the lairs for rest.

Hunting and Diet

The tigers usually feed on medium and large sized animals like sambar, gaur, barasingha, chital, wild boar, nilgai and both water buffalo and domestic buffalo. Strangely sometimes, they also prey on other predators like leopards, pythons, sloth bears and crocodiles. Occasionally they also feed on much smaller prey like monkeys, hares, peafowls and fishes.

The old, or injured and incapable tigers sometimes turn into man-eaters as they lack agility and strength to hunt normal prey. Occasionally tigers eat vegetation for dietary fiber.

The tigers used to hunt in the night, but sometimes also hunt during the day. Usually the tiger hunt alone, ambush the prey and overpower it; the body power and weight are used to knock large prey off balance.

The tiger can run at a speed of about 50–65 kilometres per hour in short bursts but can't sustain speed for long, so the tiger come close to the prey before breaking the cover to ambush. The tiger is capable of taking long leaps, the horizontal leaps can be upto 10 metres, but generally it leaps around 5 meters. Despite master in camouflage, expert in ambush, still the successful kills are rare, only one in twenty tries ends in a successful kill.

The tigers used to bite the throat of a large prey like gaur and water buffalo, the prey usually weigh over a ton and a tiger weigh around 200 kg, around one fourth to one fifth of the weight of the prey; the tiger uses its forelimbs to hold onto the prey and bring it on to the ground. The tiger continue to hold the neck until the prey dies of strangulation. For small prey, the tiger bites the nape, often breaking the spinal cord, piercing the windpipe, or severing the common carotid artery. Sometimes tiger kill smaller prey by swiping its strong paws, which are powerful enough to smash the skulls of domestic cattle.

After killing the prey, the tiger drags the kill to a safe place, begins to eat continuously for an hour, and then take rest for several hours. After rest, the tiger comes back to the kill and eats the meal again and again.

Though generally clashes do not occur, almost rare, but the tigers are capable of killing formidable predators like leopards, pythons and even crocodiles on occasions, although these predators typically avoid each other. In case attacked by a crocodile, a tiger strikes back, hit the reptile's eyes with its paws and blinding it. The confrontation between the leopard and the tigers are rare as they hunt at different times of the day. The wild dog packs sometimes attack and kill tigers on disputes over food, but the dogs pack too suffers heavy causalities.

It is strange to notice lone jackals sometimes attach itself to a particular tiger, follow it at a safe distance so that it can get a chance on the kill after the tiger completes its eating.

Reproduction

The tigers are noisy during their mating, paw swiping, growling, hissing, groans, roars and rolling are associated with the mating process. The tiger mating generally takes place between the months of November and April though it can occur throughout the year; a female remains receptive for a few days and mating is frequent during that time period; the male and female stay together for a week and then breaks for new partners. The gestation period is about 16 weeks, the female gives birth to around 3–4 cubs, each weighing about a 1 kilogram, the cubs are born blind and helpless like the puppies. The females rear the cubs alone; keep them in dens such as thickets and rock caves. The unrelated male tigers sometimes kill cubs to make the female receptive.

The tiger cubs generally become independent around 1½ years of age, and they leave their mother at around 2–2½ years of age. The females reach sexual maturity at 3–4 years, whereas males reach sexual maturity at 4–5 years.

GROOMING

Grooming is an important routine for the tiger, they use their rasping tongue to remove loose hair and dirt from their fur, which keeps the tiger coat in good shining condition.

In that bright morning I came out, moved out of the guest house periphery, looked at the magnificent forest a little distance away, Similipal forest was displaying its magnificence, great grandeurs, the mountains of mystery, the secret of youth, the call of the life, the shriek of the death, the unsolved spells. A butterfly was sitting on the ground, what a beautiful butterfly it was, I looked closely, the forewing, also the hind wing colour was bright blue with white waves at the outer edge, and velvet dark wide patch towards the head, beautiful symmetric rings were put symmetrically at the outer edge; it appeared like as if the sea had come to the body of the butterfly, such was the brilliance in colour combination.

I looked at the forests far away, a white cloud had descended onto the hill top; here the butterflies were flying, moving here and there, so many butterflies appeared, I was surprised. I looked at the colour, their movement pattern, time passed by, birds started calling from the hides, the voices of Similipal was calling me again and again.

I looked at the deep forests again, a strange Odia speaking tribe remains inside, take pride in their belief; their astounding climbing skills were fresh in my mind. I read from a book on Kharias of Similipal, the Kharias considers themselves as Sabaras, the original Sabar tribe – they are Odia speaking tribe too, probably initially lived in the coastal areas of the state and this present group might be a descendent of the original race. I read their lifestyle, on their taboos; some strange words appeared – "A Kharia cannot accept food from the Brahmins, their girl Lalita, the daughter of Visvavasu Savar had married to a Brahmin man called Vidyapati and to accept food from the daughter's house is considered as a sin, a forbidden activity in their society". I simply couldn't believe my eyes as I looked at the book, the legendary Sabars of Jagannath fame remain deep inside the Similipal, away from the eyes of the common people; I recollected the myth of Vidyapati and Lalita related to culture of Lord Jagannath, the reigning deity of the Odia people, the story as if floated from the Similipal hills.

THE STORY OF VIDYAPATI AND LALITA

King Indradyumna was a great devotee of Lord Vishnu; he had a keen desire, to see Vishnu in his most perfect form on the earth. In his dream, he got the direction, the God would be found in the perfect form only in the land of Utkala (another name of ancient Odisha). So Vidyapati, the brother of the royal priest, was asked to search for the place where the God had such an appearance and to report his findings. Vidyapati visited Utkala, after a laborious search got information that Vishnu in his most lustrous form appeared as Nila Madhava, somewhere on a hill in a thick forest, was worshipped by a Savara (an aboriginal tribe) chief named Visvavasu. In search of the deity he travelled to the dense forest, met the Sabar chief, the tribal chief offered shelter to the knowledgeable Brahmin man without knowing his intention. Vidyapati was unsuccessful in his attempt, no information about the location of the seat of Nila Madhva, a great secrecy was maintained over the location of the Nila Madhaba. The Sabar chief had given the responsibility of taking care of the daily requirements of the Brahmin to his beautiful daughter Lalita, the Brahmin man need to be given flowers for worship, proper fruits need to be offered and so. Lalita was in her full youth, beauty adorned every part of her body, music on her movement, fragrance from her open hair, attraction in her walk; she was highly obedient, performed her assigned duties with greatest devotion and purity, the Brahmin was surprised to see such devotion in the densest forest; such lyrical beauty. While continuing to stay there, he developed love for Lalita, and later married her; the marriage probably would un-reveal the mystery over the presence of the God, time passed without any result, he need to give information to his king. He watched strange routines in the house, every night the Sabara king leaves for some unknown destination and comes back the next day around noon; when the Sabar king returns smell of camphor, musk and sandalwood used come from his body. Vidyapati requested his wife to explain the mystery, innocent Lalita initially didn't tell anything, but repeated request from her husband revealed the secret – her father used to go to a secret place to worship the deity Nila Madhava. The man was extremely happy, finally he got the news about the God in his most perfect form; in the face of love Lalita had forgotten her vow – not to tell anyone about the presence of Nila Madhava. Vidyapati was pestering Lalita to see the deity Nila Madhava, initially the girl couldn't dare, but finally took courage and requested her father to take her husband for a glimpse of the deity. The Sabar king couldn't believe his ears, his own daughter had revealed the secret, but Lalita continued to request her father at the insistence of her husband. Finally the Sabar king agreed to the demand, the Visvavasu fulfilled the desire of his daughter, Vidyapti would be taken to the worshipping place blind folded, the route can't be disclosed to anyone. Vidyapati collected some mustard seeds and kept in his clothe, hidden from the eyes of the unsuspecting Sabar king. The man walked blindfolded inside forest along with Sabar Visvavasu, he dropped the mustard seed stealthily, without the knowledge of the Sabar. They reached at the place of the deity Nila Madhava, the Sabara uncovered the eyes of his son-in-law Vidyapati; the Brahmin was almost blinded by the beauty of the deity; Lord Vishnu had appeared in the land in his fullest form. Leaving him alone with the deity, the Sabara went out in search of flowers for the adoration of the God, returned and offered prayer after cleaning the area, decorating the God.

They returned, Visvavasu left for his land without telling his beloved Sabari wife Lalita, to inform about the great discovery to his king Indradyumna. The king arrived at the place following the route created by blooming mustard plants, but they couldn't find Him; the God Nila Madhava had miraculously disappeared, so the king was extremely sad. Suddenly he received a divine direction, go to the sea-coast at Puri and to draw ashore a wood log that would be floating on the waves. He moved to the shores of Puri, found the log, and the log was brought to land; the log needs to be given appropriate shapes, the body of the Nila Madhava needs to be fabricated in a befitting manner. The king brought the best sculptors from different parts of the country, none of them was able to touch the Duru Brahman (the log); as soon as they worked on the log, the chisels broke into pieces. The king was at his wits end, he pryed to the God, finally the Lord himself came in the guise of an old carpenter, told the king that he could work alone with the doors closed for 21 days to give a shape to the deity; cautioned the king not to open the door. The sculptor took the daru brahman into the temple and locked the doors.

Days passed, everyone was eager, the queen herself was coming to the closed door everyday; after 14 days no sounds of tools was heard, king was worried, queen Gundicha was worried, the old sculptor might had breathe his last. The door was opened, they couldn't find the old sculptor, but the daru-brahman had been transformed into four incomplete forms, Jagannatha, Balarama, Subhdra and Sudarshan; the present form of the deities of Nilachala Khetra of Puri.

I couldn't move my limbs, even my ears had turned deaf, the story was incredible; the taboo of the Kharia sabar holds so much legend, the reigning deity of Odisha, is linked to the deep forests, the green forests; the descendents of the Sabaras live deep inside, the Kalianai winds brought so much of unbelievable messages.

King Indradyumna prayed to Lord Brahma, but Brahma said Lord Vishnu had manifested Himself at Shree Kshetra, so only he is capable to bless the flag atop the temple; he who sees the flag flying over the disk placed over the temple will be liberated. I looked at the tall hill from a distance, the hill was transforming in the shape of a temple, the deities of Similipal were seated there, the wind of Kaliani was bringing his blessings, the white clouds were the flags of Nilachakras.

I closed my eyes, Lalita and Vidypati had again took birth in dense forest as lovers; Lalita was very angry at the treachery of Vidyapati, she never expected her lover would be so deceitful, tear rolled down from her cheeks, her clan members were so unhappy at the disappearance of Nila Madhava from their jumgle; she left for the dense forest and the love bee Vidyapti wanted to return her back, his earlier action was destined. Nila Madhava need to resurface at Sree Kshetra for the benefit of the whole world, Lalita can't be so selfish, she needs to be explained. The man looks for his beloved; I recollected some stanzas of the Kharias

Oh! Goat herds boy, Oh! Shepherds
Which side, Oh! Boys, my love has gone?
The forest is dense and deep
Hollows and hill everywhere,
Tigers and bears around.
Which way, O boys my sweet heart has gone?
The forest is dense and deep
Hollows and hill everywhere,
Tigers and bears around
Evening descend fast.
Which way, Oh! Boys, my dear has gone?
With cloth across her shoulders,
Wailing and weeping .
Where my darling went?

The Kalian wind was full with emotions of immortal souls; it carries so much of legend, I only looked at the green hills, white clouds passed over the hills, the long shadows were casted on the land.

The Image of the Receding Tides

It is the land of uncommon, some say the largest crocodile of the world measuring more than 23 feet long and entered into Guinness Book of World Records during 2006, lives here; the place is inhabited by the living fossils, the horse shoe crabs – a strange creature with an armored shell and spiked tail, and its beaches are among the largest mass arrival sites in the world. The horseshoe crabs are among the world's oldest and most fascinating creatures, estimated to be at least 300 million years old, before the dinosaurs even arrived (which was about 200 million years ago). The Earth's land have changed dramatically, species evolved, but horseshoe crabs survived, remained much as they were 300 millions of years ago.

So many firsts in the world, the mangrove richness only can be compared to the forests of the Central American country Costa Rica, it was so surprising to me. The forests of Bhitarkanika, the pictures of Bhitarkanika created so many thrills, of course before reaching there I listened a story while riding a boat.

Story of Dhumal

"Do you wish to listen to the story of hunter who turned to a Yogi," he asked me, I nodded my head in affirmation.

"Imagine the scene, the king cobra is looking at you, hissing, and bite you, it was the story of the hunter." He was dramatising, I was drawn to the world of imagination, and a huge serpent appeared from the bushes and started hissing loudly, he then described a story.

Dhumal was initially a hunter of the Bhitarkanika, knew each part of the forest very well, a shrewd tracker, he could find any animal from the deepest corner of the forest. He was so powerful that he could kill a jungle pig by hand, an animal very difficult to tackle, it has tremendous power, even a male wild pig can defeat tiger many a times. He used to catch the snakes by hand; the snakes were good as his puppet. That day he caught a king cobra, the most ferocious snake – it eats other snakes, powerful and quick. Dhumal was swift ever, but the king cobra was a difficult customer, he could catch the king cobra just below its hood, but the snake slipped a little. The snake was hissing, as if fire was coming out of its mouth, the snake was terribly angry, as soon as the man caught the snake, his fist was tightened around the snake throat, the snake slipped a little, as result he was holding sake little below than the safest catching point. Now the snake turned its head, coiled its body on his hand and tried to bite him. Though he was holding it tightly, still the snake managed to bite him on his nose. His fist was loosened, he threw the snake away, the death hid bitten him, it was then matter of minutes he would leave the mortal world, the venom of the snake was lethal, soon the venom would come to the blood flow, and his body would be immobilised, and death would come within minutes. At that crucial moment he took a decision, deep incision would be made on his nose, to be burnt, and immediately he made deep incision on his own nose using his own knife, allowed blood to ooze out, the venom would come out with the blood, the soil was covered with his own blood, a lot of blood came out. Then he felt that the portion on which the snake bite was there need to be burnt, and he lit the fire, burnt the top portion of his nose by burning wood. He escaped sure death, his nose was disfigured, he survived with burnt nose. He came back to the hamlet, informed his close associates, but the incident changed his mind, and he was no more indulged in hunting, transformed himself as a protector of wildlife, and finally turned to a Sanyasi, a Baba, a yogi.

My friend looked at the deep forest of the Bhitarkanika, the deep lines beyond the water limit is full of unheard stories, inexplicable animal cultures. The waves of the sea were meeting the turbid waters of the river, we were at the confluence; the unbound horizon was meeting the earthen limits, that was the period when I listened the story of Dhumal. I recollected the song of the roaming yogis also found begging in the fringe villages of this dark forest. They move with their kendera, which is a typical musical instrument resembling a small veena, around a feet long, from the semi-pot structure the strings attached to the corners, the song is played by moving another stick which is made to an archaic shape and the strings are attached to both ends, on the strings of the main instrument. The music is soft, resemble more like a cry, the man is crying, his heart has opened, all the songs reflect the agony in life, and advises the listener to maintain a pious and dedicated life. I closed my eyes, imagined Dhumal wearing the dress of a yogi, the singing kendera instrument was on his shoulder, was wearing gerua (brown coloured) dhoti on his waist, the cloth was falling up to his knee, on his dark body he was wearing a traditional half shirt called fatei, with no bottoms, a red Khurda gamocha (a red thin towel) was rolled on his head, which is a turban formation in which a gamocha is rolled around the top portion of the head, on another shoulder one cotton bag was hung in which a vessel made out of white gourd was kept, it is used for taking alms. The Kendera song from the book *Tika Govinda Chandra*, song of the dark forest of Bhitarkanika started reverberating in our ears.

Recite the name of Rama my son
Remember the name of Rama
Don't fail in recitation
The death God will take you....
Recite the name of Rama my son.......

The story of Dhumal was awesome, full of horror, anxiety, fight to survive. I was eager to meet the man, he had left home for taking Sanyas, to become the wandering yogis, and to discover the man, I came to the deep forests of Bhitarkanik again. I heard he had returned after a long stay outside. Many myths, many uncertainties, many unnoticed items to be explored. I not only heard about the Dhumal, about a lotus pond where once a girl was sacrificed to the crocodiles – Oriyan myth and many more; the greatest attraction was the beauty, the glory of mangrove forests.

Journey to Bhitarkanika pond

Early morning fog covered the trees that day, haze carpet covered the green lines, the crocodiles, the snakes, the wild lives were inside their dens, no sound except for the calling of the birds from their hides, others lives were still immobilised by white fog, dew on the leaves. We started early for the lotus pond, located on the other side of Dangmala, across the river of crocodiles and mud flats, the boat crossed silently, the mud flats were calm, no life in the Nalia grass, no egrets, no crocodiles, no deer, no boars too. We arrived, the low tide has reduced the level of water, the landing platform was at a higher level, more than six feet higher than the present water plane. The boatman tied the boat with the bamboo bases, the bamboo sticks were erected on the water, the cemented base of the platform was little away, bamboo ladders, wide one-almost six seven feet wide, tall as the platform was, was tied to the cement structure, a men can climb in case of low tide. We climbed, a thin layer of black mud was covering the floor of the platform making it very slippery, so we moved over the surface carefully. Ahead was leading a road into the deep forest, a kuccha one, a track for the cycles was created with regular movement of the forest guards on the track, on both sides thick impregnable forest was laid by the nature, and moving on that track by cycle was creating curiosity, the forest was unknown to me, the trees were unknown, the fear of the snakes and crocodiles were live in the mind. Little inside, it was more dark, the crocodiles might be hiding, the pythons might be hanging on the branches, more importantly the king cobra might be on the tree top. I heard it earlier, the speaker when told about the king cobra of Bhitarkanika, his eyes were protruded, the information – the king cobra of Bhitarkanika sits on the tree top, enjoy the morning sun, and here in the early morning we were moving inside the thick forests, the sun might be there on the sky, the king cobra might be watching us from the tree top, here for it some people were moving in semi dark atmosphere.

After a brief cycling, we reached at a more open area, a green temple, later I came to know that the temple was a Shiva temple constructed by the king of Kanika at olden times. The temple was not much tall, around twenty high, the door was facing the forest towards east, no flag on the temple top, with the setting of the Kanika kingdom, the temple had lost its glory. The colour was however not that old, the forest department was taking care of the ancient structure. On its side a Banadurga temple in a dilapidated condition was standing, the inhabitants of the area prays to the deity of the jungle there, the common people pray to the Goddess for their safety here, when death is few feet away in the deep interior people certainly have strong belief in miracles, in uncertainty man falls back to the goddess. The main deity was inside, alongside the door there were side gods, these sculptures were partially covered with vermillion. A tulsi chaura, a small pyramidal structure, around 3-4 feet tall with steps, and on the top the tulsi plant is planted, this kind structure one usually finds in the Odia villages, was standing outside, between the main Shiva temple, and the Banadurga temple at the corner. The crow pheasant, a beautiful brown red bird was calling 'ku ku', its voice was deep and grave than the koel, behind the branches of the baula tree. I looked at the baula tree, a very old one, fissures appeared on the bark, strangely some hanging roots came from the branches, a common sight under a banyan tree, here it came down from a thick branch of a baula tree; I was puzzled and question appeared in my look; the forest guard rectified, those were the parasites named as guluchi creeper, these creepers entered into the trunks of the old tree, appeared like part of the same tree. I walked a little, found the lotus pond; the pond I was searching for, the lotus pond was connected to the story of the crocodiles, on a lotus pond the Sadhaba of the area once left his daughter. The birds were sitting on the branches of the trees on the bank of the pond, were singing the myths of the deep forests.

The lotus pond was not big, little less than an acre of land, almost square shaped, a bund ran all around the pond. The lotus pants were in the centre, the flat and rounded leaves covered the entire water surface, and around the lotus leaves the water grasses raised their branches, in this grassy portion of the pond clean blue water was seen sometimes, the morning sky was deep blue. The hunting tower of the erstwhile king was standing on the other side of the pond; the yellow structure was casting a shadow on the pond. The tower was partially visible, I walked towards the tower alongside the bank, I was careful, the crocodile might be hiding in the waters waiting for the victim to come within the striking distance. The structure was two storied, there were two entrances, one for the ground floor, the other one for the upper floor, the doors were narrow, around three feet wide and five feet tall; the top terrace was disconnected from the rest floors. The terrace was designed nicely for putting the firearms at the right place; there were small narrow towers at four corners, small pillars were erected between the towers with open space between the pillars for facilitating the view of the hunters and for putting the firearm nicely. For the ground as well as for the first floor, there were square holes on the outer surface at many places, at regular intervals; through these holes the king's hunting party kills the unsuspecting thirsty animals. A big mango tree was coming to the roof; a neem tree was standing just next to the tower towards the pond side. A little ahead, towards west of the structure, the modern watch tower of the forest department was erected and in front of it, after a small band of trees was a wide flat grazing land, a meadow, the dew on the green grasses were glittering in the morning sun. Inside that glittering land, surrounded by forest all around, a small pond, connected to the creeks during the high tide was located, the forest guard inform with a hiss, fear in his eyes, the crocodiles remain in that pond, the animals of the meadow are hunted by the crocodiles in the water. I looked around; few cattle egrets gathered around a small water hole, their white bodies were shining. On the other side, just at the edge of the forest, towards our left two wild boars were grazing in the fields. I looked at the band of trees just adjacent to the watch tower, the leaves of the guanara tree from a distance looked like leaves of camphor tree. Some water gathered in the water channels, small fishes were playing there. Then I looked at the brown green field amidst dark forests, life ends, life begins there, with the morning sun, with the high tide, fishes flicker in the left over stagnant waters of the earlier high tide, the memory changes with the lines of those small water bodies. We returned, on the way looked at the lotus pond, the sun had come a little away from the edge of the horizon, streaks of soft rays were dripping through the openings between the foliages, illuminating the pond, the tower. For the merrymaking of someone, so many thirsty animals once died here, their love for life ended here. Few pigeons started humming, other pigeons looked at us passively and the humming of the pigeons continued. Two cormorant birds rose from the pond water and flew towards forest, the cuckoo started calling from the thick hides, the kingfisher called from the branches; The life of the forest has not changed much.

I returned through that forest road, still fog was shadowing the trees, hazed the leaves, on the side beside a big banyan tree, the forest was mixed, not all the trees were purely mangrove trees inside. The green ponds alongside the track were feared ponds, these small water bodies were filled with crocodiles, the big reptile from the creeks used to visit the ponds inside, used to wait for the prey, the animals need sweet water to drink, the crocodile then leaps at the animal closed to waterline. The green moss covered the entire pond surface, I tried to locate the crocodile, couldn't find the eyes, the crocodile had hidden itself in a dark unseen corner, the foot prints of visiting crocodile was seen, the return prints were not there, the crocodile was hiding inside, and till I reach the edge of the waterline, within the striking distance of the crocodile, I am safe. I can survive with a bottle of water, the animal has to visit the crocodile filled water to quench thirst, and there would be regular fight for survival.

I returned to the camp, there I found Dhumal, a mysterious man, around whom so many baffling stories float, was sitting below a broken baula tree. I looked at him, his lean figure was not speaking about the strength, his capability to handle the wilderness of Bhitarkanika with so ease.

He started with some stanzas of Shrremad Bhagavat of Bhaktakavi Shri Jagannath Das –

Good or bad of a life
Known at the time of his death

I knew about Bhagavata of Jagannath Das, in the history of Odia literature and culture the name of Jagannath Das has been immortalised as a leading devotee, his consummate work *'Bhagavata'* is read daily almost in every household of Odisha. His unique creation 'Srimad Bhagavata' continues of stir up spiritual feeling with an established ritual of regular recitation. Hardly there is a village where there is no 'Bhagavata Ghara or Bhagavata Tungi' and a house, where Bhagavata is neither worshipped nor recited, the Bhagavata is the companion of life and death of an Odia society. The author Atibadi Jagannath Das was one of the five comrades of his contemporaries like Achyutananda, Balarama, Sishu Ananta and Yosabanta Das who pioneered the Bhakti movement in Odisha. Shree Chaitanya, the greatest devotee of Shree Jagannath conferred the title of 'Atibadi' admirably upon Jagannath Das, highest great Bhakta Saint of Odisha'.

I looked at the man, confusion, hollowness in my mind, in the deep forests I was listening something uncommon.

He smiled, and recited again,

Body physical,
Even the God dies in earth

I was amazed, looked at him, smile in his face, hollowness in his face too, I couldn't understand the mystery in him, the myth of Bhitarkanika which I have been searching for. The man was short, lean and thin, a bigger head than his body, black beard covered his face and few white breads within was speaking of his experience and on the head the hair was not long, not uncombed and rough like a yogi; most surprisingly he was not in the attire of the yogi, he now looked like any other common man of the area. A brown muffler was coiled around his neck like the coil of the king cobra, a flower printed cheap grey shawl wrapped his upper body, a green tartan (checkered) lungi covered his waist and down, and he was wearing a full sleeved red shirt. I looked at him keenly, where was the figure of a sanyasi, where was the figure of a fearsome hunter? The passive look of course spoke of detachment, the long look at the forest spoke of his knowledge, I didn't find arrogance, anger in his face. I was perplexed, the man was talking philosophy, a man from the dark forests was reciting the verses of philosophy. I hesitated, but the question roamed inside. He understood and then he recited a stanza of Bhagavata.

Recite the name of Govinda,
You can cross the world of ocean

I was surprised, where from a rustic man like him got so much of philosophy, I was interested to know his life, I knew that he was once a worker with forest department. He opened up, started telling the stories of his life, the life begins with the shadow of the mangrove trees, the youth flourished with the animals, with poverty; there was struggle at every step, the man continued to fight. I am recollecting the story.

As a young boy, Dhumal was no different from other boys of the area, he had only one half pant that his father bought for him from Chandabali – the nearby town at those days. In his village Bankuala he joined Jay Durga Chatasali the lower primary school is called Chatasali in the rural Odisha in the coast belt, with a bag. The village schools, during those days were generally made out of wood, the roofs were usually thatched one, the wooden pillars were giving the support to the roof and many wooden desks, chairs were put in the class room for the students. That day, the teacher was late, small kids were screaming in fear, a big snake had coiled near the front wooden desk and no child could dare to go near it, the snake was hissing loudly. The kids panicked, the snake could harm, so many horror stories move in the air. Dhumal at that time was in class III, a small child, no one knew where from he got so much courage, he stepped inside the room with very slow steps, other kids peeped in, no body dared to accompany, the voices at once stopped, the young boy came closer to the snake, without alarming the snake, he slowly extended his hand between the desks, and suddenly caught the big snake near its neck. Everybody was terrified, but Dhumal caught the snake, then he slowly brought the snake outside, the snake by that time had coiled around his little hand, but he hold its body with right composure, with calm, the snake was trying to free itself, but the boy hold it properly. He brought the snake, it was a JhadaKalua snake, the king cobra is known by that name in this part of Odisha, was like a toy in his hand. Then he went to the edge of the forest, allowed the mighty snake to escape to the wilderness, every child was hypnotised, nothing of that sort ever happened. The teacher came; he was surprised to know the incident, later everybody in the village was surprised, his parents however panicked.

I looked at his deep eyes now, a middle aged man was sitting in front of me, telling the story of his childhood. I was confused, a child of Class–III could handled such powerful snake, a mighty king cobra, where from he got the courage, how it could be possible?

"I was like Ekalavya, the disciple without a guru in hand; I never got formal training on handling of the snake' in fact I had never touched a snake before that incident," he mentioned.

"Many snake charmers visit our village, I looked at them keenly, watched every trick of theirs with interest – how they catch the snake, at what place they catch, how they handle the deadly snake, the movement of their hands," he was narrating without a hitch.

"With that knowledge, I caught the large king cobra for the first time at that young age," he continued, suddenly his eyes glued to the farthest corner of the horizon, his voice turned impassive.

"Life continued under tremendous poverty, no food for the family, mother worked as a domestic help, father worked in the fields, the study ended after the Chatsali, I worked as a help in a farmer's place, but inquisitiveness with snakes continued, I watched them with caution, with curiosity, Then I started catching those sneaked who sneaked into the village from the adjoining forest. The mice in the village attracted all kind of snakes, cobra, common krait, banded krait, vipers, dhaman etc. were found in the village, king cobra of course was occasional visitor. Many slipped below the beds, many coiled around the utensils and grain baskets, many were in the roof, I caught them with ease," he was explaining his life, how a boy developed to a man.

"I got employment with the forest department for sometime as casual worker, there I handled the king cobra and other snakes, the outside world came to know about my experience with the snakes," he mused. Then he explained his techniques in catching the king cobra snakes.

"Many a times the king cobra remains on the holes inside the trees, or in hallows in the trees. If you find a king cobra inside, then climb the tree, slowly enter your hand into the hallow and locate the snake's head," he was narrating with a cool voice, as if the chill of the cold blooded reptile had brought coolness in his talk, no rush of blood in his talk.

I was speechless, my hair roots swelled with fear. I never imagined a man would enter his own hand into the hollow of a tree to catch the mighty venomous King Cobra, the king of the snakes.

"If the king cobra bites you, after all you are not able to see it inside that hallow," I asked him.

He smiled, then explained. "King Cobra can't bite your hand inside the hallow, unless it raises its hood, it can't bite, it is the trick, it is the technique, the greatest obstacle is the fear of the snake," he was describing his trick, then he continued further.

"The snake, inside the hallow would move its head while remaining in coil, then I sense its head, and catches the snake below its neck, then pull it out slowly. You can't catch other smaller snakes; cobra, krait are treacherous quick snakes, they will bit you without raising their hood, but king cobra can't do that..," he explained the behaviour of King Cobra.

"If you see a king cobra outside, in the open areas, then how will you catch it?" I asked him, he smiled and recited.

What is impossible on earth?
If a man is righteous,
Donate to the needy.
Serve the poor.
He can achieve everything for this virtue.

"I believe in Him, He is the protector," he said and then continued.

"Catch it differently, you can't enter near the snake, when the snake tries to move away tap the tail lightly, the snake will suddenly raise its hood and will try to strike at you, this big snake tries to hit the head of a man, not at lower height, when it strikes at you, you have to adjust your hand, with a sudden flash you put the hand just below the hood, the distance from the hood should be such that the snake can't bend its body, else it will bend and bite you either at your head, or at your back." I couldn't believe my ears, a man can catch the king cobra when it tries to strike at him, the lightning speed of the snake is matched with the tremendous belief he has in him, one will faint at seeing the burning eyes of the King Cobra, listening its terrible hissing sound.

"The snake should not be tightly pressed, its spinal cord would be hurt, but not loosely too, the hold should be such that the snake couldn't escape. The snake then tries to curl around the hand, you have to move with the movement of the snake; slowly it will get exhausted, then the snake can safely be kept in the snake box."

I was curious about the King Cobra, where it stays, how it behaves in the thick forest of Bhitarkanika. I enquired.

"The King Cobra used to stay in those places where food is available in plenty, mostly around rivulets, small springs, in the grassy areas – mostly Nalua grass areas. The jungle rats live on the trees, to eat them the smaller snakes move in the trees, and king cobra preys on the snakes. King Cobra used to make its nest in Pinchha forest, the large snake remain in nest, the weight of the reptile presses the leaves and twigs of the nest, thus elaborating the size of the snake," he was explaining. Then he continued with many stories of king cobra, how it eats a dhaman snake (rat snake), poison it and many more.

"The last King Cobra story," I paused, this was the story which probing my mind for so many days, incident that changed the life of a man, from a hunter to a sanyasi. Then he narrated the incident.

"The forest officer in charge of the area was looking for a King Cobra, the Nandankanan zoo authorities had asked for a king cobra for the Nandankanan Zoo, the zoo at that time was not having a King Cobra. I was trying to locate a healthy King Cobra, but the king cobras are not easy to find always. One day I was going to Bhitarkanika block along with the forest guard of the area and the local priest of the Shiva temple. On my shoulder I was carrying husked rice on a cement bag, the mustard oil was kept in a glass bottle without cover but closed by putting some straws on the mouth; and to prevent spilling the bottle was buried in the rice. Near Bhitarkanika temple, alongside the small pond, I noticed a big king cobra, the time was around 1 p.m., an unusual time to find the snakes near a water pond, and probably the snake was basking in the sun. Once I saw the snake, I forgot the load on my shoulder, the load might obstruct in my swift movement and it in fact was the reason of accident. Seeing us, the snake moved away quickly, tried to sneak through the bushes and creepers. As usual I tapped the tail, the method called 'Thukeiki Dhariba', the snake suddenly turned back, opened its big mouth and strike at me. I tried to block, the load on my shoulder prevented my free movement, in fact I forgot the load in the heat of the moment. I tried to block, but the snake slipped, it struck me along with the creepers, due to its speed the thorny creeper and snake both hit me, and there was scar from head to nose . After striking me, the snake tried to escape; it sneaked to a hole in the kochila tree. The old tree had hallows, the snake got immediate shelter. But, I as determined as ever, went after it, the snake could not enter fully, was struck half way, there was not sufficient space for this big snake in that hallow. I tracked the snake, tried to pull its body a little, this alarmed the snake, and it escaped to open ground through another deep fissure in that tree. Once the snake was out, I tapped its tail and caught the snake by tap and catch method. After catching the snake, I put the snake in the cement bag and closed the bag by tying the mouth.

Everything was over in few minutes, then I remembered about the strike of the venomous snake; the forest guard and the temple priest were requested to check the wound, they informed that there was wound at the nose tip, a deep needle-like mark with blood and water oozing out of the wound. At that moment, I suspected the wound to be from snake bite. I requested the temple priest to cut my nose in that portion; I heard from the snake catchers that if the blood flow is blocked, then the snake poison would not spread to the rest of the body. The temple priest refused, this work, cutting the nose of a live man would be an impossible task for him. The forest guard too trembled; he simply couldn't believe that I had actually told him to cut part of my nose.

Seeing both of them reluctant, time was running out too, the affected part had to be cut, I took the sharp knife, cut the top portion of my nose, a nail sized flesh came out. There was heavy bleeding and pain. I suspected it to be due to the king cobra bite, my body started trembling, and thoughts got puzzled, vision blurred; I knew, nobody has escaped king cobra bite, and my time would end very soon, so I ran to the jetty, the forest guard ran after me, the temple priest couldn't follow. The boat was on the other side, the boat man was in the jungle, we yelled, but he couldn't hear us, he was far away, by the time he would come to the boat and reach our side, it would be late. I had no choice, I wished to see my kith and kin for the last time and the time was running out for me. I jumped into the crocodile filled water, I had to cross the river, at that crisis moment I simply ignored the crocodiles. The forest guard also jumped into the river along with me, we swam safely, the crocodile didn't notice us and we reached the other side. I ran towards my village, reached the courtyard of my house and fainted. However I survived, till date I'm not sure the whether the King Cobra had really injected the full venom. Sometimes the snake always don't inject the venom." The man completed his story, and then he recited –

Till the soul takes refuge on the lotus feet of Lord,
He is unhappy and suffers from sorrows.

I looked at him, at his nose, the head of the nose was blunt, and the area darkened due to deep cut, apart from the disfigured nose there was no other deformities on the body. Listening so much, I recollected my first journey to Bhitarkanika in a moonless night, the chill of Bhitarkanika was felt on that day, of course without knowing the full story of the land.

Boat journey in creek during night

In another moonless night we travelled in a boat, to see the lights of Bhitarkanika, there was no sound, the engine was switched off, and the boat was floating towards the Dangmal jetty in the high tide. The tidal waters was pushing the boat towards the upstream, the moonless night was increasing the depth of darkness, the sound of small waves of the tide was creating a soothing sound, the call of the mangrove forest, and in that forest one tree dazzled, another tree dazzled and the banks of the river glittered with green dazzling lights, small lights of the glow worms. I did not have the sufficient words to describe the phenomenon. The forest was lighted, the symphony of the waves beating the mud bank, the sound off the night birds were filling the atmosphere, slow, touching, the sounds of the nature, the inner sounds of the heart. I looked at the those glowing lights, my colleagues were highly excited, the lights were glowing, shutting the next moment, there was no warmth, there was coolness, the size of individual light few millimeters only, low in intensity, the whole tree was glowing. On the other side, the sailor told me to be the Bani and Keruan forest, the dance of the light was highly synchronised, the whole tree glowed for two seconds, thousands of glow bulbs, on the leaves, on the branches, and on the next moment, the lights were put off, total darkness followed, and the lights again came after two seconds. What scene it was! I was taken aback; the forests of Bhitarkanika turned to a fairy land. Suddenly the sounds of the water stopped, the sound of the night birds stopped, the glow worms stopped lighting for few minutes; as if they all were dancing at the direction of a unseen magician. I tried to hold my breath, my colleagues also hold their breath, nobody wanted to break the silence, the silence of the forest had its message, untold, feel the coolness in the heart. Suddenly the lights came, the sounds of the tides came, the river was full with mild music of the tidal waters, the glow worms started dancing rhythmically, on that night the glow worms were changing their position rhythmically, their movement, to me appeared like the movements of acrobats, jumping from one branch to other, not breaking its speed, not damaging the trees also, the formation spectacular better than any presentation by the humans. I could not believe my eyes, it was so amazing, many more times beautiful than the fireworks in the event of closure of Olympics.

Our boat moved, the stars in the sky were stationary, in that silent night my colleague started telling about the uniqueness of the forest, the living land with so many unique features.

"Horse shoe crabs also called the King Crabs, the living fossils of upper Silurian age, the period dating back to almost 400 million years ago." He said and I was confused, did not know what that Silurian age means, never ever heard of a crab called horse show crab, strange names to me, of course.

"It is a crab, but does not have the shell on the body," he said again, I was again surprised. There can be crab without shells; those words were so confusing to me.

He was not narrating the stories of the bigger animals, the infamous salt water crocodiles or the world famous nesting of the Olive Ridley turtles. I heard of those beautiful creatures, those famous ones, now he was narrating the surprising facets of the Bhitarkanika, and moments ago I saw the wonders of the black night inside the forest. The black night can glow, can put its signature, can make acrobatics. My memory turned shallow, I could not recollect the words ever I listened in my life about them, never imagined such creatures to live so near to the human territory. The living fossils can't survive near human habitation, though it can survive the race even though the horseshoe crab has been imagined as an armored box that moves.

The King crabs still find their ways to the mud flats of the Bhitarkanika, out of four species of horse shoe crabs found in the world, two varieties are found in the waters of Brahmani Baitarani delta, the Bhitarkanika area, along the Gahirmatha coast. The highly priced chemical 'Lectine' used in the cancer treatment is derived from them. Sometimes, these innocent crabs are found floating in and around Gupti area.

He showed me the photograph, didn't know why, in torchlight. The crab looked so interesting, it did not resemble a crab, rather to me, it appeared like a ray fish with hardened shells on the top, long sword like organ protruding outwards from almost a spherical body, the side portion was scaled; the shells were olive green and were shining.

"The other interesting crab, the hermit crab never has a shell on its body; still it is called a crab. It occupies the dead gastropod shells, when gets larger, then enters to another bigger dead gastropod shell. What a strange animal it is?" he told.

"Very strange behaviour, are those the only crabs found in the Bhitarkanika?" I asked

"Mangrove forests are the treasure of other species of crabs too, eight varieties of crabs found in Bhitarkanika, the most prominent among them being the Scylla serrata..," he explained.

I was thinking about the crabs, the mangrove crabs can climb the trees for some time, and I knew some crabs, the appearance of the Scylla serrata crab varies from a deep, mottled green to very dark brown. The females are able to give birth to almost a million offspring, and they can grow up to 3.5 kilograms in weight and can have a shell width of up to 24 centimeters wide. Some people consider them to be among the tastiest of crab species. Their nature is highly cannibalistic; when another crab undergoes moulting (moulting or molting is the manner in which an animal routinely sheds off a part of its body, not always an outer layer or covering like crabs, either at particular times of year, or at some points in its life cycle), the hard shelled ones sometimes attack the moulting crabs and eat them. These crabs are highly active; eat almost everything, small fishes and all kinds of meat, even vegetable matters. These crabs are hardy, can tolerate most difficult water conditions.

The boat moved with the dark shadows of the forests, the bending trees were appearing like supernatural structures, the dark shadows created so many appearances, poor visibility limited the depth of vision, the big channel looked like a stable pond, such was the strange effect; the moon light created so much of illusions. Some black masses emerged from the water surface, almost blocking the route at far. I was frightened, we probably lost the way, the boat came closer, the channel took a long turn there, and we couldn't see it from a distance, the illusions in the starry night created so much apprehension.

"Once my junior staff saw a river ghost, he in fact trembled in fear," he looked at me in the dimly lit night, in the dark nights of Bhitarkanika, ghost can't hide long, he wanted to see fear in me. I was horrified, if the ghosts descend into the crocodile filled water, I can't think beyond, fear came to my eyes.

He laughed, not looking at me, but looking at the water, the memory of the incident brought laughter in him, then started narrating a strange experience.

"It was a moonless night, we were returning from Chandbali by boat, entered into the Dhamra mouth, were close to Kalibhanjadiha Island. There was no sound, except for the sound of our boat, we had also stopped talking, suddenly a strange sound came from the water, we were surprised. There was no boat, no fisherman would dare the dark night there, no one around. Strangely, the confusing sound was coming from the water, we stopped the boat, the sound was coming nearer. We switched on the strong torchlight and scanned the water surface, no sight of any animal, but the sound was coming closer, and at that time my junior screamed – Ghost, Ghost," he stopped and started laughing, the experience of that night must be amusing.

I was also amused; fearful too, the other companions were eager. I never listened about strange sounds coming from the waters in a channel in the mangrove forests though I moved in many areas full with mangroves. Is Bhitarkanika was so strange; the water was really hounded by the ghosts of the creeks? Some strange feeling seeped into my spine, I tried to figure out unusual in the water line, tried to hear any feeble sound coming from the water, but there was no such sound. Then my companion continued, he had observed curiosity and fear in our faces.

"I was also confused, when my junior screamed. I was also terrified to some extent; how can sound came from the water. But, the strange sound in that dark night was getting louder, we almost stopped breathe, someone was hitting the water. We tried to find out the reason of such sound, the torch light moved from one end of the water mass to the other end, some splashes of water on the river surface, but no life. The ghosts of the water were terrifying us, how could be there some splashes on the water surface without the sign of life, how could strange sound come from the water. Even I thought about the ghosts of the water, people says – the ghosts would create many illusions and shapes, can generate strange noises, to frighten the traveler, and lead the man to death. Our torch lights moved over the muddy water, some waves appeared on the water surface. Suddenly four Irrawaddy Dolphins sped past our boat, their backs were little visible, their quick movement created strong river currents and our boat almost lost balance in that strong waves." He narrated his river experience in a striking fashion, till his description I was ignorant of the Irrawaddy dolphins in the river mouth, this aquatic animal is an endangered species, not many are living in the world. Their strange behaviour, modes of communication, their intelligence create so much of interest in this water animal.

He showed me the photograph of the Irrawaddy Dolphin in the torch light, the water animal always created so much of interest in me. Then he explained about the behaviour of the dolphin, the probable source of the sound which might be due to the lobtailing; sometimes a whale or a dolphin lifts its flukes out of the water and then bring them quickly down onto the surface of the water and hit the water hard in order to make a loud slap. During lobtailing the dolphins remain in horizontal position and make the slap through a jerky whole body movement; and there can be several slaps in a single session. The river dolphins rarely lobtail, but it is a very common incidence amongst the dolphins of the sea. This sound of such lobtail can be heard underwater several hundred meters away from the site of a slap.

On that night we talked about the wonder animals, our boats drifted slowly, we enjoyed the night in Bhitarkanika, the fairies danced in the dark forests of Bhitarkanika. The sound of the breaking waves was creating music, matching the signature of the glow worms on the black canvas, drums were not there, high sounding pitches were not there, a vibrant music, a live design creating live designs.

Taopoi Story

Next day morning I saw a beautiful worm, red velvet in colour, less than 1 cm in length, with thin small legs, on the garden, it was moving on the sandy soil. He picked it up gently, put it on his palms, after a pause of few seconds the worm turned itself and started walking on the palm. I picked it up; it was a lovely worm, so soft to touch.

"The beautiful red Sadhababohu,

Where you are going?

Where you are going?"

He recited the rustic rhyme for me, to understand the worm better.

"This worm is called Sadhabbohu worm, the meaning of Sadhaba is the sea merchant, and sadhababohu means the woman of sadhaba, she is gorgeous, beautiful and shy." He informed. While I was admiring the beauty of the worm, he started telling further.

"Do you know once the girl of the most prosperous sea merchants was moving in the mangrove forests of Bhitarkanika helplessly, no oil was ever applied to her hair, hairs were uncombed, her body was wrapped with the dirtiest clothes, she was resembling a small bear of the forest and her odyssey was later surfaced in the form of a festival. All unmarried Odia girls now even continues with this festival, the Bhalukuni Puja"

I knew about Bhalukuni festival, performed by the unmarried Odia girls, for five terms, each Sunday at the evening the girls sing the odyssey of the girl who was once devoted to Goddess Mangala and the Goddess in turn accepted her broken rice offering (known as Khuda in Odia) from Bhalukuni, the name derived from the appearance of the girl – the girl Taopoi appeared like a bear, called Bhalu in Odia. Also since her offering was Khuda (broken rice), the festival is also known as Khudurukuni festival.

I knew the story faintly; the long disassociation with tradition is erasing the picture of this festival so famous in the rustic Odisha. Then he started telling about the festival, to refresh my memory, to make the journey more interesting.

"The story started from the land of mangroves, at Satabhaya village located at the edge of the Mangrove forest, touching the Bay of Bengal. Bhitarkanika is the same land; here the brothers came through the rivers, after their ships missed the Dhamra port in the dark night to rescue their sister," he replied

She, Taopoi, was among the most privileged, her father Tanayabant, was the richest sea merchant of the area of Righagrh, adjacent to Bhitarkanika forests, his wealth was the envy for all, had seven ships, innumerable servants.

"You may like to know the riches of the sea merchants of the Kalinga," he wanted to bring more curiosity to the subject. Then he started singing some stanza of the Taopoi festival.

Wealth in their house,
Maid savants wear Patasaree,
On her hand shines golden bangles
Women in house wear jewellery invaluable
Jewels matches their weight
They sit on the stool of quartz
Staircase made of marbles even.

The women of the Sadhabas were as sweet as Sadhababohu worm, soft and shining like it, the Sadhababohu worm surfaces during the rains, is a beautiful small worm with red velvet skin, the worm is harmless, much liked by the children. The ladies of the Sadhabas were gorgeous in their look, their riches were the talk of the society, and they maintained a luxurious life.

I was taken back, the riches of the sea merchants were unimaginable, and the glory they bring to the kingdom was unbelievable. Previous night I saw at the sky, thousands and thousands of diamond had glittered in the sky, the riches of the Kalinga had gone to the dark night sky of Bhitarkanika.

Then he continued with his story, the eager ears were listening to him keenly–

She was the only girl child of her parents after seven brothers. Beautiful she was, friendly too, she was once playing with the daughter of the minister of that kingdom. Both the friends were creating the houses, making cooking with dust, they were screening the dust using their bamboo Kulei, an handheld implement to screen small dust particles from bigger sand particulate. One Brahmin widow came, she saw the children playing with the dust, an ugly character she was, she didn't see good of others, chided the Taopoi.

"You are the daughter of the richest merchant of the area, your father couldn't manage one golden Kulei, and you play with bamboo Kulei, had I been in your case, I would have brought golden moon from my father," the Widow Brahmin lady commented, and the child wept, never she was chided by someone, she never listened harsh words, went to her father and asked for the golden moon, the parents loved her so much and the father agreed, the goldsmith was called, golden moon was ordered. But destiny played a different game, her sorrow started, she lost her father Tanayabanta by the time the moon was half ready, by the time the moon is full ready she lost her mother Shakuntala, the brothers, sister-in-laws took care of little Taopoi. Time passed on, the brothers left for the other countries on sea voyage, their ships sailed, their wives prayed the goddesses, bid them farewell and the most loved sister could not hold her tears.

That Brahmin widow came again, saw Taopoi, she was highly envious, wicked that lady, couldn't see Taopoi in happiness, told many imaginary stories to her sister-in-laws, filled their ears with ill advices, the sister-in-laws, were impressed by her, wanted to get rid of the girl. She was asked to go to the jungle with the goats for their grazing, to do all the house hold works, her condition was so pitiable. But the wicked sister-in-laws had no pity, they wanted to get rid of her, the tiger would prey on her, she would die, helpless. On a cyclonic day, the rain was pouring, wind thrusting open the closed doors, the biggest goat called Gharamani didn't return, the eldest sister-in-law was furious at Taopoi, ordered her to go the forest to collect the goat, lest she wouldn't get space in the house. Taopoi, didn't have any option but to go to the forest, she prayed mother Mangala, the most revered goddesses the girls prayed always, she heard the Huluhuli, a devotional sound made by the women and girls of Odisha, of the other girls, the girls of that area was praying to mother goddesses. She reached the place of worship, prayed to mother Mangala for safe return of the goat, return of her brothers, she had nothing to offer to the goddess, the other girls came with a lot of worship material, she only offered husk and broken rice particle which she could collect from outside. The goat returned, she had belief on the goddess. She continued praying the goddess on each Sunday of the Bhadrava (August-September) month, the worship term come on each Bhadrava Sunday.

The torture of the sister-in-laws increased, so also her belief on the goddess, they were not giving her proper food, that day the food was miserable, she couldn't tolerate, she went to the forest, looked at the riverside, her brothers had left for trade in their ships, and she cried and cried. People had placed Akashdipa, people of Odisha still used to put lighted lamps on a high pillar (Akash Dipa) near Siva temple or in front of a tulasi tree as a symbol of light house for easy navigation in the month of Kartika when the trade winds are favorable, she was looking at the lamp at far away distance in the outskirts of the village. That day the brothers had returned, they had anchored their ships at another anchor point. Taopoi didn't see that, the brothers listened the cry of a girl, they were curious, the youngest brother came in searching, found their sister in distress, they were dumbfounded, the wicked wives need a lesson, they decided. They returned the next day, pretend not to know about Taopoi, enquired about their sister, the sister-in-laws tried to fox, they were asked to worship the goddess Mangala seated at the prow of the ship, they agreed. Taopoi was waiting there, she cut the nose of the all wicked sister-in-laws, except the last one, the one was kind to her. Later the wicked ladies got back their noses at the mercy of the lord Shiva seated in this forest and the families were reunited, their hearts changed, and Taopoi turned to be a demigoddess, she went to the heaven; and thus started the tradition of the worshipping of Goddess Mangala, the Khudurukuni festival in the Odia society.

Travel to Satabhaya

I was highly inquisitive, on another winter day, in search of the village of Taopoi I travelled to Satabhaya, the village established by her brothers, it was in fact cluster of seven villages namely 1-Kahnupur, 2-Balarampur, 3-Hariharapur, 4-Laxminararayanapur, 5-Gobindapur, 6-Gopalpur and 7-Banabiharipur, all on the sea front, on the back the impregnable black forests of Bhitarkanika. The colours of Bhitarkanika, the mystery of Bhitarkanika can't be completed without the description of the village, the deity of the place, the fuming sea, of course the shade of the visiting birds, the rural landscape, the belief, the tradition. The journey now was different, the boat covered a little distance, then after a small journey on a motorcycle we came across small creek, not wide creeks as described earlier, soft mud banks on both sides of the water channel, the mangrove foliage covered much of the mud banks as usual narrowing the channel. On the side of the road, some people were waiting for the country boat to cross the channel, the big trees were raising their heads on their back, many fruits on the sisumar trees, some as big as Bel fruit; small channels on mud floors criss crossed the area like a net. On the water channel inside the creek, few sticks were strongly put on the mud floor; a nylon line was drawn across the water channel from the other side of the channel to our side connecting the poles on both sides. Some people were sitting on the boat, the boat was relatively flat, wide and low at the centre, not that narrow at the front, some people were standing with their cycles; some bags filled with varieties items were loaded at the centre. The boatman slowly pulled the fixed nylon rope, the pull pushed the boat forward and it slowly moved towards the centre of the channel, the boatman was holding the line on one hand and was pulling it constantly, he covered the entire length; the people disembarked, and we embarked on the boat. The boat moved to the other side and we arrived on a land which joins the sea front.

I looked at the channel at our back, thick green foliage were protruding into the grey water line, the muddy water was not reveling the lives within. Suddenly a bird dived as a flash into the water, the dive was almost a straight fall from the top, the long beak was pointed towards the water, legs pulled back into the feathers, a big splash occurred on the water body, the bird came out next second from the water face and flew towards a tree. The bird sat on the branch of a tree. I could now see the bird more clearly, earlier during its flight I couldn't see it properly, it was a white breasted Kingfisher, a small bird, less a feet long from the end of its beak to the longest feather at its back, and what a beautiful bird it was, the back and lower wings and tail are brilliant turquoise-blue, the head, flanks and lower belly was deep chocolate brown, the black eyes were scanning the water front continuously, the lower neck and upper chest was covered with white feathers, the bill was thick and pointed, specially designed to catch the fish and to sallow it.

It again flew over the water body, remained stationary in the air over the water body for sometime, its wings moved rapidly to support the weight, the body was still, the beak was lowered, it was not moving forward, the bird was looking for its prey. Suddenly it dived into the water body around twenty feet below and came out with a small white fish on its bill, it flew towards a tree, sat on the branch, thrashed the fish on the branch, then swallowed the fish, then it made a chuckling chake-ake-ake-ake-ake sound and flew away.

We moved ahead, the forest thinned, suddenly long vacant wet lands with grasses appeared, on both sides of the road long patches of wetlands, the left side ends at the tree line and the right side ends at the sea. I looked at the smaller water body of few acres on my right, the water appeared to be shallow, reeds emerged in between, other water plants covered some areas. On the clear water two Brahminy ducks were floating, I was totally surprised to see these migratory ducks there, in my wildest thoughts I never imagined a migratory bird in the thick forests of Bhitarkanika or nearby. We stopped for a while, two birds were floating on the still water elegantly, they were moving away from us; they appeared like floating Boita (ship) of ancient Kalinga, floating slowly, the head and the tail were raised. I looked at the bird, how elegant it was, a little bigger bird, the body was orange brown, the head was paler, and the wings were white with black flight feathers, the bill was black, also the tail, one of them was having a black collar on lower neck. I heard about this bird earlier, it was a sacred bird for the Buddhists, in Sanskrit, it is known as the Chakravaka or chakra (also Chakwa (male), Chakwi (female)), considered as "couples in harmony". From the ancient times the Chakravāka birds are considered as the examples of conjugal love and fidelity, a married couple should remain "attached to each other like Chakravāka birds". It is believed that the Chakravāka couples separate in each night and mourn; during the night the male and female birds call out to each other from opposite banks of the stream, and reunite during the day.

On the other side of the water mass, near to the road, few pond herons and large egrets were standing on water, viewing large egrets are getting uncommon, this tail magnificent bird was standing at knee deep water, and the long pointed yellow beak was pointed downward, the long narrow neck was elongated, it was waiting for the final strike, the concentration of the bird was remarkable, I recounted the stanza that inspired me during my younger days.

"Bathe like a crow, concentrate like a crane, sleep like a dog, eat a little, and leave the house; these are the five qualities of a student."

The bird was looking keenly at the water surface, the white reflection on the water was appearing like reflection on the mirror, the water was so calm, and the bird was so calm. Two white ibis came nearer, a little ripple appeared on the waterbed, the large egret was standing in deeper water and the white ibises were standing near to the edge of the pond where reeds were existing, their long curved black bills were continuously dipping into the low water. Inside, almost in the middle of the water body, on a floating branch of a tree a cormorant was sitting; the sitting was so elegant, its body structure was narrow, long and thin. On this side, a pond heron was standing still on the edge of the water; it too was scanning the water line. On the other side of the water body, far away from the road many Brahminy ducks were standing on the grass land adjacent to the water mass, on a line, their reflections on the water in fact was increasing their size. Another

five hundred meter away, the blue sea was roaring, and here the water body was full with visible lives, varieties of birds were feeding; water supports so much of colour.

We moved forward, the water bodies continued on both sides of the elevated road, suddenly I stopped, on our left side, towards the forest side, there was a huge congregation of the migratory water birds, I never saw such large congregation outside the Chilika lake, all water bodies which were little away from the human eyes support a large folk of migratory water birds. Hundreds of birds gathered on the raised areas in this marshy land, the ducks, storks, ibises, spoonbills, snipes, teals, pin tails, gooses, shoveller, cormorants, and so many, I couldn't count, were flocking. Many birds were sitting on the raised area in the marshy land, those appeared like ducks, they were preening their feathers. A towering painted stork was standing a little away, surrounded by Brahminy ducks, this huge, colourful and magnificent bird was standing alone in the colony; few white large egrets were standing at faraway places. I looked at the birds, some were swimming in open waters, some between the reeds almost in camouflaged condition, some were searching for the food in marshy areas, some were diving into the water, some were dibbling; watching those birds was a remarkable pleasure, it was so enchanting, the congregations of the birds changed the landscape; the colour tinge, the grasses on the water body was green in colour, the water mass collected the blue colour of the sky, the water birds appeared like a wide band after the water mass in grey-white and chocolate in colour, after that the grasslands in grey with greenish tinge. Subsequently again long water mass continued, long grass land continued then after towards the forest; the water birds gathered at a secured place between the water bodies which give them protection against land predators.

We moved ahead, the water mass continued, suddenly I stopped, a group of cormorants were swimming in the water, I have seen cormorants before, but they were mostly individual or two, mostly waiting for the prey on the banks, but I was surprised, here dozens of cormorants were swimming in water, between the grasses, such big gathering of cormorants were not seen by me, it was something like gathering of crows or common mynahs in the evening on the cultivation fields, the cormorants being water birds were swimming in a group. I looked at the congregation, their bodies were almost dipped into the water except a little back portion, the necks were raised like a raised snake, the heads appeared like the hoods of cobras, the pointed beaks appeared like the forked tongues of the black snakes; the birds during swimming appeared like a group of snakes raising their heads on the waterline.

Suddenly a group of black winged stilt birds raised from the land, and flew over the blue water body, their flight was so elegant, they appeared like wide thin Chinese kites, the black narrow wings were so aerodynamic, the white head was protruded forward, the long pinkish legs were joined and stretched away, they were maneuvering so nicely over the waterbed, their glide was a treat to watch, in the nature so much of beauty, so much of skill is hidden inside; a man needs an eye to watch; the formation, the shapes they made during their flight was just beyond imagination.

The beauty of the water bodies, the life inside was amazing too, so many visitors with so many colours and shapes, their behaviours were so different. Like the water body on the way to Satabhaya, there are many other significant water bodies or bird congregation points in Bhitarkanika, which are mainly Nalita Patia, Rai Patia, Hansina, Bhandatuth Patia, Bhitarkanika patia, Mathdia, Barunei Agarnasi area, etc.

I was totally surprised to see so many birds in the wetlands of Bhitarkanika; I recollected the figures of waterfowl census in 3 major wetlands of Odisha.

Year	Details	Chilika Lagoon	Bhitarkanika Sanctuary	Hirakud reservoir
2005	No. of Water fowl/ water birds (in lakhs)	9.58	0.40	0.57
	No. of Migratory species	97	48	16
2006	No. of Water fowl/ water birds (in lakhs)	6.79	1.15	0.50
	No. of Migratory species	102	101	26
2007	No. of Water fowl/ water birds (in lakhs)	8.39	1.16	0.50
	No. of Migratory species	107	101	26
2008	No. of Water fowl/ water birds (in lakhs)	8.92	1.25	0.23
	No. of Migratory species	111	96	25

The figures were revealing a new world in Bhitarkanika, this land is known as the land of impregnable mangrove forests, territory of tall residential birds at Bagagahan (heronry), giant crocodiles throng the mud flats and large snakes are found all over; but now the wetlands in this area are the winter migration site for so many species of water birds, almost the same number of species

visit when compared to Chilika lake which is the biggest wintering site of migratory birds.

We moved ahead, a cactus forest came, the Pricklypearcrop cactus called as Nagapheni in local language, grew luxuriantly on both sides of the road and these cactus drew my attention immediately, not for their luxuriant growth alone, rather for the shades they created. I looked at the cactus with sun low at my back, a simple plant, the stem has evolved to become photosynthetic and succulent, while the leaves have evolved into spines, from the bud another growth continues, and the tree grows in size, long yellow coloured thorns appear throughout the body, mostly towards the margins. The colour, shape of the cactus forest looked unattractive with sun at my back, we crossed the patch, then I looked back, the cactus patch looked different, mystic, the land looked different with sun low down at my front. Each cactus stem was now glowing, the yellow thorns on the margin were now glowing with sun at the back, a yellow hollow was created on each cactus stem which now turned dark. The rounded shape of the stem now appeared like head of the humans, the shades of light created an imaginary depth of field. It appeared like hundreds of girls with flowers on their head waiting for our arrival, they gathered on both sides of the road, were elbowing each other for space, to come to the road, but kept a safe distance, a mystic setting in the dark forests of Bhitarkanika, the angle of sun could bring so much of change in the settings.

Our road journey ended, we arrived on the sea front, the roaring sea was falling on the white sand with great force, on the side the Panchubarahi temple was standing, the village had vanished, the sea had swallowed the village, few coconut trees, few pandanus trees, few huts on a mound were the left over, people could not face the angry sea, they retreated, now settled away. The place of deity of the land, the Pancubarahi temple, the seat of power of the people, was the lone structure left. It was a small temple, the Orissan style of temple, five goddesses adorn the seat, the priest was a female – a tribal from Sabar community, it was a surprise setting too; in Orissan temples women do not work as priests, but in Panchubarhi temple of Satabhya a tribal woman was working as a priest, the goddess gave a doctrine; male will not touch the Goddess, once a Brahmin priest was performing in this temple, but lust overpowered his mind seeing the beauty of the Goddess; so Goddess cursed him and he turned to a stone. In the village of Taopoi, there is no Mangala worship which is prevalent in coastal Odisha; the Panchubarhi goddesses worship Mother Mangala on the behalf of the people of the area.

I looked around, towards my right was a big sand dune was continuing, on the front the sea was roaring, few coconut trees surrounded the dune. The sand dunes and sand deposits continued towards my left, and the old Satabhaya village now lost the place in the sea, shifted beyond the sand dunes. After a walk through the casuarinas and acacia plantations we reached the village, an insignificant one, the wealth of the past got vanished with time, the strength of the Sadhabas eroded, they were no more able to bring the past glory, retreated to cultivation and fishing. Two black jungle crows – a type of crow bigger and heavier than common crow and very dark in colour, were gathering food on the village road, and on both sides of the road the rice straw thatched mud houses existed. Those houses were low, one entrance in the front and another at the back, and a small courtyard remained between the doors, the mud walls and small posts were supported the roofs. On the outer mud wall beautiful drawings in white, mostly lotus flowers in symmetrical form, were drawn. I looked at a house, Chita were drawn over yellowish grey wall, so many lotus and other beautiful flowers were made on the wall. The ladies had cleaned the wall nicely and made their homes the abodes of flower and prosperity, the white line cluster resembling the paddy cluster shows the importance of the crop in the life, Mother Lakshmi (Goddess of wealth) comes into the house. I looked keenly at the Chita, a pitcher was drawn over which mango leaves were drawn, just over which the green coconut is drawn; a blooming lotus was drawn above that. The banana leaves, a temple, so many flowers, flowering creepers were drawn, showing the importance of those items in the lives of the common people. Few women in printed cotton sarees were sitting on the soil, some children were running on the road, the older people were playing cards, the cattle were returning, the rustic life was soothing and relaxing.

We came out of the village, a big open land with cultivation fields ran forward, many fields were water logged due to stagnation of water in low lying areas. The people were busy in harvesting their paddy crops, the paddy here had longer straw, enabling the crop to survive water logging condition, and the area was famous for Lilabati paddy – a variety of paddy famous for its taste and flavour, and of course the fishes in the paddy fields. People were returning with loads of paddy on their heads, on their shoulder, paddy was so prominent in the lives; I looked ahead, a non-conglomerated road went ahead, black drongo birds were sitting on sticks and dry branches near to the road, near to the fields where people were busy in harvesting, to catch flying insects. I looked ahead, the long green tree line was much closer, the dark forests of Bhitarkanika with mystery surrounding its colour was laying idle.

On Dangmal

After the journey to Satabhaya, I came to Dangmala, halted there in the guest house, a lovely one, amidst the green forest, decided to watch the morning in the rivers of the Bhitarkanika. As usual my friend can't sit without talking, he started.

“The place was called Dangamala, and the present name Dangmala came from that.” I didn’t know why he wanted to give me more and more surprises.

“Dangamala, means congregation of boats. The place once had a fleet of boats, pirate boats. There were many fights with the Marathas, the pirates looted the consignments of Nawab, even the ship of British East India Company was not spared. Dhamra port, one of the most active port of the earlier Kalinga, was situated the near the creeks of Bhitarkanika was the favourite hunting grounds of dreaded pirates of the creeks,” he said.

These words were so surprising, the Oriyas were famous for their merchant skills in the ancient times, also well-known for their bravery in the battle fields, the land witnessed one of the bloodiest battle in the history of India, brought the religion of peace to the mind of the conqueror. Many such words, many such sentences were so strange, immediately attracting my attention. Couple of hours ago I listened the stories of Taopoi, the most famous festival of the unmarried Odia girls, the Khudurukuni Osha, where the girls pray to the goddess for the prosperity, for the safe return of the brothers.

He then narrated the stories on the fights in the waters of Bhitarkanika.

There were fights, the creeks of Bhitarkanika turned to naval battle grounds many a times, the Marathas wanted to subjugate the kings of Kanika, who possessed inundated, unhealthy tract of the countryside. The Marathas were using wide and flat bottomed battle boats where as the King of Kanika was using the long, narrow boats with barricades, some with even having 100 paddles or oars. The Maratha fleet due to its design and heaviness were unsuitable to large streams or wavy sea front; the local boats were tailor-made) for the region. When the fleet met, the Odia boats used to move quickly, the local troops used fire from their matchlocks at the Maratha troops who mostly remain unprepared for the fight in the water in the creeks and the king mostly came out victorious. It was presumed, unless Kanika was subjugated, Kataka, the capital of Odisha can’t be brought to the knees.

The ships of the Nawab of Kataka were looted many a times by the pirates of Bhitarknika. The Nawab considered it being the handiwork of the King of Rajkanika. Once, the consignment of the British East India Company was looted by those pirates. I heard a lot about the pirates of the Carrabean Islands, also on the pirates of the different seas, the world is full with the stories of these pirates. The Somalian pirates are the recent infamous ones. In India there were not many native pirates, probably except for Kanhoji Angria (or Conajee Angria), I read it somewhere, who was a Maratha, reigned the western sea during 17th and 18th century, others were unknown. His first base was located at the Maratha fort of Vijayadurg ('Victory Fort') (formerly Gheriah), located about 425km away from Mumbai. He even established a base in the Andaman Islands, so is credited with attaching those islands to India. Around 1710 AD, he used to launch his missions from his base to attack coastal shipping, especially that of the English East India Co. and other European interests. Angria even blockaded the port of Mumbai, a ransom of 8,750 pounds was extracted from the British East India Company.

But that was a glaring brave story of the western coast, and here in the dark forests of Bhitarkanika, the stories of the Odia pirates remained buried beneath the thick foliage of the mangroves, only to be depicted by those glow worms on that dark platform.

Journey in Khola Creek & description of mangroves

Morning came, the horizon was clearing slowly, and we, as decided earlier, came to the Dangmala jetty with the first sound of the bird. The scene was superb, the muddy water was calm like pond water, the mist covered the mangrove forest on the other side of the river and extended to half of the river, appeared as if the river ended in the mist, the expanse, to me appeared as if immense, actually it was not that, but the stories of yesterday added hallucination in the mind. I, only could think of the sea, the creeks, wide, spacious, the boats of the Odia pirates moving with great speed, the sailors peddled the ores with full throttle. The sea merchants were in disarray, their boats were damaged, their hopes shattered, and the pirates were screaming in the morning, such was the hallucination, as if I was witnessing a battle in the creeks.

On our side, the horizon was clearing from our back, the tree tops were getting cleared from the white mist, the water drops were falling on the ground, moistening the ground further, the peacocks come early to the river bank, and behind the bushes the spotted deers were grazing the grasses. It was so marvelous.

We came to the mechanised country boat, approximately 20 to 25 feet long, 6-7 feet wide, a comfortable boat with sufficient sitting places. The boat started, and we greeted each other, the morning tea was served hot in the boat, the boat moved, ripples were created, the silence of the river was broken, the animals looked at us and we moved to the vanishing mist of the river. There were so many trees on the sides, the mangrove forest was getting clearer, it was a dense forest, big branches were bending down, leaves were almost touching the waters.

My friend was enthusiastic as ever, he showed me the trees and described their characteristics, they were so many, all beautiful, green, fresh, shining in the morning sun. The mangrove forests of Bhitarkanika is full with Sundari, Bani,

Keruan, Rai, Sisumar, Paniamba, Masitha trees. We were enjoying the beauty of the nature when his voice broke the silence, he had a habit of making interesting sentences.

"These forests are different, the trees are different, its characteristics are different. If I say that its root breathe, not inside soil, but above the soil, then will you believe? He created a learning atmosphere, all other persons were eager to know about the characteristics of the forest, after all we were moving in a strange land, and then he distributed a write up made by him.

Why the roots surface over the soil after all, the book has the answer. The mangrove trees grow in inter tidal zone, in unstable salty soil, mud there is as sticky as wet clay. Since the area is regularly flooded by tidal waters, the soil does not have much oxygen, so the trees breathe through pneumatophores which are pencil roots or knee roots or prop roots.

The description was strange to me, so many types of roots, how they really look like and what was their actual use? Whether they found throughout? The questions puzzled me.

The pencil roots appear like pencil, emerge from the mud; and the knee roots appear more like a bent knee because of its shape, and some trees have prop roots in which through tiny pores the tree breathes. These are simple definitions; the roots resemble the actual literary meaning contrary to the botanical terms which are difficult to comprehend. Mangrove forests generally have shallow and wide spreading roots, but not continuous tap roots, they don't have deep roots, the root system hardly go beyond one meter beneath the soil surface due to poor aeration. I was reading that book, without knowing the behaviour of the mangroves, one may not enjoy the beauty, after all one needs the eyes to see, understand the beauty of the nature, its diversities.

Suddenly he broke the silence, except for the engine sound of the boat, no other sound was there, and started saying, "If I say I have brought you to the colony of the islanders, do you believe." I couldn't understand his question, the link between the island and the mangrove was not understandable to me. I was perplexed; simply I didn't have the answer.

"Can't you see the tribal huts here on the mud flats?" he asked me, smile was on his lips.

Again the matter was perplexing, baffling to me, I was confused.

He continued saying, "You have seen the huts on the coasts, the base is raised, the house is standing on the bamboo poles, the tribal huts just at costs of pacific and Bay of Bengal are mostly on the raised platform. The base is constructed by putting bamboo into the soil, each bamboo is connected to the base, the hut gets strength from such design. During the tidal waves, the waves wash the coastline, the inhabitants live comfortably on the raised platforms," he was narrating.

But the correlation between those hut structures and the mangrove was still not understandable. Then he started explaining further, his hand was pointed towards the nearby mangrove tree. I looked at the tree keenly; its root system was in the focus of my eye.

"The roots of this tree are as thick as bamboo pole, each root is embedded deep into the mud, the main tree trunk is well over the waterline. Don't you see the resemblance between the mangrove root design and tribal hut structure on the coastline of Pacific. Many tribe took the clue, and created their dwelling houses, of course the house design here is different, the reason the people here were more civilized, adopted higher class of living."

I looked at the root system of the mangrove tree keenly. Many, many strong roots, long and tapering, uneven shaped, each embedded into the soft mud, the root system spread over couple of square meter of area and over that support system a spreading mangrove tree of around 20-25 feet balances. The water came, the base system was covered with water, the root didn't obstruct the water flow. The speed of water reduced, and it was the way how these beautiful trees modulates high waves along the coastline.

"Mangrove gave the idea to man to reach this height, your present progress owe a lot to the mangrove structure," he was making strange comments, always gap remained between his views and his expression, he had the habit of making curious sentences. We didn't have the answer, he also didn't expect the answer from us, he knew the limitation of our knowledge.

"Oil is the backbone of the growth of the mankind, you can very well see the design of the off shore oil rigs, the long poles are embedded to the deep sea, like the root system of the mangroves." He was weaving the words, and I understood the meaning – man has learnt from the mangrove structure, the design to work on marshy areas, on seas, using a support system like that of a mangrove tree.

Our boat had moved ahead, we were close to a mud flat, I looked at the forest, so many pencils like roots emerging from the mud flat, the tidal water had receded, the pencil roots were clearly seen. Innumerable roots, emerging from the slate coloured bed, more appeared like the seedling in the first stage of the life. The buds are yet to come, the tree has emerged from the seed, and after all they supply the oxygen to the trees.

I looked keenly at the surrounding, and the pencil roots. The mud surface was shining, the water had retreated by a few meters, the light slate coloured muddy was now more calm, the mud base was more clearly visible. The pencil roots appear like narrow, tapering upward structures, sharpened pencils dug to the mud, the height of these roots were not much, from the top of the mud

surface those roots might be around six inches to one foot tall. The main tree was standing at the centre, the root system had spread uniformly in all directions, however towards the deep water side, the roots were taller, much closer to each other. I zoomed my binocular to those roots, to me those roots near to the water appeared like towering structures on in a modern landscape, the line drawings on a moving landscape.

Many questions were appearing in my mind, on this unique forest, on the animals. I opened the book, some species have negatively geotropic root systems – the pneumatophores, the roots grow against gravity, and these pneumatophores develop root system that reaches the mineral rich surface layer of the clay. Some pneumatophores, for species like Sonneratia apetala, may rise upto few feet, for Avicennia species as they looked like pencils.

In Rhizophora, the roots develop from different parts of the stem, are called as stilt roots, to provide better anchorage to the tree. The lateral roots from the plant later on further divided into more arches after they come in contact with soil. These roots give strong support to the tree, as they come up in the strong tidal areas, near to the sea.

The aerial prop roots, another form of root, in some species of Rhizophora, are aerial roots, that are soft, tender, flexible with uniform thickness, descend from the branches, hung vertically down, and they grow till they reach the soil level.

In some species, like Bruguiera and Ceriops , the lateral roots bend at a height from the soil level, make a knee like curving with thickened bends and again return to the soil. In some trees like Bruguiera and Ceriops species, the buttresses are formed.

He was talking about the mangrove species, the characteristics – many were not understood by me, till now I am not confident of the mangrove forest, which were the species and how they all really looked like.

He drew small land form structure on the piece of paper, the last part touches the sea coast, little up there, then a constant mild slope land which goes further away from the sip, then finally reaches almost a flat land much away from sea. At the sea front, rather at the water front, the Rhizophora, also called Black mangrove species are established, these trees have prop root, the root system in which the roots balance the tree. This root system has been explained earlier, the idea of raised houses on platforms on the costs was probably derived from this system. Little away from the water front, the Avicennia species, also known as white Mangrove, with pencil roots gets established. The Bruguiera species, the orange mangrove, have the knee roots, establish themselves. The Nipa Palm, or Dhani palm come after them. Closer to the land not regularly disturbed by the tidal action daily the Acrostichium species or Mangrove ferns appear.

We know the root system, when I was last in schools, it goes down, provide nutrients to the tree, and gathers water. These trees are after all different; their characteristics are so different from the other trees.

I looked further, the establishment of forest in this eco system was a miracle, may be an aberration to me, my knowledge was so limited. Strangely, the seed always does not germinate on the ground, rather in some mangrove the seeds germinate in the mother tree itself, the reason being the soil is saline, and often the soil is washed in the tidal waves. So here, the germination takes place inside the fruit while these are still attached to the mother plant, fall off as soon as some root system develop, on the mud bed. The seed penetrate the soft soil and gets itself established, or floats in the water and anchor at suitable place.

I was reading my book, was looking at the forest in between, and enjoying the beauty, creating imagination, linking it to the landscape.

"Don't you see the leaves are so fleshy, the mangrove leaves are fleshier than the leaves of most of the trees?" suddenly he asked me, he in fact wanted me to get more involved to the topic.

I plucked a leaf of the nearby tree, a branch of which was touching the water and looked at it. It was fleshy, spongy too, strange leaves.

"The mangrove leaves store also extra salts, and becomes fleshy, salt gland on the leaves ensures that the extra salt exists, the root filters the salt also. The leaves of trees in mangrove forests are different from leaves of trees in other forests, the leaves here are thick, sunken with water storage tissues," he replied.

"Do you know they are the best protection against the tidal waves, cyclones, say even the super cyclones," he told, but I still don't understand why he changes the topic so suddenly.

The memory of the super cyclone hitting the Odisha coast was still fresh in my mind. I knew the tidal waves, wind crossing more than 250 kms hit the Odisha coast during 1999 and it was deadliest Indian storm since 1971. In that cyclone a tropical depression was formed over the Malay Peninsula on October 25 which moved northwest and changed to a tropical storm on October 26 which was strengthened further into a cyclone on the 27th on October 28th , it turned to a severe cyclone with a peak wind speed of 260 km/hand hit Indian coast the next day at a speed 250 km/h, sea waves as high as 26 feet struck the Odisha coast, traveling up to 20 km inland. Crops were destroyed over 17,110

km^2 of area, and an additional 90 million trees were either uprooted or broken. approximately 275,000 homes were destroyed leaving 1.67 million people homeless, another 19.5 million people were affected by the super cyclone to some degree.

Strangely the damage in the Bhitarkanika was not that phenomenal, owe it to the magnificence of the mangrove forests of Bhitarkanika. Now the message goes to the common man, here is the saviour, preserve it.

I remembered the news, the study carried out by researchers at the University of Delhi and Duke University analyzed deaths in 409 villages rural Kendrapada District of of Odisha. They found definite inverse relationship between the number of deaths per village and the width & thickness of the mangroves existed between those villages and the coastline, the villages with wider mangroves suffered considerably lesser number of deaths than ones with slender strip or no mangroves which proves that the mangroves reduced the death toll substantially.

In 1944, mangroves covered nearly 31,000 hectares of land in Kendrapada District and the average village had 5.1 kilometers of mangroves between it and the coast. Since then, nearly half the area has been cleared, mostly for rice production. Today, the average width of mangroves between the villages and the coast has shrunk to 1.2 kilometers. The mangroves act like giant shallow bowls, water flowing to the mangrove forest loses speed and spreads out. The forest arrests silt, the fine mud through its wide spread root system and trees so close to each other which works more as a trap. Apart from that this forest is the natural nursery of fishes, crabs, prawns as the water gives best protection available in a tidal system.

I was reading, also interacting with my friend, Bhitarkanika is one of the largest mangrove wetland eco system in the Indian subcontinent, its floral diversity is next only to Papua New Guinea. The Bhitarkanika has the distinction; it is an important Ramsar site, the sites of threatened wetlands. The forest locally called as Hentalabana, or the Hental forest, with Hental meaning the Phoenix paludosa trees, which are in plenty in the forest. This forest also known as Bani forest, named after Avicennia species or Sundari forest after the Heritiera species. The mangrove forests here are a two storey system, the top storey and the middle storey; and the ground storey is poor in species diversity. Importantly Nyapa palm which abundantly found in Sundarbans is absent here, and the Dhala Sunderi, the Heriteria littoralis is on the contrast absent in Sundarbans, but found in the Bhitarkanika. Some species of Sundari are not even found in the Sundarbans, are found here. Biodiversity wise this area is much richer than the Sundarbans. As per the study, 63 varieties of mangrove species and its associates are found in Bhitarkanika out of world total of identified 72 species of mangroves and its associates, thus Bhitarkanika is one of the richest mangrove heritage site of the world.

"I am giving a beautiful definition for you, if I say the mangrove builds land for you; you will definitely not believe me. See we people encroach land, they encroach sea, make colonies, and make new land for you, virgin, fertile and precious too." He commented again. Mangrove forest was so important, but his comments were so interesting, my attention was attracted once again.

He showed me the paragraph, the drawings of the mangrove trees, hanging over the tidal waves, its intention to move towards the waters, the land portion is highly congested. Most surprisingly, mangrove forest advances towards the sea, thus creating more land. It is the true land builder, they stabilizes the newly formed mud and the silt deposits in the river mouth.

Again he told, "You are moving in one of the best natural nurseries of the world, the mangrove ecosystem of the Bhitarkanika is among the richest eco system. The mangrove food chain, you will surprise to know that every part of the tree contributes to it." He commented and as usual he showed me the chapter.

Mangrove litters are the beginning of an immensely important detritus food chain, the chain initially involving dead and decaying mangrove matter, the principal energy source in the mangrove eco system. The leaves are in different decaying stages which formed food matter for many phyto planktons and zoo planktons which in turn provide nutrition higher forms of life like crabs, fishes, amphibians, etc.

He showed me a photograph of a mangrove tree; on each part different creatures have their distinctly separate niche. The tree, as per Hindu belief, each part is the living place numerous gods of Hindu mythology, likewise the mangrove tree, each part of it is the living place of numerous live creatures. The oysters, the animal with hinged double shells remain attached to the root and depend on the sea water to bring oxygen and food particles. The upper root is inhabited by periwinkle, a type of snail remain attached to the mangrove roots and feed on the algae. The mangrove floor is the play field of varieties of creatures like the mud skippers, the strange fish that can breathe in air, hops about on the mud and have strange eyes which are on the top of the head and can rotate in all directions. The prawns have ten legs and have hard outer cover for protection, and also strangely its body has the capacity to re-grow broken the parts like legs. The eel, the fish with long snake like body, breeds in the sea and its young grow up in the fresh water when adult, remains on the mangrove floor. The mud crab, the fiddler crab also remain there. Amphibians like frog are found in good numbers in this forest, reptiles

like snakes, saltwater crocodiles, water monitor found this forest as a very good habitat. On the branches varieties of birds create their nests.

I started reading about the beautiful forests of Bhitarkanika while we were moving in the waters of the creeks.

Harakancha, the herb, the local name of Acanthus species occur in pure formations in many degraded areas, can be seen near Barunei mouth in the upstream of river Baitarani, each regarded as a degraded mangrove habitat.

The fern species of Kharkhari, Achrostichum aureum are most favoured by the salt water crocodiles, they collect the leaves of this fern and other mangrove leaves and twigs for their nest building. They occur in areas where the mangrove system is highly degraded. The Banarua tree, Aegilitas species occur slightly away from the sea, but in the high saline areas, frequently forming pure patches and found around Barunei-Gahirmatha forest areas.

The Ooanra trees, the Aglaia species, grow well on soft muddy banks of rivers and creeks, towards the less saline area, towards the landward side and is most prominent in Khola creek.

The Avicennia trees, called Bani in local language, are forming thick pockets; grow along the banks of Bhitarkanika rivers and inside the creeks. The Bani trees is among initial colonizer species in the newly formed muddy islands in the sea front.

The Lata Sundari trees, Brownloiia species form thick patches on the soft muddy banks of tidal rivers and creeks, prominent generally in smaller creeks and areas away from the sea where the salinity level is less, mostly occurring Khola, Gokhani creeks.

The Guan species, Excoecaria community formations found in the borders of the mangroves and occur prominently in Bagagahan.

The Sundari trees like Bada Sundari, Kanika Sundari, Dhala Sundari, all from the heritiera community found in the less saline areas, where the soil is more stabilised and are prominent in the Bagagahana areas.

The Nalia grass, Myryostachya species, an important grass is found in pure patches or with Dhani grasses in the banks of the river.

The Pandara species called Lunikia in the local language form dense patches along the Gahirmatha coast also in the Kola creek.

The Phoenix species, the Hental trees, are in a dreaded condition found in Chinchiri mouth and form pure patches.

The Rhizophora species, called Rai trees are dominant trees in the tidal affected areas. The Rai and the Bani trees formg dominant patches towards the sea. during high tide the plants remain submerged and appears like trees floating in the water.

The Keruan, the Sonneratia species are best developed along the soft muddy banks of Bhitarkanika river. is a large tree. seen in the forefront of the rivers and creek banks. These trees can grow in both low and high saline areas.

The story of the Kanika King –

"You know about the pirates of Odisha a little. we discussed earlier?" suddenly he questioned.

I nodded my head, but the topic was insignificant, the Oriyas were not known for their piracy, if they were there, the bravery of the pirates of the black land never spread beyond the dark lines of the forests of the land. My friend was adept in studying the mind, the continuous discussions about the trees were boring, to refresh the mind he diverted from the description of the trees.

"Once the pirates ruled the waters of Bhitarkanika, the name Dangmala, known as the congregation of boats in Odia, was the hiding place of the pirates. Most surprisingly it was also associated with the establishment of the kingdom of Kanika and creation of Rajkanika, its capital.

Narendrapur was the old name, the place was located between the meeting points of the rivers of Brahmni and Baitarinin. The sea merchants used to stay there, they ruled the vast tracts of present day Kanika, their ships sail through the Dhamra mouth, located on the sea. Narendra, the sea merchant also the ruler of Chhamuks, was returning from his sailing, his ships anchored near Ramchandi peeth, the seating place of Goddess Ramachandi, near present false point close to the present day Paradeep port. The sea turned rough, the cyclone visited the coast in the night, high winds swept past the coastline. The next day morning cyclone stopped, the merchant located a stray boat in the sea, they rescued the boat, found a beautiful girl, around 6-7 years old in sleeping condition on the laps of an old lady. On enquiry the old lady informed that the girl in fact was the princess of Kujang kingdom named Kanika, and she her ayah. The order of the queen of Kujanga, the stepmother of the girl, was to kill the girl, her own mother died during childbirth. The sea merchant adopted the girl, promised the ayah to take care of the girl, would rear girl as a princess. The lady left for Kujang, she didn't wait for the sleep of the girl to break, the beautiful girl now turned to the adopted daughter of the sea merchant. The ships sailed through the Maipura river, the little girl was brought to the palace of the sea merchant and the he celebrated the arrival of the princess, now his daughter, with riches he now got a beautiful child, he had no child.

Time passed, Kanika grew older, her beauty and courage was the talk of the kingdom of the sea merchant, she had entered into her youth. The riches of

the sea merchant grew; he believed it to be luck of his lovely daughter. On Panasankranti, a festival in which the Oriyas make non alcoholic drink, offer to the same to God, to the travelers and to the near and dears. Kaniaka on that day was offering the Pana drink to the travelers, there he met an outsider, who actually was the youngest prince of Mayurbhanj, who had left his kingdom for fortune. He instantly fell in love with the beautiful Kaniaka, and to win the love of the charming lady he wished to join the sea merchant. He expressed his desire to the sea merchant, the merchant was happy to find a capable young man, he was getting older, and the business had expanded. The young man the youngest prince of Mayurbhanj performed the duty of the accountant, called Gumasta In the Odia language. Time passed on, the love between two hearts blossomed, Bhujabal wanted to marry Kanika, his position was the greatest hindrance, and simultaneously he wanted to capture the kingdom, a prince can't continue longer as Gumasta. He had a plan, he wanted to lure Narendra, the sea merchant into trap, dethrone him and take over his small kingdom. He created a story, the beetle nuts of Mayurbhanj were of better quality, the merchant should ask for the same from Baripada, it would be a part of merchandise and the same would bring more fortune to the trader. The merchant agreed, Bhujabal Bhanja send coded message to his brother – the king of Mayurbjanj, requested him to send the Sabar (tribal) soldiers to the land along with the beetle nut. The Sabar soldiers came, remained in hiding, were ready to attack the merchants at the time of his morning stroll, at the direction of Bhujabala Bhanj. The plan materialised, Narendra was seized by those fugitive soldiers, Bhujabal Bhanja expressed his desire to marry Kanika, and to get the throne. Narendra agreed with happiness, he had made up his mind for their marriage much earlier, only now the turn of the events was ugly. He handed over his daughter to the young man, the attacker too; his kingdom also went to them and then he went to the forest for Banaprastha (the stage of life when man exist to the forest for tapasya).

That was the first days, Kanika kingdom was christened as Kanikaraj, was the kingdom of Kanika in Odia. So Bhujabala Bhanj was not happy, an independent minded person like him felt himself isolated, the kingdom belongs to his wife, and he was a puppet king. One day he left the palace without telling the queen along with his Sabar soldiers, and became a pirate. He attacked many other small kingdoms of the merchants and looted their wealth and tortured their subjects; the muddy waters of Bhitarkanika and nearby areas turned to be his hunting place and used to take shelter in dangerous creeks of the dark forests. The merchant chieftains were highly disturbed at the rise of a pirate in their sea route, wanted to give the pirates a befitting lesson; so they requested the queen Kanika to lead as she only had the guns and cannons. The queen agreed, she didn't know that she was leading the fight against her own husband. Her fleet sailed into the muddy waters of Bhitarkanika, and moved in the creeks; the pirates were smarter, in a dark night they attacked the ship of the queen and before the cannons were fired from the ship and overpowered the sailors. Bhujabala went inside, his face was covered with black clothes, he was holding blood stained open sword on his hand, a sword fight resulted between the queen and the pirate king, and queen was defeated. Bhujabala turned to be the winner, he had defeated the true queen of the land, he reveled his identity. Bhujabal was the crowned as the new king, queen remained with him, now he was called the king, not husband of the queen; so started the kingdom of Kanika in the name of the king, called Rajkanika, it is now King's Kanika.

Journey through Khola Creek continues

Our boat had moved far, we were now moving inside Khola creek, a deep artificial water ways, a dug out channel created by king of Kanika for better navigation, connecting river Brahmani. The channel width was around 20 feet, was having a depth of around 30ft., almost there was no bank, the trees on both sides were covering whatever soil there, the branches were even touching the water, the channel width was further narrowed at many points. Many a times, the branches were even blocking the full channel, we used to lift the branches for facilitating the movement of the boat. He showed me Paniamba, a rare species of Bhitarkaniaka, the tree appeared like a mango tree, the flower was white but little different from mango inflorescence, and the fruit was shaped like a mango. The mashitha, sundari, kerua were the of the other prominent species, and all the trees had one characteristics common, the roots were protruding upwards, those were the respiratory roots for respiration of the tree in submerged condition. The lata sundari trees in water was having strange roots which appeared like thickened net. The sinduka, the kerua trees were towering over the shrubs and grasses, their leaves appeared like that of a jamun tree. A brown winged king fisher dived down from the branch of Sundari tree and caught a kantia fish, the fish was gasping for breath in its beak, then the bird moved over the nalia grass patch on the mud flat and sat on another Sundari tree. The pani kenduli and kauti grasses were covering the other mud flats of the mangrove forest, and beyond the flats, the taller evergreen mangrove forest was seen. On the other side of the bank the blue king fisher was eagerly looking at the water, the egrets were walking with measured steps, the heron was also waiting for its prey. The vultures were gathered on a tall tree and were scanning the whole area for food. The red fruits of the sisumar tree were hanging up to the water level and beyond that the keuti grasses had come up well on the adjacent mud flats. The Khola creek wass famous for its biodiversity, probably no other creek had so much of diversity, the place was most preferred by Baula kumbhira, the salt water crocodile, around 70 of them stayes there, some of them were as long as

18-20 ft. The crabs, mainly the madhua kankada were peeping from the mud holes, and from the tree branches the monkeys, mostly bander monkeys were looking at us with curiosity and were jumping from one branch to other branch, and the lower branches were touching the waters due to their activity when they jumped over it.

On cabs

I looked at the hand book, the crabs were attracting my attention, the mud crabs are large crabs with a smooth, broad carapace, most common form; the colour varies from very dark brown to mottled green. These crabs are typically nocturnal, spending the daytime in a burrow that can be up to 6.5 ft (2 m) deep. The flattened, paddle-like rear legs are be used for swimming or for rapidly burying itself in the sediment. This crabs favour a soft, muddy bottom, often below low tide level.

Mating occurs when the female mud crab is in the soft-bodied condition following the moulting. Female crabs incubate eggs for 2 to 4 weeks under their abdominal flap. The females can give birth to more than 10 lakhs of eggs, a huge number. The large claws of the mud crabs are used for crushing and cutting their prey. If they lose a claw, another one grows during the next moults. A mud crab can live up to 3 years. The juvenile mud crab eat planktonic animals, molluscs and crustaceans of various types and adults feed at night on a variety of molluscs having two hinged shells and gastropod molluscs including mussels, pipies, small crabs and polychaete worms, also they are attracted to dead fish.

The mangrove crabs are significant in many ways in a mangrove ecosystem, they keep much of the energy within the forest by burying and consuming leaf litter. Their feces may form the basis of a food chain contributing to mangrove secondary growth. The crab larvae are the major food source for juvenile fish inhabiting the area which in turn helps the fishery production.

They burrow the soil, these burrows alter the topography and sediment grain size of the mangrove, thus help aeration of the sediment, absence of aeration would cause significant increases in sulfides and ammonium concentrations, which in turn would affect the productivity of the mangrove forests. They are called a keystone species for mangroves; a keystone species is a species that is crucial or essential to the ecosystem's community structure.

I looked at the crabs on the mud flat; they were scanning the area with their protruding eyes from the safety of their holes located between the roots of the trees. Here mainly Nali crab, madhua crab, halua crab are found in the mangrove forest of Bhitarkanika. The crabs make holes on the mud flats, remain inside the hole, but fishing folk could reach them. People used to put a bent iron rod inside the crab hole, and the crab in anger catches the rod, the rod is then pulled outwards, the angry crab moves along with. Sometimes baited disc net traps are also used to catch these knotty creatures.

A kerua tree was leaning towards the water, my friend informed; the fruits of the kerua tree is a great delicacy of the jalanga fish, a non-scaled fish growing to a good size and a favourite food of the crocodiles, when the fruit ripens during rains, the jalanga fish waits for the fruit to fall on the water. Their competition to catch the fruit is intense. The jalang fishes even jumps from water, catches the falling fruit in air before it actually hits the water. This sour tested fruit is also liked by the monkeys; who apart from other fruits available in the forest also live on roots, soft branches and soft leaves during lean period.

I read the book, the dense forest is also the most preferred habitat of the bears, sambar, fishing cat, snakes, pythons, king cobras; the largest Indian lizard – the water monitor lizard is also found in good numbers. The creek is the most preferred nesting site of the salt water crocodiles, it nests on high ground using kharkhari and hentala leaves, away from the river waters, so that the high tide does not touch its eggs. The reason of picking those particular leaves is that these are better controller of heat and humidity, the temperature need to be maintained at a constant level. Once the crocodile lays its egg, it watches it from a distance till the eggs are hatched between 75-90 days. If the temperature rises then the eggs are not hatched, also for low temperature the eggs too do not hatch, so the crocodile egg hatching is a problem, thus hatching percentage is less too. There are no natural predators of the crocodiles; the eggs are occasionally predated upon by water monitor lizards, wild pigs and monkeys.

Moving in the main Creek

Till now we mostly moved inside the smaller creeks, the bigger main creek was not properly touched, the night journey except for expressing the glow worm dances and synchronising music of the waves, didn't reveal the true colour of Bhitarkanika. On another day I moved through the main creek, started from Dangmala to Gupti in the main creek, it looked so wide, the mangrove trees were touching the waterline in the high tide, the high water had almost entered into the forest. There was no movement in the water, no formation of small ripples even, a tranquility stage, the creek appeared to be the backwaters of a big lake, one gets this state of water in the backwaters of big reservoirs, the sun was on our left, the forest on that side looked darker, in the right the forests was illuminated in the morning sun, the forest was deep green, so many tinges of green. Around a kilometer length of the creek was visible, the waterline went straight, the trees were on both sides, on the right small mud flats were seen, on the far ahead the tree lines were seen again, the waterways takes turn at that point, the reflections of the treesin the tranquil water increased the size of the forests, made it mammoth.

We moved ahead in the creek, the main creek was a long one, around 300-400 meter wide, small mud banks were found regularly, sometimes with the protruding seedlings, sometimes the breathing roots prop from that bank.

My friend was silent for a long time, like me was enjoying the beauty of the creek, refreshing his knowledge. He looked at a crocodile and reminded me – the area is the resting grounds of the biggest crocodiles of the world, the bigger crocodile earlier used to be found in plenty, by conservative count there were more than 7 big crocodiles, all over 20 feet long. The maximum number of crocodiles, though smaller in size, generally were visible in Khola creek, Sahojara creek, Mahiasamada creek, the bigger crocodiles remain in the main river.

Some information on saltwater crocodiles

I recollected my knowledge on the salt water crocodiles. These crocodiles generally remain in freshwater swamps and rivers during the monsoon and move downstream to estuaries during the dry season, and they sometimes travel far out to the sea. Large males will establish and control large stretches of river, they may bellow for females may occur. The females are usually allowed into male territory, but the males risk severe injury if they challenge another for mating rights. The low-ranking crocodiles are forced into the more marginal river systems.

They can swim between 24 to 28 kilometer per hour in short bursts, but generally move at a speed between 3 to 5 kmph. The maximum land speed which was recorded is 17 kilometer per hour for a galloping crocodile in Australia.

The saltwater crocodile is known to attack any animal that enters into its territory, either in the water or on dry land, humans are not spared. The large adult saltwater crocodiles eat any animals within its range, like monkeys, wild boar, deers, birds, domestic cattle, pets, water buffalo, gaurs, and even sharks. The Juveniles eat smaller animals such as insects, amphibians, crustaceans, small reptiles and fish.

The crocodile is generally very lethargic, it normally moves leisurely in the water or relax in the sun most part of the day, and prefer to hunt at night. This crocodile is capable of very quick speed when launching an attack from the water; sometimes the speed for a short length is as fast as a running human.

It usually waits for its prey to come close to the water's edge before striking, and then it drags the animal back into the water. Interestingly enough, crocs on average seem to attack drinking animals just as they are prepared to leave. During attack the crocodile jumps out of the water onto land and onto its prey, grabs the prey by its powerful jaw, mostly the preys are killed by the immense jaw pressure, some animals are incidentally drowned. These jaws can bite with massive force; the force can be as high as 5,000 pounds per square inch which is the strongest bite recorded of any animal. The large great white shark bites with a force of 400 pounds per square inch, around 1000 pounds per square inch for hyena. The characteristic hunting technique of the crocodile is known as the "death roll", in which it grabs onto the prey and then rolls powerfully. This action throws besieged big animal off balance, thus making it easier for the crocodile to pull it into the water. This action is also used for tearing off the large dead animals.

During mating period the male and female will get together, female will show her obedience by raising her jaw and exposing her throat to the male. Then the male will mount on top of the female, both will submerge and mating will occur. The female then searches for a suitable nesting site on the shore and begins building a mound of twigs, grasses, etc. Then a pit is dug and there she lay around 60-80 numbers of eggs. After the egg lying, the nest is well covered up and the site is guarded for the entire incubation period of 3 months; at that time she attacks any intruder coming near to that area. In crocodile species, the sex of the young depends on the temperature; males are produced for temperature at around 31.6^{0}C in the nest and females are produced for little lower or higher temperature. When the eggs are hatched, the juveniles call their mother; the female comes up from the water and dig them out, takes young to the water using her mouth.

The juveniles remain with the mother till they voluntarily leave the mother when they reach around 1 meter size and become more solitary.

Sex and size of crocodiles

The saltwater crocodiles do not have any visible external sex organs. But, there is a marked difference in size between the males and the females; females generally don't exceed 4.0 m in length whereas, males may reach 7.0 m or more. The average size of the males within the Bhitarkanika waters is about 5.0 m. All crocodiles with length more than 4.0 m are males.

Estimation of body length from direct sighting:

If entire body is seen, the length is calculated on eye estimation; there may be variation of 1 foot.

If only the head is visible (like when part-emergence from water),

Body length = 7.2 x head length i.e., from tip of the snout up to post occipital scute.

If snout to hind leg is visible (like when Crocodile half-emerged from water),

Body length = 2 x length visible

If tail tip to hind leg is visible (like when the Crocodile is partly hidden in vegetation),

Body length = 2 x length visible

Estimation of Body length from tracks

From hind paw mark: body length = approx. 14 x paw length

I was looking keenly at the crocodile, our boat was still, the water in the creek was still too, no sound, no waves, and everyone was enjoying silence. The reptile was resting on a mudflat of around 50-60 feet long, 20 feet wide, devoid of any vegetation, the lower side of the flat was smoothened with the deposition of silt, on the upper side there was little undulation but smooth surface. Undulation due to existence of the root system of the mangrove trees, few pencil roots were propping up on the upper mudflat and a few smaller trees emerged from the surface at the farthest end and forest started beyond that. The crocodile was laying motion less, the grey shadow was reflected in the water, the foot marks of the crocodile was clearly seen from the waterline, both side of the body line, due to its crawling motion the prints were not parallel to each other on both sides. After crawling for around 10 feet the crocodile was laying motionless. Its body was parallel to the waterline, the small legs were rested close to the body, the entire body rested on the mud flat, the long tail took a light curve towards the end, curved towards the water body. The long tail was narrowed towards end, but the thick and wide spines got bigger and bigger from the base of the tail, the appearance is more like a long saw, only the tip is not pointed like needle, but little broader. The tail appeared to be formed with bands of rings of decreasing diameter, almost of equal length, jointed strongly. The lower the diameter the longer was the spine at the tail. The wider spines got shorter at the joint to the main body, and this type of small wide spines covered the entire body length on the upper side, on the side the spines are shorter, the irregular polygonal grey coloured body scales appeared. And the massive head with long jaw rested passively on the smooth mud flat, its eyes were closed, the front legs extended little forward, the big jaws were closed too.

We came closer, the crocodile noticed us, then it slid on the mud, a big log slide into the water, a long splash resulted, the crocodile disappeared into the water, bubble came, the water returned to its tranquil state again. I looked at the mud flat little ahead, a small mud flat too, but not that low, a couple of female deer were standing, they were not surprised by our visit, they were standing at the edge of the forest, thick tree line mainly comprising of

Bani, Keruan trees were standing behind them, long pencil roots of the Bani mangrove trees covered the entire mud flat, except for those pencil roots, no other life was there.

I was looking at the deer group; my friend suddenly recollected an event, the struggle for life in the deep forests of the land. The time was not long back, my friend a member of the patrolling team went for the morning patrol along with other members, in usual duty in the park; the crocodiles were basking in the morning sun at different mud flats. The water was calm, the team looked for something unusual, but the park was quiet, no change from the previous day. The team then came near to a makeshift jetty in their boat, the morning tea was poured into the cups from the flasks, and they started taking the smoking tea slowly. The water was calm, no sign of the crocodiles nearby, the last bigger crocodiles remained some hundred meter downstream. They were sipping the tea from the pots, and looking at the mud flats. A group of deer were grazing whatever little grasses that came on the mud flats, away from the water line; the chittals were shining in the morning sun, their golden brown skins were glowing. One deer came nearer to the water line unknowingly, there was no sign of crocodile in the water, or fish on the water surface; no visible danger from the water front. The birds were chirping as usual, the deer were busy in their grazing, monkeys were jumping from branches to branches; and there was no alarm or distress calls of the birds or animals, there was no presence of the hunters, else the animal and bird guards of the forest would give indications, scream; but that day the surrounding was calm, the forest was calm. Suddenly a crocodile sprang from the muddy water, it was medium crocodile, around 8-10 feet long, and it jumped at the unsuspecting deer. It was too late for the deer, the animal tried to return, but the crocodile caught the deer mouth, the deer screamed, the teeth of the reptile entered into the flesh, the crocodile was holding the struggling deer strongly, and it was pulling the deer into water, the deer was giving stiff resistance; blood was flowing from the mouth of the deer, the mud and water on the edge turned red and this red water flew down stream, and here the struggle for life continued. The crocodile was dragging the deer into the water, the deer was constantly losing strength, and finally it died after a brief struggle, the mud flat by that time was red with fresh blood from the dead deer.

The patrolling party was watching the struggle with horror, they were thunderstruck, and never experienced the fight of life and death so close, everyone was watching the event with great interest, no sound even from their noses. Suddenly, one more crocodile swam towards the battle field, its head was only visible; it was moving very quickly, like an arrow and came to the fighting place in no time and charged at the smaller crocodile which had hunted the deer in water. The new one was big, around 18-20 feet long, was more powerful, it snatched the deer from the original crocodile and the smaller one dipped into water, didn't rise.

I looked at the water, no sign of life in that muddy water, no crocodile was seen near. The boat moved forward, the mangrove forests was changing the veil at every corner, every mud flat was screened by the curious eyes, the crocodile might be hiding inside the patches of Nalia grass, or small Dhani grass fields. On an open mud flat, no grass was there, pencil roots of the Kerua trees covered the entire area, on that area a crow pheasant was standing, its eyes were searching for the prey on the mudflat, the stunning bird almost of same height of jungle fowl has a beautiful feature, the body feathers are deep red-brown in colur, a bluish–black band runs around the neck, eyes deep red, strong pointed beak, the tail bent upwards when it stands, the legs are strong and straight. I looked at this beautiful bird at the backdrop of tall kerua trees, it was standing motionless for some time, we came close, it flew inside the forest with a short nice flight, and other crow pheasant called from the hide 'Kuuuuuu', the deep calling filled the atmosphere.

Many mud flats came, on some mud flats tall grasses come up nicely; entire flat has been covered with the grasses, tall grasses, not very deep green, appeared mostly like wild paddy variety, the grasses started many a times right from the waterline. Pockets of pure Bani, pure kerua tree patches figure on the bank, the entire forest floor was covered with these pencil roots.

The tree composition was changing, we came across Rai tree patch has come deep into the water, its auxiliary root system, very long ones from the stem entered into the water, the roots are like thin flexible bamboos with straight bole, dug dip into the soil over which the water flows. Series of such roots made a root net, trapping the nutrients, creating a good feeding ground for so many aquatic animals. After this patch again the mud flats appeared, the tree line at the back, no grass on the flat but full of knee root-those appeared like stone pebbles scattered around on the flat, a small tree was coming up, and on that flat a huge crocodile much bigger than the last crocodile, was laying, its colour almost matched the colour of the flat, grey dark in colour, a huge animal. Its leg was faced towards the forest, part of the tail was hidden behind the trees, the front legs were pushed to the side, bent towards belly, the back legs were bent towards tail, while sliding down the crocodile had halted in between, the free limbs were pushed backwards. Its eyes were closed, long jaw was closed too, the crocodile was laying like a long log no life was seen around, no life on the water too, small ripples were speaking of the retreating tide, the low tide, small ripples now on the water but there was no splash, no head on the surface, the life was still with the crocodile. We switched off the engine, the boat came closer, the crocodile at once turned agile, it slipped into the muddy waters, with a long splash the whole body drowned into the water.

"Do you want to hear a beautiful local story on a crocodile?" he wanted to create further interest in the subject.

Obviously I was interested; he had been giving me so much of information, made my trip so interesting. I nodded my head, and he continued.

"Again it was story of a sea merchant."

"It appears your stories are, moving around the sea merchants." I commented, smiled at him.

"Oh! Yes, this is the area where the sea merchants once sailed their ships to far off lands, brought innumerable wealth to the and of Kalinga," he recounted the background.

Story of moving lotus –

"The wife of the merchant was pregnant, not able to take food, all the food turned tasteless, the merchant brought different kinds of food, but she was not able to take food. One day the lady wished to eat Kankada, a small vegetable found in a creeper, but the same was not available, the time was winter and at that time the fruit does not bear in the creeper. The merchant sent people to many villages, if the vegetable could be got, but the effort turned fruitless. The lady was not able to take any food, so the merchant himself went to search for the Kankada vegetable, to the forest, all the villages had been searched by his people. He reached deep forest, found a pond, the bushes covered the bunds, and inside the bush he could see one Kankada creeper, the creeper was full with the fruit. The merchant was very happy; at last the Kankada could be found. Then he went inside the pond, the creeper was almost on the water, it appeared the easiest approach was through the water. Once he was inside, the crocodile of that pond came and bit the leg of the merchant and didn't leave. The condition of the merchant was pitiable, the crocodile was about to kill him. The merchant prayed to the crocodile, informed the creature about the health of his wife, the crocodile then agreed release him with one condition – if a girl is born, then the merchant would hand over the child to the crocodile, and if a son would be born, then the merchant would keep him. The merchant had no option, he had to agree, and the crocodile left him. The merchant returned to his house, the Kankada vegetable was cooked, the lady after so many days could eat a proper meal.

Time passed, the girl, beautiful one, sweet, soft and loving too, born to the wife of the merchant, the merchant seeing the girl remembered the words of the crocodile, he couldn't throw the girl to the crocodile, and his own daughter wouldn't go to the crocodile. The merchant avoided that big pond, never went to that side, and the crocodile was waiting for him there. Years passed, fourteen years elapsed, once the flood came in the river, the low lying areas were flooded, the flood water even came to the village roads, and getting the opportunity the crocodile came near to the village, waited for the merchant at the bathing ghat and the merchant without knowing the presence of the crocodile came to the ghat. The crocodile asked him about his vows, his words, the daughter had to be handed over. The merchant explained, the girl was too small, but the crocodile didn't agree, the girl was fourteen years old, old enough to be handed over. The crocodile threatened the merchant in clear words – hand over the daughter the next day, lest the whole family would be eaten. The merchant returned to the house, informed the wife about the incoming danger, the wife cried, but there was no option, the daughter had to be handed over to the crocodile. Finally with heavy heart the parents decided to hand over the sweet girl to the crocodile, the girl was told that she would go to her maternal in-laws house across the big pond. The girl was happy, she wore her best dress, the parents cried in silence, the child was enthusiastic and they left for the pond. The girl wore a red silken dress. She looked like a beautiful sadhababohu worm, deep red, small, soft, beautiful, charming, she was radiating happiness. The father asked the daughter to wait for him at the bund of the big pond, he couldn't have digested the scene – his beautiful daughter was being eaten away by the crocodile. The girl waited for the father, he was late, and the child was getting restless, she looked around and found a beautiful lotus blooming in the pond, the best lotus she had ever seen. She wanted to pluck it, went inside, the lily was within the reach.

The man waited for a while and looked at me. I was listening the story keenly, there was silence all over except for his words no sound was there. One bird called from the mangrove branches, ripples came in the creek waters. Another call came from the other side of the creek, many many bird calls followed, as if all the souls were requesting him to complete the story.

"Have you visited the lotus lake of Bhitarkanika?" He asked me, and I nodded my head in affirmative. He asked me to recollect the blooming lotus of that pond, I closed my eyes, imagined the scene of the lotus pond inside the deep forest, the lotus pond I have described earlier.

He looked at the water of the creek, the tidal water was coming, there were many ripples, the activity in the mangrove forest was increasing. Then he narrated the further story, the daughter was inside the water,

The girl was singing then –

"I am in the knee deep water
Lotus is moving further and further."

She was not able to get the lotus, but she wanted to pluck it, so she went into the water further and sang –

"I am in thigh deep water father
Lotus is moving further and further."

The lotus was moving further, and she went further inside and sang –

"I am in waist deep water father
Lotus is moving further and further."

The lotus was moving further, and she went further inside, she was determined, unaware of imminent danger and sang –

"I am in chest deep water father
Lotus is moving further and further."

She was still away from the lotus, now she was fearful, wanted to return to the bund and before she could turn the crocodile surfaced, jumped at her and caught her, but didn't harm her, didn't wounded her there and brought to its nest in the mangroves. It wished to eat her at the right time, wanted to make a good feast of her meat at the right occasion. In the meantime the crocodile started catching the animals coming to that lake side. Slowly people, animals avoided that lake, the crocodile was hungry, but still didn't eat the girl, it managed its meal with rotten flesh. The crocodile finally decided to\eat the girl, went to the blacksmith to sharpen its teeth, the girl now understood its fate, wanted to escape. She changed her appearance, her hair turned rough, she put a got skin on her body, pasted mud all over that, took a stick and changed her appearance to a rustic old woman and started walking like the old woman, the backbone almost bent to the knees, she was walking slowly with the stick. The crocodile saw her on the way, couldn't recognise, the girl escaped into the forest, the mangrove forest was deep dense, almost\ there was no route, no path, the girl was puzzled, the roar of the tiger came from the densest part of the forest, she trembled, now there was no escape. Nearby there was a sahada tree, seeing no escape route, the girl requested the tree to give her shelter. Strange thing happened, the divinity in the forest helped her, and the bole was torn to two parts and the girl went inside, and the parted boles joined, the girl remained hidden inside, the tiger returned.

After few days the prince of the province came for the hunting, he camped inside the forest, next day morning he was breaking a small branch from the same tree for tooth cleaning. While he was cutting the branches, he listened a feeble voice –

"Cut slowly the branches Oh! Youngman,
You cut my nose
Cut slowly the branches Oh! My Prince,

You may prick my eyes,
Cut carefully my Lord,
You may break my hand."

The prince was taken back. The sweet voice touched his mind, reverberated in his heart, he returned from the hunting. During that time the king was looking for a bride for the prince, many girls were seen, but now strangely the prince decided to marry that tree, he didn't listen to anyone, didn't take food or water. The king was surprised, but finally bowed to the will of his only son. The strange marriage was solemnized, the prince married the Sahada tree in the dense forest. The prince uprooted the tree from the forest, planted it in the backyard of his palace. The hidden girl used to come out in the night, cook food for her husband, cleans the house, does all household works and returned to the tree at the end of the night. The prince kept the watch, saw the beautiful girl, was very happy to get such a beautiful caring wife. The next night when the girl was out of the tree, was doing her household work, the prince burnt the tree, the girl came back was dumbfounded to see her hiding place being burnt, the prince gave her solace, after all he was her husband. Then they lived happily.

It was a lovely story, the creeks of the erstwhile Kalinga was full with folk songs, local stories which were so interesting, makes the moment light, makes learning so interesting.

On crocodiles continue

The boat moved further down, many bigger trees appeared on the tree line, there were many ripples on the water surface. The curves on the tree lines too, the mud surface was full of irregularities, roots, branches, grasses, trees of different colour and shapes appeared frequently. The vacant spaces between the trees were full with pencil roots, the roots were providing anchorage to the tree, provides air to the tree during high tide. Slowly the boat came to the middle of the stream the horizon now looked bigger, the tree lines looked uniform, all deep green in colour, and their branches were touching the water. A mud flat appeared between the bushes and grasses, the trees stood a little away, the mud flat was a small one. A dry tree was standing in front of the mud flat inside the water with few dry branches, and there on the mud flat a huge crocodile was sleeping, its tail was curved towards water body almost parallel to the water, head towards the bush on front, it could keep an eye on the developments on the waters. Another eye would keep a watch on the forests, its leg marks were deeply engraved on the mud floor.

I looked at this big crocodile, it was enjoying the sun, its skin colour was pale white unlike most of the crocodile outside; the whitish crocodile of this area is called Sankhua Kumbira in Odia. Sankhua meaning conch white colour, its eyes were closed, mouth was closed, the snout was little dug into the mud, the soft mud had given way to its weight, a little part of its body had gone into mud, the ripples of the river water were almost touching its long tail. There were movement marks on the mud flat, now this crocodile was the lone one present, other crocodiles had moved into the river, the movement marks it was a shallow furrow, around one to two feet wide, some points the mud had come upwards and the furrow ends at the water. Little ahead to its resting place, a small patch of grassland was there, the grasses were light green in colour, might be 2 to 5 feet tall, and further beyond the dense forest continued. The mudflat was low, just above the water, the slope was gentle, also the slope of the grassland on the mudflat was gentle; the best place for the crocodiles to take sun bath. My friend told me about the crocodile sizes, the crocodile skull preserved in the museum of Kanika palace was about 3½ ft long, according to the thumb rule, the skull is roughly $^1/_7$ of the body length, the crocodile must be around 25 ft long. The giant crocodiles of this size were rare, but still were found on the mud flats.

"I knew once the crocodile population dipped; was almost alarming, so any special effort to preserve these huge crocodiles from the poachers, the big crocodile is an extremely valuable trophy, to be achieved with any difficulty, now the poachers are going to any extent to get a catch," I asked him, and then he started telling about the crocodile rearing project –

"The crocodile rearing project started from July 1975 by collecting 25 eggs from the wild for hatching in captivity. 24 young ones were hatched, the white crocodile named Gourie because of its colour, was the product of the crocodile rearing project. The hatchlings are reared in captivity in small ponds, the juveniles after attaining a reasonable length are released in the waters of Bhitarkania, around 6-7 months prior to onset of monsoons with the intentions that they should get sufficient time to acclimatise themselves in the waters, know the creeks, the flood water would wash them if they are not acquainted earlier to the creeks and channels. The Dangmala Creek, Suajora Creek, Pati Jora, Sapua Creek, Jalahara Creek, Sagunachera Creek, Ganjeikhia Creek, Mangalpur Creek, Mahisamara Creek and other smaller creeks give the juveniles better protection, they adopt slowly to the natural environment, finally disperse to the main channels. In that project the first batch of 15 crocodiles was released in the Dangmala during Aprill 1977," he narrated.

I read the reference book with me, without the help of which the forests of Bhitarkaniaka can't be understood well; after all it gives so much of knowledge. The salt water crocodiles are the largest among the living crocodiles, inhabits in estuaries of rivers where there is regular flow of tidal water. All the crocodiles of Bhitarkanika are salt water crocodiles – locally called the Baula Kumbhira or Sankhua kumbhir, the largest crocodile is 22-23 ft long; probably the largest one of the wild lives in the forests of Bhitarkanika, however the largest one ever encountered in Bhitarkania was about 30 ft long, not found in the recent past any more. Crocodiles more than 20 ft long are sighted regularly, but there are no massive crocodiles any more. In the waters, the Sankhua Kumbhira, the partial white crocodiles are also found in the waters in good numbers. The salt water crocodiles are among the most ferocious attackers, the instances of attack on humans and cattle are regular, the bigger crocodiles attack people fishing illegally inside the sanctuary or cattle grazing nearby, incidence of attack occurred when the human being or cattle enter into the crocodile habitat without precaution. Otherwise the crocodiles in wild generally prefer big fishes like vekti, khaingas, jalanga which form their major pray base, human or cattle do not form a part of regular food chain, but the crocodile attacks on human and cattle are regular. During high tides the bigger crocodiles, mostly males above 18 ft length come closer to the river banks and attacks on human occur.

The crocodiles in the estuarine area like protected creeks, those creeks open to the sea front but not facing the waves directly, and like mangrove areas which are little away from the sea face, also the side channels of the main channel to the sea with good forest growth around. These side creeks are not affected by cyclone, they generally have good mud flats; the crocodile can collect their nesting materials, usually leaves of the mangrove trees, from the forest easily. In the early stage of crocodile life, after their hatching, the hatchlings need cover against preying birds and other animals, and the mangrove forest offer the best protection because of its netted structure. The sheltered waters is the nursery of varieties of fishes, mainly prawns and shrimps, this forest system provides good food for the nourishment of the young.

The crocodiles are amphibious creature but spend more time in water than land. Sun basking is a typical behaviour of crocodiles when they come out of water to regulate the body temperature. Since they spend considerable time in water, so they lose body temperature during the cool hour of night; so in order to compensate the loss of body temperature they come out of water during the day for basking. During the winter, the crocodiles used to bask for long hours on the bank of the river or streams, or on partly exposed rocks or islands. However, during the summer months the crocodiles spend much of the time in floating or submerged in water during the day hours, they come to the land generally during the night. In the night, the eyes of the crocodiles glow in the reflected light from the torch.

Many questions appeared in my mind, the fishes make the largest prey base, the crocodile is heavy, slow and the fishes are much smaller and fast, then how the crocodile is catching the fishes. I expressed my doubt to my friend.

"The crocodile move slowly on land, but is a fast mover inside water, when crocodile swims, it also moves noiselessly in water; during the high tide the fishes come near and the crocodile catches them. It prefers non-scaled fishes like jalanga, kantia, etc and also scaled fishes like khainga, vekti, khoranti, etc. Sometimes it also eats madhua crab, which is available in plenty in Bhitarkanika, this crab is has more flesh, has thick legs, are light grayish in colour, and weighs about 250 grams," he answered.

I know the crocodile of Bhitarkanika are man eaters, but whether these attacks occur inside the sanctuary limit, I am not sure, so I asked,

"Whether the crocodiles ever caught a person inside Bhitarkanika sanctuary?" I asked the man.

His eyes gloomed, a big heave came from the wide chest, some miserable event happened in the dark forests.

Madhusudan was a forester, worked in forest for almost 25 years with long experience in Bhitarkanika, and he was in charge of the crocodile rearing area. That eventful day on 24th April 2011 he came to an old pond inside the crocodile research centre area. The crocodiles were kept under proper protection in a different area and there was no fear from them. As usual after giving the feed to crocodiles in the rearing pond area, he descended to this separate pond; a small one with around 3-4 feet of water, sat on the stairs to wash his hands and legs. As he lowered his body, suddenly a crocodile jumped at him from the water, he never expected a crocodile to be there hidden, it was far away from the creek, the crocodile shouldn't have been there. The killer reptile hold the mans shoulder and part of the neck in its strong jaw, the shoulder bones were broken, the wind pipe was partly cut open; the man struggled with crocodile to free himself, but the crocodile was strong, as he lifted his shoulders, the crocodile instead of leaving him now caught his thigh including the lower belly, the liver came out of the belly through the opening. The man continued his fight, seeing the delay Sadhuchanran, the man in charge of motor running rushed. He somehow rescued the man after hitting the crocodile on the mouth and the eye, the crocodile will never open the jaw unless there is some hitting on the eyes, beating the body has no result. He brought the man to the bund, the man was semiconscious, badly hurt, and couldn't survive for more than fifteen minutes and died before getting any kind of help. It was highly unusual for a crocodile to be there, the place shouldn't have been a nesting place, but the crocodiles in search of nesting place comes very close to human habitation, sometimes remain in very low water, unthinkable for a crocodile stay.

The crocodiles in search of food, nesting place too, sometimes come very close, in one incident one crocodile came right on the main village road inside the Dangmala village in an evening. An old villager on cloth was going to a shop without even thinking of the presence of the crocodile in that area. Suddenly in the twilight time, the crocodile jumped at him, caught the long flying cloth in its mouth, the man screamed, fortunately no part of his body came in the jaws of the crocodile, he ran at full speed fully naked.

These stories were scary, but mostly aberrations, now the people were very careful about the crocodiles, except for freak accidents like above, crocodile attack on man in park area is rare. However crocodiles caught people outside Bhitarkanika, in the small channels which connect main Bhitarkania creeks. During rains, the water of the river rises, touches the embankment, sometimes crosses it, the whole area remains flooded, the crocodiles unknowingly enter into the village ponds and smaller channels and then attacks human take place. Apart from that the poachers, many a times were attacked by the crocodiles inside the sanctuary when they descended into the channel to catch fishes.

We looked around, so many crocodiles on almost all mud flats, mostly big ones, were lying like logs, their eyes were closed, big snouts of many were wide open, but most of them closed their snouts. Many a times we came closer, the crocodiles didn't remain on their respective mud flats, they slipped into the muddy water, only remained the mark of their departure, a sliding line, deep in the middle, smooth and polished.

Our boat had covered a long distance, we were much closer to Gupti area, a long creek meets the main creek, the land mass on our right was parted, our curious eyes searched the area. A long necked large egret was sitting on the protruding branch of the Bani tree, its eyes were glued on the ripples on the waters, the bird was glazing at the backdrop of the green foliage and dark shades. I looked up, on the blue background a huge painted stork bird was flapping its wings. It was a huge bird with very wide wings, there were gaps between the feathers at the edge of the wings, the inner side of the wing was black, the body was white, neck was covered with small white feathers, at the lower belly grey feathers formed a band. The long pointed bill was pinkish in colour, the legs were tall, the bird in fact towered over the branches and other living birds of the area. It flapped its wings, the leaves moved in the wind, the bird raised its body, and then it stood in a proper shape balancing the huge body nicely on the thin branches. The bird was now fully visible, the neck was more orange in colour, round head is pinkish, then the neck is curved like egrets, small white feathers covered the entire neck, the wings now appeared partially white, lower stretch is dark and dark grey colour, the body is white, the tail is again pink with dark bands in between, the leg is white, it was standing on the white branch of the tree, the green leaves covered its lower part, the long bill and tall head was raising from the branches like flags of the Bhitarkanika forests.

I remembered the story of the painted storks, the Kouncha bird, the first shloka of Hindu literature was composed at the death of this bird, the Ramayan was composed then after by the great sage Valmiki, the killing of the painted stork moved the sage, he composed the great epic.

Once the great sage Valmiki was going to the river Ganga for his daily ablutions, his disciple Bharadwaja was carrying his clothes. On the way, they came across the Tamasa stream; the water was clear, he told to his disciple, "Look, this water is so clear, like the mind of a good man! I will bathe here today." He went down, and searched for a suitable place, then he heard the sweet chirping of birds. He looked up, two painted storks were in their conjugal dance, they were busy in the love making, the happy bird couple was making pleasant chirpings. Suddenly the male bird fell down, it was hit by an arrow; the hunter with bow and came out from the bushes. The female bird cried in agony, the male bird fell dead on the ground, the heart of sage Valmiki's melted at this painful sight, the agony of the female bird passed into his heart. The hunter was happily going towards the dead bird, the sage got very angry, the saint uttered the words with agony:

"You will find no rest for the long years of Eternity
For you killed a bird in love and unsuspecting."

Thus the first śloka in Sanskrit literature came from the mouth of the great sage with great pain. Later Maharshi Valmiki is revered as the first poet, or Adi Kavi and he composed the entire Ramayana which is known as the first kavya or poetry with the blessings of Lord Brahma.

The Bagagahan (Heronry)

I was watching the storks keenly, my friend was observing me with the same keenness, and observing my interest he started narrating about the colonial nestlings in the Bhitarknika. I did not know, the dark forests attract thousands of birds not for feeding, but for nesting, that too they nest in a place called Bagagahan. He showed me a photograph, I couldn't believe my eyes, never expected to see so many white brushes on the green canvass, firstly the canopy of the trees looked so different, it was somewhat undulating, resembling small undulating land full with small bushes, the tree canopy from top look totally different; secondly so many birds were on a single photograph, except for during flight in a group, so many birds were never seen by me. I looked closely at the photograph, so many birds, tall birds were standing on branches, almost all of them were storks, open bill storks, painted storks, many were gathered on a single nest, couples were standing together, some were standing alone, all the available places of the tree tops were occupied by these tall birds, the magnificence of colonial nesting was unthinkable unless seen in own eyes. He showed me another photograph, a close up photo of the birds, five open billed storks on a single tree top, it appeared that there were three nests, two couples were on both sides, on their respective nests, at the centre the lone stork was standing tall, and its mate was flying just above it. All the birds were looking at the left side, their long thick bills were pointing downwards, long necks were twisted a little, and their body weights on their left legs, the white chests were clearly visible, they were making some kind of strange drills as if. I looked at the bird in flight, the long neck was fully stretched, the bill was little lowered, extended forward, the body was fully stretched, the legs were stretched away backwards, the long wings, white at the shoulder and black at the outer side, were fully stretched; the bird looked magnificent at its flight.

I looked at another photograph, a close up photograph of the nest, two tall birds were standing side by side, the taller bird had lowered its neck, its bill was touching the nest, its long bill was a little open, its partner was standing very close, their body was touching each other, its bill was lowered, a white canopy had been created on the top, and below two partially grown up chicks with white feathers on their body, were sitting comfortably. The nest was created atop the tree, few branches emerge close to each other, some of the branches were broken at the top and leafless branches were seen, the nest was placed neatly between the branches, the side leaves were removed, a beautiful resting place thus was created. Near to another nest one big open bill stork was standing alone, its long claws were holding a broken branch strongly, the long claws with long nails were visible; the huge body was standing in a leaning position, the back feathers were touching the leaves, the neck was curved, the bill was huge, most strangely, the bill was closed, but there was opening between the upper and lower bills, the mud and the useless materials would come out when the bills are pressed.

He showed another photograph, a very close look of the nest, the parents were not present, three ash coloured young chicks were sitting close to each other, their eyes were closed; feathers had not come fully on their body, they had loose skins, signs of small feathers coming from the body was there. The nest was nicely made, shape was like bowel, middle portion was deeply depressed and the outer edges were raised all around. Different kinds of twigs, longer ones were kept around the margin to give the nest a better shape, support too; smaller twigs were kept at the centre; some leaves were also put, to close the gaps. There were layers of twigs of different shapes, but most of those were straight, the centre was thickened with many layers, the centre would take the maximum load. The nest was nicely made, was balanced; the chicks were very safe there.

In another photograph, a group of painted storks were standing on the tree tops, but the vegetation was sparse, leafless branches were many, these elegant birds were mostly standing alone, couples were not many. Then I looked at another photograph, the undulating green canopy was covered with white brushes, painted storks, open billed storks occupies all available spaces. I was looking keenly at those photographs, I couldn't get other birds. I looked at my friend. He clarified, the birds have three tiers of nesting, the taller storks occupy the top canopy, the middle canopies are occupied by the egrets and the herons occupy the lowest canopy, as per the size of the birds, canopies are delineated, the smaller ones can go into the middle or the lower canopy, but the bigger birds can't cross so many branches found in the the middle or lower canopy.

Once in a cloudy day I had travelled to the Bagagahan area in Shuajora creek, our boat had moved to this narrow creek from main Bhitarkanika river; in the dark sky the open bill storks were flying, those magnificent birds were crossing the creek continuously, many were with green branches on their beak, we were approaching the famous heronry of the mangrove forests. At the confluence point of the river a huge crocodile was floating on water, its saw shaped tail was coming out of water; the long body was appearing like a long thick branch of an uprooted tree. I looked at the sides, the creek was much narrower than the main creek, tree branches were coming on to the water line continuously, the mangrove forest was displaying its richness in colour and diversity, the call of the birds were coming continuously. A dove started calling, it was perched on a dead branch of a big Guan tree on the side of the creek. Its companion replied from the other side, a nonstop singing continued, it reminded about our presence, we were entering into the kingdom water birds of the forests. I looked ahead, open bill storks were perched on many trees, they were looking at us, as the boat came closer they started flying, a beautiful flight was sighted from a close distance. A small green bird came to the water surface in its fly, its wings were moving fast; it touched the water then flew back to a dry branch just over the water and looked at us, alongside it a black Drongo bird was sitting quietly. Again a dove called loudly, I looked for it, found it perched on a denuded branch of Sundari tree, these small birds were making the forest live. The boat moved through the beautiful forests on the sides, small and big birds fly over the water line regularly, a cemented jetty came and we reached the landing point to Bagagahan.

We moved over a footpath, a raised soil bund had been created over which narrow cement slabs were kept to facilitate easy walking. On both sides the small water swamps were found regularly, water was flooding the forest floor, and on the forest floor the pneumtophores of the Sundari trees were rising like small white ant mounds. The crocodiles prefer this kind of area for food, nesting too; our eyes were scanning the floor continuously for the crocodiles, the big reptile used to frequent the area during high tides. After a brief walk we approached a big metal watch tower, the huge tower camouflaged with the surrounding with its location, green paint were put over the angles and metal nets to merge with natural surroundings. We climbed to the tall watch tower, at least 30-40 feet high, reached the platform on the top; the platform was just over the tree branches, giving sufficient space for viewing, but not obstructing the movement of birds in flight, also not an eyesore in this beautiful forest. On our front huge forest runs to the horizon, and on the forest a wide band of trees, and thousands of birds were perched on different trees.

I couldn't believe my eyes, so many birds, so many birds at same time, the watch tower was almost 300- 500 meters away from the nesting site, but the view was nice mainly because of the huge size of the birds on the trees. I looked at the forest, the forest expands from the green paddy fields in my far left at the horizon to the far right, and a narrow waterline was visible at the left, the island was encircled by the water channels in all direction. The green band at the front at farthest points were green, without perching birds, then towards inner side the height of the trees were reduced gradually towards centre, and the green colour of the trees had changed suddenly to white, thousands and thousands of open bill storks, large egrets, ibises, painted storks, etc. Crowded the tree tops, not a free tree top could be noticed. They were busy, some were standing, some were sitting, the birds were descending on their nests, rising from the nests also, some were carrying the nesting materials, the peak nesting season was going on. One big open bill stork flew at my right side, around 20- 30 meter away, the bird was flapping its huge wings, appeared like a big toy airplane, it was holding a green branch on its large beak, its eyes were on the nest; I watched it continuously. The bird flew for some time then descended with long legs down and fingers claws opened and it sat on an almost leafless tree top. I couldn't believe, as I watched closely, almost all the trees were without leaves on the top, the birds had been breaking the leading shoots continuously so that the branches go laterally, creating enough wide space on the tree top for establishment of huge nests, I was told that some nests had a diameter upto 5-6 feet, so huge were the nests, the birds were big too, many were almost one meter tall. I looked at a broken tree, almost all the branches were broken, only thick boles and small branches were visible, the new nests need new materials, old nests need repairing. The heronry was close to several big rice cultivation areas. The open bill stork – the largest group of nesting birds need small snails of the cultivation fields to feed, the nesting site should not be far away from the feeding grounds. I looked at the site, the birds were continuously coming to the nests, the big wings swung, and slowly they descend on the trees; the birds were calling each other, when I didn't see the place and was on the ground, I thought that the human habitation was nearby, such was the sound, and such was the noise.

I came down from the watch tower, suddenly the Kaak Kaak Kaak Kaa sound came, the call of a jungle fowl. I was surprised, in this big gathering of the birds atop the trees, the beautiful colourful jungle fowl was present on the land, the fowl remained on the forest floor, eat the pieces of eating material like fishes, snails, etc. that drop from the tree tops; in a biological chain every where there is presence of life, interlinking of one life with other. I looked at the forest floor, a lot of small dark crabs, they had created numerous earth burrows, blankets of dry rotten leaves and numerous dark fruits of mangrove trees, water all around. Near to the channel, on the mud flats a lot of small red crabs with thick legs were seen, and with the littlest disturbances they were running to their holes, the mud skippers were rushing to the far areas.

Our boat moved, instead of going to the main channel, we stayed for some time in the Shuajore creek and watched the Open bill storks perched on different branches. The birds were a little away from their nesting site, they were standing tall on the green branches, tall brownish legs were supporting the huge body well, the strong fingers claws were gripping the branches firmly, the heavy wide beak and large heads were resting over the half S shaped neck and there were many such birds on the trees. As we came close, a bird rose from the branches, the huge fingers claws freed the branch, in flight the bird looked like a mythical shape with sharp beak and strong legs down and wings up in other direction. From another branch two birds flew, the gaps between their upper and lower beaks were clearly visible; they rose beyond the tree and flew towards the nesting island. A dove again called from a tree hide, the atmosphere was filled with long H-u--u-m sound, the Bhitarkanika heronry was bubbling with life.

The colonial nesting of large number of resident water birds and local migrants take place inside the deepest part of the Bhitarkanika wildlife sanctuary. In Bhitarkanika most of the birds nest in Bagagahan, the heronry, a place alongside the Suajora creek, around 30-45 minutes journey from Dangmala, is on the left side of the channel, and the area is famous for its concentration of birds over a small area. The place is like a small island, saucer shaped, area around 15-20 acres, big trees all around at the periphery to prevent high wind entering into the area, surprisingly the size of the tree reduces from periphery towards centre; and the birds lay eggs on the smaller trees, the food is available in plenty around the nearby fields. The birds start reaching the Bagagahan from the first week of June and the nesting continues till the end of November and the hatching occurs by August and September. The total number of birds nesting in the area usually exceeds 65,000, including 35,000 young ones and 30,000 adults of both sexes. The numbers of nests are in the range of around 15, 000 per season over approximately 5,000-6,000 mangrove trees. The breeding period generally continues between June-November months of every year.

About 11 species of birds found to be nesting at Bagagahan also called Chadheigahan, majority among them, approximately 60%-70% are open billed storks; and the other birds are painted storks, little cormorant, little egret, medium egret, large egrets, purple heron, night heron, gray heron, darter or the snake bird, white ibis and cattle egret prefer this area which is full with guan, sundari, singada and bani trees. The pattern of the nesting is very interesting, the painted storks occupy the top canopy, the Ibis (Odia word-Da bentia) takes the next lower canopy, followed by Darter bird. The open billed stork, great egrets and great herons occupy the top and the next lower canopy, the medium egret comes next and at the lowest canopy the pond herons, little egret and the cormorants nest. The place is most liked by the open bill storks followed by little cormorants.

Year	Type	Asian Open bill stork	Large Egret	Medium Egret	Little Egret	Cattle Egret	Purple Heron
2006	Nests	8,493	1,019	546	41	*	148
	Birds	36,944	2,955	2,020	205	*	604
2007	Nests	7,368	810	331	202	*	303
	Birds	38,313	4,252	1,704	979	*	1,302

Year	Grey Heron	Night Heron	Little Cormorant	White Ibis	Oriental Darter	Total
2006	240	254	854	136	88	11,819
	748	914	3,749	408	396	48,943
2007	81	273	633	90	208	10,299
	283	1,173	2,785	463	842	52,096

*Not counted

The Guan and Sundari trees are the most preferred trees for nesting. The reason for such mass colonial nesting is primarily due to good availability of sufficient food both for young and for adults, availability of suitable nesting materials nearby, and importantly remoteness of the area. The open billed storks called gendalia mostly feed on mollusks, also called genda in local language found extensively in the agricultural fields around the sanctuary. Due to such feeding of genda (the mollusk), the open billed stork is called gendalia. These birds, called as colonial birds are residential birds of Bhitarkanika, do not come from outside.

I listened so much about the colonial nesting birds of Bhitarkànika, but I was ignorant about their behaviour, habitat, even look. It was necessary to know a little about the birds, to understand their habitat, their behaviour. I opened the book and glanced through the pages.

Storks

Storks are large, long-legged, long-necked wading birds with long, stout bills, are heavily built, with wide wingspans. They used to live in drier habitats than the related birds like herons, spoonbills and ibises. The storks have no syrinx (name for the vocal organ of birds located at the base of a bird's trachea), and are mute, thus give no call; the bill-clattering is an important mode of stork communication at the nest. The storks feed on frogs, fishes, insects, earthworms, small birds and small mammals.

This bird use soaring, the gliding flight requiring thermal air currents for flying up, which conserves energy. The soaring birds can maintain flight without wing flapping, using rising air currents; many gliding birds can in fact lock their extended wings by means of a specialized tendon. The meaning of soaring is lift, which is a meteorological incident, used as an energy source by the soaring aircraft and the soaring birds. Gliding, hang gliding and paragliding are the air sports that use soaring flight.

Energy can be gained by using rising air from four sources:

- Thermals (where air rises due to heat).
- Ridge lift, where air is forced upwards by a slope.
- Wave lift, where a mountain produces a standing wave.
- Convergence, where two air masses meet.

All storks in their flight fly with their neck outstretched.

The nests of the storks are often very big, and used for many years; some nest have grown over 2 m (6 ft) in diameter and around 3 m (10 ft) in depth. The storks are once thought to be monogamous, but this is partially true; they sometimes change mates after migrations. They remain attached to the nests as much as partners.

Asian Open Bill Stork – The Asian Open Bill Stork is a large wading bird in the stork family, is a broad-winged soaring bird, however it is relatively smaller for a stork family, stands around 76 cm. This bird breeds near inland wetlands, build stick nest in trees, and lays 2-6 eggs. The incubation period is 22 days. The diameter of the nest size is around 2.75 feet; the main nesting materials are green Guan tree branches. They prefer Guan trees for roosting and nesting, in fact they do not allow this tree to grow as they constantly downsize the leading shoots near their colonies.

The breeding adults are all white, the wings are black with flight feathers, the legs are red and the bill is dull grey and the mandibles do not meet except at the tip, and thus the name this bird is derived. This stork walks slowly and steadily on the ground, feeds mainly on pond snails, sometimes frogs and crabs.

Painted Stork – The Painted Stork is a large wading bird, the name originated from their distinctive pink tertial feathers, is a medium-sized stork, stand about 93–102 cm (37–40 in) tall, the wing span is around 150–160 cm (59–63 in) and the weight is around 2-3.5 kg. This stork has a heavy yellow bill with a down-curved tip; the head of the adult is bare and orange or reddish in colour.

These large birds forage in flocks in shallow wetlands along rivers or lakes, wade along the water course, they prefer water depth around 12 to 25 cm and deeper waters are generally avoided, they walk slowly and also disturb the water with their feet to flush out fishes. They dip their half open beaks into water and make side to side movement of beaks and catch small fishes that come across. They also eat frogs and occasionally snake too. Usually they forage during the day time, but may forage late under exceptional conditions. Their nesting is colonial on trees, often along with other water birds and prefer trees on an island or in an undisturbed area. They make nests on the tops of the trees; many times birds almost push each other for these locations. Their breeding season begins shortly after the monsoons, around mid-August and generally continues till January. In hot sunny days, during the mid-day, the adults stand with wings outstretched at the nest to shade the chicks from heat.

These birds are not migratory, only make short distance flights in their range for food and also for breeding. They often make use the late morning thermals to soar in search of foraging areas.

Egrets and the Herons

The herons and egrets are long-legged, long-necked and usually long-billed birds. They feed on fishes, frogs, lizards and insects.

They use many hunting techniques, sometimes they stand still at the edge of water or in low water and wait to spear a fish; sometimes they stir the water or grass with a foot or flick the wings to dislocate the prey, sometimes walk rapidly so that the prey can be reached. This prey flushing actions of foot stirring and wing-flicking can be in combination with a slow walk or a walk-stop-walk-stop hunting. The most interesting hunting method is that of Green-backed Heron which bait a fish, it drops an insect or piece of vegetation onto the surface of the water and then catch the fish that rises to for this potential food.

Most of these species are solitary feeders.

The bittern, herons and egrets are short-tailed birds. For the herons and egrets, their long necks remain in 'S' shape with the head held back between the shoulders. During flight the head also remains in the same style, instead of being stretched which is unique to these birds, clearly distinguishing them from storks and cranes which fly with their necks stretched straight out. The herons cannot bend their necks and only move it in backward and forward directions.

Some species of herons nest and roost together in a tree or group of trees, these heronries are generally far away from feeding areas and the birds commute several times a day between the two, for their own feed and to feed the chicks also.

Many species of the heron and egrets are highly expressive birds with a wide range of display actions, such as threat displays, forward and upward stretches, bill snapping and rattling; circling and pursuit flights are made during the courtship. A male offers female a twig as a gift, the time to build a nest, and they remain in pair. The nests are usually built on the trees, most species nest colonially; their colonies are often mixed colonies with other wetland birds such as storks, Ibises and spoonbills as well as other species of herons.

Cattle Egret – This egret is found in abundant in the Bhitarkanika area, stands around 51 cm, is a small sized bird with short neck with short yellow bill, often found moving around cattle, so its name is arrived at; this bird mainly feeds on grass hoppers, lizard, small frogs and other insects. These birds arrive at the Bggagahan area around July-August. Their nest is thin, made up of very small dry twigs of Guan or Sundari trees, the diameter of the nest is around 2.75 feet. The bird lays 3-4 white coloured eggs. The incubation period is 17 days.

Black Crowned Night Heron – This bird is a residential bird of the Bhitarkanika area, also a local migratory, stands around 58 cm tall. The bill is strong, black in colour, the adult has black crown and mantle contrasting with grey wings and whitish under parts. This bird is nocturnal, is very shy, prefers nest on the lowermost part of tree, roost on the trees during the day time. These birds move in flocks during evening in search of food with quackling sound; but when in heronry the mother bird sometimes go for food during the day time too. They mainly feed on fishes, frogs and aquatic insects. Their nests are made up of thin and dry twigs of Guan trees. The diameter of the nest size is around 2.5 feet, there are around 1000 nesting population in Bagagahana heronry. This bird lays 3 pale blue coloured eggs. The incubation period is 20 days.

Great Egret – This is a big egret, stands around 90 cm, is a large white coloured bird with a long thin S-shaped neck when not extended, the bill is slim and dagger like. They are the first birds to arrive at the Bagagahana heronry, usually from the first part of June. Both parents look after the hatchlings, when one parent leaves the nest in search of food, then the other parent takes care of eggs and chicks. This bird mainly feeds on fish, frog and aquatic insects. The nesting population in the heronry is round 3500 numbers. Their nests are made up of dry sticks of Guan and Sundari trees. The diameter of the nest size is around 3.5 feet. The bird lays 3-4 blue coloured eggs. The incubation period is 21days.

Darter – This bird is rare residential bird, stands around 90 cm, known as snake bird for its snake like appearance while swimming with head and neck above water. This bird prefers tall trees for nesting. This bird mainly feeds on fish, frog and small snakes. The nesting population is around 500 numbers in Bagagahana heronry. The diameter of the nest is around 2.9. The bird lays 3-4 eggs, occasionally 5 white coloured eggs with blue spots. The incubation period is 19 days.

Black-headed Ibis – This white coloured residential bird stands around 60 cm, has black head, black neck and curved bill. They mainly feed on frogs, fishes and insects. The nesting population is around 600 numbers. The nest is made up of twigs and leaves of Guan trees. The diameter of the nest size is around 3.5 feet. The bird lays 3-4, bluish white coloured eggs. The incubation period is 18 days.

Purple Heron – This residential but uncommon bird stands around 86 cm, appears similar to Grey heron but are more slender with dark purplish brown wing coverts. This bird mainly feeds on fish, frogs and small snakes. The nesting population is round 1000 numbers in the heronry. The nest is made up of dry and thick sticks of Sundari trees. The diameter of the nest size is around 4 to 5 feet. The bird lays 3 blue coloured eggs. The incubation period is 19 days.

Grey Heron – This common residential bird stands around 96 cm, is the largest water birds of Bhitarkanika heronry. Its feathers are grey with black and white feathers below neck, and crest is on the head. This bird mainly feeds on fish, frogs and small snakes. The nesting population is round 750 numbers. The nest is made up of dry and thicker sticks of sundari trees. The diameter of the nest size is around 6 to 7 feet. The bird lays 2-4 blue coloured eggs. The incubation period is 21 days.

The Little egret (nests around 1000), Intermediate egret (nests around 3000), and the Little cormorant (nests around 3500), are the other birds found in the heronry.

The information about the birds were amazing, gave so much of in-depth knowledge. I looked down, scanned the same tree, a large egret was standing on a branch at lower height and at the forest floor, alongside the main stem of the tree a huge crocodile was laying, this crocodile was not laying in open, rather the place was sheltered, not fully illuminated, many trees, branches around. It can't be categorized a true good quality mud flat, but this huge crocodile was taking rest there, its body was grey, dark and pale shades appeared throughout, a melanin variation, the snout was facing the water. On the body long and thick spines started from the neck, spiny eruptions appeared all over the body, over the snout the huge yellow eyes were open, burning, the long teeth were visible from the side of the snout, the crocodile was watching the ripples on the side stream, one front leg was stretched forward, other front leg was pushed backward, huge back legs were stretched. The crocodile was ready to charge at the victim, be careful, it was the crocodile land.

We moved down, the stream widened, the tree lines suddenly got thinner and grey line of the crop fields and thatched houses appeared suddenly. Now no more trees colonizing the water body, the channel was transgressing to the land, brown broken landmass appeared on the coastline. The paddy cultivation was over, people in this low lying area produce a lot of paddy, silt and nutrients are carried from the higher lands during the time of flood, turns the low lying land of this area fertile. Few coconut, Chakunda (rain tree) and tamarind trees, stood alongside a small hamlet consisting of 3-4 thatched houses, on the higher lands. The paddy straws were scattered on the yard, an open place cleaned for gathering paddy, one white cow was grazing on the straws. One lady on printed orange saree with green border was walking alongside the open bank of the channel with a white aluminum pot on her right hand, her left hand was folded back, the crocodile filled water was around 20 feet away, the man eater crocodile of the Bhitarkanika was hiding in the muddy waters. I looked keenly at the house, the houses were thatched with paddy straw, roof was like isosceles triangle. On the top long bamboo lines were kept to give adequate strength to the thatching, the long straws of paddy created a thick impervious layer for water, but good for air circulation, the golden straws turned dark brown over a long period, whitish patches were seen here and there. The thatched roof was lowered significantly only 3-4 feet away from the land, the brown wall of the house was made up of silt mixed soil and pasted over bamboo posts, the bamboo gave some strength to the wall, the muddy soil gave the luster. These house are very comfortable and one gets a fresh feeling, the cow dung soil mixed thin paste used to be put everyday over the wall and the floor by the women folk, these houses are cool during the summer and during the winters the chilly wind doesn't enter. The room is warm for the humans. These kinds of houses with low thatched roofs are found all over the coastlines in and around Bhitarkanika, the people have developed eco-friendly houses from materials abundantly available in the vicinity.

Some creepers were covering parts of the roof, probably poi lata, shimba lata and white guard, the people here plant some creepers, mostly white guard, poi, etc alongside the house, a bamboo stick gives initial support to the creepers, then the creeper climbs further and reaches the roof. Every inch of land around is utilized, some small vegetable garden in the vicinity could be seen too. Two cows, one white one, another reddish brown, were tied to the bamboo posts, were sitting over the dried golden straw, their ears were stretched forward, they were watching us. A little away from the hamlet, the paddy stalk bundles were gathered, on one side the paddy straws were heaped, the paddy grains were still attached to the straw, and paddy mounds were made; the paddy part is put towards inner side, the paddy hala (the paddy bundles) are put in a circular shape, then the paddy stalk bundles heap is made, the shape somewhat looks like a circular mound. The shape is adopted for easy storage, the paddy can be safely gathered there till the paddy grains can be separated later on, the farmer is busy in other work, for harvesting of rest of the crop. The golden paddy and the straw was shining. The sky was at deepest blue, the scattered trees were in deep green colour, the soil was in brown; the water below on the channel was grayish dark; combination of so many colours in a landscape. After a small distance mangrove crop appeared, a small tree with long roots appeared, and in between the trees, not far away from the village a small crocodile was late afternoon sun on the mud flat, the smaller reptile entered into more conflicting zone, the human presence would make it vulnerable, but it had no choice, better and bigger mud flats had been occupied by massive crocodiles and it now was searcheing for a new area.

Further down, the tree lines didn't turn thicker, the vegetation was non-frequent and broken, scattered tall trees of course appeared regularly, small and bigger hamlets came often. We reached a mud flat covered with taller Nalia grasses. The bank was almost 100 meters away, the mud flat was almost hidden, some open areas appeared on the waterline. We came closer, the tall green grass covered almost the entire area, no other sign could be seen, no life, the village was around 200 meter away behind the bank. Suddenly a small opening on the grass was seen, a long, black crocodile appeared, its body was partially hidden in the grasses, it was almost hidden behind the thick cover of the grasses an expert eye was needed to identify the big crocodiles in the basking places. The crocodile was motionless, body almost hidden; part of the top portion and the part of the tail was visible.

The river turned wide, the boat moved into the deep water, now more ripples on the grey water, the huge fishes of the sanctuary were hidden in the muddy waters, suddenly birds were seen, they appeared to be floating, the white birds, we came close, some were floating, some appeared to be standing. I couldn't understand, how a bird could stand on the water, no land was visible, the low tide was freeing more areas, the receding water was exposing mudflats, the dividing line between the new mud flats and the water was almost indistinguishable unless one comes closer, the mud flat was in deep grey, the water was in light grey, the reflecting sun from the water was prominent; from the water soaked mud flat the reflection was weaker, the ripples danced on the water. The brown headed gulls, called sea crow by the locals, were standing on the new mud flat, some were swimming very close to flat, as the water recedes further they stood on the soil, seeing so many birds at one place was increasing my curiosity. Till now I had not seen so many birds floating in the Bhitarkanika waters, I watched those birds carefully, they were white in colour, size was little bigger than common crow, legs and beak were orange red, head little brown. We were watching their movement, some were pruning their tails, their feathers, some trying to find any prey on the flat, some were swimming passively. Screening the new mud flat I couldn't believe my eyes, a huge crocodile, was laying still on the new flat, the land was not even 20 cm above the waterline. The water was going down on small channels created on the flat, it had come from the waters few minutes back, was lying a little ahead of the birds colony, the reptile was almost on the waterline. Its huge body was laying motionless, snout just above the water, the tail towards the land mass, the colour was more whitish than dark, snout closed, and the yellow eyes were opened as usual. No mangrove trees was seen in the vicinity, no pencil roots, the flat was like a slate, appeared so smooth, no line, only the presence of the huge reptile. No line of its coming, the crocodile was floating on the water, the water level reduced, the crocodile simply landed on the land from top, as if the reptile parachuted on the land through water, such was the incident. We came closer, the crocodile turned active, it slipped slowly, the snout went into the water, slowly and slowly the whole body went inside, the tail was visible now, the tiny tails appeared like a saw on the water body, and after few seconds it vanished. I couldn't believe my eyes again, not even 100 feet away one ripened paddy on the field started, the water must have receded from that area; a woman was cutting the paddy crop, the man eater was not far away, the woman in an orange saree was unaware of its presence, was busy in cutting the paddy on the higher flat. Man had encroached into the territory of the crocodiles, the flat should not have been occupied, now the greedy human had encroached upon the land, the life of the reptile as well as the precious human life were at stake, the conflict goes on, the crocodile here slipped into the water, I looked at the channel, few bubbles came, next moment the bubble vanished, the crocodile was the loser, the life of the woman was at risk, but here the crocodile was pushed to the corner, vanished under muddy waters.

After seeing so many crocodiles on the way, I looked at the statistics with me on the Saltwater crocodiles.

Trend of Saltwater crocodile population in Bhitarkanika.

Year	Hatchlings (< 50 cm)	Yearlings (51-90 cm)	Juvenile (90-120 cm)	Sub-adult (120-180 cm)	Adult (> 180 cm)	Total
1976-77		61	6	29	96	
1984-85		118	13	34	165	
2005	681	290	169	107	207	1454
2006	657	283	197	122	203	1462
2007	503	368	259	135	232	1497
2008	538	343	231	143	261	1516

Note: 1976-77- Pre-release population of crocodiles
1984-85- Post-release population of crocodiles

The above figures shows constant growth in crocodile population in the Bhitarkanika areas, for the year 2008, majority of crocodiles are found in Kanika area (1141), and other crocodile areas are Rajnagar (280), Mahakalpada (77), and Chandbali (18). Looking at the different population size in the year 2008, it is seen that hatchlings account for 35.8%, yearlings for 22.62%, Juveniles for 15.24%, sub adults for 9.44% and the adults account for 17.22% of total crocodile population.

A flock of Chha chadhei passed over the river, a large group; took a short straight flight, then suddenly changed the direction, a sharp curve in the flight and they vanished in the foliage of a tree. I looked ahead, five beautiful painted storks were standing on the right, from their size and stature; they looked like soldiers of the mud flats, stood there to defend their land. They were dropping their necks simultaneously for food, lifting the beaks in the next moment. The pink shadow was casted on the muddy water, was moving with the muddy water, the birds were standing silently on the low water, at their back little away from the water line on the mud flats, the Nalia grasses were growing tall, brownish white inflorescences were coming out from each plant, giving a greenish brown tinge.

We moved ahead, many mud flats came on the way on and on them crocodiles were lying idle. Slowly the forest alongside the channel was thinned, the human habitations appeared more frequently and we reached the meeting point of two big channel, the Bhitarkanika channel and the Patashala river; to our right now was a new mangrove patch, not as deep as the earlier mangrove forests; there beyond the grass lands, inside the forest, not far from the waterline, one big crocodile was lying. We came close, the crocodile was watching us, it came quickly through the grasses, entered into the water, the body came to the water and the crocodile started swimming for some time, its snout was above water, the crocodile was breathing through the nostrils, the huge yellow eyes were above the water level, it was watching us keenly. We had seen the crocodile entering into the water, so we could make out the snout and its body, if not watched earlier, the crocodiles were many times difficult to find, it appeared like a floating log, but in Bhitarkanika all most all floating logs were crocodiles. The long snout was visible, the nostril was just above the waterline, the head was elevated a little, and while we were watching its movements the crocodile dived further, no sign, ripples appeared all over.

Further down another crocodile appeared on the other side of the bank, there was no dense forest, few small trees, the water was receding fast, some channels were created on highland and through it water was gushing into the main channel; and on that elevated land one medium sized crocodile was sleeping, from it, around 20-30 feet away towards land side a road was passing, the electric poles were clearly visible. Another 100 feet away from the crocodile, parallel to the water channel, two big ash coloured herons were standing on the edge of the channel, those big birds had long sharp beaks, body heavier than the egrets. We came closer, the crocodile leaped into the water, water parted, the crocodile entered into its safe territory, the herons looked at the splash, and we moved ahead.

The story of Bali-Basuli

"Will you like to hear a beautiful love story of the land?" He asked me, I was also looking for a break, the crocodiles, the birds by that time were capturing my thoughts, a little change might bring more interest in the topic. His eyes were glued to the reflections on the water, so much of water flowed, his eyes were lowered, my eyes too were fixed on the dancing waves on the muddy waters. He continued while looking at the waves –

"Not much away from the deep forests, two lovers, the princess of Brahmin king of Bajragarh and the prince of Kumbhar King of Righagarh laughed a lot at seeing the beautiful waves on the river, the birds were flying over them on the black sky on that day; it was a beautiful love story." He paused, his eyes moved towards the flying white egrets, a big flock was passing over our head on the black sky, I too looked at the sky, how lovely they appeared in flight when they move in groups, the colour contrast was noticeable.

Bijuli was the only daughter of the Brahmin Choudhury king of Bajragrh, a girl, but she never dreaded the dark nights, always liked to move out, roamed in the deep forests alone, never feared the fearsome tigers on the land or crocodiles in the water, or the king cobras on the trees, the daring girl liked independence, after all she was a princess of courage. Once she went to the seat of Goddess Jayadurga in the forests, was praying to the goddess there, offered fresh flowers from the forests. With her astounding beauty she was looking like the goddess of love and Bali, the prince of Righagarh was surprised to see such a beautiful young woman in the deep forests; alone, she was offering prayers to the goddess. Both met at the seat of Jaydurga, they expressed their mind, the prince and princess fell in love before the goddess, Bijuli imagined Bali as her husband before the goddess, Bali accepted her as beloved in his thought. Bali was extremely happy to know about the mind of the goddess of love, he was in the other heaven, both lovers returned to their respective parents.

They spoke to their respective parents, the parents were shocked at such news, they were from different castes, the princess was Brahmin and the prince was a Kumbhakara, a lower caste than the Brahmins. But Bijuli was adamant, she didn't budge to the pleads, threats from her kins, her close ones, her decision to marry the prince was final; the Brahmin king finally gave in to the determination of his only daughter and arranged for the marriage.

Bali came with his full marriage team from his kingdom along with his father in their royal boat with great splendor; they arrived at the Bajragarh and were received well by the host king, father of Bijuli. The Brahmin relatives of the host king had already conspired to eliminate Bali, without the knowledge of the father of the princess, their own king; a Brahmin girl can't marry a Kumbhakar boy, even though he was a prince. Bali and his group were treated very well not seen in the land earlier, they were extremely happy at the behaviour of the Brahmin king. Bali was taken to a different place; the bridegroom had to be treated specially, he was separated from his own kins, the groom was the happiest man in the world at that moment, he was to marry his dream girl. Once was separated from other persons from his kingdom, the unsuspecting prince was killed in cold blood, the place was filled with his scream, the conspirators were ready for the moment, they spread the message – Bijuli was not a simple girl, she in fact was a goddess, a human can't marry a goddess, so the goddess herself had killed the prince. A lot of noise was created to give the killing the shape of wrath of the divinity, the Brahmins at that time created myths around them, in that melee the persons from the prince's side were highly confused, had there been an attack they could have understood the conspiracy, but after getting such a good reception they were totally confused; the people from palace were fleeing the area, rumour spread in no seconds, the goddess had turned blood thirsty, who would come on her way would be killed. All fled the area in panic, the young man was murdered in cold blood, the foods were buried to give the incident more dramatic turn, the Goddess was hungry and blood thirsty. She had even eaten the entire food.

Innocent Bijiuli saw her dreams shattered at the hands of her own kin, on whom she had unfathomable belief, they killed her lover in cold blood; she had witnessed the killing, the dagger of the killer pierced into the heart of bali in front of her and she couldn't react. She couldn't take the pain, the treachery was too much for beautiful young girl to bear; she ran to the Goddess Jayadurga, the girl cried before the Goddess, there she killed herself, on the feet of the Goddess.

The tragic story ended, slowly people forgot the incident, the Bhanja kings later captured Rigahgrh. Once in the dream of their king dreamed the soul of Bijuli appeared and informed that she was lying as an idol in the forests around the Goddess Jayadurga and expressed her wish – build a temple for her and celebrate the event. The king searched for the idol, recovered a stone figure from the nearby forest, and built a temple for the statue in the prenatal home of the Bijuli at Bajragarh. A tradition started as per the wish of Bijuli in the dreams, the Goddess of Bajragarh would marry mortal Bali every year; an earthen figure of Bali would be brought from Righagarh in a traditional boat to Bajragarh, a coconut would be given the shape of the bride Bijuli, both would sit on the marriage place, but before the marriage could be completed, the earthen figure of Bali and the other ceremonial items would be buried in a nearby pond; the memory of the incident thus passed from generation to generation; now take the shape of a celebration.

My heart turned heavy at the tragic incident and treachery, the young lovers could not meet, the emotions flowed down the waters, the memories turned faint, none of their ancestors remembered, they were lost with time, the ancestors also lost their identity.

I looked at the sky, on the dull white background huge open bill storks were flying, they flapped their wing for some time and floated in the wind; as the huge wings moved in the air a suu-suu sound was created drawing the attention of the onlookers. I looked at the bird keenly, what a shape, huge white coloured wings with black bands towards back side and also towards outer side were wide open, the long neck was stretched outward and the legs were extended fully backward; the picture of the bird appeared more like the birds of the Hollywood film *Avatar*; the thick and wide pointed beak attached to a large head was bent a little down; the bird on flight looked spectacular.

I looked at them, few feathers fell on the water, and I remembered the stanza

Udigale gendalia, Jhadidele para
Rajajhia Kandedekhi aha budhabara

(The open billed storks were flying away, the feathers were falling on the fields, the village girl was looking at the birds, her marriage was fixed, but the groom was older, she was unhappy, but she couldn't say that to her parents.)

The rural settings of olden, golden Odisha were reflected in the song, the birds, the animals were placed so close to the life of rural Odisha, in the songs, in the stories they appear frequently; life turns dull with their absence, accepts colour with their presence. The rural Odisha celebrate the Chitou Puja to offer cakes and other eatables to the snails of the ponds and fields. Let snails and fishes grow, the magnificent birds will get sufficient snails to eat, let the black sky is filled with them, let them fly and drop their wings. One open bill stork was flying low, very close to the top of a thatched house alongside the water channel, its wings were wide open the neck was pulled towards the body; it was almost touching the coconut tree alongside the house.

Then I looked at the flock of flying birds, the black line was drawn on the cloudy sky, the birds were returning, slowly they vanished behind the foliage lines, the sound of the ripples were coming from the creeks. Suddenly a long but non conspicuous sound came.

Gaan-gaan-gaain-maaaain-gaaanaaa, the crocodile of the creek was calling its mate, the water ripples continued to hit the boat, the banks, the water of the creek was rising.

The Northern Visitors.

Story of Shari & Description of Boita

Shari looked at her Boita, a floating vessel of ancient Odisha used for maritime trade, as if the bird of the far off countries was floating on the blue waters. She took a long breath, satisfaction was in her heart, the Boita was strong, sea worthy, beautifully designed; the carpenters of Kalinga were expert in making sea worthy boats. She looked at the long sky, the sea was merging with the sky at far off distance, her uncontainable desire to conquer the new land created a small fleet of strong Boitas, the sailors were strong, dedicated and adventurous, all were courageous, no fear for the sea, death even. She looked at the waters, beautiful birds were floating alongside her small armada, her Boita looked like huge birds, equally colourful, the shapes were matching with the floating birds; her Boitas were light like the birds, would float on the wavy waters, could pick up the speed of the floating bird, there was stamina to fly to the distant unseen world, to conquer the new land.

Suddenly a big group of birds descended on the waters, all big gooses, the migrants from northern lands, they were floating elegantly on the green-blue waters. At their side her Boitas were floating, dancing with every small wave, a light upward thrust and light fall, the dance of the birds and the Boitas were synchronized nicely, as if the same soul ran in the body of the birds and her Boitas, a smile passed on her shaped lips. The Boitas were nicely built, shape was matching the floating gooses, the front side was curved, crafted in the shape of head of a bird, beak, eyes were well formed on the wood, nicely coloured; the wooden birds were looking at the distant land. Materials, arms were fully loaded on the low decks, almost filling the decks; with full boats the bodies of the boat resembled that of the birds. The back of the boats were raised too, like the tails of those beautiful floating birds.

Shari again looked at the horizon on the south, blue waves were dancing, the far off sea was calling her, she wanted to fly like the birds of the horizon, her world had expanded with her imagination. Shari wanted to explore the new land, her uncontrollable spirit was looking for more, looking for new. Her father, her friends were on the bank, waving their hand, waving their heads, their young brave daughter was leaving her country to conquer new land, see new land; the kingdom of warrior sea merchants can't sit idle, the boys, the girls had to go out to win the new world. Shari looked at her friends, they all stayed with the green line, now she had boarded her Boita, she looked at the articles, diamond, pearls, topaz, turquoise, quartz and many more, father had given her sufficient wealth to survive, to trade. Enough provision of water and food, the workers were screaming in happiness, lot of enthusiasm in their work, the sailors were highly experienced, the Kurahadias and Kodalias – a group of people with arms, expert in creating troubles in other countries, and of course some expert swordsmen were bubbling with energy. To entertain the team, dancers, comedians, magicians accompanied the armadas, in long sea journey the group need to be entertained, need to be kept in best shape, they after all had aimed to conquer new land.

The princess was sitting on a gold covered chair studded with precious metals, her servants had put a long decorated umbrella over her head, she again looked at the dancing waves, her Boitas were about to enter into deeper waters, the birds were floating in low waters, she smiled, the birds of the far off countries had given her the courage, the birds were small, so they float in low waters, her heart was bigger, she floats in endless waters with her Boita, the wind was slow but pleasant, drifting her Boita into deeper waters. She was an expert in sailing, fighting, horse riding, archery, swimming, no prince of her land could match her skill, her courage; her father gave her the best education available, made her capable to win the world, after all that was the tradition of ancient Kalinga. The girl changed her dress, to look as a perfect sailor she wore the dress of the captain of the ship, golden earrings on her ears – the Kalingas wear earrings on their ears, the long pearl necklaces were running up to her waist, diamond rings on each of her fingers, on her crown she was wearing a big diamond; she now appeared like a wealthy sea merchant, but with a long sword at her waist she looked like a prince too she was not known by her people as Bidar Nayaka – the man who never fears anyone. She was adept in politics, made good friends. The courageous lady sailed her armada, the beautiful birds remained far away, they halted at many small ports, an expert in management of kingdom, she made friendship with the Tiger king, the Barha kings, later in a her adventure she might need their help.

They arrived at Srilanka, planned for conquer of the island, she wanted to have her own kingdom, at her direction the Kodalais and the Kurhadias entered into the kingdom and created trouble. The Dalimba king was surprised to see such trouble, came with his army to the camp of the Bidar Nayaka. The truce between the king and the sailor was not effective, a battle was resulted. Bidar Nayaka called for help from the Tiger king and the Barha king; her own people were highly expert in fighting too. Dalimba king of Srilanka was defeated, Shari was the winner, and she seized the kingdom, imprisoned the king, and brought the loser king to her Boita. Her people were surprised at the courage of the leader, Shari was extremely happy, strangely she fell in love with the imprisoned Dalimba King; but she couldn't tell her heart, a winner princess of Kalinga can't marry a loser king. She was much close to her land, the green lines were visible, the green waters, the hills, the orchards; she looked at her land, a smile reflected on her face, but next moment her heart turned heavy, she looked at her Boita, the wooden armada was dancing in the blue waters. She was taken aback, the birds were leaving, she had come back from the distant land, the birds were leaving for the unknown land, her heart turned heavier, tear rolled down from her cheeks.

I turned the page of the book, reading the stories of Shari, I simply drifted in my imagination to the olden times, I felt as if I was a member of her famous armada, a tiny one, but strong one. I looked at the front, a group of strange birds were swimming in front of her boat, except for that small group no other birds were visible nearby, the birds were flapping their wings, they were preparing for the departure, her Boita came closer, the birds flapped their wings and the whole group rose and flew towards the north. I imagined, Shari then looked at the flying birds, the line was getting thinner, the green lines were getting bigger, tear was streaming from her eyes continuously, her hands were now unsteady, and she lost control on the steering. Suddenly black clouds came, the birds now vanished behind the hills, the green water was not dancing anymore, bigger waves came continuously; and Shari instead of controlling her Boirta was looking at the long north, towards the direction of the vanishing birds, and her Boita got drowned, her win, her love, her defeat got drowned in the deep waters of the sea.

Journey to Nalaabna Island

The boat jumped a little on a bigger wave and next minute fell on the water with a big bang. I regained my consciousness, I recollected my position in the boat. I was looking at the birds, hundreds, thousands in front of me, like the beautiful Boita of Shari, the birds were floating on the green waters, jumping and falling with the tides, as if the armada of Shari filled the water mass; wherever the eyes goes hundreds and hundreds of birds. On my front hundreds of ducks were floating, almost the whole waterline was covered by them, their black head and partially white body was quite conspicuous, they were swimming leisurely; waves almost hidden part of their bodies, only dark heads were visible, for those on the crest the white body was visible. These ducks were appearing like group of naval soldiers, disembarked on the waterline for a fight, their heads strangely were away from our side, the naval soldiers were going for a mission. On the air, above the flock, a big group of birds were flying; they were looking for a better feeding place, their position looked like an umbrella over the floating ducks below, such were the numbers, such were the positions.

We came closer, the Nalabana sanctuary was a little away, another big group of birds, and our boat came closer. I was sampled overawed by their positions, their flying. The ducks were trying to move away from us, some simply ran for some distance over the water, the splashing water was creating white patches on the green waters, the birds were capable to take flight from water, unlike the domestic ducks who are incapable to take flight from water. I looked at a speeding duck, the head was elongated over the water at an angle towards front, remained above water; the small wings were moving fast, the legs were pushing water in backward direction, the wings were giving upward thrust, the legs were giving the forward motion; strangely the bird appeared like a rocket in a slanting position. The fully open wings at the lower body looked like fuel tank, the body was fully elongated, the upper head appeared like tip of the rocket, the splash on the water body appeared like initial rocket propulsions on the ground; such was the flight, such was the shape. We looked at the group, one by one the members started getting speed in that manner, and the entire group got airborne within a minute or two, the water surface was filled with splashes. The birds flew for short distance; the air was filled with so many brackets and irregular shapes, the heavy body was supported by strong motion of the wings, the wings moved from top to well low down, now the sky colour changed slightly, the dark and white lines moved over the blue sky; then they disembarked on the water, well away from any disturbance.

Slowly, the waterline changed, now a faint brown green line appeared on the front, the landmass in front of us was the famous Nalabana island, the blue water mass created a new world from the water a small white blue coloured structure appeared from the land mass, we were close to the Nalabana. Small pockets of land mass appeared here and there, wherever the eye went there were small small non contiguous land masses, long straight grasses covered all the protruding sandy landmasses with little soil, wide waterways were laid between them, it appeared like the lotus leaves on the water, only here the colour was brown. The masses were more elevated from the ground; the water appeared to be quite shallow there, not fit for navigation, the birds used to flock in those areas. We looked at the Nalabana sanctuary, our boat had anchored at deeper water, a small wooden boat was used to ferry us towards the land mass, the big boat can't come close, heavy weeds on the floor, only knee deep water prevented our movement. The small boat however moved on the manually created small deeper water channel, an easy way to reach to the Nalabana area. As we came closer, the water depth decreased further, small pockets of grass lands appeared more frequently, the wooden structure was more clearly visible standing just next to the deeper waterline. Smaller black winged stilt birds were standing on low waters just next to a small water mass surrounded by water, their long pinkish legs, long pointed beak were most suitable for feeding on low waters, for easy walking; those small birds surprisingly were not floating, they were walking on marshy land, they in fact feed on small water insects, mollusks, small seeds; for them with few inches deep water were the best feeding place. I zoomed my binocular on a bird, the small bird was standing on couple of centimeters low waters, weight on one feet, another feet was slightly lifted, the small black eyes on the relatively large head were looking forward, the pencil sharp black beak was pointed at an angle towards the waterline, the bird was ready for a strike. Like it, many birds of the same group were standing over small area with low waters, all looking at the small waves carefully, ready to pickup water insects.

We came closer, almost a stone's throw distance from the bigger Nalabana island, low green land appeared, to our side a group of white brown water birds were standing on the water, size and shape appeared to be similar to the doves, the marsh sandpipers were standing in hundreds in very low water, some almost on the protruding landmass. These small birds, around 25-30 cm with long pointed beaks were wader birds, waiting for the prey insects, small mollusks, were flocking in a big group, all were aiming towards the deeper water, with each small wave new foods were coming to them. Towards a little right, little away from them another big group of Bar – tailed Goodwit birds, a relative smaller bird, a wader group too, were foraging on low waters, like the marsh sand pipers they were all looking keenly at the low waters, the waves bring new varieties of food for them. Different groups of wader birds appeared frequently, where ever we looked different varieties of small waders in big groups flock the low waters.

Our small boat moved through the artificial channel, on both sides the grayish dark soil was covered with grasses, on the waterlines many small earth balls and furrows were seen which showed the presence of crabs on the muddy floor. The size of the grasses diminished as we entered into the bigger landmass, the big long grasses were much less, the vegetation evolved as per the need, with open land the necessity of long grasses was not there, the flat lands was covered mostly with short grasses, and short vegetation. A small isolated landmass appeared between bigger masses, separated by very low stagnant water body with small floating plants; on it a single black coloured Common Moorhen was standing, its size was almost size of a cock, was looking at us with curiosity; these birds live in swampy areas, are non migratory, are omnivorous, feeds on aquatic plants, insects, small fishes, mollusks, frogs. Seeing a residential bird of the Chilika in the emerging Nalabana landmass increased my curiosity, the emerging landmass supports both migratory as well as non migratory birds, in search of better foraging ground, the local birds also come to the Nalabana.

We covered some distance inside the Nalabana area through small navigable water channel, the movement on the boat was easy in the island, this mode of transportation in the Nalabana was quick, didn't disturb the water birds due to the movement in the 8-10 feet wide defined channel. On our both sides, the land masses with very low grasses extend up to the horizon, 1-2 tall dry trees appeared here and there, probably those pockets were not submerged during the rains.

On the water channel, a small area was secured with nets, sticks were put in a rectangular shape, nylon net was tied to the sticks, creating an enclosure on the low water, a bird rescue centre. I looked inside, few birds were floating, all ducks, some Pintails, some Shovellers; they were rescued from the different areas in and around Nalabana and were treated in the small enclosure, would be freed once they were cured.

We moved to the lone cement structure in the island from the water channel, the watch tower for the protection of the birds was created so that a watch and ward on the birds can be kept without disturbing them. In this light green coloured single storey watch tower, the flanks were covered with stone and cement to give strength to the structure during the submergence period and a cemented staircase ran to the watchtower portion at first storey from the land. We climbed to the watch tower, watched the beauty of the Nalabana area, the land was not very big, not many land forms were there, it looked insignificant, uninteresting; but the idea changed in no time as we spotted different birds on the landmass. Varieties of ducks appeared on the land – some were taking rest, many actually feed during the afternoon or evening. The area was almost flat land, like a plain football field with very low stagnant waters at pockets, as the water recedes, low lands were getting emerged, free of waters. I looked at a small group of Brahminy ducks near to a very low stagnant water on the open land, some were sitting on the grass with their belly down, some were standing, their pink legs were visible; this bird is the most respected bird of the Chilika, the Brahminy ducks associated with the legend, they are symbol of fidelity, also with their arrival the storm stops in the lake. To their left, in the stagnant low waters another big group of white grey birds were flocking, I couldn't distinguish them from such long distance, after them again the land mss continued for long distance till it met the blue waters of Chilika. Just little above the land some birds were flying, some descended on the land, some raised from the land, the birds were busy in their daily chord.

After watching them for some time we returned through the same water channel, the birds appeared continuously at different places, on the land, also on low waters. A depth measuring post-coloured in white and red was erected on the water, to inform about the depth of water in that area, over which a Pallas's Fish Eagle was sitting alone. This dark brown coloured bird is a threatened species in the lake, rarely found, is one of the hunting birds of Chilika, is around 80 Cm long, it mainly feeds on fish, water fowls, water birds, snakes, frogs and turtles. The food chain in the Nalabana starts from the vegetative matters and ends at the hunter birds like the eagle here, all are interlinked.

We came deep into the waters of Chilika, big group of Common Pochard diving ducks appeared in deeper water, they dive deep around 10-20 feet water in search of food. I looked at them, the number reduced, many dived, many surfaced next moment. We came closer; the birds tried to move away, to gain speed they almost ran on the water, the position of the legs and the heavy body needs time to give right propulsion in the beginning, they flew for short distance and descended on the water again.

Seeing so much of the birds at Chilika, I thought of knowing a little about Chilika, unless the information is available, Chilika wouldn't be understood so I tried to refresh my knowledge.

General Information on Chilika lake

The Chilika lake is a low coastal wetland, is the largest brackish water lake in Asian continent, also the second largest brackish water lagoon in the world, and most importantly this lake is a combination of marine, brackish (this water is more saline than fresh water, but much less than seawater due to mixing of seawater with fresh water) and fresh water ecosystems. The lake environment supports wide variety of flora and fauna, over 540 vertebrates and a number of endangered species. This large lake extends over the present districts of Khurda, Puri and Ganjam, is around 64.3 km in length and the width varies between 5-18 km; the water mass area also varies between 906 sq. km to 1165 sq. km depending upon seasons. The lake can be divided into different habitats like marshlands, mudflats, coastal areas, fresh water and open water habitats with varying depth of salinity and the vegetation includes 1-submergent (a type of plant which is completely below the water surface. Most these plants are strongly rooted in the soil, 2-emergent (a type of plant which grows in water but is partially in air), 3-mixed, 4-reed beds and 5-grass lands.

The northern sector of the lake is the shallowest part, is mainly a fresh water zone and area wise is the largest with diversified flora. The southern sector of the lake is smaller but deeper. The central sectors have depth and water salinity between northern and southern sector. The water depth varies between 41-448 cm at different locations, the deepest portion towards the outer channel and minimum depth is found towards Bhusandpur area in the northern sector. With the rains, the water level starts to increases from July, and highest water level is observed during the month of September; the lowest water level is recorded in the summer months.

The Eastern Ghat hills starts from the western and southern periphery of the lake. Some small important islands like Parikud, Barkuda (Honeymoon island), Nalabana, Somolo, etc. are located inside the lake. A 32 km long outer channel connects the lake with Bay of Bengal near village Sipakud.

Some distributaries of river Mahanadi like Daya, Bhargabi, Nuna discharge their water into the lake and accounts for largest volume of fresh water inflow in the lagoon. The other smaller rivers like Ratnachira, Kani, Malaguni, Dhanua and Salia in the western side also discharges water into the lake. A total of 52 numbers of rivers and rivulets drain water into the lake.

The lake is the largest winter visiting place for migratory birds on the Indian sub-continent. The water birds include water fouls, shore birds or waders and sea birds who use this wetland for the nesting, feeding and roosting. Apart from those birds other wetland dependent birds mainly raptors, kingfishers, etc. are also found. Many of the water birds are migratory; undertake annual journeys in well defined fly ways between their breeding and non-breeding grounds. About 129 water bird species belonging to 19 families are found in the lake; the lake supports about 7 lakhs to 9 lakhs water birds annually. The lake plays an significant role in the life of migratory and non migratory birds, and acts as a resting and feeding places for the migrant water bird species, The lake system plays as the breeding grounds for some residential birds.

The birds congregate at different areas in the lake, the prominent among them are Nalabana island and Mangalajodi. The Nalabana was declared as a sanctuary during 1987, is a small island with an area of about 15.5 sq. km, and is located in the central sector of the lake. The Nalabana area mostly remains submerged in water during the rainy season and emerges in the winter months and dries up during March-April, this area used to remain under four- five feet of water at the beginning of the arrival of the first migratory bird which starts from October; that time only few small land masses come out, the major masses still remain under water. This kind of emergence is important for higher biomass production which in turn attracts a large congregation of birds of different species compared to any other area of the lake; it attracts over 60% of the total bird population of the lake. The winter birds use this area for resting, roosting, feeding and moulting; over 450000 water birds have been recorded in this portion.

Mangaljodi is another prominent bird congregation site in a fresh water zone adjoining the northern sector of the lake with marshes, areas with emergent vegetations. The Mangaljodi area is much bigger, is around 58.59 sq. km, and the area is dominated by reeds and about 11.78 sq. km. area is marsh land and wet meadows. The fresh water birds like common coot, moorhens, rails, crakes, migratory warblers and bitterns are generally found in this portion.

As per a survey conducted in the lake, 45 per cent of the birds are terrestrial in nature, 32 per cent are waterfowl, and 23 per cent are waders. This Lagoon also houses 14 types of raptors, around 135 rare and endangered Irrawaddy Dolphins and about 37 species of reptiles and amphibians

The lake is important from international angle, as per the Ramsar Convention, a wetland is considered as internationally significant if it regularly supports 1% of bio-geographical population of one species or sub species of water birds. For 45 species of birds found in the lake, the population exceeds the 1% threshold population (it is the minimum number of birds necessary for a particular service can be provided in an area); in 5 species over 30% of the threshold population has been recorded which proves the significance of Chilika lake.

The birds play a major role in the Chilika eco-system, the birds help recycle of nutrients back into the ecosystem through their guano, the quantity guano dropped into the lake eco system by the ducks and geese is estimated to be equivalent of around 33.8 tons of nitrogen, 10.5 tons of phosphorus which results in higher biomass and fish production. The water birds clip the aquatic plants when they eat, helping in fresh sprouting of tender shoot, thus increasing the fish feeding base. Also due to the foraging by the water birds, the vegetation get thinned which facilitates movement of fishes.

It has been observed that the docks and geese are the prominent migratory birds, they account for around 85% of total migratory water bird population followed by wading or shore birds which are the second largest number. Most of the migrating birds of Chilika breed outside the Indian subcontinent; some birds of course migrate from Ladakh, Kashmir and sometimes central and eastern Himalayas. Most of the migratory birds come from far off areas in Eastern Europe (Belarus, the Russian Federation from the Ukraine,) the Western and Central Siberia, South West Asia, from Baharin, Turkey, Uzbekistan, Western Asia (Western part of Russian Federation bordering Caspian Sea, Central Asia, Afghanistan to Uzbekistan, south Asia from Bangladesh, Bhutan, Nepal to Sri Lanka), Eastern Asia from China, Korea, Japan to Russia.

During the year 2007, nearly 840,000 migratory birds visited the lake, out of which 198,000 were found in Nalabana area. Another bird census during January, 2008, estimated 900,000 birds arrival out of which 450,000 were found in Nalabana. There has been a significant increase in the migratory bird population; the primary reason for such increase is the removal, especially of invasive water hyacinth species, a freshwater aquatic weed plants, and also due to restoration of salinity of the lake by opening new mouth.

Among the birds, big flocks of Greater flamingos from Rann of Kutch in Gujarat, also even from Iran, have been noticed in the shallow waters; and other-long legged waders like Goliath Heron, Grey herons, and Purple herons, Lesser Flamingos, Spoonbills, Storks, Egrets and Black-headed Ibis are also found. Many birds are rare like Asiatic Dowitchers, Dalmatian Pelican, Pallas's Fish-eagles, and very rare migrant species like Spoon-billed Sandpiper and Spot-billed pelican.

Many raptor birds like the White-bellied Sea Eagle, Pariah Kite, Brahminy Kite, Kestrel, Marsh harrier, peregrine falcon are noticed in the lake.

The short-legged shorebirds like Plovers, Dunlin, the Collared Pratincole, Ruff, Snipes and Sandpipers, Larks, Wagtails and Lapwings are seen in large numbers on narrow bands along the shifting shores, and also on the mudflats. In the deeper water long-legged Avocets, Stilts and Godwits are also found.

In the higher vegetated areas birds like Coots, Moorhens and Jacanas are found; along the shores birds like Pond Heron, Night Herons, Little Cormorant, Kingfishers and Rollers are found. In the waters, flocks of different ducks like Brahminy Ducks, Shovellers, Pintails, Gadwall, Teals, Pochards, Geese and Coots are also found.

The bird groups were highly confusing, I find it so difficult to remember, and those difficult names were very hard of course. Every year bird census is carried in Chilika. I opened a page, the migratory waterfowl census during 2008 gives some interesting figures about the arrival of different migratory birds.

Species	Population during 2008
Gadwall	169,506
Lesser Flamingoes	56
Northern Pintail	113,915
Bar headed geese	1,274
Shoveller	107,998
Brahminy duck	1,927
Pochards (Common, red crested)	69,910
Grey lag goose	161
Coots	73,665
Small pratinocole	7,003
Wigeon	68,211
Black tiled Godwit	33,233
Gargeny	41,065
Bar tailed Godwit	27
Greater Flamingoes	1,624

Reading so much about the birds, I was thinking of the summer areas, so far away, at the northern extreme points of the world in Siberia, so much of land, so many terrains, hostile atmospheres, and still the birds find their ways to this lake, and also other wintering sites, the phenomenon is a mystery. I refreshed my knowledge on migration of the birds.

Bird Migration

Migration from one place to another place is important in the life cycle of many birds, not all birds of course migrate, and without this yearly trip many birds would not be able to raise their youngs properly as food, water, and a protected place to nest and breed are the necessities for a bird's survival. In the same place there could be stiff competitions and with change of season, sometimes a comfortable living environment transforms to a hostile place to live in; so birds migrate to find the, most abundant food sources that will provide them adequate energy to nurture their young.

Different types of birds like the waterfowl, sea birds and land birds, migrate to suitable places annually, and they usually migrate at night, not during day. Many large water birds use customary stopover places along their flyways and come again, year after year, to the same nesting and wintering areas. Their flight is dependent on bird's preferance to fly in clear skies and with a good tail wind; and under suitable conditions they can cover several hundred kilometers during a single high-altitude flight. Compared to other types of birds, the seabirds are very well-adapted for very long distance migration over long oceans. The land birds too migrate as far as weather is less severe and most summer land birds migrate at night.

Many species of birds move in flocks may stay together for the entire journey. The young birds learn the routes of travel and layover sites from the experienced adults.

Flying over such a long distance is a strenuous activity, a lot of energy is needed for the long journey. As the migration time approaches, length of the day changes, metabolism changes takes place in the body of the bird and fats gets accumulated under its skin, or some species that make longnonstop flights, the amount of fat deposited can be equaling half their body weight or more. It is extremely essential for migrating birds to find good, steady food supplies before and during their journey.

The migratory birds may shift to appropriate altitude to find the proper wind "conveyor belt"; the wind at higher altitude sometimes move in the reverse direction than the wind on the ground, and usually blow strongly. The larger birds depend on thermals (hot air) rising from the land in the mornings to gain proper altitude by soaring,the Bar-headed Geese even crosses the Mount Everest during its migration. The waterfowl and shore birds generally fly at higher altitude; sometimes they fly at 10,000 feet or even as high as 20,000 feet when they are making long, over-water flights.

During migration, the birds adjust themselves to the compass points using the location of the sun and the stars; they are capable to know the magnetic north. They also use other signs like image of the land, smell of the sea, sound of waves on shores and winds through mountain passes. Different important tools he migrating birds depend to orient themselves appropriately during migration are as follows.

Sun Position – Many birds negotiate the proper direction if a clear view of the sun is possible. The night migrants also use the sun as a sign, as most start during the twilight.

Star Position – The night migrant adjust themselves in the right direction under clear, starry skies, they learned to orient as per the position of the constellations.

Recognition of Odour – Some short-distance migrants, usually the land birds, recognizes the odour of nesting and wintering sites.

Magnetic Compass – Many kinds of birds possess a built-in magnetic compass to use during cloudy days.

Arrival of Migratory Birds & Behviour of local birds

With the onset of winter, the migratory birds arrive in group, usually comes from north and few from south direction, their arrival is mainly concentrated in the northern areas of the lake, some birds also land in nearby areas like Bhusandpur, Kalupada, Panchakudi, Jarman, Chitrakuti. It is observed that from mid October the birds in small groups starts appearing in the sky and their arrival continues up to the month of November. During the flight they fly in the formation in the shape of V, the wide open space towards the far end and the shape closes towards the front. The group size usually varies between 100 and 500 plus numbers; rarely the size is as small as 15 and while flying some sound like S-U-U-U-U used to be generated. These migratory birds used to arrive during night, generally during the moon period, not during the dark period. Among the birds, the docks used to arrive first and the Brahminy duck used to arrive last, within a month of arrival of the first migratory group. The arrival of the Brahminy duck called Panda in the local language, some also called it Chakua-Chakoi, shows the end of the rains; the people are then sure, there would not be any storm, the Chakua birds have arrived.

Looking at the pattern of arrival, it is seen that the female birds arrive first, followed by the males after almost a week or two. The Nalabana area is initially filled with the females of different species, ugly looking birds found swimming all over the water mass; in bird community the males are more attractive than the females. Similarly, when the birds return, the female returns first, the male returns after a week or two.

When the migratory birds arrive, the local residential birds congregate in Nalabana, as if to receive the visiting migratory birds; which is a matter of surprise. The residential birds of Chilika are scattered around the villages, still they fly over the water body and gather at Nalabana to greet the migratory birds, and their behaviour is just like the human beings, happy at the arrival of the distinguished guests. No aversion is shown for the new comers, rather the local birds welcome the migratory birds, and there used to be no fight for space and food.

Departure of birds

With the advent of southern wind, the number of waves in Chilika increases, and Chilika waters become more and more unstable, the birds prepare for their departure journey. Before their departure birds of the same species gather together, the harmoniously living species like Pin tail and Shoveller grouped differently without any reason. Birds of the same group suddenly move upward, fly a little and descend thereafter. Sometimes, the same species of birds sit together, flap their wings together, and prim their feathers together. They size their feathers, swim together, bath together, and suddenly fly to the air as if they are leaving, take V shape in air and descend after sometime; this drill continues for some days and in one day they suddenly leave the lake for the summer place in far north.

The water bird groups including the residential birds have been made for the lake, the groups in Chilika are as follows.

Water bird groups in Chilika

Bird Group	Bird Group
Cormorants and Darters	Pelicans
Cranes	Plovers, Lapwigs
Ducks, Geese and Swans	Pratincoles
Flamingos	Rails, Crakes, Moorhens and Coots
Grebes	Sandpipers, Stints, Snipes, Godwits, and Curlews
Gulls, Terns and Noddies	Skimmers
Herons, Egrets and Bitterns	Stilts and Avocets
Ibises and Spoonbills	Stone Curlews and Stone Plovers (Thick Knees)
Jacana	Storks
Painted Snipes	

Different types of aquatic birds are found in the Chilika lake; some information on the birds category is given below.

WADING BIRDS

Generally they are long-legged birds, such as a cranes herons or storks, which frequent shallow water in search of food. The distinguishing characteristics of these birds are as follows:

The Wading birds show several distinguishing physical characteristics which are mainly:

Legs: All the wading birds have long, slim legs and expanded agile toes which help them to maintain balance in swampy areas, generally muddy, thus unstable. The longer legs also help them to forage in deeper waters.

Bill: The wading birds generally have long bills, frequently with typical shapes for efficient foraging. The bills can be sharply pointed, or have distinct curves, sometimes take spatulate shapes depending on the nature of foods these birds live on.

Neck: The necks for these birds are long, agile, and take different shapes as per the posture of the bird. The neck muscles are powerful which help wader birds such as egrets and herons to hunt effectively by spearing the prey.

Foraging: During hunting, the wading birds are highly patient and can stand without motion for long periods, waiting for prey to come within the striking distance. When they move for the prey, they remained very careful; the steps are slow and deliberate with an intention not to scare the prey.

Flight: During flight, these birds typically extend their legs fully to the rear, the feet often the legs stretch past the tail. The necks may be contracted or extended in flight depending on the species; the neck positions are useful for identification of the bird in flight.

DUCKS

The ducks are relatively long-necked birds, not as long-necked as the geese and swans, their body is broad and elongated; the body shape of diving ducks is more rounded. Their bill is usually broad, with serrated lamellae; which are required to filter mud and water from feed. These birds have very strong but generally short and pointed wings.

Most of the migrant birds coming to Chilika are docks species, which are divided into two categories:- the dabbling and the diving species.

Dabbling Ducks

The dabbling ducks are a type of shallow water ducks which feed mostly on the surface of the water or by tipping headfirst into the water to graze on aquatic plants on shallow waters. The important dabbling ducks are the gadwall, the garganey, the pintail, the shoveler, the teals, and the wigeons. These ducks generally do not dive deep and are usually found floating in shallow waters where they can reach for food by up-ending without getting completely submerged. These ducks are fast fliers. They often forage near the shore for seeds and insects. These birds have flat broad bills. In these ducks the males are usually little larger and more attractively coloured than the females.

In dabbling ducks, compared to other types of ducks, the legs are placed more towards the centre of the body, which enable them to walk well on land.

Diving Ducks

The diving ducks, commonly called pochards or scaups, are a category of ducks which dive deep into water and swim underwater to feed on water plants, insects and sometimes small fishes. These ducks are very good swimmers, can dive into deep waters for protection. Compared to dabbling ducks, their legs and feet are situated further back on the body which helps them with their propulsion in the water. However this position of the legs makes their walking difficult on land, so not many are actually found on land. The diving ducks are heavier than the dabbling ducks, their weight helps them to dive easily, but they find it difficult to take off for flying.

These birds used to go deep into the water in search of food, usually found floating in areas with 16-20 ft deep water, and occasionally diving into the bottom for weeds. The presence of those birds in deep water confirms availability of food materials, particularly weeds in that area.

The most noticeable difference between dabbling ducks and diving ducks are the size of the feet, for dabbling ducks the feet are generally smaller as they do not require the extra propulsion to dive for their forage, for diving ducks the feet are larger. Another important difference is how they take off, the dabbling ducks jump straight up from the water and where as the diving ducks need momentum to take off; so these birds must run across the water for a short distance to gain flight.

The ducks feed on a variety of foods such as grasses, aquatic plants, fish, insects, small amphibians, worms, and small molluscs.

The ducks are usually monogamous, usually a duck pair remain attached to each other for a year. The duck species mostly breed once a year and they make a nest before breeding.

Some important Migratory Birds:-

Godwall

This duck is a migrant bird from Central Asia, and is one of the commonest wintering duck found all over India, except for south India where it is rare.

The male during the breeding period is dark brown and grey with whitish belly, light chestnut wings and a black tail end. In Gadwall duck the male is slightly larger than the female, weighing on average 990 g.

These ducks are generally found in marshy areas with plenty of aquatic vegetation cover. These ducks form only small flocks and are a fairly quiet group.

This duck mainly feeds on seeds, shoots and tubers of marshy plants and aquatic weeds and grains of wild and cultivated rice. Occasionally they eat insects, worms, molluscs, etc.

Northern Pintail

This bird is a migrant from Central Siberia and Central Asia and is around 56 cm long, is among the most widespread migratory ducks in entire India. This duck is a relatively large duck with a long pointed tail.

The male has elongated body, slender neck and long pointed pin like central tail feathers, The colour of head and throat are chocolate and the hind neck is black; a black white band runs down on either side of neck.

This bird prefers brackish lagoons and estuaries; they nest on the ground, often a little away from water. They are highly sociable, form large mixed flocks with other species of duck.

The Pintail feeds mainly in the evening or at night, and spends much of the day resting. This bird mainly feeds on grasses, corns, shoots, and seeds of aquatic plants. Sometimes it also feeds on molluscs, worms, water insects and larvae.

The Pintail walks comfortably on land, has a very fast flight, with its wings slightly swept-back, not straight out from the body like some other ducks.

Shoveller

The Shoveller is a common and widespread duck, has a large spatulate bill, the colour of breeding male is glossy metallic, has dark green head, the breast is white and belly is chestnut, also the flanks. These ducks are around 51 cms long have a wingspan of 76 cm, and weighs up to 600 g.

This duck is a dabbling duck, dabble for plant food in low water by swinging its bill from side to side and use the bill to pull food from the water. Their wide-flat bill has well-developed lamellae – a small, comb-like structures on the edge of the bill which act like a sieve, it enables the birds to skim crustaceans and plankton from the water's surface.

They nest in grassy areas away from open water.

This duck is a fairly quiet duck.

Common Pochard

The pochard duck is of the size of a domestic duck and is around 48 cm long.

The adult male has a long dark bill with a white grey band, a chestnut head and neck, a black breast, red eyes and has a white grey back. The adult female has a brown head and body and a narrower grey bill band. The triangular head shape is distinctive feature of this duck.

Their breeding habitats are the marshes and lakes where water depth is one meter or more.

These docks form large flocks in winter, often mixed with other diving ducks.

These birds feed mainly by diving or dabbling. They eat aquatic plants with some molluscs, aquatic insects and small fishes; often they feed at night.

Coots

The Coots are medium-sized water birds, around three quarter size of a domestic duck, around 42 cm long, have slate coloured black feathers; the bill is pointed and ivory white in colour. The bird is a common resident and winter migrant to places all over India. They have rounded wings.

These birds are vegetarian; mainly take plant material, but sometimes also feed on small animals. During the breeding season they are very aggressive on territorial occupation, otherwise they are often found in sizeable flocks on the shallow vegetated lakes.

These birds require a great deal of effort to become airborne, pedaling across the water with their feet before lifting off.

These birds are frequently seen swimming in open water. They can dive for food, also are capable of forage on land.

Wigeon

The Wigeon is a dabbling duck, is around 42–50 cms long and has wingspan of about 71–80 cms, and weigh up to 680g.

The breeding male has grey flanks and back, the bill is blue-grey with black tip, with a black rear end, dark metallic green speculum and a white patch occur on upper wings. This bird has a brown pink breast, white belly, and a chestnut head with a creamy top.

This bird is generally found in open wetlands, and usually avoids deep water. It feed on different aquatic plants, algae, grasses, seeds, it sometimes also feeds on water insects, molluscs, etc. This bird nests on the ground, the nesting sites are found near to water and are under cover.

THIS BIRD FORM LARGE FLOCKS

Garganey

The Garganey is a small dabbling duck, it migrates from West and Central Siberia, and is one of the commonest winter migrants occurring all over India. It is of the size of a domestic duck, the length is around 41 cm.

The adult male has brown head and breast and has a broad white crescent over the eye. The rest of the plumage is grey. These ducks have a grey bills and legs.

They prefer grasslands adjacent to shallow marshes and lakes.

This bird generally feeds on seeds, arable crops, occasionally aquatic insect larvae, and molluscs. These birds feed mainly by skimming rather than upending.

In this species, the male has a distinctive crackling mating call.

Black tailed Godwit

The Black-tailed Godwit is a large, long-legged wader, is around 41-50 cm long with a wingspan of 70–82 cm, has long and narrow bill. The bird migrates from Central Asian Siberia, its size is similar to a domestic hen, and is a common winter migrant to entire India. The males weigh around 280 g and females around 340 g, the female is around 5-10 % larger than the male, and the bill is also 12-15% longer. During the breeding season the bill has a yellowish or orange-pink base and a dark tip; otherwise the base is pink in winter. The legs of this bird are dark grey, brown or black, the upper part of the body is grey-brown.

This bird prefers inland jheels, shallows and mud banks of rivers, lakes and reservoirs, sometimes also brackish lagoons, tidal waters.

This bird is carnivorous; feeds mainly on molluscs, crustaceans, also seeds of aquatic plants.

Brahminy duck

The Brahminy duck is a large orange-brown coloured duck, around 58–70 cm long with a 110–135 cm wingspan. The head is paler than the body; the wings are white with black flight feathers. The legs and beak are black in colour. During the breeding season, the male has a black ring at the bottom of the neck. They give a loud wild honking call. This bird is generally found in pairs, sometimes form small groups, and very rarely form large flocks. These birds are omnivorous; feed on grains, tender shoots and tubers, molluscs, aquatic insects, small reptiles, etc.

They prefer large open lakes, rivers with large shingle banks and mud flats.

They used to arrive late, during last week of October to first week of November, usually after the arrival of other migratory birds, and leave the lake quite late, almost after the departure of other birds, stays upto mid April.

Interesting story about the flamingoes

We left the Nalabana island for Parikud island. I looked back at the Nalabana island, a group of flamingoes were foraging in little deep water, my companion told me an interesting story about these birds, a bird can really create a miracle.

Bhgirathi Dev, the king of the small island of Parikud in Chilika lake was extremely worried, he simply couldn't think of a war against the mighty Khordha kingdom. He never thought Khordha king would send the army to his kingdom, he was after all a small landlord, can't dare the power of Khordha. He had already lost to Khordha king in the battle at Banapur, fled from his kingdom and took refuge at remote Parikud Island. Those words were heartbreaking, the behaviour of the large king was insulting, a Khaysatriya man can't tolerate such words, such behaviour. There were not many paths before him, fight and get killed in the battle and attain martyrdom, people would remember him for his courage and his bravery for the small land, or live like slave and get tortured continuously; he choose the first path. It was better to fight a battle, though an unequal one, but better to die once in a battle field, let the last drop of the blood redden the black soil of Chilika. He looked at his soldiers, few hundred men, can't be a match for the mighty Khordha army, gloom in their face, they knew – they were going to die, they might kill many, but before the flood of soldiers, they didn't stand a chance, but they were Paikas, the warriors of the land, they would fight till the last blood ooze out of their body.

The Dalapati was busy in encouraging the soldiers, the morale need to be high, was explaining the war strategies, which Vyuha need to be formed. The Ardhachndra vyuha, the soldiers of Khordha would butcher them from distance using their bows. The Vajra Vyuha appeared to be better, but the flanks were weakened in this formation, it was better to form Garuda Vyuha, the defensive posture, the front forces can be effective during attack, the bird formation appeared to be better; he had to adopt both defensive and offensive postures. The Dalapti looked at the flying eagle; the huge hunter bird dived deep in air with great speed and caught a bird prey in no time from a big folk, before the prey bird actually knows, before the folk reacts. The king discussed about the formation, he was not very enthusiastic about this type of formation, he was terribly upset, they were going to die for the cause of respect. His army was not well equipped as the Khordha army. His weaponry was limited and not as modern as the Khordha soldiers, but he had to show a courageous face.

As per his direction, the spears men came to the front, at the beak side with their long spears, they would reach the opposite force from longer distance. The swords men remained at the centre, at the body portion with their swords and axes, on the wings the spears men were ready with their spears. A very small number of archers were kept at the back, all need to be involved, they were only a few, were facing thousands; but the formation was like an eagle, the most powerful bird of the bird kingdom, they would harm the opponents.

The battle was scheduled to be fought at Gurubai nashi in Chilika area, a place generally gets dried up during October, and remains submerged during the rainy months. The Khordha soldiers were coming by boats, the messenger had already given the message about the size of the army, the weaponry at their disposal, and their expertise. The Khordha Paikas were well armed with bows and arrows, spears; they were capable of striking them from a distance. The foot soldiers were well-armed, body armor covered the entire body, head gears on the head, the katha was covering the neck, cross belts, kavachas, vahutti, kalingi, hata on the arms and forearms and were holding strong shields; they were well armed from head to toe with weapons like chakra, gupti, dagger,noose, vajra, caltrop apart from swords.

Bhgirathi Dev was getting nervous with each news, the messengers were coming contineously from the opposite coast, he knew all would be killed in the battle. He looked at the green waters of Chilika, the waves were dancing, the birds were flocking, so many colourful birds, they were flapping their wings, some were diving, some were flying just above the water. He knew, next day he wouldn't be there to see those beautiful birds. He went to his palace, Mother Kali was the reigning deity of Parikud, now more popularly known as Mother Kalijai, for her help in the battle; let the death come without fear. After offering the prayer to the Goddess, the king proceeded to the battle field and waited for the arrival of the Khordha army from opposite side of the lake.

The Khordha Paikas slowly appeared in the northern horizon, their body armors were shining in the bright sunlight, all were well-dressed, and their war cries was coming from such long distance, carried by the wing. The king looked at the direction of the seat of the Goddess Mother Kali. She could only do some miracle; and strangely miracle happened, they never thought of it, never understood it too.

As the king bowed his head, all the soldiers bowed their head at the direction of the Goddess, a large group of big flamingos alighted from the sky at the same place and started foraging. The soldiers raised their heads; they saw so many birds, numbering more than few thousands, were standing in a line, foraging in front of the them in knee deep water. The huge size of the birds and with bright colour, the flamingo flock appeared like a big army from a distance.

The Khordha soldiers were still little away, not within the striking distance of the arrows of Parikud soldiers, the war cries of the Khordha soldiers were filling the atmosphere. Suddenly the war cries stopped, no sound came from the big boats coming from the northern side. The Khordha Dalapati was crest fallen to see such a huge well dressed army in front, Parikud, they knew as a small kingdom, incapable to raise a big disciplined army; at that time, to them, the flamingos appeared like naval soldiers of Parikud; the miracle of Goddess Kali worked, the Khordha soldiers could not distinguish between the birds and the actual soldiers of Parikud, they were overawed by the sheer size of the army of Bhagirathi Dev. The Khordha commander was at his wits end, his land soldiers were not ready to face such big group of naval soldiers, they can't simply land on the battle ground, the dismemberment means sure deaths to the soldiers; and as an wise commander he decided to retreat, the Parikud king would be taught a lesson at right time later. He withdrew his soldiers, Parikud was saved, massacre was avoided because of the flamingos; and the people still believe, Mother Kali had directed the flamingos to alight at the battle ground to create confusion in the mind of the Khordha king. These are strange group of birds, found always in a line, no flamingos ever goes ahead of another flamingo, and never snatch food from the fellow colleagues; this behaviour of the bird confused the Khordha army.

We were approaching the Parikud island. I lost the track of time as the story was so interesting, I never thought a bird could confuse the group of seasoned soldiers, the bird must be unique, I looked at a congregation, at the backdrop green tree lines a big flock of flamingos were foraging, hundreds of them, were standing in low waters. From coast lines towards little deeper waters, everywhere the white pink birds were standing, some on low waters, some little deeper water, their long feet held them well above the blue waters. They were almost in line, almost a orderly formation, on same depth a group was standing, their long curved beaks were almost dipped simultaneously into the water, the upper body little curved, appeared like the body of naval soldiers, the beak and long throat appeared like long swards, they appeared more likely a human formation from a distance.

Flamingoes

Earlier the flamingos used to remain throughout the year except for 3-4 rainy months, in Chilika. Now a days it has been observed that they, though not in larger number but in smaller number, remain present during the rains and summer too, stayed near Nalabana after it is dried up during summer, sometimes they are also found at Sunada Nashi near Parikud.

The flamingos, also called Era in the local language, are the tallest birds of the area, there are two varieties of flamingos, the greater flamingos and the other relatively smaller to them, are the lesser flamingos. The lesser flamingos are more pinkish than the greater flamingos. The bigger flamingo stands at around 4½ feet, its neck is fairly long, beak is red in colour and curved at the end, the red coloured legs are very long. The red-pink part of the feathers remain hidden behind the white wings, so the bird appear to be white while standing, these birds are actually of three colour – white, black and pink, while flying in the air, it appears pinkish, while standing it is white.

The flamingos form large groups, big groups are found on low sandy areas, they prefer sandy areas than muddy areas; in Chilika they are generally found around Nalabana and nearby areas where sufficient green algae, their main diet is available and also they feed on brine shrimps; their beaks are specially adapted to separate mud and silt from the food they eat. The flamingos are a noisy flock, before eating their food they generate a noise which sounds like woah-woah-woah.

Flamingos are often found standing on one leg, the other leg is pushed beneath the body. It is believed that the flamingo has the ability to let half of its body to go into sleep when one side is resting; then they swap the legs and the other half goes to sleep. Some researchers however believe that standing on one leg allow the birds to conserve more body heat, as the bird stands for very long period in cold water; also due to long standing at a place, the flamingos trample their feet in the mud to bring food from the bottom.

The distinguishing pink or reddish colour of flamingos comes from some protein called carotenoid proteins in their diet; the flamingos whose only diet is blue-green algae are darker in colour compared to those who get it from secondary source like feeding on fishes which eat that plankton.

Flamingos are social birds, live in big colonies numbering in thousands; large colonies help them to protect against predators, also due to their movement in group foods come out of mud easily.

Before breeding, the flamingo colonies are divided into smaller breeding groups of around 15-50 birds; in the group both males and females perform coordinated customary displays. During display, a flamingo group stands together and display to each other by raising the neck, followed by calling with head-flagging and then flapping the wings.

The Story of Kaliaji

We left Parikud quickly, the journey would be long, the Kalijai portion of the lake was deep, different types of boats appeared more frequently in the route. The water become little turbulent in the open areas, the wind speed increased, more ripples were created, the rolling and pitching of the boat were more apparent. In our front a small green island surfaced from the water mass, on the little protruding side of the lake a temple was standing. As the boat moved in to the deep waters, the water splashes were created more frequently, almost wetting us fully. The small island in the deepest part of lake was increasing my curiosity.

Kaliaji hill was close, the colour of the water changed, now a dark green colour showing the depth of the water in that area, we were in the deep waters of Kalijai hill; the Kalijai temple over the hill on an island inside the Chilika lake lies about 18 km away from Balugaon in south east direction, is the sitting place of Goddess Kalijai. The horizon was suddenly little darkened, my eyes were getting closed, the stanzas of the famous poem *Kalijai* written by well-known poet Pandit Godabarish Mishra was reverberating the horizon, as if the song was coming from the hill.

Sail carefully Oh! Boatman,
Sail carefully
The girl fears the water,
People in the fort are waiting
The girl goes to her bridal home.

The beautiful rustic girl named Jai was going to her husband's place in the Parikud Island for the first time after her marriage. The girl was feeling lonely in the boat, thoughts crowded her mind, and she was thinking about the past; her friends, known faces were far away, she can't see them anymore, grief almost choked her chest. The boat was flying like wind, her eyes were fixed on the known hills; the memory was getting fainter, and she was getting fearful of the unending water of the lake. The father was cautioning the boatman to be careful in the waters, they were new to such wide waters, they had seen the waters of Salia river, but here the water was the sea.

Slowly the boat reached the deep waters, the boatmen started rowing the boat, the boat was getting unsteady with the waves, but they were expert boatmen. Suddenly dark clouds appeared on the Bhaleri hills, within no time covered the Jatia hills and entered into the lake; strong wind blew and the storm captured the entire deep waters. The boatmen couldn't control, the people on the boat screamed, the boat drifted fast and crashed on a rock on the island. The storm stopped after some time, bright sun appeared from the clouds, mild wind started blowing and the survivors started looking for each other; all were present except the bride. They searched for the girl, no sign of her; the father searched for the girl frantically, she was hidden in the deep waters. The grief stricken father returned, the boatmen returned with heavy hearts, Jai vanished from the eyes of the mortal world.

With time many boatmen passed by the hill, never such strong storm swept the deep waters of the lake; they always listened strange human voice coming from the hill. In the last passing hours of the day, the soul of Jai appears in the hill, moves on the hill alone, tear rolls from the eyes, it tries to control the storm, and never ever a boat capsized in the deep waters of Kalahari hills, the soul of Jai modulates the high wind. The boatmen, the common people started worshipping the Goddess, people of the area later constructed a temple on the island, worshipped her as Goddess Kalijai –

When the sun sets
And the day falls silent
Jai roams on the hill all alone
Tears trickle from the eyes
Her face shrinks
She moves hand, controls somebody.

The melodious voice of Jai came from the hills. I looked at the sky, night stars slowly appeared in the sky, the evening star was shining brightly, Chilika is protected by Mother Kalijai, the visitors of the north are protected by the seating Goddess.

The Green Malis of Damanjodi

I listened about the colours of the crystals, minerals exhibit special colour characteristics at different temperature and under different circumstances; during my college days I had seen beautiful colours of different minerals in chemistry experiments. How can I forget the beautiful blue colour of Copper Sulphate, the first crystal I had seen in my life. The optics experiment was interesting, the colour of the light, sharp color is exhibited when reflected in different planes, after so many days, still I remember these colours.

The Borra Caves

This passion for the colours brought me to the southernmost flanks of the famous Bauxite deposits of the Eastern Ghat hills, on the Odisha Andhra border; my passion for the colour encouraged me to explore the beauty of the cave. The famous Boara caves of Araku valley was still away, we were moving through narrow but beautifully maintained mountain roads through Ananthgiri hill ranges, tall green mountains, beautiful valleys, nice coffee plantations were filling the landscape. The Borra Caves, also called Borra Guhalu in Telugu language – in the local language 'Borra' is something that has bored into the ground and 'guhalu' means caves, are located in the Ananthagiri hills of the picturesque Araku valley, with hill ranges elevation varying from 800 m (2,624.7 ft) to 1,300 m (4,265.1 ft) in the Visakhapatnam district of Andhra Pradesh. The caves are limestone structures extending to a depth of 80 metre, considered as deepest cave of India, distinctly exhibit a variety of impressive cave formation with secondary mineral deposit with spectacular shapes ranging from very small to big and irregularly shaped; the stalactites – the structures are pointed pendants hanging from the cave ceiling from which they grow and the stalagmites – the structures are the "ground-up" counterparts of stalactites, often with blunt mounds. The percolating water from the roof of the caves dissolve limestone, water trickle drop by drop to form stalactite at the roof; and the same water then drip down to the ground to form stalagmite. Due to weathering many interesting formations like Shiva–Parvati, mother–child, crocodile, temple, rishi's beard, human brain, mushrooms, etc are formed in the calcium carbonate deposits.

"The professor would ask you to go around the campus, spot the girls, probe the colour of their sarees, then come back to the laboratory and search for that colour in the crystals and minerals," Mr. Sreeedharan recounted his golden olden days, simultaneously he enflamed passion in me, to learn about the colours.

I looked at the stalactites column in the semi-lighted cave, the natural light was far back, the interior of the cave was illuminated at points by artificial lights, the people as they walk on the well-laid stair cases will be able to see the formation of the stalactites well, appreciate the bounty of nature buried deep inside the earth crust. The pillar was wet, beautiful white marble like structure, tall around 20 feet high, many carving on the body formed due to chemical action of water with lime stone, so many fissured lines, to me appeared like pillars of a big palace, long semi pipe like structure are joined together and the pillar is formed; the most striking feature is the symmetry of the structures, no flaw, the symmetry of crystals world was fascinating. As the body was smoothened due to wetness, the structure was shining in bright artificial light, again increasing my quest for the crystal world to an unmanageable extent, my eyes keenly searched for every corner of the cave, new structures were getting added.

I looked at another corner, these structures were exquisite, the visitor's imagination wired there, the stalactite formation were hung from the roof, symmetrical long icy rods were joined together, formed a group; the endpoints, were razor sharp, and as light fell on them some pinkish-white glow were coming out of that structures, the chandelier of nature exhibited more colour and variations than the dead quartz crystal in a big hall of the emperor Sree Krishnadeva Raya of Vijaynagaram kingdom. The artificial illumination in fact had increased the depth of the cave, the exquisiteness of the crystals colours had been exhibited, the golden orange glow, the white blue shadow, yellow streaks, the greenish tinge added life to the colourless crystals.

I never imagined about the variations in the crystal world, my knowledge was limited, just confined few descriptions, I knew a crystal is a solid material whose constituent atoms, molecules are arranged in an orderly repeating pattern extending in all three physical dimensions; the snowflakes; diamonds; table salts are common examples of crystals. Sometimes the material couln't achieve the crystalline structure and the molecules are not orderly due to different physiacl reasons, then the material is called amorphous, vitreous, or glassy material.

I looked at the entry to the cave, and at the light sources, the electric bulbs were shining like stars, the entry to the outside world was shining like bright china rose leave painted on black background. The trees which grow on the entrance of the cave appeared like veins of the leaf in that cloudy day.

I was thinking of the colour of the crystals during our return, the dazzling colour of the cave formations, the stalactites, stalagmites which were hidden beneath the green Eastern Ghats hills. I was in my imaginary land my eyes were searching for uncommon in those beautiful hills, narrow paths, and green valleys. The rocks look black and big, sometimes massive, the varieties of earth forms, so much of variations. My quest was increasing, to know about the beautiful land, the rock forms of the Eastern Ghats and Mr. Sreeraman talked about the geological history of the mountains, the rich mineral hidden beneath, on the top too. The brief visit to the crystal world was unforgettable, the Eastern Ghats holds so many colour, I was thrilled, my journey to the highlands of Damanjodi from Andhra side through Sunki was taking me closer to the colours, the beauty of the crystals were implanted in my mind. Throughout my journey I was looking for the colours, green, blue, I was finding innumerable colours in the green forest on the way, so many tinges. The journey through the mountains of the Eastern Ghats, not far away from Damanjodi, was memorable and I was moving in the Salur Ghat area in the borders of Odisha-Andhra.

Journey from Salur Ghat to Damanjori

I looked at the plain lands of Andhra way below; we were climbing to up-lands of Damanjodi, light green carpet, deep green isolated islands spread all over; the flat cultivation lands were shaded in light green and the orchards in dark green. The landscape was fascinating, from the curve of the hill road, the beauty of the land below was astounding, on my right the green hills on Odisha side with trees of medium height, and on my left the vast sea of greenness expanded to the horizon, hazed towards the far left, lost the border; above the clouds from the mountains hovers with shades of blue and black, the gaps gave the blue tinge and the cluster clouds turned darker. Seeing the low lands from a height takes the mind to a different plain, the arrogance of haves ends with the vastness of the vision. Some small mountains peaked above the white clouds far away, their colour darkened in the diffused light; and here near me the light green coloured small bamboo was jungle, the colour contrast of green, and grey were unparallel. I looked at the beauty, I travelled to the uplands, many beautiful places, every place was different, this journey was different, but the beauty was no way less than most talked about routes of India, only this route is less known.

Slowly we climbed further, the green fields of Andhra were no more visible. The road took several turns, small hills appeared frequently, between their folds occasionally the flat lands were visible, and slowly the sight was lost, we entered a new land, much different from the low cultivation lands. The hills turned more beautiful, the rain had shaded every open patch green, so looked more beautiful, deep green pockets of bigger trees scattered all over, bamboo and bushy forests are less green, the mans greed has denuded the forest at many places. Slowly we climbed, with a right turn the road enters into the folds of the hills, not to resurface again towards the side of the low lands, now the roads were more bumpy, green cover was more apparent, the trees turned bigger, springs with flowing water appeared continuously, shorter, hills appeared frequently, some of them with large light green patches, some intact, and between the hills there are very barrow valleys with some agricultural lands on steps; the agriculture land were light green-grey in colour, the denuded hills took further deeper green tinge, the bushes and herbs took little lighter green, and the bigger trees took dark green tinge; to understand the shade of an individual colour, the forest is the best place to look at, particularly during the rains the shades of green are apparent.

Many narrow valleys came, we arrived at the last bordering town Sunki of Odisha, located between the mountain folds, almost on the joint of the hills; houses were with tin or asbestos roofs, their number be around a hundred, and on the road there were not very long queues like that at Girisola, or Jamsola, few loaded trucks, mostly ration trucks, and few other vehicles. The long hills continue behind the township, the green fields slowly got converted to deep forest above the town.

We were entering into the uplands of Koraput, the land of people under whose legs the earth remain unsteady, the worlds remains unsteady, the evenings of the tribal hamlets gets filled with the sounds of Damak, the dancers perform dances in the moonlit nights; dance is life, song is life. The sounds were coming as if, the Dhangda and Dhangdis were getting ready for the Dhemsa dance, the Dungudunga dance, the Laga dance. I closed my eyes, the whole village was performing the Dhemsa dance, the sounds from the musical instruments like Damak, Dhola, were filling the tribal horizon, every one was dancing, the sounds of the hearts were filling the atmosphere.

I was also entering the land of myths and beliefs and also the land of bears; bears visit houses in Damanjodi, comes to the markets of Koraput in broad day light, the hills were once reigned by the bears. I remembered a story, bears hardly got such prominence in the stories ruled by tigers, lions, elephants, rabbits, and snakes; bear generally remained at flanks, but here bear took the prominent position.

The Story of Bear queen

The old couple was unhappy for not having children, finally she gave birth to a bear child, a bear girl; the couple was sad, but finally consoled themselves. God was kind to give them at least a child, though in the form of a bear. The bear child grew up; she used to remain as bear throughout the day. with the departure of the day she was transformed herself to a beautiful girl. She grew up, her beauty was unparallel, the fairies of the heaven wouldn't match her.

The king of the area heard about the beauty of the girl. came to see the girl in disguise, and decided to marry her after seeing her; the next day the King came to the old man's house with proposal of the marriage. The parents agreed. their daughter would be the queen and the marriage was solemnized.

The girl went to the palace with the king, performed her duty as a queen well; the king was very happy with her, her beauty and mannerisms was the talk of the kingdom. The queen used to remain as a girl in the night, but with the coming of the day the girl used to leave the king and transformed herself into the shape of a bear.

One day the king was moving in his garden, saw a big bear inside. He directed his soldiers to catch the bear and kill it in the forest. The soldiers caught the bear, took it into the forest, when they were about to kill it, it cried and begged the soldiers in the tone of lady in human voice, not to kill her and offered to give them some riches. The bear was docile, had not troubled the soldiers on the way, they too fell pity on the bear, decided not to kill the bear and frred it inside the jungle and returned to the king.

In the next night king looked for the queen, but she was not there; for many days and nights the king went on looking for the queen, the king and his servants searched for the queen, but couldn't find her. The minister was ordered to search for the queen, the intelligent minister gauged some mystery in the disappearance of the queen; to solve the problem he visited her parents, and the old couple divulged the birth details to the minister.

The minister came back, was unhappy too, the king had already given order for the killing of the bear, still he enquired the matter from the soldiers and the truth came out; the soldiers had not killed the bear, the minister was assured of recovering the queen.

At the order of the minister, the soldiers went to the forest and searched for the bears, the direction was to find out the bear which transforms herself to human shape in the night; one group find such bear, in the evening the commander went inside the cave and saluted the queen and requested her to come back. The queen agreed, there was no mistake on the part of the king, the king didn't know about the form, knowingly he didn't harass her wife, so he gave such senseless order to kill a bear. The bear queen returned to her husband and lived happily.

A simple story, not much message inside. The theme of the story is the prominence given to a bear, once the uplands of the undivided Koraput was full of bears, so the stories evolved with bear as the main character; a new man creates imagination with the wildlife, lives with prominent characters around.

We travelled further, slowly the landscape changed, the true beauty of the uplands of Damnjori surfaced – the colour, the contour, the contrast of the shades, all created weird imaginations, a visual treat. The tall hills had reduced their height, the slope of the hills were not steep, rather gentle, a boy can easily run to the top. Now appeared so many small valleys, flat sloping lands, small broad hillocks, no rock cliffs, no steep slopes, the cultivation lands were longer and broader, the landscape transformed me to a child, a naughty one, I stopped frequently, filling my memory with the colour. I halted, my world halted for a minute, I watched, no thought was going in, a narrow road ran forward, the road was constructed on the slope of a small broad hillock, grasses and lichens covered the exposed black rocks. Few water channels brings excess moisture in the form of small springs, the cloud descended on the hillock, almost covered the entire hills, the road was covered too. After a while, the cloud moved away, visibility improved, I looked ahead, so much beauty, unparallel landscape, so many, so frequently they appeared, I was taken aback. On my right a wider valley ran along with the road for a long stretch, the cultivation fields almost covered the entire valley. Each bigger yellow field is surrounded by green border, the non cultivation areas gave rise to the growth of green grasses and bushes, few big trees appeared in the fields, the trees gave a superb colour contrast to the fields which were extending up to the middle of the hill range with massive black rocks, the hillocks appeared to be formed by single rocks at many places which were covered with grasses on borders and the exposed rock portion were shining due to wetness.

I couldn't move, my eyes stopped. I paused, on my front was laid a big valley, beautiful, wide, mild slope and a great collection of colours and contrast. Wide flat lands almost covered the entire setting, big trees mostly mango and tamarind dotted the yellow a landscape, the fallow lands with darker shade of green appear in-between the yellow ground. The hills on the right, left too were covered with low clouds, the small broad hills lost their identity in the white clouds, a white ceiling hanging from the top, and below it a long yellow carpet. The shape of the valleys were mostly like rounded plates, flat at the centre, and the hills form the edge. Absence of visible human habitations in almost all valleys increased the beauty of the yellow setting, gave the land the true colour; irregular habitations and big human population denudes the natural beauty of a system. We moved valleys after valleys came, with almost same land form, long valleys, low mountains on both sides, mosaic of green, yellows and black colour. The small Potnangi came with few establishments on the backdrop bigger hillock almost entered into the clouds, the town was standing in front of light green hills. No tree was on the hill, and the thin soil over the rock had given rise to growth of grasses.

We moved forward, on the way we came across a tribal haat, a weekly market place, people, mostly tribal, gathered there with festive mood, the weekly meeting place for merry making; the tribal haats are the place to meet, to enjoy glasses of Lanja (country liquor from ragi), Pandom (country liquor from rice) after marketing. The market starts early, ends just after noon, people have to return to their far off places inside the forest; the necessity of the terrain has been taken into account; also the evenings in the tribal villages are musical, are full with the sounds of heartbeats, the sounds of Damak fills the atmosphere; the Parajas need to return to their hamlets early.

A little ahead, a group of ladies, most of them are middle-aged or old, one two may be little younger, were sitting in a line, big aluminum pots with covered mouths were kept in front in a line, besides each bog pot small aluminum bowels of different sizes were kept, the smaller ones were used for drinking. Most of the ladies were in single saree which moved around the neck and comes back to the chest covering the chest but exposing the arms; some however were wearing blouses or bangles. I looked at a lady, she was looking gorgeous with orange gold saree and with her necklaces and bangles too, one beaded chain was wrapped round the neck tightly, another wide necklace was hung loosely, came up to her chest. She was wearing three gold rings on her wide nose, which in fact widened her nose, and were touching the upper lips, the beautiful white teeth was shining below the golden ornaments; on each ears she was wearing two rings. Her saree was not wrapped around the neck, rather folded backwards exposing her arms and neck. She had wide circular tattoo on her forearm like a ring, above the elbow; on her lower arm she was wearing single red bangles on each hand. Her skin was shining, her coiled rough black hair was combed backward and folded back and wrapped back. The other women were mostly wearing one nose ring, hung from the centre of the nose, and of course the ear rings. All the ladies have tattoos on their exposed hands, around six inches below the shoulder; the tattoo was in circular shape. Many of them were wearing silver or white metal bangles, which were glowing over their dark skin, and on their fingers at least one wide silver ring was there. The sarees, most of them were wearing white ones with wide border, and few small prints, the sarees covering the lower portion of the body, put across the chest from right waist to left shoulder, and then went down, bound properly at the waist, exposing the arms and the neck.

A female customer was sitting on the red ground and was drinking Pandom, the country liquor made from fermented rice which these women were selling, in a steel can. All kind of pots were used for drinking, her eyes were glued to the white drink, her dark skin was glowing in the bright sun light, lips dipped to the drink, her short nose was even touching the liquid, such was the passion for the drink. At another place an old man, in his half pants and bare body was dipping his hole mouth to the drinking bowl, his hairs were only visible, the face was almost hidden behind the bowl. At another place two women with coloured sarees were sitting on the ground and were enjoying the drink, their head with well combed hair were only visible. The smiles were exchanged between the sales woman and the customer, the customer sits near the sales woman, drinks Pandom and leaves the place. Surprisingly, there was no shouting, no one was talking loudly, no fighting, the tribal society was enjoying the haat, the hospitality of the sales women. The tribal society gives immense respect to the ladies, no loose talk, no lewd gesture or filthy remarks.

On the other side, the haat was going on in full swing. The merchandize was mainly vegetables, bitter guard, saru (esculent root), guanar, jahni (ridge gourd), beans, tomato, maize, brinjal are kept in medium sized bamboo baskets. The vegetables were then kept on the front over plastic mats on Bhaga (making quantities of equal size, and the size is priced, not weighed) basis, vegetable of same variety are grouped together and then sold per bhaga (group), the vegetables are not weighed. Many ladies were sitting with tamarind, a delicacy here, a good merchandise here.

I looked at a group of young people, simple smiles in their faces. World was not critical for them, a place to dance and make merry, heart opens there like a blooming lotus, fragrance spreads like the simple words of a young woman. I imagined the young lovers wants to marry, many forms of marriages are there but this form impressed me much; the young woman wants to remain with her lover, she goes to her lover's house and expresses her desire to stay in the house. All the female folk come out of the house, looks at the girl with affection, the mother of the young man looks at her, this young woman chooses her son as her partner, she smiles and remembers her days few decades back. Then she offers her some mandia (ragi) drink to her, the girl drinks the mandia porridge and starts living in the house; so simple is the desire, so simple is the tradition, the society accepts the girl as the bride. In the name of tradition, we complicate the matter, in the name of nature they maintain simplicity, in the name of new we bring complex to the life, in the name of belief, they retain unpolluted life. The days starts with a life, morning starts with smile, days contains life and smiles, and evening gets sounded in the Damak.

The time passed noon, the customers were returning, many on jeep, all the visible part of the vehicle was covered with human bodies, many were hung from the whatever support they got. At least five were sitting on the bonnet, ten on the roof, fifteen inside, and ten were hung, a small jeep meant carry six people was carrying at least thirty people. Many of course were walking, their collection were neatly tied to a bag, placed over their heads on a cloth support. Though I felt the bags would fall off at any time, but surprisingly she walked with good steady pace on undulating land, and moved ahead. I enjoyed my time in the haat, it was so new to me, the people appear so contented, so happy, it was visual treat to me, the people here are uncomplicated. Love the life as it is, enjoy today.

By the time we arrived the Shaila Niwas, the afternoon descended in the white metal town, the dry pine leaves on the floor turned red, the sun was setting behind the green mountains. My mind was roaming around the colour of the land, the white metal was the greatest attraction. I came to see the bauxite mines, I was excited, somehow I liked the area, earlier listened about the minerals atop the tallest hills and below the beautiful valleys are laid symmetrically; the tallest hill looks like a place in a different world, just above the low cloud line. They told me about the thin vegetation over the red soil, strong wind, and the football field like long plain lands and I heard about the Panchapatamali mines, the phoenix species, each to me was the surprising face of the nature, not yet seen by me; the plateau at the top, the habitat of the black bears of the Damanjodi forests, all were so exciting.

My first evening in the Paraja land was coming fast, I closed my eyes, the songs of Parajas were reverberating with the beats of the Damak. The evening was going to musical in Paraja villages around, the evening brings energy in the legs, energy in sounds, energy in emotions.

The dances are filled with life, young Paraja Dhangra (young unmarried boys) and Dhangri (young unmarried girls) continue to dance in the moonlit nights; the air gets filled with the sound of DunguDunga, Madal (double drum), Damak (single membrane drum), Dhola, Dibdibi. The Dhangras, the Dhangris stand in a line. The black feet are bare; the saree starts around 6-7 cm from the angle, wrap the body and goes to the shoulder. The right hand a girl goes over the back of her immediate female companion in right and rest on her upper forearm; the left hand goes over the back of the left companion and holds her waist, the dancers holds each other so the line performs in unison, no discord in movement. The dancers stand in queue as per the height, the man in the front holds the long peacock feathers, make movement, the group moves forward, comes backward, raises the heads then bend forward down, with the tune of the Damak the speed increases; initially the speed is slow but as the time passes the dance peaks up speed, the young lives are full with energy and music. They praises mother nature, through their dance, the beauty of mother nature got reflected in their songs.

Evening at Shailniwas

Here at Shailniwas, the evening shadow lengthened, dark evening brought chilly wind, the pine leaves around the guest houses shivered in cold, the light glowed in the rest house, the yellow wall glowed in the neon light. Inside, in the warmth of a cozy room, the evening came to life, they all laughed, pairs of black eyes suddenly fixed on Mr. Singh, his heavy turban grew longer as they joked.

"Why? You still tell – *Sardar ka Baara baaj jata hai,* Sardar's watch turned twelve. You know a senior officer, well learned one, once asked me the same question, and could you believe what could be my reaction." Mr. Birender Singh, a Sardar, told me, on one hand he was holding whisky filled glass, and on the other hand pieces of fried chicken. He took a full bite of the chicken, then gulped almost half a glass and looked at me.

"It was so stupid, how a person like him could make such a comment. The sardars are the humans like you, and how could there be an event at 12 o' clock and the sardars would be at their wits end." He was explaining the audiences. Other mines managers were sitting around him in that dimly lit room, the fragrance of the fried chicken, salted cashew and of course the glasses of whisky at every body's hand were increasing the depth of discussion.

Nobody answered his question, everybody in-fact were looking at Mr. Singh to tell the reason. He looked at the group, all mesmerised, he was instant attraction, knew the trick to draw the interest of even most unwilling listener. He looked at his glass, it was almost empty, he raised his arm, the glass touched his lips and in one gulp he finished the rest of the liquor. The serving boy in spotless white uniform was standing at a side, instantly he came forward. Mr. Singh nodded, and then he made an extra large peg, to which he added cold water and ice cubes, didn't touch the soda bottle at the side, the white glass turned golden brown, the eyes of Mr. Singh glittered.

"The Sikhs were endoctrined to protect the Hindus, eight of them took the first oath, sports the beard, wore the saffron turbans and then took revenge on the oppressive Muslims. The Muslims during that period had one agenda – convert the country to Islam, the Punjab province bears the burnt, the young girls were abducted, snatched from the families and were kept in the harems. The first Sikhs then attacked those oppressive mass during the dead of the night, rescue the hapless ladies from the lust of oppressors. That time, every body knew, at dead of the night at 12, the Sikhs would attack the Muslims and punish them for their guilt. Form that time onwards the saying of *Sardar ka baara baaj gaya* has come. The *baara baajgaya* means the Sardars during that period would do daredevil works to rescue the hapless," he finished, the bravery of the Sardars was known to everybody.

Everybody was enjoying the evening. For the miners, their life starts early at the mine, with machines, dusts, hazards round the clock, and for them the evening is the time to cool themselves, enjoy the glasses of whisky in the cozy comfort of the sitting room. They were chatting, the glasses were filled instantly, without any delay, the snacks were served regularly and Mr Singh took the discussion to the period of independence, their migration from West Punjab, and their plight, their fight, their rise to prosperity and success, and everybody was enjoying. Mr. Singh was highly particular about the events, how the Pakistanis were defeated, his description, to me also to other officers, appeared like live commentary, as if he was present right at the spot, witnessing the whole event in his eyes, listening to the closest conversation betweens the generals. The other members were simply saying yes sir, yes sir to Mr. Singh, the words of appreciation to the speaker, the words of acknowledge to the person for his in-depth knowledge. He laughed, at least five pegs were consumed by that time, the discussion was continuing long, but no body wanted to leave. In that group, I was the only, non-miner, and I was enjoying every seconds of their gossip, their chatting.

Mr. Singh looked at me, he was looking heavier in his huge green turbans, the beards were glued to the chin, the long mustaches were twisted at the end, appeared like knives emerging below the nostril, his voice turned heavier now.

My attention was again drawn to the sentences of Mr. Singh, no way I could divert my attention.

"You know, how we behave when there are so many alternatives, but how we behave funny," he asked the people around him, no body had the answer.

"When I go to the market to purchase a shirt, I used to go the beast shop, my wife in fact directs me to go to such shops, she though never helps me, still asked me to see the lot, and I look at the full lot, almost 50- 60 shirts, then finally choose one, come back to the house with the new shirt, with the satisfaction that I have bought the best, but when it is opened in normal day light, it appeared to be a bad choice. In office too, when we see so many alternatives, we usually chooses the worst," he commented.

His comments were very interesting, everyone was involved, still I went to the balcony door, opened the door a little; a gush of cold wind pushed me, the warmth of the room was lightened. The night was dark, bright stars were shining in the sky, the dark shades, the trees were moving slowly, the hills, trees were coming to life. I returned back and closed the door, the evening was still warm, everybody was enjoying the company of Mr. Singh, he was store house of interesting information.

"You know, I had seen bears here, can you believe," his voice was that of a naughty boy. Everybody knew the answer, but I didn't, I looked around, was all were smiling.

"Right below the window here, right below the balconies of Shaila Niwas, the NALCO rest house at Damanjodi," he told the reply.

I went to the window, looked thorough the glasses, no sign of bear, the sodium lights was casting golden shadow on the well-maintained thick garden, the teller trees at a little distance were hiding the lights, the darkness started just around fifty meters from the lamp post.

"I am here since nineties, left for brief period to other places in between, now came back, I always saw bears on the way. The bears here have very good philosophy – live and let other live too. Only aberrations are there when the mother is with the child. That time the elephants used to be single, now I found them in families, father, mother and the child in a group, they roam freely in the lonely patches in the township. You come late, around 11 p.m. the family would be on the road, resting on the black road comfortably, not disturbed by light and the sound of the vehicle. I shall frankly confess, the bears here are very simple bears, not like arrogant bears of other places, they don't attack. The bears are found between November to March, rest of the months they go to the cashew nut forests for their food. But I always say they have gone to their mother's place. They behave like civilians of the town, almost harmless, in Damanjodi township, during the last ten years, there were only two attacks, that too due to extreme carelessness of the people. Can you believe they come to the kitchen, sometimes to the dining hall, after all they are Sharif bhalus – the well mannered bears," he laughed. Wildlife was also a subject of interest to me, I enjoyed the stories of wildlife.

"Any incidents with you," I asked inquisitiveness was reflected in my voice.

"Once I was coming to Damanjodi during late night, I was on the driver's seat, my driver was sitting at the back, I asked him to sit at the back, I was enjoying driving the vehicle during dead hours. I saw a bear on the road, I want to make some fun, drove the vehicle near the bear, it was not leaving the road and I instead of blowing the horn, downed the glasses, and touched the bear. It was angry, it turned furious, it attacked our vehicle and we drove away. The bear was angry – if you play mischief with us, then we would not leave you, treat you the lesson. Then onwards there was no incident with bears, saw them many a times on the road, but avoided them, Mr. Singh spoke.

"From which side of the town do they come," I asked, I knew it would not be easy for the mine manager to tell the name of the forest, but he could very well tell about the side from which the bears come , and later on I could gather the information about the forest from other sources.

"Generally from the red pond side, the bears come to the Damanjodi township. Usually they do come around 7 p.m. congregate around the VIP guest house, probably the location was chosen, so that everybody can see wildlife from close," he narrated.

Then he talked about the behaviour of the bears which he knew which is quoted below.

The bears, also the local tribes prefer Mahula, a fruit; unfortunately the confrontations are frequent, the bear attacks takes place during the early hours, around the Mahula trees, or when people come back during late evenings. During early morning and late evening, the bears are highly active. Once confronted, the bear will attack without provocation, the most important part of the in-human body is the eyes, strangely then after the genital organs, almost all the victims of bear attack have one thing common, the bear attacks them without provocation and the face, particularly the eyes are damaged." Mr. Singh was taking a long breath; the long talk had drained his energy a little. The evening again turned warmer, the cold outside couldn't penetrate the thick walls. I wished to look at the pine trees below the guest house, opened the window, the fresh cold air entered, no sign of bear, my eyes were searching every dark corner for a common but fearsome animal, then I recollected my accounts of the bear.

Bear – Short Details

The sloth bear is a medium-sized bear, has long, untidy-looking hair which is black in colour, often with a brownish tinge, or occasionally brown. On the chest, it has a V-shaped or crescent mark. The muzzle of the bear is long; the jaws are small and have bulbous snouts with wide nostrils. It has short hind legs, the claws are hooked and ivory white in colour, the lips are long and the lower lip can be stretched over the outer edge of the nose, the tongue is long and flat. It can suck up large numbers of insects. In bear family, the males are larger than the females. They are omnivorous; diets include both plants and animals. The claws are used for digging, climbing, tearing and catching prey.

These bears are found in moist forests, also in dry forest such as thorny woodlands; also in grassland areas.

An adult sloth bears in general weighs between 80-145 kg, stands at around 2-3 feet when four legs are on ground, the body length is between 5- 6 feet.

The females are shorter than the males, and are more hairy between the shoulders.

These bears are mostly nocturnal, but sometimes may be seen active throughout the day. The females with cubs are active during the day; the reason may be to avoid other bears or predators.

People hunt them for food and products such as their bile and claws.

Behaviour

Many a time adult sloth bears are found in pairs, and the male is generally gentle with cubs.

This bear walks in a slow, lumbering motion, while they, walk noise is generated because of their peculiar motion. However, they can run faster than humans. The sloth bears are excellent climbers, can climb the trees to feed and rest, are capable of climbing on smooth surfaces, sometimes hang upside down. The bears are good swimmers. They sometimes scrape trees with their forepaws to mark their territory and rub against them with their flanks.

They produce sounds such as barks, screams, grunts, roars, snarls, wickers, woofs and yelps when they are angry, trying to threaten or when fighting. When they hurt or afraid, they shriek, when feeding, they make noisy wheezing and sucking sounds which can be heard over 100 meters away. They also produce gurgling or humming sounds while taking rest or sucking their paws. They are also very noisy during mating, make loud melodious sounds.

These bears stay in a cave or den in hot weather as well as during the rains; in cooler dry weather they usually sleep in tall grass or in shade under trees. The females use a natural cave or dig out a den for rearing the cubs.

Reproduction

They usually mate in the months of April, May and June, and give birth during December and January. The gestation period of female bear (sow) is about seven months, and the mother gives birth to 1-2 cubs, sometimes 3 cubs. The cubs start walking after a month of their birth and gets independent at around 24-36 months, attains sexual maturity at around 36 months.

The female sloth bear remains in a protected den with her cubs for six to ten weeks. When it leaves the den, then she often carries the cubs on her back as a protection against predators.

Diet

This animal has an excellent sense of smell, even better than most of dogs. It turns over rocks and logs to reach for the ants and termites and break open termite mounds with its powerful claws, then blow the debris away and finally suck out the termites. This bear may dig 1.5 m deep to reach large underground ant colonies. The sound of such feeding can be herd from distances almost 200 meters away.

The bear is a good climber, climb trees to reach for honey bee combs, sometimes for fruits. Generally they eat the fruit when it falls on the ground. This bear also eats different fruit and plant matter, the fallen petals of Mahula trees, mangoes, sugarcane, jack fruits are the favourites.

Relationships with other animals

The tigers sometimes prey on sloth bears and the tiger generally seizes sloth bear from the back. When confronted front to front the sloth bear many a times charge at the tiger.

Sloth bears sometimes scavenge on tiger kills.

The leopard is also threat. The wild dogs (Dhole packs) sometimes attack the sloth bears.

The elephant, also the rhinoceros do not tolerate the presence of sloth bears in their vicinity.

All bears are very powerful, can attack a person fatally, but usually they are shy, easily get frightened and avoid humans. However many times, in search of food they come closer to human habitation, where the bear encounter generally happens.

My memory went further, I closed my eyes, tried to figure out the habitats of the bears in the Damanjodi town, to understand the bears around the town it is necessary to get an account of the Damanjodi town, and its surroundings, it will give a better idea of the habitat of the bears and its co-existence with humans. On the industry side, the forest were disturbed, most of the mountains were with much less vegetation. The main industrial set-up is divided into three parts, one for the collection of the ore from where the ore is transported to the industry site through conveyor belts from Panchpatamali mines which is around twenty kilometers away, then the other part is the coal dump yard, the coal is needed for producing electricity and finally the main mechanical set up; the portion where the red bauxite soil is converted to alumina, the white powder. The bauxite soil is treated with alkaline solution, and washed thoroughly, the alkaline water along with the red slurry is transported to the red mud pond through pipes. The chimneys of the plant site were very tall, almost triple the size of the rest of the structures. The railways line, specially constructed for the NALCO to carry alumina to Visakhapatnam, also to their plant at Anugul, was going alongside the wall of the industry complex, over the line, the white coloured, specially designed bogeys, each form a distance looked like big cement blocks, wide at the base, flattened at the top, connected to each other by joints for strength, were driven by a single diesel engine. The red pond site was on a raised land, created by making artificial dam, was around one kilometer away from the plant, and the green mountains started just beyond the red pond; there were innumerable small peaks with caves the hiding places, the habitat of bears of Damanjodi. The black pond is at other side, the coal wash is transported to the site, again by pipe and a black pond is created along side the red pond.

Next morning we went to the Baunsuali goddess place, around 1-2 kilometer away from the Damnjori town. There was no formal temple, a gate was erected, over which the face of the goddess was painted on white and yellow. The background was coloured in green with trees and hillocks on black and dark yellow, on the back of the gate the thick bamboo bushes existed through which streaks of light enters the gate top. The name of the goddess was interesting, 'Kantabasuani' meaning the goddess of the bamboo with thorns. We looked through the gate, a kuchha road entered into the bamboo bushes, people had put red religious flags alongside the kuchha foot path; the curved road moved alongside the bushes, care was taken to preserve every bamboo clusters, bamboo grow in clusters, and there used to be some gap between the clusters. In the bamboo cluster there were many individual bamboos, thorny branches came out from bamboo nodes, and series of irregular thorny branches virtually made the bamboo cluster impregnable, almost impossible to enter, a very safe place for the shelter of small animals, the sharp and long thorns prevents the hunters from entering into the cluster. The devotees had wrapped red clothes with golden foils over individual bamboos, almost all the bamboo on the side of the path were wrapped with the clothes giving deep green bamboo culms a beautiful wrapping. The clumps however didn't cover the entire area, between the bamboo clumps, the open areas were covered with light coloured bamboo leaves, a good contrast, dark-green bamboo clusters were surrounded by light coloured bamboo leaves. The bamboo clumps looked beautiful, the bamboo forest has interesting feature, below towards ground, the individual culms struggles for space, virtually no space for a new shoot, the individual culms protrude upward for 10-15 feet, the cluster expands its size, then the individual bamboos spread at upper side, long straight bamboo grow upward, between them some openings are created, through which light penetrates, a beautiful soothing atmosphere is created through the diffused lights.

I looked at the setting, with so many bamboo clumps around, the impregnable bamboo bushes with long and thick nails, but inside so much of open areas, the individual shoots form the sky above, no light for new shoot at the ground, thus a good resting place created for the wild animals. I knew, the elephants prefer this kind of Bamboo forest, they took shelter, also the larger animals like bear took shelter in the bamboo bushes. While I looked at the thick bamboo bushes, I listened about the attack of the bears, the bear was taking rest in the bamboo forest elsewhere and the people disturbed it.

Bear attack stories

Bear attack in Deopotangi village, Pottangi Block.

The time was in the dawn, the people of Potangi used to wake up early and goes to the work early. With the call of the birds two young men went to the forest adjacent to the village, they were collecting bamboo shoots for food, here in the tribal belt bamboo shoots are delicacies. Bamboos occur in the forest in cluster, individual bamboo stems rise from the soil, then from the rhizome more number of bamboo stems emerge. The younger stems, the initial period of emergence are used as vegetables, the material is fleshy, soft and have good taste. The tribal cook the stem, some times they dry it alter and use it in other vegetables. As usual, the unsuspecting young men were searching for the bamboo shoot, they were going from one bush to the other bush, and sometimes the shoots are little inside the bush, so they need to cut the branches to collect the shoots.

The morning sun had just come out from the tree line, soft sun rays was illuminating the leaves, giving those light orange tinge. Few people were cultivating in their fields, the cultivation field in the hilly areas are on the slopes, bushes appear on the field, they toil to clear the land from bushes, and burns the bushes at the site, then break the hard soil with great labor with minimum tools at their disposal. The bush cutting sound was coming regularly, the two friends were busy in collecting the bamboo shoots, the birds were calling from the hides. The first man was between two bushes, bent down to collect the shoot, and suddenly one black bear jumped at him. The man was very close to the bear, he stood straight, the bear was in front, suddenly the bear pounced on him, caught the throat of the man by its claws, its long sharp nails pierced the flesh, and tore his face, the man could hardly scream. The other man seeing the sound rushed to the spot with a stick, the bear at that time was on the first man, it was busy in tearing the face of the man and the skull had come out by that time. Seeing the other man in this condition, the second man tried to divert the attention of the bear from the seriously injured first man. The furious bear, instead of fleeing the scene attacked the second man and tried to catch the man, the man tried to evade the claws, tried to hit the animal, his effort went futile. The bear was trying to catch the man, he tried to evade, and was screaming; listening the screams the other two men rushed from cultivation field, but seeing the bear in such a mood they didn't dare to come near and they called for help. The villagers, armed with laths, bows and arrows rushed to the site. Here the fight between the second man and the bear was continuing, the furious bear finally caught the man, tore the calf muscles, made the man immobile and then tore his chest and body. Both the men were now dead, the blood drops were scattered all around, raw flesh was scattered all over, the blood from the two dead men had coloured the black bear, the hair were turned red, yellow teeth were visible as it opened its mouth, the eyes were burning. When the villagers arrived the bear at that time was sitting over the body of the second man and was eating the human flesh. Seeing the site, the villagers though were in a group were terrified, still they decided to rescue the corpses from the final rites. One young man moved forward with a big lathi, the lathi can't harm the thick skinned and well padded bear, but he felt that the bear can be scared; the screaming group at his back would definitely scare the bear. Alas! they were wrong, seeing the advancing young man with lathi, and the scream of the villagers, the bear, instead of fleeing charged at the young man with a roar. The villagers were at their wits end, they could not use the bow and arrow in the melee, and the roar of the bear was reverberating from the adjacent hill. The villagers were terrified, they fled leaving the young man alone, the man was now at the mercy of the bear, the highly agitated bear roared at ran at the man, the man couldn't flee, he was very close to the beast. The bear entered its sharp claw onto the chest of the man, the man fought, he tried to push the animal, but the strength of the bear was higher. He tried to hold the hands, using its back leg the bear tore his calf muscles, the man and the animal were on the slope land, they were rolling, sometimes the bear was on the top, sometimes the man was. Finally the man couldn't hold the claws of the bear, the sharp nails entered into the face of the man, the bear tore the entire face, plucked the eyes.

The villagers were screaming the last cry of the young man was freezing the blood; they ran hither and thither. The bear after killing the young man charged at the fleeing villagers even though they were few hundred meters away. The charging bear caught an old woman at the end of the forests, after that more open lands continued; the old woman was the mother of the first man killed in the bear attack. The animal tore the entire body into pieces with fearsome force, the helpless lady couldn't scream.

Message of the bear killing spread quickly, the local forester couldn't dare to come near to the bear, the villagers were highly agitated, at that time around four five hundred people had already gathered, but they couldn't dare to come closer. The forester sent the message to the Range Officer, fortunately he prevented people from coming close to the bear, else there could be more casualties, at that place where bamboo bushes were plenty, the villagers couldn't have escaped a charging bear. The highly agitated villagers were shouting, the Range Officer arrived, the mob was almost uncontrollable. He somehow controlled the situation. Kerosene cans were bought, long bamboo sticks were brought over which old clothes were wrapped and kerosene was poured and fire was made. About thirty people moved towards the bear with those burning sticks. The bear at that time was sitting on the corpse of the last man and was eating the flesh. Seeing the people closing the animal roared in fury, charged at the group, the group instead of fleeing moved forward with the burning sticks, the bear seeing the determination of the people fled from the site and hid itself in the nearby hills; and the corpse were rescued from the attack site. The people were extremely angry, they wished to kill the animal, the Range Officer tried to control the mob, immediate monetary help was given for the last rite, the villagers were prevented from going towards the hill, the obvious reason – a highly agitated bear is more dangerous than the tiger. For three days watch was kept, the bear came to the attack site many a times, but was scared by the watchers in the same burning stick method. We came out of the bamboo bushes, took rest at an open space, not covered with bamboos. I looked at the road leading to the Damanjodi town, the township is just a kilometer away, the area once was frequented by the bears from the malis, bears from the bamboo bushes, the ferocity of the bear was scaring then I listened the other stories.

Bear attack on the road

The corpse of a cow was thrown in an eucalyptus plantation area, and adjacent a cashew plantation was standing & lone bear seeing the corpse in a secluded area tried to eat the flesh. Some villagers were passing that side, they found the bear with the dead cow, seeing the villagers disturbing him, the bear charged at the villagers with anger. They ran, the area was not undulating and bushy, unlike the earlier one where the accident happened in hilly area with many bamboo bushes. Other villagers gathered, they charged at the bear, pelted stones at it. The bear, seeing so many shouting people, ran for cover from the plantation area and found a passenger rest shed next to a pucca road and it went inside. The passenger rest shed was a small structure with cement roof. A cement bench for the passengers were made inside, on which the bear sat. The mob had gathered on one side of the road and were pelting stones at the passenger shed, the bear was highly agitated at that time. Suddenly a man came from the other side of the road in a motorcycle, his small daughter was sitting at the front, on the petrol tank; the people from this side shouted loudly at him to not stop, they were warning. Unfortunately the wind was blowing from the other side to the mob, the man couldn't hear the warning sounds properly, and most unfortunately the man stopped just in front of the rest shed without knowing the presence of the bear there. The mob were frightened, the bears could charge, the man was standing in front of the shed, he was looking at the people and suddenly the bear jumped at him, the young girl ran. The man had a terrible fight with the bear, other people didn't come for his rescue, they couldn't pelt stones at the bear, and the man could be injured. The animal killed the man after a bitter fight, the blood was spattered over a large area, Seeing the cruel killing in front of them, they pelted stones at the bear, and killed it.

Listening to those scary stories created anger as well as fear in me, the bear is so cruel, but whether we really understood the animal, the confusion was there I my mind, then the accompanying Range Officer described a story, which really changed my views.

Another Bear story

It was early summer, in one morning of April, 2005, the Range Officer Malkangiri went to the Shiv temple around 20 km away from the town, located deep inside a mixed forest, atop a hill. It was the time of Mahula, the people were gathering Mahula flower at the foot of the hill, no other people except for few Mahula flower collectors. The Range Officer, a devotee of Shiva, was climbing with flower and coconut at around 7.30 a.m. in the morning, no other person was also walking that time. The temple priest had already walked to the temple, the priest used to remain there for a brief period, and then he comes down, very few devotees visit the temple daily, but the priest used to go there everyday for the daily worship of the God, remains there for a brief period and then comes down. The path was full with round stones, the path was covered with trees, many a times disappearing behind the bushes. The Range Officer was climbing slowly, after a long walk the man wanted to take rest. One small stone floor was existing just adjacent to the foot track, he sat there for some time, the temple was another half a kilometer climb from the place.

The location was covered with trees all around, the black stone floor was a small one, around five feet wide and seven feet long, few bushes were standing at the edge, around 20 feet away a bamboo bush was located, and suddenly a huge bear emerged behind that bush, it was a huge bear, the white V on the chest was prominent. It suddenly charged at the Range Officer, at once the officer jumped from the place and started to run. In a bear attack, the best escape is to flee from the site, the bear is too powerful to be killed by a man, it uses its claws, teeth to tear a person. A tiger generally attacks the neck and shoulder, but the bear inflict injury at any part of the body, mostly defaces a person. Suddenly the Ranger Officer slipped, he couldn't run fast downhill over morum and gravel. The bear was roaring, charging at him like a barking dog, he again jumped and started to run, but slipped again and fell on the ground. Now the bear was very close, no chance for the man to run, he can't run as fast as the bear over that gravel filled land; suddenly he remembered – if one lies like a dead man, then the bear will not attack. So he pretended like a dead man, the bear stopped, the man was lying motionless at around 4-5 feet away from the angry bear. The bear didn't attack; it turned back and vanished into the jungle. The range officer remained motionless for a longtime, the bear might be watching him, once he was sure that the bear had in fact left, he slowly woke up and slowly descended. In the meantime the priest had completed his daily cord at the temple and descended to the foothill. Not seeing the Range Officer, the Mahula gatherers enquired about the Range Officer, the news of visit of the Range Officer was a surprise to the priest. They sensed something serious, they knew that during Mahula period, the bears used to remain close to the human habitations, and many bear attacks took place during the early hours. Then they climbed up in a group, the Range Officer was found coming down slowly, he narrated the incident; it was a miraculous escape for the Range Officer.

The bears used to attack the front part of the body, particularly the face and the eyes, with sharp nails in all four legs, the attack on the human turns scary, with fleshes coming out of the body almost at every parts. In the night my memory searched the caves in the hills around the Damanjodi town, in my imagination, I saw so many bears on the streets of the town, I was excited to go to the hills, and the journey to the Panchpatmali hills was a great surprise to me, I was going to a mali, meaning the hill, the bears live there; to get the real picture of the bear habitat.

Journey to Panchapatamlli hill top

Next day morning we travelled to the Panchapatmalli hills, it is a range with five peaks, the hill peaks are called as malis locally, is the among tallest mountains around, around 25 kilometers away from the township of Damanjodi. The hill top, contrary to my belief, did not end on a point, it was flat, a few kilometer patch of open plain land, totally flat like a well-leveled football field, only the small phoenix trees, the natural species occurring in the area, the indicator of the Bauxite was scattered all over; portion of the area has already been mined, the rest area was with, virgin, the landscape is still intact.

I was stunned looked at the wide sky in front of me, long rainbow, not a short one of the towns, much bigger than the rainbow of the green fields too; over the hill top with vast expanse of flat land, other hills were well dwarfed, the rainbow looked terrific, the white cloud line just above the land holds the left arm of the rainbow. Just on the edge, below my vision, the rainbow started from another hillock covered with white rain clouds, the outer red and orange colour hazed at the lower portion, but the inner blue and green colour were much sharper, in fact the rainbow was looking sharper and clearer because of uninterrupted light grey green grassy landscape on the front; the rainbow took a very long arch, passed through little darker individual clouds hanging on the top, the blue sky was too looking prominent on the back, the blue colour of the rainbow was not that deep blue, rather it was Prussian blue, with violet inner border, the colour was looking astounding, the natural arc at that height was unparallel.

I came to the edge, looked below, surprise was stored, on my left lies long picturesque valley, not very wide, the positioning of the small and big hills, cultivation lands in between, was a treat to the vision. A huge landscape, I once saw the photographs of the beautiful cultivation fields of Japan, the photograph was fantastic, the cultivators through initial planning planted paddy of different varieties and colours, when the field is looked from a wider angle, beautiful unbelievable shapes came, a horse with a rider, a monk, the advance planning creates picture perfect; and now those photographs in front of me were picture perfect too. The recently harvested paddy fields were light golden brown in colour, the islands of grassy land in between, newly ploughed land in red colour, the smaller hillocks were without tall vegetation, only with small grasses, giving the land a green tinge. The bigger hillocks too were without taller trees, recently passed monsoon had brought bright lush green outfit to the smaller and bigger mountains on the left side. I looked at the landscape, last monsoon cloud was passing over the land, November was late, but the last dark rain cloud was casting the long shadow on the clean lands; and I saw a ferocious bear carving its head from the taller hill, bending to drink water from the flowing stream. As the clouds passed so many shapes were figured; the dance of shade over the valley below took me to a different world, imaginations changed so frequently, watching the clouds play on the vast stage of lower lands, watching the game from the balcony of hill top was unforgettable.

I recollected the belief of the Parajas, they are living in the land off God. I remembered the story of Dangar Devi, the Goddess of the uplands, the hills, how much belief they have on natural forces, they believe every landform, every tree, every forest, is the seat of a God or Goddesses, the divinity look at the welfare of people and helps them, one such story came to my mind; their containment in life created story – how happy they are in the uplands.

The Dangar Goddess and the Tiger Mother

An old couple was staying in village for a long time, the couple was very greedy, they had no child still they went on gathering the wealth in their house, so the whole villagers criticized them – their greed had made them infertile. However, the God had pity on the couple, the wife got pregnant. One day the couple went to the forest to collect firewood, there the woman got the labour pain and gave birth to a child; to cut the embroical chord the knife was required which was not there at that time.

The man rushed to the house, found his house was full with the wealth and grains. He was surprised, but rushed back to the jungle and explained about sudden appearance of wealth in their house. The woman was happy, a celestial message came – the wealth would remain with them if they leave the child in the jungle and the greedy parents left the child in the dangar and returned to their house.

The young boy was playing in the jungle, the Dangar Devi (Goddess of the uplands and hills) came in that way, handed over the child to a tigress and directed her to rear the child properly. The tigress was very kind, she reared the child with utmost care, she used to raid houses or markets in search of clothes and food for the little boy. Slowly the boy grew up and reached the marriageable age, he had been seeing people below and had been thinking of visiting the villages, so he expressed his desire to his tiger mother, and the tigress with a heavy heart agreed and allowed the young man to go. He went for the village, on the way met a monkey who was also interested to visit the village; the young man agreed to the request of the monkey, the monkey took the shape of another young man and both went to the village. The monkey was a naughty soul, always tried to put others in difficulty. They visited the village, made friendship with villagers, choose two beautiful girls, married them and settled in the village. The young man was very hardworking. They worked very hard on the fields. He always used to get bumper crops. The monkey on the other hand was lazy and used to waste his time in gossip, so his crop was always bad. The monkey got envious of the young man and in order to harm the young man, visited the crop field of the young man in the night and damaged the crops; as a result the crop of the young man started failing and his in-laws were very unhappy. The man now decided to find out the miscreants and guarded the field with his bow and arrow, in one night the monkey was in his field, so the young man shut the arrow at the monkey and killed it. The man ran at the intruder, found it to be his old acquaintance, the monkey, and since the husband of a village girl died, the young man sensed trouble, so he decided to return to the dangar with his wife. The girl agreed to accompany the man, both climbed up the hills and went to the forest and returned to their tiger mother, the tigress was very happy and gave them good houses; they were very happy too, their children started the lineage of the Kandha Parajas.

I looked at three huge land roofs in front, three ranges with flat wide top ran parallel to each other, the top of the ranges was a surprise, absolutely plain lands with negligible undulation on their top, how the formation could be so plain, no big tree, no tall bushes, almost devoid iof significant vegetation, except for some small shrubs and herbs. The light red-grey haze was prominent at the backdrop of light green haze from the side of the mountains, the slopes were covered with small bushes, steepness mild, were dotted with bushes and there were many small folds which were relatively dark green in colour, signifying the water availability, the folds works as water channels. The nature had created magnificent land forms at the top of the hill. I remembered my journey in the higher hills of Eastern Himalayas, there I saw sharp land forms, the cliffs were so steep, almost vertical, any thing on the land will fall onto the deep gorges, and over the cliff the human habitations existed, the people there cultivate on flat lands, the slope of the land on the cliff was not steep at all; and here the cliffs are not steep, but the land form is superb, so many flat hills with beautiful green slopes. I have moved in almost all hill stations of India, Shimla, Darjeeling, Gangtok, Shillong, Ooty etc, the present land forms and the beauty of the hills were no way inferior. The long land form with such flatness is unique, unseen elsewhere. God lives in the highlands, the God of the Kondhas of the Damanjodi lives in the beautiful lands of the malis.

I was lost in the beauty of the land, new and more land forms appeared continuously, again a beautiful hill, without any vegetation, lush green in colour, the sides were covered with velvet green grasses, ran into the haze far away, the long slopes were uniformly steep, some folds were the only interruptions, but like beauty spot on the face of a beautiful girl, to increase the beauty of mountains; and the mild orange white haze at the top adds to the mystery of the land. The hilltop on which we were standing was covered with small bushes, mostly Phoenix, and with some grasses and some small herbs with many long light violet inflorescence, the inflorescence emerged from the branch, flower cluster occurred towards the end, beautiful small flowers starts from the base and goes towards the top; and the red-brown exposed rocks were covered with lichens, bleaching the colour at many places. I looked at the phoenix bushes, the bushes were appearing continuously between the rocks with white patches, but didn't cover the entire land, occur intermittently, these were small bushes, had Khajur like leaves, the light green leaves emerge from the base. The phoenix bushes are in plenty, the roots are the staple food of the bears, the slope of the hills are covered with these bushes too, small light grey grasses fills the void existed between the bushes and the small rounded rocks. I looked keenly at the rock, many small holes on the top and on sides too, these were the effect of weathering, the colour was reddish grey, the white patches were prominent, which were shaped like brain corals; the small eruptions on the white patch are like the eruptions on the arms of the octopus, the chemical reaction on the bauxite rich rocks is casting beautiful shapes on the rock.

We were moving on the flatlands of Panchpatmalli hilltop, an expanse of around 25 kilometers, unbelievably, long, orange grey tinge was coming from the land, the phoenix trees were adding green shade, over the head dark clouds were moving regularly and our land was growing further and further till the clouds in the other mountain. The long rainbow was still there on the side, now brighter with distinct colours. I was looking at the shape, clouds slowly thickened, the right arm faded at the far mountain, and in this mountain a lone big tree looked mystic at the backdrop of the white clouds, the green mountains on the other side had already lost the colour. The tree looked mysterious, grey grasses with reddish tinge on the ground, one two rocks protruding their heads from the land, no bigger trees, not even phoenix on the land, and at the edge the lone tree with green leaves was standing as the magician of the land, looking at the distant mountain, chanting the spells, the scene is mystic, mystery shrouded in the hills of Panchpatmalli. On the side, on a dry branch, near to that mysterious tree, a light ash coloured eagle with orange tinged feather was sitting motionlessly, its head was large, chest wide, and the light black coloured back feathers was narrowed backward; was looking at the faded mountains. I looked at the mysterious clouds, the mysterious settings, probing life, probing strange events. Suddenly my eyes spotted a jackal towards the left of the tree, it was sitting on the ground, its grey coloured feature was almost camouflaged with the set up, its head was protruded upward, like the eagle, it was looking at the mysterious mountains. The cloud rose further, the green mountains vanished below the rain cloud, the eagle flipped its wings and flew to the white clouds, the jackal rose from the gasses, ran at full throttle to the phoenix bushes at the far left, a strong wind started blowing suddenly, the clouds were rising, but the rainbow was still there, the colour didn't vanish, and below the colour deepens for the tree at the edge.

I looked at the other side, vast expanse of flat land at the high hills, the mysterious settings remained to the left, beyond the phoenix bushes the gray land with orange tinge continued. The white rising clouds were now replaced drifted to far away hills, on the ground the occasional small water holes with little water were looking lush green. I looked down, strange little flower just on the ground without any vegetative part, I didn't know the name, it looked strange. Around 12 fleshy greenish white coloured petals, each floret is circular towards end, soft and long pinkish spikes towards the edge on each floret; rain drops glued at the end of the spikes were dazzling; a beautiful flower on the dark ground. I looked forward, the eagle was now sitting on a big rock, its head was oriented towards the far sky below, the jackal suddenly rushed out from the phoenix bushes and again ran at full throttle to the small bushy forest far away; again a strange setting. I looked at the jackal, its slim body was jumping with each step, the long thick tail with dark hair was moving almost parallel to its long body, the head was raised little and the small ears were erect; the jackal vanished into the bushes, the eagle also flew upward, moved in the same direction of the jackal, it too vanished into the clouds.

I was watching the life on the strange hills and was slowly moving towards the edge of the mountain, to see the distant land, again I stopped, a small bird, it didn't flew as we came nearer, its head turned, it looked at us, a stranger to its world. The bird was grey coloured, with white and dark long aligned patches, like house sparrow, the belly was ash grey, legs were pinkish; the bird looked much like a house sparrow, but here swiftness was not there, again the bird was a land bird. We came closer, the rounded heads rose further, it jumped a little into the same grass land, but couldn't fly, and hopped to safe distance on grassless area; it lowered its head, the shadow of the bird was falling on the land, blunt beaks to collect food from ground. At a distance, the jackal was again seen, it was standing in front of phoenix bushes, body partly hidden, and the long face was watching us keenly.

Suddenly I recollected a story of a birds, 'Liting Piting' its name, the cry of the bird changed the behaviour of naughty children, so much of love for the wildlife the Parajas are carrying in their heart.

The story of Liting piting

A beautiful bird made a nest at a Sal tree alongside a road, on the outskirts of a village and, laid four eggs and was very happy, always used to dance and sing 'Liting Piting'. Her eggs were about to be hatched, she could listen the sounds coming out of her eggs. A group of children went in that direction, heard the song of Liting Piting, found the interesting bird with the eggs in the nest. The children were naughty; the beautiful song of the bird did not impress them, they climbed the tree, drove the bird away and brought the eggs down.

The embryos of the eggs cried "Mother, Mother, the wicked children are taking us from the nest. Please protect us". The Liting bird was very unhappy and cried "Liting Piting. Liting Piting, what can I do children? I am unable to protect you; the naughty children take you down." She flew over her nest, low over the heads of naughty children and cried, but the weep of the mother and chicks didn't enter into the mind of the children. They took the eggs to their houses, the little bird followed the children; the naughty group didn't care for the bird's presence and broke the shell.

The embryos once again called "Mother, mother the naughty children are breaking us, please protect us." The mother replied "Liting Piting I am crying for you, children, they are breaking you; I am unable to do anything." The bird continued crying 'Liting Piting'.

Then the naughty children broke the eggs and little undeveloped chicks came out, the naughty children did not feel pity on the small chicks, they caught them and started cutting them. The little birds cried "Mother, Mother, they are cutting us." The Liting bird cried "Liting Piting. I am unable to do anything. I am crying for you." Then she cried.

Then the naughty children cooked the little birds and the little birds cried, "Mother, Mother, they are cutting us and cooking now." The mother bird cried "Liting Piting. What can I do children; I made a nest on the way of the people, so they took you." She cried and cried "Liting Piting".

The naughty boys cooked the little birds and started eating, the tiny little birds cried "Mother, the naughty children are going to eat us." The mother cried "My dear children, I am crying, I made a mistake, I made a nest on the way of the people, so they find you." then she cried and cried "Liting Piting", all the birds and animals were very unhappy over the sorrow of the little bird, the forest God was very unhappy.

The children ate the meat of the little birds, from their stomach the little birds started calling for their mother, but the mother was far away. So they continued calling their mother. The children and their family were terrified to listen such voices coming out of the stomachs of the children; they prayed to the God and promised that in future they would not harm little birds.

The story illustrates the love of the tribal people from the little creatures around, a very simple story but carries so much of meaning.

Cave & Bauxite formation

On the top of the mine, I looked at my friend Mr. Sreeraman, without knowledge of the geology, forest, its history, understanding of the environment will be incomplete, my interest, apart from the bear, the natural surroundings, also on the bauxite minerals of the Eastern ghat, the types of rock we encounter are generally called Kondolites. The name derived from the name of Kondha, tribe of the districts of Koraput, Kalahandi etc, is metamorphic rock, originated from sedimentary rocks. These rocks are very tightly isoclinally (series of lines with the same slope) folded, and due to weathering, one will not see the peak of the folds, but vertical walls, inclined almost perpendicularly, around 800 from the horizontal, are found often.

These rocks have different mineral composition. Every piece of rock is different, band wise there are differences, some bands are rich in aluminum minerals, some are rich in iron minerals, so degree of weathering differs as per the chemical composition of the band, for softer minerals the weathering goes deeper and for harder minerals it remains near to the surface. So, though the rock surfaces are equally inclined, still the weathered surface is very irregular, somewhere it is very deep and some where it is very shallow. As weathering increases, the softer mineral portion gets weaker and weaker and thus weaker zone is formed, and rocks collapses occur. The softer mineral portion being weathered deeper, they get washed away during the weathering process like leaching, rains etc. and the hallow portion, or the cave is formed. These types of caves are not very deep, generally 3-4 meter deep, but wide enough to shelter wild animals, particularly bears.

Bauxite Formation

My interest in the minerals was increasing, the white metal, the Bauxite was the subject of interest. Mr. Sreeraman was continuing on the subject.

The Bauxite formations are available in the hills of Koraput, Kalahandi and Rayagada. Though the average depth is around 14 meters in Panchpatamalli hills, the bauxite formation is some where few centimeter thick and somewhere about 60 meters thick. In a bauxite profile the percentage of iron on the surface is higher on the surface; as we go deeper the iron percentage get lesser and lesser and for aluminum the percentage is lower towards top and as we go deeper and deeper the aluminum percentage goes on increasing; the reason purely because iron has more affinity for the oxygen than aluminum so in the colloidal form it rises and pushes the aluminum molecules down and occur near the surface, where as aluminum being less oxygen demanding than iron occurs below the surface. When iron comes to the surface, minerologically it is called hematite Fe_2O_3, the colour being dark brown to blackish and as we go deeper where aluminum richness happens, the iron tends to be limonitic which is yellowish in colour, like turmeric, it is again Fe_2O_3, but minerologically it is more amorphous than the hematite. When one encounters this kind of bauxite soil, for sure the soil is rich in aluminum Al_2O_3, and if the colour is brownish to darkish like steel grey colour, then the ore is poor in Aluminum.

After listening to the Bauxite formation theories and the flat lands, caves of course, my eyes searched for the strange landforms. The cloud had cleared the slopes of the hill ranges, the parallel flat land were seen again, the green slopes were clearly visible, every dark spot was creating more interest; small cliffs were found at many pockets. I looked at a cliff, a small one, fifteen twenty feet tall, few darker areas were seen, the caves of the bears; finally I discovered the caves of the bears; the cave was around hundred-two hundred meter away from the human tracks, located on the cliff, on the top the flat lands starts after ten-fifteen feet from the cave face on the upper side, in fact it is impossible to imagine cave below the flat upper land. In the cave on the cliff the top portions were arched, then another arch, a hallow then follows, the hallow appeared to be five-six feet wide, the mouth was dark. Inside maybe the cave was extending couple of feet. On the lower side, small bushes almost cover the mouth, the bushes continue from the mouth in all direction. Laterally, after around a hundred feet another cave was seen, a smaller one with one single arch, with narrow opening on a vertical cliff, and as usual bushes covered the mouth and adjacent areas.

In this land the bears inhabit, the green mountains give them shelter, food, water. The sound of the wind blowing through the valley was creating a soft sweet sound, the sound of the small spring was composing a beautiful music, the sun was setting, the scary tales of the bear was puzzling me, but I knew how simple those animals are. We simply misunderstood, reacted unnecessarily, all the situations could have been easily avoided had we taken little precaution, had little understanding of the animal, but we are never taught about co-existence.

I closed my eyes, the Gods of the hills, forests are looking at us, the Nishani Munda of the Paraja land was looking at us, other Gods of the hill ranges is looking at our activities, all our action is been judged by Him. The Jani has invoked Gods of the Dangar, the Dissari is performing the rituals. The Shira Kalisi is finding out the reasons, the Gurumai is performing the rituals; all the powers of the Paraja world are looking at us with open wide eyes, with curiosity.

I looked the rising clouds, then came to the other edge of the mountain, the green mountains were more clearly visible, the mystic shadow had been lifted, between the mountains one hamlet was visible, contrary to the green cultivation field settings and barren hills with green tinge, this side the forests are greener, the trees are taller, the sounds of the springs were louder. Between two hills, a narrow flat land with red tiled houses were seen. The houses appeared to be made up of bamboo, small timber and red soil, and the roof was made up of red tiles. There were many houses, all in one cluster, few cultivation lands on steps surround the area, one-two Salap trees were standing near to the hamlet, and the tribal community enjoys Salap liquor. The long shadow of the taller mountain lengthened further, touched the outer limit, the evening would come soon to the hamlet surrounded with mountains, tranquility would come soon.

We came to the other side, the sun had traveled past the head, the mountains were turning darker, the sky turned white, blue and dark shades had disappeared, the mountains were constantly turning darker, haze covered all the mountains, the smaller mountains appeared like turtles and so many of them. I looked at the sky, the sun was hidden behind the clouds, some openings were created, the sun ray tickled through openings, round blue patches appeared in the sky, flood of light came rushing and increased the brightness of the green mountain nearby; at the far side, the mountains were getting darker, so many big rocks raised their heads from the soil; the Gods of the Parajas, the Nishani Munda were sitting in an assembly.

Driven to the Last Shelter

Part-A

A. The elephants drive in Dhanbad

Sanjeeb then looked at the unfinished paintings, a tribal girl with an earthen pot on her waist, feathers of the jungle fowl around her head, and was standing in front of a thatched hut. The girl looked live on the off white canvas, the painting showed the expertise in bringing the lines to life. The youthful smile depicting the energy within, the expressive look showing the heart within, and the standing pose again, describing the language of life, the passion. Was attracting the thoughts of an indifferent onlooker, like me, instantly and I couldn't turn my eyes. In that dimly lit room, where the shadows were coming to life with words, I looked at the beauty of the girl on the canvass, the green forest at the background, at the flying birds in the sky and at the dark shadow of the elephant herd at a distance.

"Such a good painter you are, I never knew that!" the words of surprise came rushing from my throat automatically.

"You are so forgetful," Sanjeeb smiled at my ignorance, but didn't reply to my question and started singing his favourite song and the passion of life flew to the eyes of that girl in the canvass.

"Kabhi, kabhi mere dil mein khayal aati hai……."

(Sometimes in my mind comes the thought, you are made for me…)

The melodious voice of Mukesh was coming to life again, and Sanjeeb as I knew for decades was a good singer, the melody in his voice again brought the inner heart to the forefront, to tell the truth of life.

He sang, I listened, also listened the portrait of that tribal girl of the Sal forest. I didn't utter a single word, the echo of this song touched all corner of the room and of course touched my soul, even if I deny to others, but truly, it touched me within. I looked at the girl on the canvass, the smile, the shine of the passion was glowing in her eyes. She was after all listening the melodious voice of her creator, a person, with the hues, a lover with the songs.

"Sanjeeb! I always yearned to listen to your songs, I, if chance would be there, I would come and sit in the shadow of the Sal tree and listen your songs, your heart for hours, non-stop. Only the wind of the distant mountains would be there, the coolness of the deep Sal fo rest would be there and from every word there would emerge a flowing river with hundreds of tributaries and it should pass through my heart." Again a person, I, who was listening to the great melody after a decade told to himself, and some of my words might have reached his ears too.

He didn't reply for a moment, the song, the melody continued, and his eyes opened slowly, his first glance went slowly to the girl on the canvass, on the picture she was smiling. To me it appeared Sanjeeb has won her heart, the creator has given her the endless love.

"Did you forget my painting exhibitions in Mussourie when we were together?" Sanjeeb asked me a question, little pain was in his voice, as I did not remember his exhibition, and for not remembering the astounding applause he got from the friends.

"But, but you created a statue, I shall not say it a lifeless painting rather I shall say a stone marvel that you have brought to life in the Sal forests of Jharkhand. The green forests, rather I shall say the tinge of life which you have shown there is simply marvelous and I envy if I could do the same," I told him. I didn't have appropriate words to express my feelings.

His eyes were glued to the canvass, his hand on the lip, Sanjeeb was deeply involved in his paintings, the used colour bowls on the table, like his mind were eager to give the correct touch once again, to the life of Jharkhand. His hand moved, the pointed brush moved lightly on the canvass and the shadow of the elephant came to life, the light dark structures were further darkened, looked like a granite stone of Jharkhand and the raised trunks looked like the hands of the God, to bless the worshipper. I looked at Sanjeeb, the songs of legend singer of Hindi films, Mukesh, was coming from his mouth and with the words his emotions were taking shape on the canvass.

"It was a true story, not imagination alone, I saw the girl at the backdrop of the rampaging herds in Dhanbad," Sanjeeb uttered few words for me. My interest grew further in the canvass, in the story, after all the girl, so beautiful, depicting the energy of the forests, beauty in her face, emotion in her eyes, was looking at the dark herd at the horizon and with the strokes of the brush, the canvass was telling more stories.

I was deeply impressed by the photo of the elephants, the dusky creatures had developed some kind of attachments, passions flowed from my heart too. I was eager to know about the elephants of the area, I knew with the herd so many stories float in the air.

"You will be surprised, some of the elephants behaved in strange fashion, thoughts simply beyond our comphrension, the stories are so interesting." Sanjeeb induced interest in me by saying the words. I was eager, much interested to know further, those stories were my obsession, then he narrated the story. He confessed, the stories were in the air; some sweet coating might be there.

Blacksmith & the elephant

It was the story of Betla tiger area; to me, that time too, appeared as a filmy story. There was a village, a remote one, just on the boundary of the reserve forest. The houses were in cluster, almost all the villages in Jharkhand have house clusters, individual houses are few; those are created due to lack of space in the original village. In this village the house of the blacksmith was a little way from other huts.

Once an elephant herd moved into that village; remained in the adjacent forest, in that herd an adult elephant was injured by a big bamboo shrapnel, a splinter entered into left front leg and remained in it in broken condition; as a result the elephant was getting tremendous pain, the injury almost crippled it, it could not collect food properly and the leg got swollen too. One evening, the injured elephant came to the village with the support of two healthy elephants; they came to the lonely house of the blacksmith. The blacksmith, his family, also the rest of the villagers were frightened at the site of the huge elephants in the village roads; massive figures were standing in front of the house, trumpeting, but not destroying the house, or eating the banana trees at the backyard. It was baffling, the family of the blacksmith somehow sneaked out, ran to safety, other villagers watched the three elephants from a safe distance, but the poor blacksmith could not escape. The elephants trumpeted again, probably some message in their voice; inside, the blacksmith trembled like a windblown tree. The elephants however did not break open the door, the injured elephant sat on the ground and trumpeted continuously, and occasionally gently tapped the front door with its legs. The blacksmith had no place to go, finally he opened the door and found the injured elephant next to his door. He looked at the injured elephant, prayed to the God with trembling hands; the elephant stood as soon as it saw the blacksmith, lifted its injured leg and then sat on the ground, low growl came out of its throat; the blacksmith understood the message, the elephant need his help. He went inside, brought a long forceps, stood near the sitting elephant and slowly removed the bamboo splinter from the leg of the injured elephant. The elephant screamed in pain, the man trembled in fear, the escorting elephants waved their ears, but they did not trample the man. Then he burned some clothes, put the ash into the hole on the leg of the elephant and made a bandage. The elephant stood up with great difficulty and slowly moved to the jungle with the help of its friends.

The next morning brought some unpleasant surprises, the village headman, the richest man of the village was hitting at his door, was scolding the blacksmith with dirty words, the whole surrounding was hot, people gathered all round his backyard. He woke up, came out and found a lot of paddy bundles at his backyard. He was surprised, the headman was humiliating him for stealing the paddy from his backyard, and his innocence was not heard by the villagers. He was sad, the elephants must have brought the paddy bundles, they tried to repay for his service. But nobody believed in his explanation, the justice – the blacksmith would carry back the entire paddy load to the backyard of the village headman; and the poor blacksmith carried the loads of paddy to the backyard of the headman throughout the day, and returned tired at the end of the day. With the dusk touching the village, the humiliated man went to bed without food. Next morning brought further humiliation, the morning again started with the scream of the headman, shouting of the other villagers. The same scene was repeated, the paddy were gathered at his backyard, suspicion reflected in the eyes of every person, the blacksmith, driven by poverty stole the paddy again, stolen the paddy, he became a shame to the village; unfortunately nobody noticed the elephant dung on the paddy. The poor blacksmith again carried the paddy back to the yard of the headman, tear was dropping from his eyes due to his misfortune, everybody was scolding him, cursed him for such misdeeds which actually he did not do.

The evening again came as usual, the hamlet went to early sleep as usual, the stars twinkled as usual, the village dogs barked as usual, the villagers went to early sleep as usual; but there was not total calmness. The headman got a soft tap on his front door, initially he did not open his eyes, no visitor should come in the night hours, and nobody in his house opened their eyes. The tapping became heavier, the whole house trembled, the headman opened the front door, and dark shadows came from the darkest corners. He looked at the shadows carrying the paddy bundles from his courtyard to the courtyard of the blacksmith, the man couldn't open his mouth, and he understood the shadows. The next morning came as usual, the blacksmith opened the front door with tottering hands, the villagers now started cursing the blacksmith for his regular misdeeds, but the headman was absent, the most louder voice was silent. The headman came with trembling legs, his age appeared to be increased by another ten years, no sound came from his mouth. At that time all were scolding the blacksmith in their loudest voices, the eyes of the headman were full of repent, he came near the blacksmith and knelt before him with folded hands and beg his pardon. Everybody was surprised, all sounds stopped, the blacksmith was surprised, nobody could open the mouth; the headman then narrated the story of the dark figures in feeblest voice. The Ganesh God was kind on the blacksmith, and again he bowed his head on the legs of the blacksmith. Now the villagers praised the blacksmith for his courage and also for his service. The next night came, the huge black shadows again moved in the village, no tapping of the doors occurred, the whole village was awake, everybody saw the shadows, everybody prayed in mind. In the following morning, the blacksmith found a big log in front of his house, and again the dung of the elephants on the spot proved that the log was a gift of the elephants. The man made implements, made doors and his broken house got a new shape, after all the elephant herd felt pity for the old house of the blacksmith; also they wanted to repay for his service. Other people understood the greatness of the elephants and they too came forward and helped the blacksmith in constructing a new house. The elephants guarded the village, and never a theft happened, the thieves were unhappy.

A strange story it was, so uncommon, unheard of too, but it was such a lovely story, the elephants can be so kind, but to me it appeared like the material was derived from a fiction, but Sanjeeb, I knew never jokes, his voice was telling the truth and I had no reason to disbelieve.

While we were discussing, the tea was served, nice lemon tea, I took a sip, again looked at the painting, it appeared the shades were moving on the canvass, the elephants were coming to life.

"Many incidents took place, to me if you say now, some appeared to be scenes in a drama, can you believe some people loose sense when the elephants are around, seeing the herd at so close they used to feel the elephants can be handled as domesticated buffaloes, can you believe once a man had caught the tail of the elephant." Sanjeeb was creating more interest in me, and started laughing.

Man holding the elephant tail

The story was again about the arrival of the herd at a village, a lot of spectators gathered, encircling the elephants from all sides, the scene was highly disturbing for the elephants. Sometimes the villagers lose the sense, they feel that they can handle the wild elephants at will, can give the direction, for some fools the elephants are the big brothers of the buffaloes. One villager, around 54-55 years of age, came near to the herd and suddenly caught the tail of a big elephant, curiosity, wild beliefs were turning to reality; all were frightened; the eyes of the onlookers were expanded in disbelief. It was late afternoon, the sun was slowly going back to the caves, the elephant with the sun at its back was looking bigger than its actual size, orange rays were coming from its body, depicting the anger stored within and the man was holding the tail of that elephant. The elephant turned on him, the man understood his folly, stood motionless with folded hands; the elephant only pushed him lightly by its trunk, the man fell on the ground but came out unhurt, to his greatest fortune he was not trampled or tossed to the tree tops.

I was amused, the stories were so interesting, and the softer mood of the elephant was getting unfolded, I was laughing.

"Many unfortunate events too happened with the elephants, their social behaviour is a matter of praise, they love each other, care for each other." Sanjeeb told me and then he narrated another story.

Mourning of an Elephant

Once, two elephants strayed into a village near to the forests. A high tension wire was passing near the fields, just over the earthen bund created for the purpose of water storage; the high tension wire were hanging very close to the ground at that point, only few feet above the ground. The happy elephants were moving, they climbed the small bund, the smaller elephant at the front, it easily passed below the high tension line, but the bigger elephant couldn't so while crossing its body touched the live wire and got electrocuted. While the elephants were passing, some people were cultivating in the fields, few hundred feet away from the bund, they witnessed all the events. At that time the smaller elephant had gone down, the other elephant was falling dead at the other side of the bund; the smaller elephant turned back, could not find its companion and searched for the bigger elephant, found it laying on the bund motionless. It tried to pull the bigger elephant, push the dead elephant and even sat near it, it continuously tried to wake up the lying elephant, for it the bigger elephant was sleeping. The small elephant then went to the nearest water source, collected water in its trunk, poured water on the dead elephant, tried to pull it's tail; it was a long try but yielded no result. The small elephant left the place, moved around the village for some time, but didn't leave the place, the companion was in deep sleep. After sometimes it again came back, pushed the dead elephant and the process continued for more than twenty four hours. Seeing no result, finally it brought a trunk full of water and poured over the body of the dead companion, threw some soil and green leaves over the body and left the place for ever.

The story was full of agony, full of emotion, so much care for others, I never imagined an animal could be so sensitive. A lot of discussions continued on the elephants, the stories were refreshing, my beliefs on the elephants were changing, they are so curious animals. I looked at the herd on the canvass, the beautiful was smiling girl on the canvass, the girl was singing, her smile was seductive, I remembered a poem of the area, I read it somewhere, there was so much obsession with nature, so much emotion.

Don't marry me off in the land of Sal forests
Don't send me off to the land of Mahula trees

So much cold in the Mahula country,
The bones froze in the deep night
The sun shines in the Sal country
Sunshine enflames the day.

I recited those lines for Sanjeeb, he was amused, in the heart he was a lover, a creator is always a lover, passion is always in the eyes, belief is on the brushes, and conviction is in the words, in the figures. I was immersed in my thoughts, my eyes were glued to the herd, Sanjeeb knowing my interest continued further.

"This herd came to Dumka, their number increased with birth of a new born, but finally we were able to drive them away to safety of the Giridih hills," Sanjeeb told me. In that evening I did not listen the story of the elephants only, also listened to the songs of life too, looked at the beauty of the girl in the canvass and how the life evolved in her society, as if the drums of the Santhals were reverberating in the room, the music was trickling from the Sal forests on the canvass, from the created hills. I remembered another song of the Sal forest.

Comes the days of thunder and rain –

The dark cloud cover the Sal forest
River flows, touches the banks
Water flows with sea of dreams
Village girl reaches the youth
The time never returns
Dance, dance and make merry
Life is full of happiness

Interction with Jallauddion

The next morning came with golden light, and I got a knock at my door, on opening the door found Jallauddion, a forest guard of Dhanbad with broad smile on his face. He, on that moment, for his contagious smile, attracted my attention.

"Jai Hind Saab, how did you enjoy your first night in Dhanbad?" he welcomed the new morning, welcomed me and wanted to be closer. He, after all a friendly person, not indifferent like other staffs and was highly courteous. I looked at the hills in front of me, thick wavy green line extended from one end of the horizon to the far end. The lush green colour of the mountain, an uncharacteristic view to me of course, I expected a bald, wounded forest area to stand there; after all Dhanabd is a coal town, black coal everywhere, black dust everywhere. But, to my pleasant surprise, I was sitting in front of a green hill range. Jallaluddin too looked at the hill and started speaking.

"Saab, the mountain was once full with elephants." I was not that interested for the dusky creatures hounding villagers and rampaging everywhere. I took a sip, the tea was not very strong and sweet, but having a lovely flavour.

I was indifferent to the story of the elephants then; my eyes got fogged with the smoke rising from the tea cup. I was enjoying the tea, the chirping of the hidden birds were coming from the eastern side, also the golden streaks of the new sun. The light cool breeze was blowing from the hill, was bringing the life from the green lines.

Jallaluddinn, though clever by his standards, still did not fathom my indifference and continued telling, he was talkative by nature, knew the ways to make the days beautiful and bright.

"Our state Jharkhand is full with elephants, small, big, elephants of all sizes you will get here. Sometimes the elephants also come from Bengal." He looked at the rising sun; the orange rays were falling on his face. He was a man in his fifties, not tall, with medium height, strongly built and beard covered his somewhat square face, the strong biceps was showing the strength of the man and the un-fallen eye lids showed the determination.

Again I sipped tea from the cup, the light touch of the porcelain, like the touch of the beloved, was touching my heart and new emotion seeped into me and my impassive eyes opened further.

"Our Saab, Sanjeb Kumar had made a canvass showing the elephants," he told me. Instantly my eyes opened, I wanted to listen the story of the girl in the canvass.

"The canvass of the girl with the elephant herd was a true picture. Our Saab on that day was in the field, supervising the driving away job and we saw that girl, in front of the rampaging herd. She was not fearful, like other villagers, rather she was calm, her eyes were shining like a star and my Saab captured that girl in his canvass." Jallauddion, the forest guard was telling the story. In the previous night, Sanjeeb was telling the story of the rampaging elephants, and today the forest guard was narrating the story of the rampaging elephants. My interest grew further, and the speaker in front of me was equally eager to tell the stories of the elephants and he started narrating the events associated with the herd.

Elephant drive Story as listened from Jallaluddin

"Saab got the information about the arrival of thirteen elephants from Bengal at Gorga village under Nirsa Forest Beat, a place thirty kilometers away from Dhanbad town and in the eastern direction, towards Bengal. There was no earlier incidence of elephant's arrival in that area, in fact that was not the area frequented by the elephants. Saab and others rushed immediately to the area, as they anticipated the elephants to be a splinter group strayed into the area and they might damage life and property. They persuaded the villagers not to disturb the herd, else the herd might harm life and damage property, and the villagers were asked not to go near the elephants. The crowd had never seen the wild elephants, and they thought the herd to be same as the tamed elephants, tender, soft and docile. The crowd had surrounded the wild elephants, and the elephants were in irritated conditions we persuaded the crowd, they agreed with reluctance and retreated to a distance. The herd was standing in a small forested block, mostly dotted with Palash trees and the ripened paddy fields were adjacent to that forest. The village, a tribal hamlet was having mud houses with burnt earthen tiles on the top the village was highly vulnerable to elephant damage. The villagers again came closer, one elephant mock charged at them and they retreated. Suddenly one mischievous person threw a burning masal at the elephants and the full herd charged the crowd. They ran for shelter, the elephants trumpeted, and the forest officials with great difficulty controlled the situation, persuaded the people not to disturb the elephants.

The elephants then went to Dumka, and were later traced at Jamtada. News poured in, during evening, message came about the movement of the elephants towards Tundi block. The villagers of that area were informed accordingly, asked to maintain calm and not to disturb the herd. The staffs of Dumka and Hazaribagh were sent for patrolling duty on rotation, directed to stay alert, put their camps inside the forest and wait for the direction from the higher office." Jallaludin was telling the story of the herd, later came in the news paper, which was the inspiring force for the creation of the girl in the canvass.

"It was decided to drive the elephants away from Dhanbad, and a driving party was formed. The driving technique was not that complex, simple, but needs a lot of patience and skill. The elephants used to be driven away during the night by using burning torches, and bursting firecrackers and giving them a direction to retreat a lot of skill is required to give the direction; else the herd would damage the houses." The man was continuing. But, to me it was a dramatic beginning, an exciting story. He, without uttering a single word, probably understood my feelings in my eyes, continued.

"Throughout the night we remained close to the elephants, and the new dawn came with a new member, a new calf was born during the previous night and the number of elephants increased to fourteen. The herd was moving towards Barbadgand village under Maharajganj Forest Beat under Tundi Range, stayed near Khalia village for the day. The public as usual gathered around and the herd was disturbed. There were many young members in the herd; and the group was frightened at the presence of such a big crowd around and they were charging at the people at intervals. In between the elephants broke two houses in the village and damaged few paddy fields. The greatest challenge before us was to escort the elephants to a safe place and ensure that no houses are further damaged and no life is lost. The elephants were moving in a thickly habited area and dense forest was nowhere near. The compensation for the crop can be paid, but losing a life would be a great risk the compensation in fact is very low and the affected people were highly agitated on earlier occasions for such crop loss and were very angry on the department and in anger could harm the elephants. The department asked for a team of masalwallahs from Bengal who were considered as experts in driving the wild elephants away and giving them proper direction, the herd do not come near to the village or crop fields. Those masalwallahs took position, allowed the elephants to go in a pre-determined direction and ensured that the elephants do not come closer to villages or towns, were directed to the less inhabited areas and the herd moved ahead." Jallaluddin took a break, galloped water from the steel glass, looked at me and continued further.

Earlier I knew Jallaluddin to be an interesting person, he knew the tricks to make the discussions lively, he fathoms the mood of the listener, also tries to remove the boredom in a narration. He suddenly changed the topic, brought a new event to the horizon.

Other elephant stories told by Jallaluddin

"There was an unusual elephant in herd, unlike others it used to disappear exactly at 11.30 pm in the night, and the elephant was very particular about the time and nobody could trace it further in the night. The driving party, till recently tried to get the disappearing elephant, but were at wits end due to its mysterious disappearance in the night exactly at 11:30 pm. As usual the driving party loses the track at 11:30 in the night, the elephant then moved to the hamlets and run amok, broke huts. I was made a member of the newly formed driving team and was given the direction to track the elephant, not to allow it to disappear at 11:30 a.m. We, the forest guards, foresters looked at the recently broken cottages, the Santhal lady, skin next to the bone, without any visible flesh, with torn clothes was sitting on a Charpai. Her child, again a thinly clad, poorly nourished, was sleeping next to her, poverty reflected in his tender body too. Those hallow eyes of the lady spoke about the difficult period they went through; they had to pass for days and nights like that. Saab, if you would ever visit the Santhal village, then you would only be able to understand the plight of the people there. The houses are built with mud walls, roofs thatched with paddy straws, or leaves from forest, sometimes tiles, these houses are never an obstruction but play items for the rampant elephant. The dried tear on the shallow cheeks, on the corners of the eyes narrated the plight to me, she appeared like a statue of destitute. The elephant had broken her house three days back, ate the little crop she had, and now they were left homeless, remained starved, with no hope for getting food and shelter from any quarter. Most of their neighbours met the same fate, and the poor Santhals didn't have sufficient food to eat in the next day." The gloom of the Santhal village was reflected in the eyes of the forest guard. The plight of the woman was reflected after so many days in the eyes of the speaker. He paused for a while, looked at me, eagerness on my face encouraged him to speak further. He moved his hand over his sized, mehendi dyed beard and started telling.

"They were no different, all victims of the rogue elephant, the Santhal villages were the victims of the rampaging elephants. The people were hapless, and strangely during that period the eyes of all villagers were hallow, helplessness reflected in their faces, and they had resigned themselves to their fate. Is not it better to die once, rather being victim of the rogue elephant every day? I told the villagers, to me of course, to increase my determination. We were firm in our belief the days of rampaging elephants in the paddy fields of Santhals is over. We persuaded them, and the villagers agreed to be part of the team to tackle the elephants. It is better to die than to leave everything to the destiny and they were showing the sign of courage and zeal to drive away the elephant from their homeland. But how could it be? The elephants were wild, rouge too and were not leaving the fields. The villagers tried to drive away the elephants using the fire crackers, but met with terrible failure, the elephant charged at them, they fled and the herd almost ransacked their entire village; they were in dilemma, we coaxed, they agreed, the courage returned, all the villagers would stay united. It was the story of Khathikund, a forested area, near to Dumka." The forest guard was telling the stories of his liasioning, a success, a small one, but for the villagers the party was like a group sent from the heaven, to emancipate them from the fear of being trampled by huge legs. He paused, took a long breathe, the fresh air was filling his lungs, and his face was glowing in excitement, tinged red with colour of the morning sun rays.

Elephant drive story continues

He then continued further, "It was late night, people with us were many men, all Santhals, they are not strongly built like we people, are usually lean, medium built, but they have good stamina to move for hours. We moved forward, nobody spoke, and there was no light around. The moonlight was falling on the ground and giving shapes to the trees, stones. The elephant could be anywhere, waiting for our arrival, they had no fear for human, and were looking for the opportunities to harm. Our eyes touched all black articles, moving or stationery and then we saw the elephants. They were two in number, standing on a damaged paddy field, the golden paddy crop was illuminated and the black structures of the elephant was giving it more contrast. The paddy crops were fully damaged, and the poor owner, a member of the party, could not control his tears; but he did not cry, only drop of his helplessness rolled down from his eyes. The elephants, probably had a good meal, now were more interested to play and they did not notice our arrival, so cautious we were. They were hitting their feet to the ground, making the soil loose and powdery, and then collect the loose soil by feet, taking the same into their nose and finally throwing the soil onto their back. A structure, aura around the body, was created with the next movement. The elephants were busy in their soil gathering game, and the trekkers came closer and closer. Suddenly, one of the elephants looked at the group and raised its trunk, the other elephant raised its trunks too. We listened to some hissing sounds; probably the elephants were communicating between themselves." The forest guard stopped. I was imagining the herd in the canvass. The sweet face of the girl came alive in my memory.

Then Jallaluddin continued further.

"We are around 40-45 people, 25-30 torch-men and the rest were staffs. The torch-men, called Mashalwallahas, were from Bengal, and they used to drive the elephants to a distance of 30-35 kms in a night. The Mashalwallahs are divided into two groups, around twenty people lead the group with longer Mashals and the smaller group of around fifteen people followed them with smaller Mashals. The other staffs also accompanied the Mashalwallahs. We were never tired, there was always a thrill and of course intension to keep the elephants at the right place so that common people are not harmed and the elephants live happily. Packed food was served at 11 pm, we finished food and proceeded ahead.

Sometimes the common people used to join us, but usually we avoid those people as they are untrained and instead of directing the elephants properly, they create more chaos. One elephant lifted its trunk a little more, others followed and they trumpeted together. They knew the arrival of the intruders, the echo came from the forest, the peaks of the mountains answered the calls of the elephants. Again the elephant trumpeted, and it was more deep and more chilling, the people around were frightened, the villagers involuntarily of course, turned backward at once and almost started running as if the deaths are nearing, who had the courage to see the sight of dusky elephants in moonlit night standing at the edge of the forest and trumpeting together and charging at the human gathering, after all they had seen the ferocity of the dusky elephants. We tried to prevent them from running away, their courage has to be regenerated again, and they have to fight their own battles in future.

We know the nature of the rowdy elephants, they would charge as soon as the human group scatters, run hither and thither and everybody would be in serious trouble. We shouted at the fleeing Santhals to stop, not to disperse, the fleeing Santhals stopped, the charging elephants stopped too. We then lighted the torches but on that night we had not enough diesel with us.

It was somewhere 3.30 am in the morning, the chill of chilly morning was trespassing our thickest clothes and the Santhals, had little clothing over their bodies were unable to prevent the chill wind penetrating deep into their bones they were practically shivering. Sighting the burning torches, tall flames dancing with wind, the elephant herd stopped, their trumpet fell silent. If the torches would be extinguished, the fear of facing the most dreaded group in a dark chilly night was disturbing us. To deter the elephants from charging, more diesels were poured into the flame and fire rose higher. The flickering flames swung with the wind, the orange light fell on the dust covered elephants, and their tiny eyes glowed in anger, in our side, the eyes of the villagers glowed with excitement, shined with determination. They would drive those rowdy elephants away from their village and would send them to Dumka forest. After all the elephants were sighted after so many days and the group should not stop at the instance of not having much diesel. The In-Charge forester radioed the message for more diesel, at least 100 litres, more for the flaming the torches for the rest of the night, and the affirmation came and the group gathered further courage. I looked at the crowd, it now swallowed to almost hundred in number, and one of our forest guards was having a 303 riffle and the Santhals were armed with long lathis. The crackers busted, the elephants moved to the direction of less noise, and the party followed them, our heartbeats jumped, our legs jumped longer and the vibration of the flickering flames increased further. One of our forest guard shouted, Oh boys, you are the sons of the Lord of Kapilash, don't be angry on the small creatures like us, don't charge at us. Retreat, retreat to the jungle of Deogarh. The morning was still far away, the eastern horizon was yet to be lighted and the dark night sky was filled with twinkling stars, we were escorting the elephants away from the human habitation." The forest guard stopped a while. My eyes were also glowing, I could feel the warm blood rushing to my ears. His eyes were now shining like bright stars. Then he continued further,

"The crackers busted again and also increased the number of trumpets of the elephants. The men with the burning torches flocked together and came closer to the trumpeting elephants and were hardly few meters away from the elephants which were known for their terror. One man threw a high sounding cracker at the elephants and it burst with a bang near the ear of the biggest one and it flipped its ears violently. That was the elephant most visible, the rogue one which never cared the burning torches or the crackers. Its eyes were burning in anger and in hatred too, but it could not dare to charge at the huge crowd with burning torches and high sounding crackers. On torch-man came near to the big elephant and hit it with sharpened rod to frighten the elephant further."

"Hit the rowdy elephants with a rod!" I exclaimed, could not believe the story of the forest guard.

"Saab, I didn't tell you about the Mashals, the burning torches. It is not like a small piece of burning wood, you can't go near the elephants with a small wood. As I told you earlier, the Mashals have a ball of fire just after the sharp end." The forest guard paused, and then continued after taking a long breath.

Mashals

The bigger Mashals is usually seven to eight feet long iron rod, pointed at the front end, just after that jute bags are tightly bounded to the rod by iron wires, on which diesel is poured and then fire is ignited, diesel is preferred over kerosene for the simple reason that the diesel burns for a longer period than kerosene because of thicker texture. As the ball catches fire, the pointed portion gets hotter and hotter and become red hot. It gives a terrible punch to the unwilling elephants. As one put diesel, the flames rose further and it swings with the movement of the drivers. The mashals are like a wave, from a distance appeared like crests and toughs of an oscillating wave. Apart from the bigger Mashals, smaller mashals of same materials, each around three to four feet long, are made which are used to throw at the charging elephants. The Mashals are the best instruments to drive away the most unwilling rogue elephants. The people with longer rod move in the front, the people with smaller Mashal follow at the back.

When the elephant charges at the driving party, at that time the front drivers are in danger, then there is action for the people at the second line with smaller mashals, they throw the mashals at the attacking elephant; the red hot portion of the rod becomes the most potent weapon in the hands of the driving party. The elephant, in great anger touches the swinging ball of fire by its trunk and it gets burned and the most unwilling elephant retreats. It is most frightening moment for a wild elephant; the smaller mashals are reigning on the body like cannon balls with sharp ends, the bigger mashals working as the sharpest spear. Sometimes the elephants don't move despite of the burning mashal, in that case, the people in the front touches the body of the adamant elephant with the hot rod, the touch is extremely painful, the unwilling elephant moves further.

I was seeing a different world, the driving method was so elaborate, the forest guard continued,

"The party also busted the firecrackers. The firecrackers were of bigger size, used to produce a lot of noise, the sound and the flash terrorizes the elephants. Sometimes some angry elephants do not care the burning rod and charges at the people as happened earlier in Dhanbad district two years back." The forest guard paused, now I was a keen listener did not want a break.

"What happened?" I asked the person in front.

The forest guard smiled, he was very happy to get such a keen listener, and continued,

"That time we were driving the elephant, a huge male, in the night; it did not care the burning Mashal, caught it in anger, twisted the red hot iron by its trunk and the torch-man, most fortunately got the time to flee from the scene. But the hot iron had its toll on the elephants; the trunk got burnt, the elephant screamed in agony; Saab, you will be surprised the at the sound, the sound of a goat came from the mouth of the tallest elephants of the district. The elephant ran towards the vacant land, and the crowd, seeing the snatching of the mashals by the elephant ran in the other direction. So Saab, the mashals were the most potent weapons. Now I am coming to the most recent story." He stopped and looked at the bamboo bushes nearby; bamboo is the most sought after food of the elephants. After some time he continued narrating the story.

"We were following the elephants throughout the night, were very tired at the end, did not have energy to lift the legs, the crowd too were extremely tired we had been pursuing the elephants from midnight non-stop, without any halt, without any rest. In came a strong wind and the torches were extinguished suddenly, may be due to wind, may be due to intentional act of the people, those who didn't want the job further. The forester in charge shouted at the torch man. They trembled, fumbled the elephants were lost in the darkness was the meek reply.

At the direction of the controlling forester, they again lighted the torches and the group continued its search for the vanishing elephants. We tried to encourage the tiring group to complete the drive away job, and in that night the elephant herd had to be driven out of the district. They promised, nobody would take roti unless the herd was driven away. The new enthusiasm was there in the air and till the herd would be driven out, they would not stop for food or water. The group shouted at full throttle, the firecrackers bursted again and again with the loudest bangs and the whole night sky was illuminated again. Suddenly we sighted the elephants; they were standing in the middle of ripened paddy fields. As we came nearer, the elephants ran away, our group ran along with. We were near to the border of Deogarh, and our job was going to end soon. Most unfortunately, the diesel stock was fully consumed and we had no further fuel, more and more torches started getting extinguished; only four from the total thirty torches were still giving light. In our front, the elephants were standing near a well and the crowd was on the other side; to our left the ripened paddy fields ran for almost a kilometer till the jungle, and to the right, the sleeping hamlets were located, only hundred meters away. We were apprehensive, if the herd changes the direction towards the hamlet, then it would damage the huts and there might be casualties, a graet risk. SOS message was sent for further direction and in came the return message from the mobile van; the fuel was reaching us shortly. The group shouted and their cheers echoed from the mountains, the villagers in the slipping hamlets also roared and the standing elephants trumpeted, no rage, but the sound of defeat in their trumpets now. The mobile van came with the diesel, the extinguished torches were lighted again, the orange flame flickered and the atmosphere was again filled with the sounds of the fire crackers and the shout of the villagers. The terrified elephants ran towards the darkness again, our group was in hot pursuit, we didn't know when the elephants crossed the border of the Dhanbad district and entered into Deogarh district and the border was sealed". The forest guard completed the story. I was surprised. Satisfaction was reflected from his eyes, smile on the face.

Sealing, it is a strange word in the language of a forester. I didn't know the meaning.

"What does it mean really?" I asked the satisfied forester. He took a long breathe, to fill his lungs again, he had pursued the elephants a long way.

"Sealing means putting the camps on the border and keeping the burning torches lighted throughout the night and then guarding the border day and night for few days. It is a known fact that the elephants follow a definite pattern of movement, they prefer the same path which they have been using since long. If some kind of obstruction is put on the path then they can't move in the same direction and it is called sealing. If the elephant starts from a place, then it comes back to the same place after some time following the same path." The answer was given.

"Why did not you try your driving process during the day time, the herd would be visible better?" I asked the forest guard. I was ignorant of the elephant driving process.

"During the day time, the elephants used to go to a particular place and stay there throughout, only they move in the night in search of food. When we pursue the elephants, the crowed was cautioned not to disturb the elephants further, allow them to remain still at a place of their choice." The forest guard was replying.

"What happened further on that night?" I asked the man.

"Slowly and slowly the eastern horizon got brightened, we, the shouting groups were extremely tired and all sat on the ground. The atmosphere was filled with chirpings of the morning birds. Our torches were still burning, but the flame was getting fainter with the gradual arrival of the morning light. The horizon was getting clearer and the elephants were more clearly visible; most of them were around ten feet tall, skin lightened due to dust deposits, trunks down and no more fire in their eyes. The tired and terrified elephants were driven out of the district boundary." He was giving the finishing touch to his story. After taking a long breathing, he continued further.

Other elephant stories told by Jallaluddin

"Many interesting incidents happened during their transit; after all they were the most covered group for the news papers and electronic media." Jallaluddin wanted to add spices to the story. I was amazed to listen, the marauding elephants, not only left the broken houses, but created so many stories.

"They liked the hadia drink the most, among the eatables available in a Santhal house." The forest guard was opening the unknown habit of the elephants.

"Really!" I could not speak further. I knew the hadia, also called handia, a country brew made out of rice, is the most sought after drink of the Santhals; a Santhal loves to consume little hadia, it is a drink of life, brings immense joy, the Sal forests dances with the feet, the birds sings with the sounds of the drums; and the elephants too like the taste of the drink, they developed the same love for the drink. Jallaluddin then started telling an incident.

The elephants used to be attracted towards the hadia, many a times breaks houses for it, drinks it, sounds surprising but it is true. There was a big elephant, a huge one, it developed a strange taste for hadia, it used to search for the drink in the tribal hamlets. The big elephant once came to a village along with other group members; the village was consisting of around ten mud houses with earthenwalls. The herd got the smell of the hadia, did not go to the courtyard for eating gathered paddy, rather they entered into the compound of a house where the hadia was kept, the small fencing around was not an obstacle. The bigger elephant pushed the mud wall of the house with its head, the wall felled a little and an opening was created. A small elephant was pushed into the opening, it went inside, collected the hadia pot with its little trunk and handed over the same to the bigger elephant, and the bigger one drank the brew immediately. Others also searched for the drink, all the houses where they got the smell of the hadia were raided, the hadia were consumed by the elephants." Jallaluddin, the forest guard was smiling at the memory of the elephants love for liquor. Like human being, the elephants like to be drunk in some part of their life, to forget being chased by a group of Mashalwallas, to forget the knowledge of their lost habitat, the forest guard thinks so.

"Saab, the herd was very kind too, if you are reasonable and kind, they would be kind too. I listened, it did not happen during the chasing process," again Jallaludin was unfolding the inner life of the elephants. My eyes expanded in disbelief, my ears were eager to listen further story.

"Saab, they obeyed us so much, they recognise the forest staffs, our directions are always followed, our presence is recognised by the elephants." Jallaluddin told something unbelievable, I was interested to know further, didn't want to break the flow of the words, might there be some coincidences, and the elephants are highly intelligent creatures. He continued further.

"It was another incident, the time was late in the evening and the elephants were standing in front of a house. The herd was about to damage a cottage, the owner, an old woman in her late 60's came out in tottering legs and bowed her head with the folded hands. The herd did not damage the house and were returning, suddenly a person from the house threw a burning fire ball made of paddy straw, at the elephant and the elephants returned with anger, destroyed the house. The prayer of the old lady went in vain." He took a rest, drank a glass of water and continued saying –

"The elephants understand the emotion of people; they are intelligent creatures. Once one elephant was not listening, I went closer and told the elephant that what kind of God he was and why was he destroying the houses of the poor people: strangely it understood and did not destroy the houses further. Once, one elephant did not listen to us, the DFO Saab was around, he went near to it with a stick, it understood, bowed its head in reverence to the DFO Saab and slowly left for the forest." The forest guard looked at the sky, it was clean and bright; many stories were so created, I was surprised, amazed at the stories, at listening the narration on the elephant behaviour.

Looking at my interest, Jallauddin also got some momentum, he wanted to bring more encounters of the forest staffs with the elephants, the man was charming, and his robe was full of interesting stories.

One more elephant story

"The forester in charge of the beat was a lean and thin man, a person hardly had the enough energy to run at a faster pace, and he once turned a dare devil, showed the rampaging elephants the way." He ignited the dying interest, my ears were eager for further narration.

"Oh! Really?" I was astonished. Then he started telling –

"That day the elephant herd was resting at the outskirts of the village, Dinanath, Forester was in charge of the area, he was given the job to control the mob, also to control the elephants; the task, for a person of his caliber looked impossible. The message had gone to the driving party about the presence of the elephants, their arrival would take some time, and till that time mob need to be controlled. People were shouting at the elephants, some were coming closer, the ears of the elephants started fluttering, the forester Dinananth fathomed danger, the herd might charge, the option before him, either take the mob away from the elephants, or take the elephant away from the mob, and he picked up the second option. He had some novel ideas, he knew, the elephants don't harm naked person, thinks it to be monkey, after all he was a stunch disciple of Lord Hanuman. Then for him Hanuman was much superior to Ganesji, the elephants. He removed all his clothes, was in his underwear, and kept his uniform wrapped on a big stick at one end, the stick appeared like a Gada (club), the most preferred weapon of Lord Hanuman, and went near the elephant herd despite of warning from everybody including his own subordinates, all requesting him not to do such a folly," Jallaluddin paused a little, looked at me, I didn't understand the humour associated with the event, where as he was smiling at the memory of the event.

"Ganesh baba follow me, he begged, after all no harm in bowing the head before Lord Ganesh, after all Hanuman knew how to give proper respect to other Gods. To the greatest surprise of all, the herd followed him, noiselessly; the herd understood the meaning of request. The man was moving in front, the whole herd was following the naked man, and they were leaving the village territory.

One man in cycle came from the otherside, he didn't know the episode till then, he shouted at the naked man, asked him to wear the dresses, to behave in a better manner before the villagers. The elephants were terribly angry, they didn't tolerate the arrogance of the new comer and the humiliation of the undressed man, they caught the cycle, the man escaped, ran for his life, the angry elephants broke the cycle. The group moved further, no body dared to speak a word and they met a child, he was also naked, was sitting on the ground, face and body were covered with dust, he was crying; one elephant gently carried the boy by its trunk and kept him at a comfortable place, no harm was done to the boy," Jallaluddin completed a new chapter on elephant behaviour.

It was such an interesting story, never in my wildest thought I ever could believe a man to behave like Lord Shiva and direct the elephants, but it happened in the real world, I had to believe the man in my front.

Looking at my interest Jallaluddin was also encouraged to go further, his real story, the elephant drive in the district has not been completed. Jallaluddion was also eager to tell further stories.

"The elephant herd was around the Murlipahadi village, our driving group was a little distance away, some naughty boys of the village unnecessarily threw firecrackers at the herd, the high sound irritated the elephants. That time I was taking food, was sitting on the ground, behind the jeep. Horrified, I saw two elephants running at the jeep, but fortunately they did not turn the vehicle, so my life was saved. The driving group rushed to the hamlet, it was devastated, four houses were broken, and the elephant herd had shown their anger for unnecessary disturbances. The fields around the village were damaged and the villagers were terrified, fortunately there were no harm to life." He was slowly and slowly unfolding many stories associated with the herd.

"Sir, you have seen the smaller elephants, immature males, sometimes Makhnas, they are much bigger than the buffaloes, and in a dark night one cattleman mistook the elephant as a buffalo," his presentation style was so interesting. I nodded my head; I was interested to know about the incident.

Cattle Herdsman & the Elephant

A cattle herdsman went to forest along with his herd of cattle, evening started casting the shadow, but one buffalo did not turn up. He was puzzled, a buffalo was a big money for him and he searched for his lost buffalo in the thick forest in that dark evening. He tried to gather courage, why not few glass of country liquor, he thought and drank few glasses of Hadia; in between his buffalo came and entered into the shed and took rest; but the inebriated man didn't know, went out to search the missing elephant. In the twilight zone of the jungle, he lost direction and reached the bamboo forest. An elephant was taking rest there, he could not differentiate between the buffalo and the elephant in semi-darkness, thought the resting elephant to be the buffalo, the bigger size of the elephant looked smaller to him and he came to the bamboo forest. The elephant was sitting after a small bund, the man climbed the small bund could not understood further depression ahead, he was at level with the elephants, to him the big beast appeared like his dark buffalo, the buffalo needs to be taught with a lesson, so he hit the sitting elephant with his stick.

"You naughty buffalo, you troubled me so much, you need a beating," he screamed and hit few blows.

"I am so troubled for not getting you, and you beast, you are taking such a good rest here," he was terribly angry. Those were his last words, the angry elephant caught the inebriated man, and trampled him, his friends were looking at him from a distance, they could not do anything for him, couldn't dare, they ran for their life, escaped certain death.

"What happened to the original elephants, those were to be driven out of your area?" I asked him.

"We had arrived at the boundary of Deoghar, the elephants entered into a different territory, the Conservator of Forest of Deogarh was informed about the arrival of the wild elephants; and the Deogarh Forest Division got themselves readied for the new challenge. The driving party bade farewell to the rampaging herd, their work had been completed, the elephants went to the other side and the party returned back to their respective working places. Before returning, Ladu and Puri were kept on the ground, an offering for the elephants to pacify, a ritual of course but a practicing tradition, followed by all.

"Where did they exactly land up at the end? The driving process never ended there, I knew Deoghar is a relatively open land, not much area for the big herd like this," I asked the question to Jallaluddin.

"The final solution – let the elephant go of its own, let them not be disturbed on the way, let them not be given direction for movement, let them roam peacefully, the humans have encroached there area, only few hundred odd souls to be adjusted in such vast land." The man resigned himself to the events, he was too perturbed by the plight of the elephants, and he couldn't hold his views.

Part-B

Elephants drive in Deoghar

I listened many stories on elephants; mostly the stories were created during the process of elephant drive at different places in Jharkhand. Once I listened to the elephant driving stories at Deoghar in the state of Jharkhand. I knew about Deoghar, in this place the Satguru asramas of Nigamanada sect is located. It is Badidynathdham, an important place of Shaivite Hindus, the revered Trikut hills is just adjacent, thousands of devotees converge to the place, and the roaming elephants were once required to be driven out of that territory, that time their presence would have been life threats to many people.

That day I was sitting with the forest officials, during the discussion the stories of the rampaging groups came out, the group that moved around in the hinterlands of Santhals.

Elephant drive from Deoghar to Banka

It was April, 2007, the news of the arrival of the herd was flashed in the local newspapers, a group of sixteen elephants had arrived from Banka in Bihar and the congregation was reported at Tulsitand, a place located between Banka & Jamui; so the forest staff rushed to the spot. That time was night, the Deputy Commissioner called up the Divisional Forest Officer, the media people started enquiring about the animal from the Conservator of Forests, Deoghar, from every quarter the message started pouring about the movement of the herd. In the thick night, the elephant herd could not be located; the team again went in search of the elephant in the morning and found that the heard in fact had come near to Deoghar college during the previous night, the information was a matter of panic for the inhabitants of Deoghar, from there they went to Bhawan village, rested there for the entire day near a flowing stream surrounded by scattered trees. As usual, the common public was unmanageable, belief, mischief and sometimes foolishness of the people was making the situation extremely tense, thus increased the difficulty of the forest officers. The people were restless, the forest people called police for public control, they arrived, the onlookers were pushed to safe distance, the people were restrained from going close to the elephant.

The people had mad beliefs, some reached with thali (steel plate) and flower, the Ganesh Bhagwan had come to the village, need to be worshipped properly. They were somehow restrained from going close to the wild elephants. They had seen elephants that remained close to the people, not the wild ones, the Mahabat used to move with the tamed elephants in the village. For the common people, the elephant from the wilderness, not under the control of any human being, are the real Ganesh Bhagwan; so there was excitement in the atmosphere, thrill at the arrival of the Ganesh Bhagwan. It was decided to drive the elephants during the evening, a prevalent practice, however towards late afternoon the herd started moving towards the stream. The officials requested for the experts from Dumka, those people actually worked with the elephant chasers from Bankura of West Bengal on couple of occasions, later got some expertise, so were frequently hired by the forest department for the elephant chase at different places.

There were many hurdles, the major hurdles came from the common people as usual, and they did not understand the gravity of the situation, and sometimes many were alarmingly coming close to the elephants. The elephant group movements were regularly monitored; driving was put to halt till the night fall and the driving started in the night. The villagers were alert but careless, to ensure that the herd wouldn't come to their village, they created many kinds of fires, as a result all the villages on the way were illuminated as if Diwali had come once again in April, they had made a lot of makeshift marshals. Controlling so many villagers in night was extremely difficult when the villagers were so much excited at the driving process; watching the retreating heard was matter of great thrill, but most importantly the villagers did not know how to handle angry elephants, a simple mistake, there might be causalities. In that charged atmosphere, giving the elephants a suitable direction was a great task, a great challenge. Some villagers were keeping vigil by putting burning tyres or burning logs in front of their villages, some in front of their houses, the elephant would be frightened, would not come near their habitation. Few people even put fire to the standing Khajur trees by pouring kerosene and diesel over it, the branches of the Khajur trees, sometimes the entire trees, were burning; the villages were getting brightly illuminated. Now, everywhere the Khajur trees around the villages were burning, a terrible scene, at the backdrop of black horizon, the orange flames were creating terrifying figures, the shouting of the villagers were echoing from all quarter, the environment was there confuse the elephants, and the task – to give the elephants a proper direction was getting increasingly bigger and taller, much tougher challenge now. It was a great relief; the elephants did not raid the villages on the way.

The elephants marched faster, the driving party missed the elephants somehow, and the group could not sight the dusky elephants in that night, probably the elephant had marched ahead, but after a while, it was found out to be wrong information. Confirmation came, the controlling party got the message, the herd had been divided into two parts, the elephant herd generally avoids splitting at the time of crisis, but here they were divided into two groups, the members must be highly frightened, must be in highly agitated mood, much more care need to be taken. Noise came from a distant village, Oh-Ho-Ho, Oh-Ho-Ho, suddenly the screams of the villagers came from all angles, the scared elephants, the smaller group comprising of a tusker and one young and rest females were following the major herd, and were coming towards the control party who were in a jeep, the vehicle was parked just outside a village. By the time they understood, the elephants crossed, the driving party couldn't believe their eyes, the elephants ran alongside the jeep, almost touching it, but did not harm the sitting people, they went to a crop field and started eating there. The driving party was immediately called, others were asked not to disturb the elephants, and the owner of the field was informed about the compensation for the crop damage, somehow the situation was brought under control. After a brief rest and food, the splinter elephant group was pacified; they were then escorted to the main herd by the driving party.

Now the people were relaxed in Deoghar, but the elephants were not far away from the Trikuti hills which is a group of three hills with some vegetation, an important religious place, a pilgrim centre and a lot of devotees gather in that area throughout the day, the driving party was apprehensive, the elephants should not be allowed to go towards the Trikuti hills, else situation would go out of control. The elephants entered into scattered bamboo forest, sat in that area, the message was understood, now the elephants were taking rest and they would not move, also driving them through the bamboo forest would be risky, the forest was full with bamboo splinters and shrapnel; entering into that forest in darkness would have been foolish. The elephants were allowed to take rest throughout the day, again the driving started in the next night, and finally the herd was driven to Dumka border, towards the wooded areas of Kathikund, near Nanihat, the only living place for the elephant herds.

While the elephants were being driven during that night, the control party received a call from the confidential cell of the Deputy Commissioner's office – the elephants were again sighted near Jasidihi, a unlikely place of retreat for the elephants near Dumka border, and apprehension in the air – the splinter group might disrupt important railway services, also the villagers around were highly terrified. All were nervous; the splinter group of the elephants might have avoided the net of the driving party, escaped towards Jasidihi, without the knowledge of the driving people. Jasidihi police station was again contacted, they confirmed, the message had come from the villagers around, so the villagers were contacted – the elephant news was all around, people were sitting with Mashals, but nobody could give concrete information. A lot of troubles around, the control party reached the police station, again got the confirmed report, the elephants were around the Jasidihi over bridge, the new cemented bridge over the main railways track, a matter of serious concern to all. All over the black roads, burning tyres were kept, again a new Diwali on that night, the people of Jasidihi were celebrating the night of light, not with joy, but with apprehension. The people were contacted, no one had in fact seen the elephant, the people from other village shouted, they believed, and shouted too. A man was coming on a motorcycle, was asked about position of the elephants, he expressed his ignorance, but he had procured fire crackers from the market to drive away the elephants from his village, also procured kerosene for the mashals. He left, a strange situation was around, everyone was in the state of fear, and nobody had actually seen the elephants. Finally, it turned out to rumour, elephants were not seen by anyone.

Coming back to the actual driving, on that night, the elephants were finally pushed to Dumka. The people of Deoghar took a sigh of relief, but trouble started in Dumka. Later, the driving party of Dumka also pushed the elephants to Banka in Bihar, the bordering district of Deoghar.

"Where, the elephants went?" I asked the group, pale smile appeared on the face,

“The elephant had gone to Lahore,” the local Range officer told, means the elephant had gone out of his territory to other’s territory, was the answer.

“Then what about India,” was my second question.

“The next day’s information came, the elephant had come to India, reached Amritsar,” was again the faint reply, a reply of disbelief came from them. Those were the strange words to correlate places with elephant movement.

I looked at them, gloom over their face, they were confused at the subject. I looked at one senior officer,

“What happened to the elephants finally?” was my question, any one ignorant of the area would ask same type of question, we were taught to get an answer in the form of yes or no.

He didn’t answer immediately, only a sigh came, a retreat from belief, his confidence was biting dust inside, and he spoke in a tame voice, a recorded voice in very low pitch,

“This particular herd has been moving between Jamui, Tulsitad, Nunihaat, Kathikund, and Banka. They are also searching for a place to stay, but there is no permanent place for the elephants. The elephants are also looking for shelter, for space, to live peacefully with their young and old, but no place for them to live in, the humans have encroached upon their territory, and their voice never got reflected in the newspaper headlines. The truth is that the elephant has no place to go – their living areas have been encroached upon by the humans, the movement corridors are totally broken, for them dark frightening nights are coming again like waves in the sea, no place to retreat.” His voice was gradually turning inaudible.

The elephants by nature migrate from one place to another place; the herd cannot remain stationary at a place. The earlier jungles have been converted to fields and human habitations, it was not the fault of the elephants, rather the fragmentation of the migrated route resulted in straying of elephants to human habitations resulting in casualties both in human side and from elephant side too.

Where the elephants will go? There is no living place for the elephants, nowhere to go, the elephants are to be thrown out of the boundary, Tadiipaar, the most appropriate Hindi word for the driven away elephants. The elephants are not to be seen.

Part-C

Earlier I have described the stories on elephant drives in the state of Jharkhand, the plight of the elephants, their agony, the elephants are always refugees in their own land. While moving in the Raygada district in Odisha, I witnessed the elephant drive in my own eyes, the elephant driving process was different here, instead of waiting for the night, the party was driving the elephants during the day time, may be terrain of the area was totally different in comparison to the Jharkhand where the location is highland with not many hills in between, the valleys there are far wide, and in Raygada, the terrain is difficult, the hills are interspaced with narrow valleys, and the density of forest is more.

Elephant drive at Rayagada

On that day an elephant driving under the direct command of the DFO, at a place called Hazaridang, under Gunupur Range; the executive magistrate was standing along with the police force from Odisha Reserve Battalion to control public; five Range officers from different ranges and almost twenty forest guards were busy in locating and driving the elephants. A special wildlife team headed by Mr. Purohit, and the trackers of Chandka Wildlife Sanctuary bordering the state capital Bhubaneswar, were already in the job, trying to track the elephants hidden behind the bushes and trees. The villagers, also people from all nearby villages gathered on the road, the newspaper correspondents from Gunupur, Rayagada too were there with their cameras, small children came along with their fathers, the women folk and very young ones of the villages were sent to their respective relatives houses in other villages, the elephant raid was imminent. Some courageous villagers were already on the hill, clinging to the biggest banyan tree there alongside a big rock, I could see them through my binocular, few were also standing on a big rock, all of them were pointing at the elephant location down below, in the valley. Ahead, the low roofed, earthen tiled houses of the tribal hamlet existed, the houses were deserted, the able bodied ones were witnessing the driving process. Towards the right of the village, thick forests consists of tamarind, mahua, asan, and other trees continued, curved right and went towards the hill where the people were watching the elephants from a height. Behind the forest, towards the left of the village, there was a minor irrigation project dam, a place where the water was collected for future use; the driving party was aiming to drive the elephants in the next night to that area, and from there those would be given direction towards the forests of Paralekhemundi, most preferably Lakhari wildlife sanctuary.

The driving party was very tense, the herd had been in Gunupur Range for the last ten days, had already killed five people, devastated many villages, the crops in the fields were raided with impunity and the houses were broken with ease. The people, mostly tribal, many were shundhis – a group of money lenders, and the rest were people of other castes; were clueless, the place does not form a part of the regular migratory route, also the area doesn't figure as an elephant habitat; they were at their wits end, scared, angry and frustrated. The local forest department failed to drive those elephants towards Lakhari, the expert team came from Bhubaneswar. Some members of the driving party were carrying high sounding fire crackers and rocket bombs, the Public Relation Officials were moving with megaphone, cautioning onlookers not to go near the wild elephants, not to disturb the elephants by making unnecessary sounds and to follow the instructions of the expert group. The DFO was constantly communicating with the Range Officers, experts over his Motorola wireless handsets, was looking tense, sweat was streaming down from his face. He was standing below a tree with his ACF, who too looked tense, and they were constantly changing their positions, going here and there, taking the stock of the situation, any time the elephant might come, might harm the onlookers, the staffs too. The DFO was an old man, about to retire within a year or two, was sort in height, had little mustache, was having a felt cap on his head, was almost running, his tension was getting unbearable, his directions were getting louder, even clearly audible to persons without a handset; the time getting late, the elephants were not coming out of their resting place.

Earlier Events

The memories were fresh, earlier the elephant had killed two persons in Khaira area, under Gunupur Subdivision couple of days back. Two small time business men, both vegetable sellers of Ghatana village, were coming from the haat. The weekly village market places, the time was evening, still little light was there; other people on the road tried to dissuade them not to go further, the wild elephants were noticed ahead of the village, they did not listen, thought they could easily avoid the elephants and proceeded further in their cycles. They met two big elephants and a young one on the road, face to face; they instantly ran leaving their bicycles on the road, ran towards a nallah, saw a dip, and hid themselves there; but there hiding did not escape the notice of the elephants, the smaller one was inquisitive, it came down, broke the cycles, and tracked the people on to the nallaha, caught one person by its trunk, and trampled him there. Seeing his friend being caught by the elephant, and later being trampled, the other person ran for shelter at neck break speed; he somehow escaped. The elephant was busy in trampling the first person, did not pursue the second, so he reached the safety of the village, narrated the horrible story, and then fell unconscious due to trauma.

After trampling the man there, the herd moved to the Khaira village, two kilometers away where one dog barked at them, the elephants were agitated by such barking, ran after the dog, and the dog ran towards a hut located in the outskirts of the village, around a kilometer away, located below a Mahula tree; the hut was constructed to collect Mahula, and the dog hid itself below a khatia (a make shift bed). Unfortunately in that night one person was sleeping on the Khatia, the time was summer, weather was hot, light wind was blowing outside so the man was sleeping outside in deep sleep. The elephant killed the sleeping person in anger, broke the wooden bed. After that, the elephants went to Gajapati district, only to return around 8th May, 2007, came up to the engineering college at Gunupur, remained in Narasimhamunda hills nearby.

During the next day the herd descended from the hill, came near the police station, then moved ahead and gathered near the gas godown; around seven thousand people, almost the entire Gunupur town gathered there to watch the elephants. When the elephants are agitated, less noise should be made, lest they would be more agitated, could damage life and property. Only the drums were beaten, no crackers were used, the elephants were in highly agitated state because of constant presence of people all around, somehow they were pushed away from Gunupur town. The people guarded the town with burning mashals, firecrackers and the elephants moved towards Turkani, and took rest in a mango orchard, where again people started frightening the elephants. The elephant used to make false attacks when cornered, but if they feel actual danger, then they charge which may proved to be fatal.

On that day one mango plucker came near the elephants with a fire ball, with an aim to frighten the elephants, to drive them away. The elephants made false attacks, came charging at him, only a few step forward, then returned to the group. The man was felling courageous, came much closer, tried to terrify the elephants, but unfortunately that did not happen, the elephants turned at him, he was going to collect his chapels in front of the charging elephant, he could not escape, the elephant trampled him, before the eyes of hundreds of onlooker. It happened in a flash, before others could react, the man was trampled, his body was rescued, but the man was dead by that time. The elephants then moved to Ambagudi, seeing the ferocity of the group, carelessness of the people, the executive magistrate was deployed along with the police, any further accident should not happen, the people should not get close to the elephants. The public relation officers, forest officials moved to the villages, the villagers were warned not to go to the forest after 4 p.m., not to stay in the lonely huts outside the village. No further incident happened, the villagers were scared, they drove the elephants, but Executive Magistrate was deployed throughout.

The elephants first arrived in the area during second week of March, 2007, were roaming here and there, going to Gajapati district, and some time were coming to the Gunupur forests; their habitat in Lakhari Wildlife Sanctuary has been disturbed by extensive podu cultivation and they getting homeless in their own land. Again the people tried to drive away the elephants, pushed the elephants away from their traditional migratory route, as a result they strayed, moved away from the migratory route, and the result more damage to crops, human lives.

Coming back to the driving process, the loud call of the DFO was audible to the Range officers through wireless, all of them were inside the forest, some were tracking, some were taking strategic positions as per the advice of the expert group. The expert team and others were divided to three groups, the DFO was controlling from the cross road, the one road was going towards the present village, the others going to other villages a little distance away. The driving groups was trying to track the elephants, they were almost invisible in the forest containing trees of all sizes, small, medium and big, also the current rain spell had brought new leaves to the trees, so tracking the elephants was extremely difficult in that forest. The Range Officers were briefed by the expert, and then the party went into the forest and took strategic locations.

The time was getting late, the expert signaled, the actual elephant driving process was going to start. Inside, the thick foliage of the trees was hindering the views, even from close quarter it was difficult to sight the big animals, leave aside the smaller ones. Suddenly, the biggest elephant, the leader saw one party, S-a-an, S-a-an, a low pitched sound came from the elephant; it was opposing the party from coming closer. The experienced team leader understood the attitude, restrained other team members from going closer to the elephants, they retreated few feet back, allowed the elephants to cool down. Further movement of the elephants was not noticed, the time was getting late, inside the forest the darkness was increasing early.

Slowly the afternoon shadow was fading, people were getting restless, nothing was really happening. From inside, the tracker party gave the signal, the time was getting delayed, and the real elephant drive had to take place. The driving party decided to use the crackers, and two crackers were fired into the sky, with a whistling noise the cracker moved upwards busted there with big b-o-o-m , the hills shivered in that noise, the elephants trumpeted, the earth trembled, people were alerted, the elephants driving process had begun. The elephants were by then divided into two groups, stood motionless for some time. The crackers were fired from the Gunupur direction, with the aim that the elephants should not move in that direction. One person was on a Mahula tree, watching the elephants, the people on the top of the hill were signaling at the direction of the elephant, the people on the plains were now getting increasingly alert, the elephants were moving at their direction. The police personnel stood on alert, the magistrate came to the front, the onlookers were pushed towards the village, the roads were instantly cleared, the motorcycles, cycles were shifted immediately. Further movement of elephants did not happen, the party waited for another twenty minutes, the expert advised for firing of another burst of crackers to ensure the movements of the elephants. In came another whistling sound, three more crackers busted, the elephants roared again and again, their movement was getting faster, the elephants started moving in a group in a corridor between the hill and the road, the bigger elephant was in the front, followed by the females and at the back were the young ones, but contrary to the expectation, the elephants did not move in the direction in which they were supposed to move, they took a different route, the sound, presence of people confused them. The lens-men got themselves ready for the pictures of the charging elephants. The light faded fast, the rain cloud hovered on the top, the elephants were not seen, and they did not come to the road, moved near the foot of the hill, the people on the top of the hills showed the direction. In that forest, it was almost impossible to see the elephants, how many had actually gone ahead and how many were in the back, or which elephant was going in which direction. A minor mistake would cost lives of driving party members, lead the driver straight to the feet of the enraged elephants. One Range officer on the hill was constantly giving the message about the movement of elephants, he could see the elephants clearly from the height. The driving party came rushing towards the control point, the elephants were to be given better direction, else they might damage the houses ahead. The elephants walked faster, the driving team members had to run, the elephants within no time crossed almost two kilometer, the message came from the nearby village, the elephants reached there.

The elephants moved ahead, the tracking party could not follow them, they simply vanished, their movement was very fast, and people on foot could not follow. The leader of the party, came rushing, for the further direction, he then went ahead in his vehicle, the DFO and others followed, the elephants were near another village, the villagers of that village panicked, on megaphone they were cautioned not to go near the agitated elephants. The team members reached that village, moved to the adjacent cashew forest, looked at the forest floor, on the sands were the foot prints of the elephants. The footprints were fresh, the elephants had moved recently. As they were checking the footprints, eleven elephants passed in front of them, they were only fifty feet away from the herd, were alarmingly closer to them, the herd did not pay heed to their presence. The elephants then moved upside of the hill, moved towards the minor irrigation project dam, drank some water, then started climbing another hill. The driving team was constantly on their chase, they were watching every movement of the elephants, suddenly the summer hail storm started, big hail stones started falling from the sky, the forest was getting wet, the branches started breaking in the strong wind, the broken branches, the leaves, started falling on the bodies of the members. They decided to come out, the forest was practically getting dark, no further chance of following the elephants. The team members came out, they had been with the elephants throughout the day, no on toward incident happened, the day passed off peacefully.

I didn't remain with the driving party for the entire length of the driving, I was eager to know the fate of those elephants. Some strange news came in the newspaper, they migrated to Andhra Pradesh, they were branded as the elephants from Odisha, a strange definition to me.

Some of the news extract from Andhra Pradesh is given below.

> "Hyderabad, Oct 23 (IANS) The forest department in Andhra Pradesh Tuesday launched an operation to chase away rogue elephants that enter the state from Odisha with the help of five trained elephants.
>
> Wild elephants have created havoc in the Srikakulam and Vijaynagaram districts of the state, bordering Odisha. Since last week, nine people have been killed in clashes with them.
>
> Forest officials have named the operation 'Gajendra'. Five trained elephants were brought from Assam, Odisha and Karnataka for disciplining the unruly pachyderms and chase them back to their habitat in Odisha.
>
> Since August, about 17 people have been killed and over hundreds of acres of crops destroyed in elephant depredation.
>
> "VISAKHAPATNAM: The reason for the death a female elephant which was found on Tuesday near Darsininvillage falling in Jammu reserve forest in Gummalakshmipuram mandal of Vizianagaram district could not be diagnosed..........................
>
> It is said that the dead elephant earlier entered Andhra area from Odisha with multiple injuries. This gives credence to the belief that either it might have received injuries while being chased by some people or attacked by them with firearms in Odisha. Forest officials are tracking down the movement of the herd comprising 11 elephants - eight female, two male calf and one makhna (a sub-adult without the tusk).

Tusker deployed

Jayant, a trained tusker from Chittoor, has been deployed in the forest to drive the herd back to their home in Laksheri sanctuary, about 75 km. from Andhra border. The herd was sent back towards Odisha but again it took an arch shape return to Gummlakshmipuram. Wild elephants get scared on facing a challenge from a domesticated elephant along with some human beings and make a retreat. Jayant is accompanied by a group of trackers, mahouts and trained personnel. "Catching the herd is ruled out as nowhere it is done. It will cost us at least ₹1 crore and feeding itself will entail an expenditure of ₹3 lakhs to ₹4 lakhs per elephant."

BERHAMPUR: News of death of another elephant of the herd that had strayed into Andhra Pradesh has reduced hopes among forest officials about safe return of this elephant herd to Lakhari sanctuary in Gajapati district in Odisha.

"Experts said the relocated elephant could have died of negligence.

The herd was not leaving the area due to the earlier death of a fellow elephant at Darsi."

The news like above, will always be the constant headlines, the elephants have been moving in their own land, and have been branded as raiders, their fate remain highly uncertain, they have turned to rootless migrants. People are getting killed, the elephants are also being killed, but the population of elephants is few, the number is reducing with time, the magnificent animal is fading in the black horizon.

Some Important Information about Elephants

Elephants are the largest land animals.

The Indian Elephant are light grey in colour, with de-pigmentation on the ears and trunk. Large males generally weigh about 5,000 kg. At birth an elephant calf weighs around 120 kilograms and they live for 50 to 70 years, the oldest recorded elephant lived for 82 years. African elephants are distinguished from Asian elephants in several ways, the most noticeable being their much larger ears. In addition, the African elephant is typically larger than the Asian elephant and has a concave back. In Asian elephants only males have tusks, where both males and females of African elephants have tusks and they are usually less hairy than their Asian counterparts. Different types of elephants found in the Indian forests are as follows.

Calf	Shoulder height up to 4 ft (120 cm)
Juvenile	Shoulder height above 4 ft up to 5 ft (121 cm to 150 cm)
Sub-adult Bull	Shoulder height above 5 ft up to 8 ft (151 cm to 240 cm)
Sub-adult Cow	Shoulder height above 5 ft up to 7 ft (151 cm to 210 cm)
Adult Bull	Shoulder height above 8 ft (Above 240 cm)
Adult Cow	Shoulder height above 7 ft (above 210 cm)
Makhna	Bull elephant without tusks

Important physical characteristics

Trunk – The trunk of an elephant is a fusion of the nose and upper lip, and it becomes the most important and versatile appendage of an elephant. According to biologists, the elephant's trunk have more than forty thousand individual muscles, some say may be a lakh, making it sensitive enough to pick up a single blade of grass, yet strong enough to break the branches off a tree.

Except for the very young, the elephants always use their trunks to reach for their food and then place it in their mouth. They graze on grasses also reach for high branches of trees to grab leaves and fruits. If the desired food item is at higher height then the elephant wraps its trunk around the tree or branch and shake so that fruit get loosened and fall on the ground, sometimes they knock the tree down altogether.

The elephant uses its trunk for drinking; it sucks up water into the trunk and holds up to 14 litres at a time; then blow water into its mouth. The elephant also suck up water to spray on their body during bathing. On top of this watery coating, the animal sprays dirt and mud, which later dries up and acts as a protective sunscreen. While swimming, the trunk is used as snorkel to breathe.

When elephants meet each other the known elephants greet each other by entwining their trunks, much like a handshake in humans. They also use the trunks while play-wrestling, caressing during courtship and mother-child interactions, also during dominance displays when a male raises its trunk as a symbol of warning or threat, a lowered trunk can be a sign of submission.

An elephant trunk has highly developed sense of smell, by raising the trunk up in the air and moving it from side to side, like a periscope, it can find out the location of friends, enemies, and food sources.

Tusks – The tusks of an elephant are its second upper incisors teeth; these grow continuously; an adult male's tusks grow to about 18 cm a year. The elephant uses the tusks to dig soil for water, salt, and roots; also to debark trees, to incise into softer trees to get at the pulp inside, and also to move the trees and branches when clearing a path. For Asian males, the heaviest recorded tusk is 39 kg.

An individual elephant can be identified on the basis of its tusk characteristics. Male elephant have only tusks and female does not have, but sometimes the female have small tush (tushes are thin, small and seldom crosses the trunk). The males are (a) tusker with single tusk (Ganesh), tuskless (Makhna), with or may be without tusks. The Makhna is a heavily built elephant with massive trunk, big forehead and no tusk may or may not have tusk.

Skin – The elephant is a thick-skinned animal, skin is very thick and tough around most parts of the body and measures about 2.5 centimetres thick. However, the skins around the mouth and inside of the ears are paper-thin. Normally, the skin of an Asian elephant is covered with hair, as they get older, this hair darkens and becomes spars; however hair remains throughout on their heads and tails.

Legs and feet – The legs of an elephant are like strong straight pillars to support heavy weight. The elephant needs less muscular energy to stand because of its straight legs and large padded feet. Beneath the bones of the foot, is a tough gelatinous material that acts as a cushion or shock absorber. Under the elephant's weight the foot swells, but it gets smaller when the weight is removed, thus enabling an elephant to sink deep into mud, but it can pull its legs out easily because its feet become smaller when lifted.

Elephants swim well, but cannot trot, jump, or gallop. They have only two motions; a walk; and a faster walk that is similar to running, they can reach speeds up to 40 km/h.

Ears – The large flapping ears of an elephant are important for temperature control. The elephant ears are made of a very thin layer of skin stretched over the cartilage and a have good network of blood vessels. On hot days, the elephants flaps their ears constantly, creating little breeze, which cools the surface of the blood vessels on the ear, then the cooler blood gets circulated to the rest of the animal's body.

The ears are also used during displays of aggression and also during the mating period. A well spread out ear increases the size of elephant, the animal looks more massive, and this is a display of dominance and intimidation.

Social behavior

Elephants follow definite social order in their lives, the social lives of male and female elephants are however different. The females spend their entire lives in tightly knit family groups made up of mothers, daughters, sisters, and aunts. These groups are led by the eldest female, or matriarch. Adult males on the other hand mostly live solitary lives. The female group size may range from five to fifteen adults, as well as a number of immature males and females. When a group size gets too big, few elder daughters break off and form their own small group. However, they remain aware of their origin herd and hierarchy therein.

In contrast, the life of the adult male is very different, as a baby gets older, he begins to spend more time at the edge of the herd, sometimes going off on his own for hours or days. Eventually, somewhere around the age of fourteen, the mature male, permanently leave his biological group. Males primarily live solitary lives, but occasionally form loose associations with other males, called bachelor herds. The males spend much time in fighting with other males for dominance, only the most dominant males breed with cycling females. It is usually the older bulls, forty to fifty years old, do most of the breeding.

The dominance battles between males sometimes appear to be fierce, but actually little injury results. Mostly battles are in the form of aggressive displays and bluffs. However, during the breeding season, the battles may take ugly turn and some injury may happen. During this season, known as musth, a bull fights with almost any other male it encounters, spend most of its time hovering around the female herds, trying to find a receptive mate.

Musth – Musth is a periodic condition in a bull elephant, characterized by violent behaviour, accompanied by a large rise in reproductive hormones – testosterone levels can be as much as 60 times higher than the same at normal times. The Musth phase mostly occurs during winter. The reason of Musth is not fully known; scientific investigations are greatly hampered as otherwise docile elephants turn aggressive, try to kill the humans.

Often, elephants in Musth discharge a thick tar-like secretion called temporin from the temporal ducts on either side of the head. The swelling of the temporal glands; and this may lead to aggressiveness too, causes acute pain comparable to severe toothache. However, Musth is actually linked to sexual arousal or establishing the dominance, but this relationship is far from clear.

During Musth the domesticated elephants are traditionally tied to strong trees, and denied with food and water, or put on a starvation diet, for several days, after which the Musth phase passes.

Communication – The elephants make a number of sounds during communication, they otherwise are famous for their trumpet calls which they produce when the air is blown though the nostrils. The elephants also create rumbling growls when greeting each other, the growl becomes a bellow when the mouth is open and turn to a moan when is prolonged; can turn to a roar when bullying another elephant or another animal.

Elephants can communicate over long distances by producing and receiving low-frequency sound (infrasound), a sub-sonic rumbling can travel in the air and through land much farther than higher frequencies in jungle conditions. These calls range in frequency from 15 to 35 Hz, sometimes as loud as 117 DB, allowing communication over many kilometers; the maximum recorded range is around 10 km. This sound can be received by the sensitive skins on an elephant's feet and also by the trunk, which pick up the resonant vibrations. To listen, an elephant lift one foreleg from the ground, and face towards the source of the sound, or often lays its trunk on the ground. The lifting of leg increases the sensitivity of the remaining legs.

In the forests, the best places to watch the elephants are near the water bodies or meadows or salt licks where elephants used to come during the afternoon and the night. Elephants sometimes remain very silent but their smell draws our attention when we pass by them. The elephants also produce very mild but distinct grrh…grrh… sounds; sometimes, the elephants trumpet.

Diet

The elephants are herbivorous animals, and spend up to 16 hours a day for eating. Their diet is highly variable depending on the season and habitat range. Elephants are primarily browsers, feed on leaves, barks and fruits of trees and shrubs, but they also eat considerable volume of grasses and herbs. An adult elephant consumes around 140–270 kg of food a day.

The indirect evidence of elephant presence is to find out the elephant dung. The elephant defecation rate is around 16 piles per day.

Reproduction

A female usually starts breeding around the age of thirteen. For the females, the mating season is short, they are only able to conceive for a few days in a year. When she comes into estrus the females gives smell signals and produce special calls. The females prefer bigger, stronger, and, most importantly older males; such a reproductive strategy tends to increase chances of survival of their off springs. Being lighter built, the female can usually outrun most of the males, she does not have to mate with every male that approaches her; she only mates with the most productive male.

Elephants display a range of affectionate interactions, such as nuzzling, trunk intertwining, and placing their trunks in each other's mouths during courtship.

After a twenty-two-month pregnancy, the mother gives birth to a calf which weighs about 115 kg and stand over 75 cm tall. The elephants are born with few survival instincts than many other animals and rely on their elders to teach them what they need to know.

Baby care

Elephants within a herd are usually related, and all members of the tightly knit female group participate in the baby care and its protection. After the initial excitement, the mother selects several full-time baby-sitters, also called "allomothers", from her group. An elephant is considered an allomother when she is not able to have her own baby. The more the number of allomothers, the better is the calf's chances of survival. A benefit of being an allomother is that she can gain experience or receive assistance when caring for her own calf in future.

Estimation of height of elephants:

The approximate height of the elephant = 2 x circumference of the front foot. The height of the elephant is treated as the height at the shoulder. The elephant has 5 toes on the front foot and four toes on the back foot. The front foot is bigger than the back foot. The front foot is bigger and circular whereas the back foot is smaller and elliptical.

Kalinga, the Path Ahead

We tried to avoid the flood of lights, retreated to the lonelier lands of the Chandka, the torrent of illumination was less, the horizon in the southern sky was shading the stars, but otherwise the night was dark, in the modern life getting a dark night is a luxury. Haze and glow masks clarity, from the madding crowd of the city we were looking for difference in the jungle, it apart from it being abode of the nocturnal animals also the island of tranquility, to pacify the random mind in the darkest corner of the sky. The evening sky was full with stars, Mr. Dey was showing me the constellations over our head, so many shapes, and I really find it difficult to conceive a figure. In that starlit night, little away from the crazy crowds of the capital city, I was looking at the stars, seeing the stars differently as per the guidance of Mr. Dey. The evening star, the Venus had crossed the sky, the other stars, less bright in colour, but strangely Mr. Dey was able to find some colour in those stars, all were blinking, calling us to explore the infinity above us.

My knowledge was limited in the subject, I knew in the olden days when there were hardly navigational instruments, the sailor look at the stars to find their way to the land, goes for sea voyage to different unknown lands. Now we know our position by using the modern GPS, and in those days even compass was not available, the unbound spirits set sail for the strange lands, conquer seas, and bring bounty to the country.

"If you look at those stars, you will see hundreds, thousands in a faded zone, they were so far away," his eyes were glued to the perforated screen above us, the knowledge trickled with faint cosmic rays, charged particles. I too fixed my eyes on the stars above my head, many colours, the hottest stars were shining bright in blue white colour, less hotter stars in white, and the colour goes from white – yellow white-orange- red as the temperature of the stars drops drastically; the blue white stars are more than five hundred times hotter than the red or orange stars.

"I have a binocular, a heavy one, and never imagined to find so my stars, galaxies in the outer space," he was highly enthusiastic, his eyes were gleaming; I as a disciple was listening to his words keenly, my eyes were fixed in the glowing stars and I was trying to imagine a new world. Cool breeze was blowing from south, winter had not retreated fully, still little chill in the wind even though the southerly wind had started blowing slowly. The Bhubaneswar town was a little away, the lights of the town was illuminating the southern sky, like northern lights, a faint haze in the long nights. The darkness has descended into the northern pole, the charged particles of the space were colliding with the magnetic particles of the earth, and the awesome colour was getting produced in the process. The tall buildings were protruding their heads from the orange illumination like glitzy mountains.

At times I was looking at the sky, at the flood of stars, new and new stars were coming as I looked at the sky, my eyes were getting tired in the process, and then I used to look at the city landscape; new and new structure were appearing in the semi dark backdrop.

"This is definitely Kalapurusha," he was full of energy, his eyes twinkled as the morning star. He was showing the constellations, describing the shapes.

I looked at the stars, he showed me a group of seven stars, some stars were bright, some were dim; he asked me to draw lines on a piece of paper; I drew as suggested, an amazing shape was coming out. I was amazed, Mr. Dey took the paper and drew few more lines, and surprisingly an ancient hunter came out; club on his right hand, shield on the left hand, a sword hanging from the west, he was ready to attack. I was baffled; the sky is full of imaginations, and this constellation is named as Orion, the 'Hunter' or Kalapurusha in Indian language.

My eyes were fixed at the burning stars; now in a dark corner of an advancing city I was totally involved in the colour of those stars, many were bright, some blue, some orange, now I started seeing the colours of the stars in the jungle of Chandka. Mr. Dey went on narrating his involvement with the stars, how he started knowing the stars in the Koreya rest house, inside the deepest jungles of Chhattisgarh where light stops in the night except for the star lights, the true colour of darkness is known only in the black shades of trees, lone shadows of lone sand dunes, vast expanse of the waters, far away from the human population.

He then drew many lines, many shapes came out, horseman with a spear, a big dog, a bull, a man with a sword on the right hand and a severed head on the left hand, a twin, a lion, huge scorpion and many more. The ancient men drew so many comparisons, when paper was not there; they created shapes in memory, passed the knowledge from generations to generations.

Mr. Dey was a avid sky watcher, his knowledge was unparallel in the subject, suddenly he recited an old rhyme about the direction of the stars.

Orion's belt from Taurus's eye
Leads down to Sirus bright;
His spreading shoulders guide we east
Above Procyon's pleasing light.

I looked at the northern sky, I was looking for the pole star, the star that gives the northern direction; and here Mr. Dey was also tired after a long deliberation on the stellar objects, a break was needed, my untiring eyes were however probing the darkness on the opposite side, and the long backdrop had no breaks, black colour spreads and finally merged with the illuminated sky on the southern horizon. I was taken aback; my eyes were fixed on a small circular object at the opposite sky, not far from the black land mass below, around 3-4 kilometer away from our sitting place on a watch tower. The object looked stationary, it was not twinkling like star, it was stationery, hazy illumination was coming from its all side, initially I thought it to be telephone tower with bulb at the top, but Mr. Pattanaik clarified, there was no telephone tower in that side. We all looked at the object, it was still stationery, floating like a balloon, and orange lights were coming from it intermittently. We were curious, what could be the object, was it a mysterious flying saucer and are we the lucky ones to locate it first in the city. The idea of hovering flying saucer on the skies of Bhubaneswar was chilling my spines, was increasing my anxiety. Topics changed, aliens enter to our imagination, the thoughts roams around the alien world.

Pattanaikbabu was taking a long sigh, his eyelids were lowered, eyes were half closed, and he was in different world, I was surprised; in the world of aliens where is the place of long sigh? I looked at him, his eyes opened, then my long sight extended to the floating object in the northern sky, Mr. Dey was immersed in his thought, and new object was increasing his curiosity. A star grazer like him was very busy in his thoughts, he was talking to himself, and his eyes were glowing like gold.

"Oh! Kalinga." Pattnikbabu whispered, his sound moved with the southerly breeze, was sailing towards the floating object in the air.

We were in our thought, but nobody till that time uttered a single word, as a curious onlooker I was watching my friends, they were in different worlds. The reaction of Pattanaikbabu was a strange, what he was uttering, I wanted to know, but I didn't want to disturb him, I want to see them in their world.

Slowly and slowly the object came closer, the long light beams pierced the black sky, and vanished at a distance, the window lights were more clearly visible, the blinking lights were coming frequently, the floating object turned out to be an aircraft, due to land in the Bhubaneswar Airport.

I looked at friends of that evening, Mr. Dey was looking at the aircraft, but strangely Pattanaikbabu was looking at the dark forests on the northern side, the aircraft had already crossed the northern dark boundary, was more clearly visible in the city haze. His behaviour in that evening was mysterious, I knew him to be a nice gentleman, and seeing him in such a pensive mood was increasing my curiosity.

"Oh! Kalinga, you should have been alive" words were choking his voice cord, I was surprised at his behaviour, something serious was choking him, I was confused, in such beautiful evening with live friends around how could Pattanaikbabu drifted into wooded loneliness.

Mr. Dey also looked at him, he was surprised too, to see such change in the mood of Pattanaikbabu, the star grazer tried to read the inner mind. We were silent, Pattanaikbabu was pensive as usual, we didn't utter a single word, the breeze was touching us gently, a strange feeling on my body, joy of being in solitude, joy of being with such good company, anxiety to see the change of mood.

"Oh! Kalinga, you should have been alive." Once again Pattanaikbabu repeated his words, his eyes opened, he was nodding his head slowly, was immersed in his thoughts. I looked at the floating aircraft, the aircraft had approached the aerodrome, we were not able to see the headlight any more, and the machine descended and after few seconds and disappeared from our vision. On the town front the sky was illuminated as usual, the orange glow was filling the southern tree line. I looked at the sky over my head, the sky was clearer, so many stars, the black sky was perforated so much.

"I am sorry," Pattanaikbabu spoke few words for us, his behaviour was a mystery to me.

"I was thinking about Kalinga" he paused; again I found so much of sorrow in his words.

I was ignorant of Kalinga. What was this Kalinga? I looked at Mr. Dey, he was perplexed, ignorant of the matter like me.

"You are such a small baby, why we rescued you?" he was talking to himself.

The mystery deepens; Mr. Dey couldn't sit long without asking further questions.

"Who is this Kalinga," few words came rushing from his throat.

Pattanaikbabu looked at us, understood the gaps in his sentences and tried to fill the vacuums in sentences.

"Kalinga was the name given to that baby elephant of Chandka; we rescued it from the Kalinga studio area, so we christened it as Kalinga." He unrevealed the mystery. Now we were eager to know about rescue, I remembered, the forest officials rescued a baby elephant couple of years back, but it was a small news in the backdrop of so many big news filling the newspaper; and I didn't followed it keenly; with time the incident faded. I was not involved in the incident, but when the man who rescued the baby started talking about the incident, I was keener now. Then Pattanaikbabau continued.

It was the year 2007, the new areas of Bhubaneswar was flooded with uncommon news, a herd of elephants from Chandka forests entered into the habitation areas, just outside the boundary of the sanctuary; arrival of elephants from the nearby sanctuary was regular news decades back, but with town expansion, the roaming areas of the herds reduced. They retreated to lonelier areas, but their arrival again into the habituated areas was creating interest in the minds of common citizens of Bhubaneswar. As usual there was a stream of the onlookers, lens men came with flashing cameras, the onlookers on the busy road parked their vehicles and peeped into the premises of Kalinga studio, the only film making unit of the state. The studio was located just outside the limit of Bharatpur part of Chandka Damapada Wildlife Sanctuary, and adjacent is the Suiviculture farm with lot of trees resembling a small forest. A blacktopped road runs alongside the western boundary of the Sanctuary, a busy road now, vehicles ply continuously, new township is coming up at Kalinganagar, Chandaka and other areas, Bhubaneswar is expanding fast, the wilderness of Bhubaneswar is sinking fast too.

A group of five elephants with a baby sneaked into the Kalinga studio area on the night of 3rd May, 2007, and the group couldn't return to the sanctuary and remained in the complex area. The onlookers gathered; the herd was standing in the complex, confused, no return path, all exits were blocked by curious citizens; also the elephants usually don't move during the day time. The day passed, the 4th night draws the elephants to the adjacent silviculture farm in the vicinity. The people followed the group for some time, further events were not recorded, but the baby female elephant felled into a cemented water tank inside the Siliviculture research complex; the herd couldn't rescue her, the terrified group finally fled leaving the baby in the tank. Next day morning, the staffs found the abandoned baby, and informed the sanctuary staffs for rescue; the sanctuary personnel duly responded and from the cement tank. The onlooker were requested to leave, road blocks were created with the police help, the baby was left alone in the place for some time as the herd was nearby; the staff hoped that by listening to the call of the baby the herd would come for the baby elephant. In the beginning the officials tried to push the baby to the herd, but the herd was panicky, they didn't come towards the studio, and the baby was stranded. The distress call of the baby went unanswered; the herd moved away in other direction, finally the baby was abandoned by the group. The road blocks can't be laid for long in the Bhubaneswar city outskirts. Here, around the baby people were uncontrollable; many tried to touch the baby, to get the feeling of wilderness through a wild elephant.

The baby was around nine-month-old, a small animal to live in the forest alone; usually the baby elephants remain with their mother for almost two years, the female remained throughout with the group; the independent behaviour develops after two years when calf doesn't need the mother for its feeding. It was a small elephant, about 4½ feet tall, grey in colour, not deep black, her trunks were down, she was not able to call her mother anymore, empty mouths had drained the energy out of her. Finally, it was decided to transfer the elephant to Godipada in the Chandaka Wildlife Sanctuary for her safe keeping, an ideal place for the treatment as well as for its feeding. She was not panicking anymore, rather she was giving thanks to the sanctuary staffs for rescuing her in her own language, she was relieved of stress, looked more relaxed with the sanctuary staffs. Two persons put their hands on her forehead, just after the long ears, they were standing very close to the body and another two persons pushed her lightly from back to give her direction to walk; they were acquainting her with human behaviour. With that escort group, the baby elephant was brought to the Godipada part of the sanctuary, a good place to comfort the baby for some time. The huge gate opened for the new comer, the cemented elephants above the gate looked at the baby as if they were coming to life, the stone tusker raised the trunk, the mother was comforting the stone baby, the forests of the elephants will shelter its baby again, at the soothing comfort of the human company, not the elephants. The baby entered into the sanctuary, she was given medicinal bath, to cure her wounds as she was bruised at many parts.

The baby was hungry, she was fed with milk using a baby milk bottle, she raised her little trunk, the animal keeper opened her mouth a little, hold the lower lips and the mouth opened further; the man slowly pressed the milk into her thirsty throat. She suckled the milk, few full bottles, after so many hours she got the milk to drink. The staffs don't want to keep the baby in a zoo, rather they were interested to release the baby with the group she came from; they tried to rear her in a natural environment, resembling the habitat from which she came from. There was a great fear, the wild elephants don't accept any member who comes in contact with the human beings; the sanctuary staffs tried to give the natural touch in their rearing as far as possible; also the baby shouldn't miss her wild survival skill.

The baby elephant was playful, always wanted to play, she would raise her trunk at the arrival of the keeper, the man used to feed her milk, also takes care of her. The little eyes glowed at the arrival of new visitors and she tries to play with them. Now milk need not be poured into her mouth, she was more accustomed to drinking from bottles; she would suck the milk from the bottle once the nipple was inside. She would also suck water from the bucket by her trunk, used to play with water; her playful nature earned her numerous admirers. She also learned how to drink water, she would suck trunk full of water, bend the trunk and blew the water into her mouth, the basic skills of living was taught to her. Human scent was a great threat, the wild herd wouldn't not accept her in future, the forest officials frequently applied ayurvedic pastes made from jungle herbs over her wounds and also on her body, the human scents would be suppressed. The baby was more adaptable now, she would run after the keeper, sit with legs, move with the keeper, but within the open enclosure. Days passed, the baby had grown a little, she was christened Kalinga; the name derived from the place of her rescue, the Kalinga Studio. The baby was more stable now, but a bigger challenge remains ahead, how to release the baby in the wild, how she would adjust in the elephant herd, but effort has to be made. The baby was brought to Bharatapur watch tower, a regular visiting place of the wild elephants of the sanctuary, the reason being water is easily available there, the forest department had created a water hole for the wild animals near the watch tower, the water comes from the water supply pipe lines passing near the tower. The water hole is a small one, but clean water is available, the leaks from the pipeline makes a water fountain, the water forms a tree, falls as an umbrella, and this water umbrella is a favourite place for the wild elephants; the availability of bamboo bushes in plenty is another attraction too. The baby was now in Bharatpur area, she was not chained there, was moving in open, the keepers were anticipating a miracle, the wild elephants would come a day and would accept her; they were keeping watchful eyes on the movement of the baby elephant.

One day a big tusker came, it was marching on the patrol vehicle track, its long curved tusks were aiming upward, the trunk was hanging passively between the tusks, with medium bamboo bushes at its back the figure looked massive. Another female elephant was walking in front of the male; both were moving slowly towards the waterhole, a usual way of coming to the water hole. Seeing the elephants closing in, the watchers climbed the watch tower and from the roof watched their movements. At that time Kalinga was free, roaming here and there around the watch tower, it never left the company of the keepers after her capture. The tusker came closer to the waterhole, the female was a little far away, the male took the regular foot track to reach the hole, the female took a little forested route, and they however didn't notice Kalinga. The male went to the water jet, the water drops wetted him, the dusky skin suddenly turned dark, and the elephant looked bigger with this new black outfit. Slowly and slowly other members of the group arrived; others were a mother and a older calf. Both mother and the son took bath under the shower, they played for some time, the baby male put its trunk over the shower, the water jet filled its trunk and then it threw water on his body, the mother was drawing water from the waterhole, not from the jet. After some time the mother pushed the baby and filled her trunk with water from the jet and poured water on the body. One female suddenly trumpeted, the bathing baby rushed towards the mother and both of them came to the open area. The whole group arrived, they were eighteen in number, male, female and young, all were close to each other, pushing each other through the bushy forests, and were coming to the open areas in front of the water hole. Many trumpets came from their mouths together, they were herded near to the water hole; all now were females, the tusker had left the bathing place and went behind the bamboo bushes. Kalinga at that time was moving around the watch tower aimlessly, the arrival of so many elephants was a surprise, she was confused also, it didn't run towards the herd; at that time his human friends took shelter on the roof of the watch tower, she had no place to go, she can't negotiate the turnings of the staircase.

The group was enjoying their time near the water hole. The young members descended to the water body, a small one for a such a big group, they had to bathe one by one, not all at a time, two young were bathing in front, their mothers were standing on the back. Another female member was standing on the track, waiting for her turn to take bath and was moving passively. She noticed a small elephant roaming aimlessly around the watch tower; she was surprised, how a mother could be so careless and allowed such a small elephant to move out of the group. Kalinga was looking different, regular bath had increased her glow, she was darker, the dark skin was shining in the afternoon light, her legs were however little dusty; in contrast the visiting elephants were mostly grey in colour, dust had shadowed their colour, black now turned grey. The young Kalinga was moving away from the group, her trunk was almost touching the ground, the tail was down, she was walking slowly away from the water hole. The big lone female was curious; she came near to Kalinga, came very close, almost at a touching distance, her trunk swung, but Kalinga moved away, the approaching legs of the bigger elephant stopped and the smaller elephant moved forward.

On the other side two young elephants were playing in another small pond across the road, it was a really small pond, not much water was there, but they were playing; the smaller one was kneeling on her back leg, the bigger one was pushing her. The smaller baby was partly wet, the bigger one was totally dry, the smaller one gained strength, lifted her legs from the mud and came to the dry ground and pushed the bigger one to the mud, and they muscled at the small pond on the opposite side of the water hole. They were pushing, locking their trunks to each other, sometimes they were lowering their heads and push each other, nobody was however fully wet. On the other side, near the water hole the full group was standing, the tusker was however nowhere seen, there were six elephants now at the water hole, each one was pushing the other for the water jet, a small baby, almost same size of Kalinga was pushing its way to the jet, and the hole group was enjoying the shower.

The first female who noticed Kalinga, came closer to wandering Kalinga and tried to caress the little one, she put her long trunk lightly on the baby, but the baby moved away, Kalinga appeared to forgot the loving touch. She didn't leave, walked side by side matching the steps of Kalinga, occasionally she was putting her trunk lightly over the baby, touched her trunk lightly, a way to console the young one. Kalinga was not comfortable, she was changing her ways often, the bigger female was following her constantly, trying to take her to the herd, but Kalinga was refusing, was moving away. The effort continued for almost half an hour, Kalinga didn't accompany the group, she was trying hard to convince the kid, but the kid was unimpressed. After bath, almost after one and half long hours, the herd started leaving the area, the persuasive female retreated dejected, Kalinga didn't accompany; Kalinga moved around aimlessly of course. The keepers were watching the full event from the safety of the watch tower, they were very happy, their effort was giving result, the young Kalinga was getting some attention from the wild elephants, she was not shunned by the wild colleagues, a positive sign, Kalinga would probably return to her wilderness. The keepers watched the retreating group, slowly they vanished behind the bushes; the last female was moving away, its grey figure slowly vanished behind the bamboo bushes, her movement appeared like an action in slow motion. Kalinga at that time was standing on the path, all alone; her eyes were glued at the retreating female elephant. She walked a little towards the hidden figure, followed the foot prints of the caring female, she entered into the bushes, the female had vanished, she looked around, not finding her she returned to the watch tower.

Few days passed, the watchers were hopeful, the original herd of the little one would definitely arrive a day, they were constantly watching the area, the trackers were watching the movement of the elephants. Suddenly a group of twenty-two elephants arrived, the whole group was walking on the jeep track, they were in all age classes, old females, young males and females, and good numbers of babies. They were marching slowly towards the water hole in a regular manner, except for the babies all were heading towards the waterhole. The group was actually two groups, later the keepers came to know that; an eighteen elephants group and the other one was a four member group. They were moving differently, the smaller group was much close to the water hole and the bigger group was a little away, and here the small Kalinga was moving aimlessly as usual around the waterhole. The smaller group came near to the water jet, all were looking at the water hole from different directions and the water jet was spilling water into the air, creating an artificial rain in that area, wetting the standing elephants at the edge. Suddenly all elephants trumpeted and charged at the keepers, the two groups were ambushing the keepers, the men ran for cover and climbed the watch tower, it was a surprising behaviour, the wild elephants never charged the keepers inside the sanctuary. Full forty minutes passed, the keepers took shelter on the watch tower, all twenty two elephants were trumpeting, the keepers locked the room and couldn't dare to come out; some baby could climb through the stairs. The trumpets ended after some time, the keepers came to the roof top after almost forty five minutes and tried to locate Kalinga; but the smaller elephant was no more, they searched for the elephant baby behind the bushes, the baby couldn't be found, the smaller group – probably her group, took her away, the baby was re-united with her mother after ten painful long months.

The sanctuary staffs were very happy, but were apprehensive too, the baby might have forgotten the wild behaviour, she might be harmed by the herd, the herd might reject her and abandon her, and she might find it difficult to eat. They were trying to track the baby, the people around were alerted, watchers were kept at all the exit points of the sanctuary to keep the track of the group, baby elephants too. A full day passed, the baby couldn't be traced, and the anxieties of the staffs were increasing. Finally the news came; three elephants with a baby were sighted in the afternoon, they were near to the watch tower. The baby was mingling with members freely, she was jovial as usual, moving ahead of the mother, the youthful energy was apparent, the joy of the union was visible; the mother was following her, the baby was playing hide and seek behind the bushes. The keepers were not sure, whether the baby was really Kalinga or some other baby, the skin was now dry, turned grey, the same colour as other members.

Next day the same group again resurfaced, three big female elephants and a small baby. The baby was surrounded by them, and all came to the water source below the watch tower. The keepers were sure, the baby was definitely Kalinga, and they knew the movement of Kalinga. The baby came to the cemented staircase, it is the confirmation of course, the baby was definitely Kalinga. The keepers watched the group from the roof top. The elephants were standing on the left side of the water hole, their long legs were appearing like tree trunks, the water jet was spreading water on them, below their bellies Kalinga was standing, she looked so small, the females were filling their trunks with water and were pouring water on the little baby; she was not allowed to move away, always she was kept between the legs. The older females were putting their trunks lightly over the baby, caressing her, fondling her, consoling her, the long shadows of the group was falling on the yellow road, the baby and the mother turned to one entity, the mother would not allow her to leave alone. One bigger female put her mouth just above the jet, the water was filling her mouth, the baby was standing just below the mouth, water drops were wetting their entire body.

One female raised her trunk, the other female followed, the first female took a back step, the other female did the same, the small Kalinga tried to do the same, her legs slipped, and she felled in the water body; the long trunks lowered at once, caught the baby and helped her to regain her feet on the slippery ground. Slowly the baby moved out of the small waterhole to the dry ground. The big three females were circling around her, protecting her from all eventualities; Kalinga was not allowed to leave, she need to be raised well at any cost, she need to be educated on group behaviour. The mother and the child went little further, into the bushes; Kalinga came under the belly of the mother and tried to suckle milk from the mother. She was raising her little trunk, put her mouth below the front legs, the breasts of the elephants were located between the front legs, not between the rear legs. After some time she lowered her trunk, lowered her head, then after a few seconds raised her trunk again and started sucking milk from her mother. The keepers were very happy, finally Kalinga coped with the group, the mother was feeding her, a great sigh of relief.

The group remained near the water hole for three days, the keepers were watching each movement of the group with great interest. Kalinga was not allowed to move alone, she was walking between the legs of her mother, she was escorted to the water jet by other females, she took bath along with others, but never was left alone. The last sight was superb, two elephants were coming side by side, the water jet was going quite high and the water droplets were falling continuously. Strong wind started blowing, the water drops were scattered over a longer distance from the source, forming a white veil, Kalinga and her mother were behind the veil, a white fog covered both of them for a brief period, the other elephant was outside the fog, was clearly visible. The faint light was not casting the shadows; the little elephant was finding the cover of her mother finally. They took bath, the baby moved between the legs, and finally the herd moved away, they left the Bharatpur water hole area slowly, and the keepers were watching the departure keenly with great satisfaction in their mind, tears dropped from their eyes, the tear of joy, joy for the final successful reunion of the daughter with the mother. Slowly and slowly they vanished from their eyes, they faded with fading light, sun was going down, the orange shadow of the drooping sun was bringing happiness to their minds, the breeze was so pleasant, the sanctuary was filled with the evening calls from the birds, the time to retreat to the nests, time for rest.

The group was tracked continuously; the sanctuary staff wanted to study the behaviour of the group keenly, the keeping of Kalinga was an experiment. Few days passed, on 26th June, Kalinga was not sighted with the group, the monitoring team panicked, the whereabouts of Kalinga was not known, whether the group had finally abandoned her after a try, whether she met with an accident again, no one was sure. The name Kalinga, by that time, was known to everyone in the state, all were keeping a watch on the well-being of Kalinga, and her new family was the biggest news for the wildlife lovers. The weather was very bad, torrential rain swept past the state for some time now, the search team tried to locate her, tried to come close to the group; but the small elephant group was not allowing the human beings to come closer. The weather was worsening; the continuous rainfall was making movement in the forest risky, with so many aggressive elephants in the vicinity, no body dared to come close to the group.

The forest trackers were trying hard, they tried to dodge the elephants, but the agile elephants were not allowing them to come closer. They tried repeatedly, without attracting the attention of the agitated elephants and they came close, the rain was pouring from the sky like strong shower, all foot tracks and jeepable roads were overflowing with water, the big elephants were guarding the roads. The bigger elephants started trumpeting at the sight of the onlookers, the team was determined, they waited for the guard elephant to calm down, the elephant turned her head, the search team came closer. They were shocked, a baby elephant was laying dead on a small pool of water, her body was decomposed beyond recognition, her trunk was twisted towards the mouth, the little head was partly drowned in water, the eye was wide open, now the small eye was looking bigger, the front leg was twisted a little towards the back leg. The entire area was cleaned off bushes, the bigger elephants had cleaned the area. The group trumpeted together and moved into the forest, totally dejected, their little baby wouldn't rise again. The forest officials conducted a postmortem, the stomach was filled with food, the baby was killed by pneumonia, a prolonged rainfall caused pneumonia and ultimately killed the baby. A long sigh filled the hearts, the long effort went in vain, the beautiful baby didn't last long, she died, but a new chapter in the wildlife behaviour opened.

I looked at the horizon, our hearts were heavy, the long narration increased the weight of the hearts, the Chandka forest was saddened by the demise of the child, the vanishing wilderness of course.

Mr. Dey turned philosophical, he was an ardent J. Krishnamurthy follower, he quoted –

> "So let us decide whether you want a shelter, a safety zone, which will no longer yield conflict, whether you want to escape from the present conflict to enter a condition in which there shall be no conflict; or whether you are unaware, unconscious of this conflict in which you exist. If you are unconscious of the conflict, that is, the battle that is taking place

between that self and the environment, if you are unconscious of that battle, then why do you seek further remedies? Remain unconscious." 1934 3rd Public Talk, Ojai, California.

These words were highly complex, in fact the inner meaning of most of the verses went past me, and I could hardly comprehend life in those sentences.

I looked at the stars, the evening had deepened, the night calls of the birds were not audible any more, the stars were shining brightly, the Lambada Oronis, or Mrigasira in Indian language, star was glowing brightly. Suddenly the city sky sparkled at the southern horizon, the tall Swati Premium Hotel building was prominently occupying the landscape, the orange glows of the street light was giving orange tinge to the white building. I turned my eyes to the black sky again; the stars were shining like diamonds. Again orange glow swept past the night sky from the southern end, the southern sky was illuminated by rapid bursts of firecrackers. Red rays spread from the centre, another cracker exploded and green rays flooded the sky; the horizon was livened with the fire crackers, marriages were solemnized in the big hotels, clusters of big hotels were located there. The horizon was illuminated, red, blue, and green and so many colours, the city was prospering, everybody was enjoying the joyful moments; the sky of Chandka sanctuary was washed with the red carpets, the Aura Boralis had descended over the sky for a short period.

The Land With No Barriers (Blackbucks of Buguda)

The beauty unparallel, mesmerizing; Ravana, the demon king of Lanka, looked at the unbelievable walking statuette from the hide of a dense tree, he couldn't believe, the charming golden figure was moving like a deer of the forest, elegance in walk, beauty streamed to the flowers she touches, passion adorned her body. The robe of fibres was thrown over her shoulders, concealing a part of her bosom, appeared like a veil of yellow leaves enfolding a radiant flower. Her lip was appearing like the tender leaflet; pink and soft, her arms resembled two flexible stalks; the youthful beauty was shining like a blossom, in its spectacular display. The charming eyes were moving gracefully over the flowers, like the brush of an artist, capturing the colour of the flowers. The damsel was fatigued by touching so many flowers on the cherished plants, her arms graced with palms like fresh bloom, hung carelessly down; her bosom was heaving with strong breathings, then she plucked a flower from the tree and smelt the fragrance, and the happy–bee, touched the corner of that eye beautifully, was trembling; approached the tip of the ear, murmurs as softly as if whispering a secret of love; while she was waving her lovely fingers over the flowers. Ravana was peeping from the hide, how short a moment it had been blessed with a sight of the incomparable beauty, he couldn't divert his mind from the sweet occupation of gazing at her, the restless heart was running back to her; fluttering with the wind of passion; with every look at her the lust in Ravana was increasing.

And then he directed Marrecha, tricked the young men in accompanying the beautiful lady, take them to a far away place, the beyond belief beauty need to be alone. The faithful servant took the shape of the golden deer.

The golden deer disappeared as if with fear, and again it resurfaced between the bushes, the hide and seek game continued, Rama was lured into the trap, he was going away from the hermitage. The golden deer was observing him over and again, was running away, into deeper part of the forest, and Rama was in hot pursuit, the golden deer appeared in the next moment, came right in front of him in its marvelous form, the deer was glazing in the light. Then the golden deer ran away at amazing speed as if to circumvent the arrow, and at times it was stopping only to tantalize him; sometimes it was springing into the skies, bewildering the man in pursuit, then it was disappearing somewhere in the thickets of forest, and appearing elsewhere in those thickets.

Thus the golden deer drew Rama far away from his hermitage in this hide and seek game, it maddened Rama again by reappearing in his close-by, surrounded with other animals of the forest, and then ran towards him and next moment vanished again as if with extreme fear only to emerge out of the thick trees. On spotting it in open, Rama decided to fell it and he held the arrow that was similar to the flare of the sun, put it on his sturdy bow and targeted the golden deer alone, then released the blazing arrow, it moved like a hissing snake and severed the heart of Maareecha, the demon which took the form of the golden deer. The demon sounded a blaring shriek, vaulted up to a height of palm-tree, and fell down on the ground and made a voice that is a sound alike to Rama's voice and yelled 'Hey, Seeta..., Hey Lakshman...'

The Ramayana story continued, the abduction of Sita, and the final destruction of Ravana followed which started with appearance and the fall of the golden deer.

I was reading the poem of golden deer, composed by Biswanath Khuntia.

"Hema Harini, Dhire Dhamante Sundara Dharani–"
(Oh! Golden Deer, your run makes the land beautiful)

The steps of the golden deer was elaborated in so detail, and then I looked at the golden deer in my front, on the vast expanse of the plain lands of Buguda, and compare their movement with the description in the poem. The deer was taking a graceful walk, the golden figure was shining, suddenly the animal jumped, a high jump, not expected of such small animal, then it ran at full speed, within seconds the animal was far away.

Like prince Ram, I couldn't take a proper look at the beautiful creature immediately, the animal was swift, flew in the air like a feather, appeared like a big bird moving close to land, the legs were as if not touching the golden earth; getting the proper glimpse of the animal in its motion was so difficult.

I looked forward, in my front a vast light undulating land was laying with light green grasses, little raised bunds; the bigger trees were standing close to the village, away from the grass land; and at the back a big hill with many black rocks was raising the head in to the blue sky. The beautiful Palm tree, with long dark trunk and long leaves at the top dotted the village periphery; around the houses the green impressions of the coconut trees were visible and the mango and other big tree with good foliage were almost mixing with the shade of the green hill at the back drop. In the late afternoon the sun was soft, on the field few blackbucks were busy in grazing grasses. A big dark male was standing little away, it raised the head, smelt the air; the group of female blackbucks were however busy in grazing. Few blackbucks came close to a big mango tree, almost came to the canopy area, but stayed outside. The long brownish guguchia grasses were creating a haze from a distance, the legs of the blackbucks were almost hidden in the grasses, the upper bodies appeared to float on the brown water.

I looked around, was searching for the words, a girl was walking with water filled earthen pot on her head, water drops were trickling down with her lyrical steps, wetting her shoulders, her upper body. She was wearing a golden yellow saree, it was folded a little, just below the knee level, the way dhoti or lungi are folded sometimes, the folding frees the legs. Lyric was there on her walk, song was on her steps, the dust coming out with her steps was creating a stage, the golden sun was on the other side, the orange rays were falling on her, an aura around her body; she was glowing in the afternoon light. The saree was getting wet with each step of her, the wetness trickling up to her chest, re-depicting her shape again, the shaped breasts, the curves were more apparent. The brass ring on the legs above the ankle, the golden necklace, the bracelets, the golden ear rings, all were giving further golden tinge to her shape. The sun took a further journey, the rays were turning reddish, the golden shape was slowly getting fainter, and the horizon was getting opaque, hazed. I looked at the footsteps, the songs of the rural Odisha was getting written with her foot prints on the dusty road, the songs reverberated from the mountains far away, the beauty of the countryside was casting the imprints on the golden land.

Songs echoed at my ears, I was looking at her in that uncommon land, the words of Kabisamrat Upendrabhanj was coming to my ears with the wind, her smell, the smell of the wet dust was reaching me.

"I saw the young maiden today,
If I would get the amazingly beautiful girl,
She could be like a necklace to me-------"

The feeling was coming to me on the land of poems, the emotions flew with her movement, the golden rays carried it to me, changing the world and my world turned too backwards, I went to that period, closed my eyes, the handsome prince, poet was sitting on an asan with lekhani on his right hand, the goddess of knowledge standing on his side, and he was composing, his eyes were glued on the girl, she was walking, emotions in his eyes were taking shape of the words on the nib; then she looked at him, he was into his deep thought, the feelings trickled on the palm leaves.

The sun was going to touch the mountain top, the rays are more reddish, she had come much closer, I looked at her, her face was wet, looked reddish, the colour in the horizon had brought its own tinge to her beautiful face.

At that time I also thought, like Upendra Bhanja,

"I saw her
glowing in the past sun,
steps turning gold,
her fragrance turned me mad.

She came closer
enslaved me,
moved along with her,
her hands around my neck,
the evening filling my heart,
no space for the wind even."

I felt many a time, if I could express my feelings in a poem, then what a beautiful place the world could have been.

On that afternoon I looked at the walking girl again, she was coming closer and closer, the golden sun was inking her turmeric paste applied yellow skin with reddish tinge, the girls of Berhampur apply turmeric paste on their body so that the skin remains youthful. I looked beyond, the blackbuck herd was running at full throttle, the males at the front, the females little back, they were jumping into the air, their legs hardly touched the ground, the dust on the earth was creating a narrow band over the soil due to their movement, the diffused red light created a golden reddish band over the earth and over it the golden-black deers were flying, and at their front the golden girl was walking, strange; no sound, but the footsteps were creating a music unmatched, the light breeze fluttered the leaves and created an unforgettable symphony, and I was looking at the setting, at the beautiful creatures.

I thought of going to the girl, she was much closer, I looked at her, her eyes were half closed, my feelings, my emotions were touching her, she was walking slowly on the dusty road. I was standing almost on the road, as she came closer my heart started agonizingly throbbing in excitement, I was feeling my heartbeats at every nerve, was totally lost on her thought, every step of her was vibrating, creating a music in my heart; and she came closer, only a few feet away and surprisingly I followed her, mesmerized by her beauty, like the character in the story where the man imprisoned by her thought turned to a sheep, speechless, to satisfy her lust in the night, she was mesmerizing. I was hypnotized, turned deaf and dumb.

On the backdrop, those blackbucks were springing into the sky, walking gorgeously and then running at full throttle, I looked at them; the beautiful afternoon sun was setting behind the hills, the golden rays falling on them, turning them to golden deers.

"Oh! My dear blackbuck,
Wait a little,
Golden sun is calling you,
turning you a golden dream,
White cloud made you so light,
Blue horizon gave you the speed,
And my beloved made you so beautiful
Left her imprints on you.'

I looked at them, tried to describe their beauty in my words, if I could express at all, my words were totally insufficient, I didn't have strong vocabulary. They were standing, in group, their eyes turned on me, as if they were finding the describing words in my lips, tall thin legs standing still like golden bamboo at her backyard, all straight, no folds, the hoops to me looked like feet adorned with beautiful golden shoes, matching the colour, the black line on the hoops was the most modern design, the legs designed for grace and speed. I looked at them more closely and was praising their shape, the shape in-comprehensible like one of the beautiful maiden, the beauty surrounded them like the glow of the girl of the country side, the shape was soft, the steps created rhythm, the fragrance incites emotion, the look invokes attraction, the teasing thought brought intimacy, the idea itself closes the horizon. I couldn't open my eyes further, tried to imprint the golden creatures in my imagination, in my thought, their shape, their movement, their fragrance and that evening all were bringing my beloved closer to me, and I was drawn to the imaginary world.

I turned to a young teenager instantly, new world resurfaced, and beautiful flowers all around, everything new and charming, full of new fragrance, new attraction. I found myself in the embrace of my beautiful beloved, her eyes were closed, so also my eyes, we were in embrace, no sound, our heartbeats were turning to stone, and we were motionless, only the thoughts, the aura of closeness moved in the air.

I remained in her embrace,
no one to disturb,
I asked her drop the thoughts,
the disturbing ones,
it brings the insanity.

She remained in my embrace,
her body pressed against mine,
shaped breasts pushed so close,
I felt her
her thought turned mine
breathings mixed

heads touched
The stone depicted
Me, me only,
no presence of any other
the shapes changed.

These golden deers were hypnotizing me, their movement spectacular, their walk lyrical, their energy limitless, their expressions brings many unbound thoughts. I looked at the black bucks, two male bucks were grazing a little away, the males were standing in that Guguchia (a type of grass) filled grass land, the lower body with white belly was almost losing its identity in the grassland, it was looking at the partner, a beautiful look, the head was raised to the maximum height, the dark rounded thick neck was covered with small dark brown furs giving the neck a brownish glow at the backdrop of dark green trees. The ears were raised a little, aligned towards the front side, the dark eyes were surrounded by a band of faint white-brown fur, giving eyes a long depth. The curved horns were elongated backwards like the crown of a king. The other male was almost having the same posture, it had turned its head to the right, the face was more clearly visible, a wide dark band passed from the side outer of mouth over the forehead towards the horn on the other side, the bands crossed each other just between the eyes, located at the front head.

I read some text on the animal, always I feel, without understanding the subject or animal, it is almost impossible to grasp the scene, the importance of the animal, most importantly how we really need them. The golden blackbucks remain in a limited areas in Buguda areas of Ganjam district, the open space is surrounded by hills and forest, the physical limit of their movement extends to fourteen villages. The villagers protect these magnificent deers like their own children, the strong belief in tradition; if the blackbucks are harmed then Mother Laxmi-the Goddess of wealth would leave the village, hunger and misery would follow; if the black bucks thrive, eat paddy this year, there would be bumper crop next year. If the blackbucks damage gram, black gram, kandula (a type of gram), and other winter crops; the farmer used to get bumper harvest even though there are some initial damage to the crop. There is also another belief, in case one kills a blackbuck, then he will turn infertile, no offspring will be born. The villagers, even though the blackbucks damage their crops- paddy mostly, never drive them away, allowed the golden deer to graze peacefully. During the lean period, when food and water are not easily available in the forest grass lands, or in fields, many a times the blackbucks come much nearer to the houses, even damages the vegetable crops at their backyard gardens. Sometimes these shy animals even drink water from the earthen pots kept outside the houses. The blackbucks, to them as their own pets, not to be harmed, to be protected from greedy hunters, in case they know about the presence of hunters, then they guard the blackbuck herds, and night vigil is kept, message of hunters pass from village to village.

By conservative estimates, there are five to six herds in the area, each herd comprises up of 50-60 adults. These blackbucks are easy to find during the early morning, or late afternoon when the sun is soft; and during the day time they usually take rest in the not so easily approachable mango grooves in the village.

I looked at another group of three blackbucks, they were looking at us keenly, three bucks were at one place, their narrow tall legs were holding their beautiful shape, the female was light brown in colour with white belly, the body little elongated, the neck was narrow, the ears were raised, the head looked like a narrow triangle with black invert vertices. The fawn was standing between the male and female, almost half the size of the female, light brown in colour, the same appearance of the mother. The male looked elegant before two innocent females, it's figure was much bigger than the female, body colour deep dark brown, the belly was more white than the females, the neck was heavy and curved, and the spiral horns were growing side up ways increasingly away from each other, and most importantly its ears were down, not like the female and the fawn, the territorial male had the confidence.

After a while I moved to a watch tower constructed below a banyan tree, the long straight wooden poles were holding the wooden structure over which a thatched roof was made, a thick branch of the banyan tree passed over the roof, the foliage was camflouging the structure some extent, but the long vision of the grass land was not hindered by the leaves. I looked at the blackbucks and started reading about the blackbucks.

Information on Blackbucks

There are many varieties of blackbucks in the country, the blackbuck of the northern and western parts of the country used to be taller and heavier, the height of the male blackbuck varies between 73 to 85 cms and the weight remains between 31 to 39 kgs. The blackbuck from the central, eastern and southern parts of the country have slightly smaller body and horn.

All the blackbucks are capable of high graceful leaps and can sustain good speed for a long time; they can run over 80 kms per hour and can leap over 4 meter high bush. Their long leap and sustained speed make them so spectacular during their run.

The male buck has stunning look with the spiraled straight shallow horns have circular rings, the number of spiral not always proportionate with the length of the horn; and for some animal there can be four spirals for a horn length of 55 cms, and for some animals there can be three spirals for a longer horn length of 72 cms

The female blackbucks do not have horns, are light brownish in colour, the under parts of the body and the tail and reminder of the legs are white, with a similar coloured patch around each eye. The males are similar to the females in coloration when immature, but the colour deepens with age, and in certain individuals the colour become almost black in sharp contrast to the white on the nose and lower muzzle, eyes, chest, belly and legs.

Habitat

The blackbucks prefer flat areas with short grasses, around 40 cm height, but certainly not more than 70 cm tall; in the nearby fields the agriculture crops should have low height too; the vision of the blackbucks should not be obstructed and the movement of the predator should be easily detected. They avoid close proximity to bushes or shrubs which might be possible hiding places of the predators. The blackbucks, during peak summer drink at least twice; so generally they remain within a kilometer or two from the water sources. The blackbucks when suddenly disturbed, take high leaps

Distribution

The blackbucks were distributed in many parts of Indian subcontinent, from Peshwar in the north to point Calimer in South, covering a contiguous habitat all along the Indo-Gangetic plains upto the Siwalik ranges, which once extended upto plains of western Assam. These animals don't inhibit the mangrove forest areas of eastern coastal Bengal and Odisha, also there was no evidence of their occurrence in the Sal forested areas of the eastern ghats.

At present the blackbucks remained in the different scattered habitats in the states of Rajastahan, Punjab, Haryana, Uttar Pradesh, Bihar, West Bengal, Odisha, Andhra Pradesh, Karnataka, Tamilnadu, Maharasta, Gujrat, Madhya Pradesh. In Odisha the blackbuck population is distributed mainly at Buguda and Aska ranges of Ganjam district, and Balukhand sanctuary along Puri-Konark marine sea drive.

Observation in herd population at different areas brings out the fact that in general the adult population is between 60-70 %, the sub adults are in the range of 20% and the rest are fawns. The male female ratio is generally between 1:1.7 to 1:3

Group Structure, Birth and Mortality

The black bucks have specific social behaviour, which is complex as humans. The blackbucks are found in different groups, as per the following ways.

1. Solitary female, usually close to parturition.
2. A female with one or two off springs of different ages.
3. Females and young groups with or without immature males.
4. Solitary male, usually mature and territorial.
5. Bachelor group of males.
6. Mixed herds of one or more mature males with females and young, either in a harem or in a quasi harem situation.

The bachelor group in the blackbuck population are interesting groups, the males comprise of yearling age group up to older males who have passed their prime. When the large male groups rests, the immature males usually sit on the periphery and the larger dark males sit in clusters, almost touching each other.

In a mixed group, in an area with sufficient food availability, the dominant male is always present with the herd and makes constant effort to cut off the extended movement of the herd, a harem formation where the females are confined to a small territory. In a quasi harem formation, the territorial males remain behind their respective territory and allow the herd to move to the other pastures.

The territory formation in a blackbuck range is interesting too, the territorial males are deep-rooted to their occupation areas, the location of the territories is influenced by the availability of food, and the frequency with which the females are likely to pass through the territory. The territory of a single solitary male is adjacent to the territory of the home range of female herd, or of the territories of other male. These territories are not occupied throughout the daylight period, the blackbucks sometimes leave their territories for periodic grazing, or to drink water, otherwise the males occupy their respective territory throughout the period shortly after the sunrise to half an hour before sun set, and next day the territorial occupation may change.

Reproduction

The females used to conceive after two years and a male mates usually after 3 and 1/2 years of age in the zoo condition and remain productive up to 12 years of age. In the harem and quasi harem situation in the black buck ranges, the breeding is largely carried out by males of the age group of 5-7 years.

Seasonality of births

In blackbuck population, mating has been observed through out the year, a female can come into estrous at any time of the year; but usually well before monsoon and majority of births take place prior to the monsoon.

PREDATION

In India, the major predators of the black bucks are the leopard, tiger, jackal. The jackal through not the big carnivorous, but is the main culprit for large reduction of blac buck population in many places. The jackals used to follow the gravid female till the fawns is born, and they attack it in the first hour of birth when the fawn is almost helpless. The stray dogs too chase the blackbucks, they are mostly predator fawns.

MORTALITY

The average life of blackbucks is believed to be between 7-8 years and the mortality rate increases after 7 of years of age; however in captive condition the male may live upto 15-16 years.

DIET

The blackbucks used to feed on grasses, sedges and herbs and varities of agricultural crops like rice, jowar, bajra, barseem, moong, gram, arhar, moth, urad, cotton, ground nut, guar, lucerne, etc; The average daily intake per adult in captivity is approximately 2½ kg to 3½ kg. The blackbucks use artificial mineral salt lick extensively.

It was a long reading, I was looking at the field below, there were so many groups in the field, some males in a group, lone or two males in other group, group of females, young and females forming a group with large territorial black male. I watched a male keenly, it was standing near a long earthen mound, a big palm tree was standing close, the legs and belly were almost hidden the black elongated well formed body was aligned to the mound, and it was watching a herd of grazing cattle which were little away from it; the white cattle were grazing much close to the hillock with many big boulders, near to the small woodlots. A cattle grazer with round bamboo hat on its head surfaced from the bushes and the male blackbuck watched the cattle for sometime then moved backwards, and came near to the group. In its group the females were grazing the grasses undisturbed, some of course were looking at the cattle at times, the male however was keeping constant watch on the movements. A little away from them two young males were locking their horns, their colour were yet to be blackened, their heads were down, mouth almost touching the grassland, the spiral horns were tilted towards the opponent, and the horns were locked, the heads were not touching each other; and they remained in that position for sometime gauged their respective strength, some movement in forward and backward direction with locked horns; the playtime of the young were continuing.

Again I looked at a small group of females, the male was not guarding them in the vicinity, probably it was chasing an intruder, their standing posture was giving them a beautiful look in the light undulating landscape, two females with deeper brown tinge were standing in the front, a small fawn was little back, another darker female was standing on a small green mound, all looking at the open cultivation fields ahead, their heads were aligned towards the cultivation fields in their front, their ears were raised and spread, the alert position of the females was a joy to watch, so much of postures the blackbucks were having on that day.

Another group of females were standing in a small group, close to each other, no alertness, they were calm, no more feeding, the sun was setting, the light had reduced, the feeding time was getting over and the herd were about to take rest. I looked at the group, almost of similar size, the females were of almost similar colour, no female with darker colour. A large dark male arrived from the left side, the group didn't panic, it came close, its head was raised, pride in its walk, arrogance in its look, the females lowered their heads, accepted the authority of the male, I was praising their posture, their shape. Then I started reading the book.

Social behaviour

The group formation has been described earlier. Among the females, there is an acceptable individual leader, from whom the herd has started. When a few animals move in a particular direction, others used to follow; some animals who appear to move in different direction initially used to follow the big group. However in bachelor group, there is less co-ordination in movement, feeding or fight.

Hierarchy

The dominant male, also called the alpha male of a mixed group remains top in the social hierarchy, even if he is a territorial male who is a temporary member in a quasi harem situation. The dominant male, even some times the mature sub-alpha males, prevent the movement of females in certain directions by blocking their path and displaying head up display and ward them off. Interestingly sometimes they trot or even run after the way ward females and bring them back to the group.

In a mixed group, the male hierarchy is decided by the horn size, colour and age of the black buck; males with larger pairs of horns but a darker coloured pelage than other males take the highest status.

In bachelor group, the hierarchy is not so well defined as in a mixed group. The age, horn and body size are the factors for pre-eminence of certain males over the others, the darker the colour, the higher is the status.

Among the adults, the closest bonds are seen between the male pair living by themselves, they graze together and their movements are coordinated. The adult blackbucks used to ignore fawns unless they are unduly disturbed. The female don't show special interest in other young other than its own fawn. In females the bonds with the mother continues even after the birth of another fawn.

Again I looked at another group of males, they were taking rest in the field, almost all were laying on the ground, all with good horns, but some were darker than the rest showing their age and maturity. I looked at a matured sitting male keenly, the Guguchia grasses were almost touching its mouth. Its body was looking like a dark stone, the ears were parallel to the ground, it was looking at us without any alertness. The lesser darker males were taking rest a little away from the darker males, all were however relaxed.

Play

Most common play for new born is short dashes with two or three intermittent straight upwards high jumps which can go up to five, then descending with legs slightly bent and these jumps usually in quick successions and sometimes the youngsters too occasionally jump vertically by pushing the soil hard with hind legs. The early morning time is the most common play time for the young black bucks.

Vocalization

The blackbucks make low but deep clucking noises, as the 'kn, kn' or 'click call'. The call of distress, when wounded or caught by dogs, is a long drawn' baa' sound. The fawns emit an 'ooo' bleat which brings the mother close.

Daily movement & rest

The black bucks feed at different times of the day, the early morning feed starts a little before dawn, and they take pre-noon rest, in the summer months the pre-noon rest period is timed at around 10:30 a.m. After the pre-noon rest, they usually move a shorter distance for food and take rest in the early afternoon. During the late afternoon and the dusk, the black bucks go for intensive feeding. In open areas, the blackbucks stand still rather than sitting and when bedded down, they often extend one of their forelegs forward instead of folding it below.

I read for a long time, looked at the vast field in front of me, the area was clearly visible, the blackbucks were grazing the grass continuously, the sun was descending fast, two males were running away from us, towards the hill, in front of them was lying a vast tract. The male black on the front was almost in air, its colour was yet to be darkened, a young male is approaching its puberty, the front legs were stretched forward, neck stretched forward, it was moving like an arrow; on its heels was another dark and heavy buck, its hind legs were raised upward, the front legs was touching the grassland, the dark neck was not that stretched and long spiral horn was not fully raised upward; the territorial male was chasing the novice away from the females. The chasing continued for some time and the novice was driven away from the herd.

Territorial Behaviour

The males occupy vacant territories, many a times new area are carved out of existing territories or sometimes the older occupant are driven out from the existing territory.

When a new territory is carved out, or the old occupant is driven out, the new member shows aggressiveness, it often involves protracted displays and fight, ritualized but some times real if the female is around, and the winner male chases the looser. The territorial male doesn't remain with the bachelor groups, it sits slightly apart. The territorial male displays aggressiveness with the sight of another male and he ends up in chasing away the intruder.

When a female group approaches the territory of a territorial male, the territorial male goes to the edge of its territory greets them and then addresses the females present in his territory. For a mixed group, the dominant herd male moves to the flank of the herd and accept a secondary position to the territorial male. However, the actual mating does not take place during the transition.

Territorial markings & association

The territorial marking is interesting, the blackbucks maintain small round or oval territories adjacent to each other and the average size of each territory is around 8-9 ha of area. The black buck make territorial markings by creating pellet piles in certain selected strategic spots along the periphery; over the pellets urination is done and the male buck usually sits on those pellet sites. They also make some olfactory marking by wiping the secretion of the pre-orbital glands on major reeds, twigs and grasses; occasionally rub the glands against the tree trunks and leaves, this strong smelling lasts upto 3 days in dry weather.

Colour Changes

The colour changes in black bucks is noticeable too, there used to be distinct colour changes during different phases of blackbuck life. The new born is brownish in colour, turn to fawn coloured in few weeks and the colour darken with age in both sexes. However, there is seasonal colour change with the approach of the peak rutting periods; this darkening is noticeable in the dominant males of mixed herds and the next most darker males are the territorial males.

DISPLAY & RESPONSE

The blackbucks exhibit different aggression while scaring other males, following females; the male blackbuck thrash saplings or bushes with horns, which shows its aggression. When he scares another male, the neck is compressed, the ear is forward but down, walks with deliberate steps and occasionally breaks into short trot towards the offending male, the head and horns move up and down in unison to the body movements, a short series of harsh nasal grunt-snorts comes out, the head is raised.

In combat situation, the horns are locked, they push each other, the eyes bulge under strain, however, rarely fight lead to any physical injury other than broken horn tips. The disengagement takes when one of the loser males run away from the fight being chased by the winner.

Some combat characteristics are displayed during the courtship, the male halts near a female and raises the upper lip, partially expose the upper teeth and gums. The female in estrous is singled out for mating .

I turned little wiser at understanding the animal, these studies were of course not taken on the black bucks of Buguda, taken somewhere else, but definitely holds good for the blackbucks of the land. I looked at the blackbucks, they were no more scattered, coming close to each other, then I looked at the girl in front, she was going towards the house, her house was near. I looked at the house at her village. Evening was descending on the dusty narrow course of the village, the earthen houses with red walls and straw roofs were looking magnificent, a light cloud of mist was hazing over the straw roofs, the trees were losing their shapes and colours, the sounds from the villages were getting silent, the stars were appearing on the sky, the burning wicks from the houses emerged.

I was looking at the evening beauty of the rural Odisha, looking differently at the land brings so much of inquisitiveness, so much of joy, a different feeling all together. Then she came out of the house, she had changed her saree, was wearing a dry cloth, the burning earthen lamp was on her right hand, and she came to the Chaura, put the burning wick on the soil and bowed her head before the Chaura. Her head touched the ground, she was worshipping the Tulsi Chaura, the deities were to be remembered, revered, let them go for rest.

I looked at her, faint orange light from the burning wick was falling on her charming face. I couldn't believe my eyes, the beauty of the girl multiplied many a times in the faint light. In my imagination she turned of to the golden girl, soft and sweet, her beauty was shining like the blossom of a fragrant plant. I searched for her in my dreamland; I recollected the song of the olden times.

Sapanara pathe pathe Sandhyare Dine Gali

(I moved in the land of dreams in one evening, to see her, to get back my lost love, the girl was coming with the evening earthen lamp with burning wick, the surrounding was full with her fragrance. I was searching for my missing love, couldn't hold myself, went to her, asked for her name. She looked at me, a soft look, full of emotion for me, and she told her name, "Preeti" and she was my lost love, I looked at her, the beautiful face was looking astounding in that evening, the golden light of the earthen lamp increased her beauty many a times, an unbound love for me was dancing on her face.)

Kharsel, the Name of Transformation

I was sitting in open, in front the silence of the Sal forest extending beyond the length of my sight. The evening birds were calling from their hides, the chill of the November evening was coming with the gentle northern wind. I was picturising a massive figure, ears fluttering as it speeds, legs thumping on the ground, the white tusk protruding from the head like a spear of the Spartan soldier, body well-shielded behind the thick skin, the tall helmet and the feathers of the soldier now takes the shape of the raised trunk. The movement, criss-crossed one, of course due to the presence of the trees on the way, the massive Spartan soldier was charging at the intruder.

He again told me to imagine, I closed my eyes, and tried to depict the description, an animal almost eleven feet tall; the heavy beast is charging at you, its deep breathing sound fills the entire forest, the trumpets are coming as thunder, the branches, twigs are breaking logs below its feet, the sound coming like the drums of the charging troupe, high beats, clear and loud, the trees and bushes giving way, the husky shape running at you, the little red eyes are burning in anger, the small tail is straightened, its trunk is raised, folded and the whole forest is coming to standstill; and he told the jungle thieves could not simply dare, they run for cover, and the jungle is safe, the animals gain safety, the trees are saved.

He recited the Ganesh Strutee, the mantras to pacify Lord Ganesh, the elephant god, to ask for His blessings.

Vakratunda Mahaakaaya Suryakotee Sama Prabha
Nirvighnam kuru mey Deva, Sarva kaaryeshu Sarvadaa

(Oh! God of large body, curved trunk, Oh! Ganesh you have the brilliance of a million suns, I pray, always make all my work free of obstacles.)

The Ganesha mantras are siddhi mantras, the mantra contains certain cosmic powers, when chanted with the proper posture and rhythmic breathing and with sincere devotion, good outcome results. The Ganesha mantras wards off all evil and bless the devotee with abundance, prudence and success. I couldn't understand the reason of such mystic ways of presenting a subject, but later the results came in a strange fashion.

Elephants, always they draw my imagination, sometimes, to me they are the soldiers, sometimes a docile animal behaving like a small baby, and other time they are so playful, and in my imagination I always see them as one of the most jovial creatures on earth. Each of their movement, I rather say, they take calculated steps, to play, to enjoy, to seduce, to take part in a particular role. In that evening he categorized it as a jewel, of course I had nothing to disbelieve, but he had, because he knew so many stories of the elephants. But still toady he continued with his belief, the animal was totally innocent, for others it was a rogue, killer; but he didn't believe them, rather he believed the elephant, after all he was the man who captured the elephant. This is the story is of an elephant; a story of good, bad and ugly and finally the total transformation.

The elephant was captured from Kharsal Reserve Forest near Bolangir and the animal was named as Kharsal elephant, the new name, matching the place of his new birth. I listened to the full story then.

The mahout had brought the elephant from Banaras for display in the countryside of Odisha, a begging elephant is a common sight in interior districts of Odisha, also in the states of Chhatisgarh, Jharkhand etc., the intention is to get some money by invoking religious sentiments; after all elephant is considered as a form of Ganesh, the elephant God of the Hindus, so the offerings like paddy, rice, coconut, banana, etc. come in plenty; the villagers worship the elephant god. The elephants and the mahouts move in the villages, collect offerings and they stay outside the village limits for the entire course of the journey. The mahouts used to bring the elephant on lease after paying the fee, money is between 50 thousand to one lakh rupees, and takes the elephants to country sides of Odisha, Bihar, Jharkhand, Chhatisgarh, etc. Many unwritten codes need to be followed, the mahout has to maintain a strict disciplined life, the man should take vegetarian food only, should remain single, no female to accompany during the tour, strictly no liquor. That day the elephant was kept in the open, in front of Padamapur court, the location is a favourite the place of the wandering Indian gypsies, they usually halt there at times. That night the Mahout stopped there, but violated the code, went out, only to return in inebriated condition, the elephant didn't obey the command, he directed again and again and used ankush(elephant hook) unnecessarily. The elephant was furious, killed mahout after breaking the iron chain and escaped to the green Gandhamardan hills, the dividing hill range of Bolangir and Khariar forest divisions.

The elephant moved inside the Gandhamardan hills, frequently came to the villages, but the tamed animal was changing to wild one and was showing peculiar characteristics unheard of the elephants – if it was damaging the bananas trees in one night, then it would go on damaging bananas trees throughout that night; if it was damaging paddy crop then it would only damage paddy crop, no other crop would be touched on that eventful night, the sugarcane was also no exception. Unless the people showed aggressiveness, it would not attack; however its crop raiding frequency started increasing, so also the worry of the people; and people started resisting which culminated in human causalities.

This behaviour was creation of the circumstance, there was a house on in the vicinity of the forest, a good maize crop was standing around the house, and the owner was proudly owning an unauthorised a hand loading gun, proudly in the sense that even though it was an unauthorised one but he was the owner of this kind of fire arm in that area. Once the elephant was in his field in one night, he fired at the massive figure, it really didn't hurt much, but the elephant roared in anger, smashed the house and searched for the man. While the elephant was breaking the house in anger, the culprit escaped sure death. The elephant destroyed the whole field, roared in anger, and returned to forest. But the anger of the elephant was so much, whenever the elephant passes passed alongside that broken house, it used to stop, used to destroy whatever new crop comes came on the field, used to trample the broken house structure again and again and used to roar in anger. The elephant, unless harmed was not a threat, but human behaviour was more unpredictable than the behaviour of the elephant. The people were told not to interfere with the activities of the elephant, they didn't listen. Once an old woman threw hot water at the elephant, it turned back, caught the old lady by its trunk and crushed her. The elephant had liking for watered boil rice, once using its tusk it made a hole on the walls of the earthen house and ate the pot full of boiled rice through its trunk; next morning people saw the house, except for the hole there was no damage to the house. But there were many unfortunate events, once it was breaking the house to eat the watered boiled rice, a commonly available food in rural areas, The house owner came closer, shouted at it, it didn't tolerate interference, it turned back, then threw the man away, the man died instantly. Kharseil was a problem for 10 years, many people died in the process, houses, and crops were raided regularly. Initially the people ignored the problem, but as the death toll rises, more properties were damaged, there was regular demand from the public, mostly from Bolangir area, to capture the elephant.

Then he recited the Bhajans of Salabega, the great Musalman poet of Odisha, though he was a Muslim by birth, his songs were devoted to Lord Jagannath, the patron deity of Odisha and I was drawing so much of similarity in the story.

(Ahe Nila Shaila, Prabala Matta barana, ------------)

(The massive elephant was in great danger, the gigantic crocodile was holding its feet in deep water, and he prayed to Jagannath, the God cut the head of the crocodile using His Chakra and the elephant was saved.)

In this case, the elephant cried, sure death in front, God transformed the mind of the hunter, the animal was saved, and then the total transformation took place.

Agitation mounted up, there was constant pressure to declare it rogue, the forest officials resisted vehemently, but finally gave in under tremendous pressure and it was decided to eliminate the elephant. There were many to hunt the elephant, hunting was a game for the royals of the Gadajat (hinter land) and other kingdoms, one such man volunteered and he went on tracking the elephant. He continued with his talk,

The man was in full hunting dress, round hat on the head, the long moustache was rounded at the tip, full-sleeved brown shirt covered the body with khaki half pant and on the legs was the soft padded jungle boot. The man was appearing like Jim Corbett, the famous tiger hunter of India, only this man had long rounded moustache. He pursued the elephant with loaded riffle was on his hand, went after the elephant for days together. On that eventful day the elephant was standing on the edge of the forest, in front of the paddy fields, near a Mahul tree, the sun was shining in front, and the hunter too was standing on a rock below the sun. The elephant saw the hunter, the man too saw the elephant and raised his gun and aimed at the elephant, the massive creature was around 50 feet away, and the massive head was straight on sight, the target was big enough – not to be even missed by an armature. The elephant understood the situation, it understood that the final time had come, so it raised its trunk and folded it at the top, a sign of showing reverence, it used to respect human in this way, tear rolled from its eyes, the sign of total surrender. The hunter looked at the elephant, the golden ray was falling on the dusty – husky figure and the sign of submission on the posture; and the hunter was moved, he lowered his gun, understood the folly in the decision in of hunting, the elephant had no unnatural behavior. Later he described his experience to everybody, everybody moved at the incident.

While one group was advocating for total elimination of the elephant, one other group led by Shri Pattnaik, a wildlife exponent and a forest officer too, of the state, was preaching for rehabilitation of the elephant after tranquilising it. Good sense prevailed, the voice of the hunter was too loud to avoid, and finally it was decided to tranquilise the elephant at Bolangir side in view of easy terrain there. The elephant was given a bait, dried Mahul flowers were procured, the elephants used to get attracted towards Mahul flower, the smell, taste get them intoxicated; the man with Mahul load was sent to the forest with the direction to run at the sight of the elephant, the Mahul was to be scattered on the ground, a stage managed show; the elephant wound not believe it to be a trap. The game was played again and again, the elephant came close many a times, but didn't eat Mahul the tranquiliser team from Bhubaneswar was getting restless.

One evening the elephant was sighted at Kuladiha village under Bolangir district, message came, the elephant was standing below a Mahul tree; the tranquilisation team rushed immediately. They found the local Range Forest Officer standing near the elephant, around 30 feet away. The team came closer; the elephant was now around 15 feet away, suddenly it started throwing sand at the intruders, the forest officers, using his front leg. The team had a challenge, the elephant had to be moved to proper position so that the tranquiller dart can to be fired, care need to be taken, else it would result elephant causality or grave injury might happen. The elephant then made mock charge, its intention was not to attack, only it took few long steps; the team understood the behaviour, they were after all experts in elephant psychology, the elephant would not charge at unless the group disperses and runs hither thither. The team was in right footing, they advanced further, now it was the time of the elephant, it suddenly turned back and tried to flee. The team was then sufficiently close; and the tranquilization dart was fired at the back of the elephant. At once the elephant turned back, again made a mock charge, but it was getting drugged, and then it ran towards the forest. After a brief run it halted, and leaned against a standing tree. The elephant was semiconscious, further dart was fired and elephant was fully tranquilized. Then the elephant was chained on its legs, front legs were chained together and the hind legs were chained by iron rings which were finally tied to bamboo clumps, the only strong available trees available there. The front leg chaining would not allow the elephant to run, the hind leg chaining would allow the elephant to move forward, backward and lateral too, it would prevent its escape. Once the chaining process was over, the revival injection was given to the elephant and it slowly regained consciousness. The elephant stood after a brief period, found itself chained, roared and tried to break the shackles constantly.

I recollected the extracts from the famous book *'Gulliver's Travels'* a novel written by Anglo-Irish writer and clergyman Jonathan Swift in the eighteenth century. Gulliver's encounter with the Lilliputians was interesting, the present human forms were like Liliputians for the elephant, but now it was chained; the situation looks so similar, I recollected the extract.

When Gulliver wakes up, he finds his arms, legs, and long hair, all have been tied to the ground with pieces of threads. Now, he can only look up, the bright sun prevents him opening his eyes, from seeing anything. He feels something to move across his leg and then over his chest. He looks down and finds a six-inch-tall human carrying a bow and arrow. At least forty more little creatures climb onto his body. He is surprised and shouts loudly, frightening the little people away.

Gulliver tries to get loose and finally succeeds in breaking the strings binding his left arm. He loosens the ropes tying his hair so he can turn to the left. In response, the little people fire a volley of arrows into his hand and violently attack his body and face. He decides that the safest thing to do is to lie still until nightfall. The noise increases as the little people build a stage next to Gulliver about a foot and a half off the ground. One of them climbs onto it and makes a speech in a language that Gulliver does not understand.

The group was apprehensive; they never thought the elephant would be so ferocious, also never in their life saw such a powerful elephant. The elephant was trying to uproot the trees, and with each effort, some bamboos were either broken or getting uprooted. After three days of chaining the elephant finally broke the chain, freed itself, but couldn't go long as its front legs were chained too, and the same was not broken. The desperate elephant ran for cover into the forest. A brave heart from forest department came forward, it caught the elephant by its tail, but the elephant was running for cover, Nila, the brave boy was hanging from the tail. It was a terrific sight, the elephant was carrying the man by its tail, not by its trunk, Nila had a remarkable elephant tail drive that day. Today, when this incident is remembered, Nila laughs and laughs, after all the elephant now has turned to be his best friend, and Nila is now his mahout. Nila continued his association with the elephant from that moment till today. Strange part of the incident was that Nila had never handled elephants earlier, and in a matter of frenzy during that moment he got associated with the elephant and had a tail ride, and he continued his association with the elephant during the entire course of capture and subsequent taming and training. During the entire capture period of the elephant, Nila used to take care of the elephant, used to clean the area using very long handled brooms and used to apply medicine to the wounds of the elephant as stated later. It was found out that Nila was the only person in the area who could handle the elephant to some extent; the elephant only listened to the direction of Nila in Bolangir.

The team frantically searched for the escaped elephant, due to its chaining it couldn't go long and was later found at Baidehipalli, in Patnagarh area. The present location was an open area, no tall and strong trees suitable to withstand the power of the elephant could be found, the elephant would be captured and would be chained for few days to a strong tree. An appropriate area was looked for, was found it nearby, so a directional drive was made, the elephant was pushed to a suitable place with few trees. The team loaded Immobilan, the medicine used for tranquilisation. Seeing the size of the animal, even though it was large, but the fact that it was chained which was an advantage to the team, so lower doze was thought of and a 3ml doze was loaded into the gun and the dart was fired at the elephant. Very soon the elephant lost its control, but it didn't lose its consciousness, was in semi-sedated condition, the team brought the elephant through drag and push method to the right area. Now it was decided to chain all the legs of the elephant, earlier the elephant was chained on the back legs and it escaped. So all the legs were chained, the four chains were tied to four different trees, the elephant could stand, would not generate sufficient force in one leg to break the chain. It tried, trumpeted, the strong chain didn't break.

The elephant remained in chained condition for almost a month, day and night watch was kept. Giving food, water and medicine was a great problem for the resource starved area like Bolangir. With great difficulty elephant food could be gathered and the elephant was fed with branches of banyan tree, banana was in its meal every day, and water was offered in a big tub, and a water tanker was pressed into service so that regular water supply could be maintained. Due to long chaining period and its sustained effort to break the shackles, its legs were wounded. The elephant destroyed food and water vessel many a times, and it remained in the agitated mood mostly. The sea of onlookers every day agitated it further; its natural aggression coupled with irritation at the presence of the onlookers was adding the misery of the elephant, its anger was rising. The media attention was focused on the elephant, both electronic and the print media came with stories frequently. The forest officials were not finding clues to tame the elephant, treat it and then bring it back to normal condition.

Then the officials thought to tame the elephant using trained female elephants, two trained female elephants were brought from Nandankanan zoo. Seeing the approaching female elephants, it at once sexually aroused, in fact it wanted to mate. In an aroused state any elephant turns aggressive, an already agitated elephant will definitely be more hostile and that happened; the experienced Mahouts tried to coerce the elephant, tried to come close with the female elephants, but it charged at the approaching females, moved its trunk violently, the aggressiveness increased with each step of the approaching female elephants. The tactics of seducing the captured one failed, the elephant could not be tamed.

In the meantime infection of the legs worsened, swellings were visible and pus was oozing out of the wound. The authorities were anxious; worsening of the wounds would draw adverse media attention and situation would go out of control. The Mahouts couldn't dare to approach the elephant directly, one tried to be close, tried to apply the medicine on the wounds of the chained elephant. Since the legs were chained in four directions, one Mahout tried to put himself under the belly of the elephant and tried to apply the medicine.

This attempt angered the elephant; it tried to sit on the man who was under his belly. Seeing the aggressiveness of the chained elephant, the Mahout ran, and the forest department was at wits end to control the elephant. They devised a method, loaded the antibiotics into an agriculture spray, then from a distance sprayed it, a jet of medicine gel rushed towards the elephant, and a portion of it fell on the wounded leg of the elephant. To disinfect the animal, they used to spray Dettol anti-bacterial liquid from a distance using the same method.

Apart from taming the elephant, shifting it to a suitable place and subsequent training were the need of the time. In the beginning it was decided to bring the elephant to Nanadankanan zoo near Bhubaneswar, but the authorities there were reluctant, they had a sad experience, a bitter one. Earlier one rogue elephant was brought from Sambalpur area, it couldn't be controlled properly, the elephant that time broke the enclosures, cages, and finally it was shot. The authorities were not interested to take up this problem once again, the media highlights were beyond their control, and again the presence of so many persons would agitate the elephant further. The alternatives were searched, the area should be close to Nandankanan and there should not be public presence. The reason for bringing the elephant near to Nandankanan was to give better treatment to the captured elephant, the wild animal doctor were only available in Nandankanan, and the doctors can't visit Bolangir frequently in view of other pressing engagements at the zoo itself. So finally it was decided to bring the animal to Chandka, a wildlife sanctuary located at the outskirts of Bhubaneswar city, adjacent to Nandankanan too.

It was decided to transfer the elephant from Bolangir to Chandka by closed trucks, a normal practice to transfer the captured elephants from one place to another. A team from Nandankanan zoo arrived and as per their advice a sunken ramp was constructed, the body of the truck and earth surface was kept at the same level and the attempt was made to load the captured elephant on it. The chains of the front legs were then lengthened with longer chains which were tied to the truck body; the chains of the back leg were loosened little by little. When the front chains were tightened a little, and the back chains were loosened proportionately, the elephant was pushed from behind, this processes only ensures the forward movement of the elephant. The elephant was brought to the edge of the ramp, but it didn't ride the truck base, the elephant didn't even put its leg on the truck body. The team then pushed the elephant further; the elephant in a rage broke the wooden walls of the truck. The team was determined to transfer the elephant, so they pushed the elephant from the back, the elephant came inside, it was furious, it shook the whole truck, put its trunk inside the front cabin and broke it. It was the testing time, the team decided not to transport the agitated elephant in the truck this time, other alternative had to be explored. Further cffort would be harmful for the elephant, on the way there would be dense forests and isolated patches, the elephant can't be controlled on the way too, the smell of other elephant on the way would aggravate its mood. So they abandoned the transfer program for the time being and the team returned from Bolangir to Bhubaneswar.

A long discussion ensued, judging the mood of the elephant, its strength and size, it was decided to transfer it by trailer truck, probably the open structure would help it to calm down, and the total iron structure of the truck would be too strong for the elephant, it can't break it. The trailer truck was arranged from the Chauliganj area of Cuttack town, the owner of the vehicle was apprehensive of the transportation of the wild animal. But he was convinced, also he allowed new fabrication on his trailortrailer truck, and also agreed for longer waiting time, the transportation process was uncertain, might take long processtime, and only night transportation to happen, the team would avoid day travel. The vehicle was brought to Baranga, the place where Nandankanan zoo is situated, and the fabrication work started and an iron cage of 10½ feet was erected with suitable supporting bars. The truck was tested with other captive elephants at Nandankanan, it had sufficient length and breadth to accommodate the a big elephant. Then the trailer truck was driven to Bolangir, on the way the party faced many challenges, at many places the truck body was touching the live electric wires, however with great difficulty they arrived at Bolangir, many snapping of live electric wires happened on the way, so the team didn't dare to take risk with a live elephant, electrocution would bring catastrophe for the handlers. The frame was again fabricated, around 6 inch was reduced, and the wielders of Bolangir worked day and night.

Seeing the unusual structure the people of the town descended down around the parking site, the crowd control turned to be a nightmare for the police and forest officials. The local officials decided to transfer the elephant during night hours, else there would be heavy rush of people on the way, and it would be difficult to control the crowd. With passing of everyday the curiosities of the people were increasing, the imminent transfer news was spreading like wildfire, even people from far off villages also came to watch the live circus, an uncanny elephant would march through the streets of Bolangir in a closed enclosure. The transfer warning was coming repeatedly, everybody was apprehensive.

As usual a sunken ramp was again created, as per earlier described procedure, but remained the most difficult task – the animal had to be brought into the truck. At early evening hours the team readied themselves, a group of people pushed the elephant to the edge of the trailer truck, the elephant was totally uncompromising, was opposing tooth and nail, it simply refused to board like a arrogant naught child:, the party tried hard, the regular pushing, thrusting was not working. Suddenly the elephant turned aggressive, it tried to break the truck, it banged its huge head against the truck body, the truck shook, but the iron structure withstood the onslaught, the truck didn't break. Now with every pushing, the elephant was banging its head against the truck body, the sound of its bringing was loudly audible, the party now felt danger, and the elephant might hurt itself. As its effort to break the truck went in vein, the elephant froze itself; it didn't move an inch even, no forward or backward movement; now the loading party came to their wits end.

A novel method was suggested; lure the elephant into the truck by offering food, a food bait is generally a trap for the wild animals, and this elephant love food very much. Then banana, coconut, Mahul etc., were kept on the base of the truck, total silence need to be maintained, and the party retreated to an actionable distance from where then could watch, the distance also would be able to act quickly. They waited for the right moment – the elephant would enter into the truck, then they would come near the truck and close the door of the cage. It was a beautiful designplan, luring a rogue elephant for capture. The elephant first collected the food scattered in nearby areas, outside the truck limit, using its trunk. After some time when the food at the reachable portion got exhausted, it sat on the ground, the trunk now reached a little longer distance, reach extended into the back portion of the truck and it collected the food from that distance. Once the food was exhausted in that radius, then it put one leg over the truck body and ate food from that portion, but it didn't enter into the truck. The team was getting restless, the elephant was taking too long a time, also they need to leave the town by day break; everyone was watching the steps of the elephant keenly, to them it appeared like a very slow movie action in very slow motion. The eating process continued from 9 p.m. to 1 a.m. in the night, the elephant was very cautious to move into the cage, the party was watching from a distance, from a hide around 100 meters away. The moonlight was falling on the truck, the shapes were darkened in the dim light, and the moon was on the other side, silhouetting the elephant. The darker structure was moving cautiously into the cage. When the elephant body was almost ¾th inside, the team leader got alerted, it was the time to act. He moved very cautiously along with a mohout to the front side of the truck, the elephant was busy in eating delicious foods, the sound of its eating was coming in the silent night, and they pulled the chain forward, slowly tightened the front chains of the elephant, now the elephant can't return. Then he signaled, other members rushed in, they were shouting, screaming, and then they pushed the elephant into the cage within no time. It was the breaking point for the elephant, the elephant understood, its strength was defeated by skill.

The time was late night, only few hours from the day break, everybody was cheering, but another task was left, the elephant had to leave in the night before darkness vanishes, it had to be carried away from the limits of Bolanghir town. The team acted swiftly, the cage was properly tightened, one strong iron mesh was kept on the back and it was strongly fitted to the iron cabin, the journey started, several times the electric wires were snapped but care was taken to avoid the live lines, and by the morning break they were out of the turmoil of the town. All the collectors and SPs on the way were informed about the transportation of the captured elephant. On further journey it didn't create any problem; the range office party was apprehending problem, the elephant even in cage, could topple the vehicle. Nothing untoward happened. They had followed the golden rule – if an elephant is to be trained, then its strength has to be defeated, its arrogance has to be broken.

The truck moved in the night, drove continuously, finally reached Chandra the special training place. A sunken ramp was created there beforehand, the elephant was pulled from back, the elephant strangely cooperated, didn't create any problem, it came backward, slowly the entire body came out of the cage. The elephant finally arrived at its new home at Godiabri in Chandaka.

Now, a new beginning started in the life of the captured elephant, the handlers christened it as Kharsel elephant. Kharsel was the place from where it was captured. The medical team was ready in advance, a team of vertenary doctors thoroughly checked it, the tusk of the elephant was broken a little, pus was oozing out from the root, the legs were also wounded too. Proper antibiotics and other medicines were given to the ailing elephant and it slowly recovered from wounds, shock too. Nila, the boy who strangely was with the elephant from the first day, accompanied the elephant and he was given the task to treat the elephant, he only had the better understanding with the elephant. Nila applied the antibiotics on the wounds using a stick, then slowly came closer to the elephant. Now occasionally he took the elephant for small stroll. During the movement the elephant was cross chained on the front legs, and on the back leg long trailing chains were attached, the precaution was taken to ensure that the elephant didn't escape. Now the elephant was following some commands, probably the elephant recollected its olden days as pet elephant, many simple commands were given to it long years back. Proper care was taken, occasionally Nila took the elephant for bathing, and as per the advice of the animal experts from Nandankanan he started giving the basic training for sitting, standing, etc. to the elephant and strangely the elephant responded nicely to the commands of Nila, to everybody's relief. However, to use the elephant for other fruitful duty further training needs to be imparted.

Some Information on Elephant Training

When a wild elephant is captured from forest, the elephant is tied to a wooden frame or between two tree trunks the mobility is restricted. The elephant tries to break the chain or rope, move its trunk violently. In order to break the captured elephant, it is repeatedly stuck with an elephant hook and beaten and at the same time the mahout communicates with it in a calming voice. The elephant is then denied with food and water for some period, at the same time its violent action is controlled by beating and striking it with elephant hook; slowly fear, pain, thirst and hunger finally forces the elephant to give up all resistance. When the elephant accepts the mahout, then the mahouts give it a bath in a river and offer some food to eat; all the while the elephant is continued to be under chain and accompanied by earlier trained elephants.

After a few weeks, the captured elephant is tamed sufficiently, but still remains under chains and supervised by several mahouts, but now the working elephants are withdrawn from the taming process.

After this "initiation phase", the elephant starts its proper training to become a working elephant.

A good elephant keeper or animal trainer need to know the animals very well. He needs the powers of observation, sensitivity and determination. First of all he should see how elephants behave among each other, how they resolve conflicts, how they quarrel and fight.

The basic training of an elephant is never to push its keepers, press them against the wall or kick them by its feet. If it tries to do so, the elephant keeper has to defend himself, gentle but determined smack of his hand or by the elephant hook gives right direction.

The basic steps for training an elephant, for any other animal are as follows –

1. The trainer gives command in one of three forms: 1 - a spoken command, 2 - the visual command, and/or 3 - the touch of a guide on the body. The commands are methods to direct the elephant what it should do.
2. After getting the command, the elephant responds with all or a small portion of the desired behaviour;
3. The trainer then gives reward for the elephant's response in one or more ways, like: provide food, gives praise.

Every time the animal does something correct, it should be given a reward (like banana, jaggery); if the elephant deliberately does something wrong, or disobeys the command, then to control the arrogant elephant there can be a blow, a pull or a strike by the elephant hook or the whip. This action gives substantial pain to the elephant, so the elephant tries to carry out the command correctly. The elephant keeper has to prevail on the elephant; else a little disharmony makes the living difficult for the keeper as well as for the elephant.

The trainers must be skilled person in giving right direction in right way so that the elephant is able to understand. The reward should be given at right time, if timed wrongly, then the elephant misunderstood it, thinks is being rewarded for a different behaviour than the expected behaviour.

Trained elephants along with their mahouts were called from Assam to control, tame and train this captured elephant. The training course began, the new elephant was kept under strict control throughout the day, many directions were given, and the trainee elephant was directed to follow the command, and punishment used to be given at the sign of little arrogance, disobedience. The trainer used to be friendly to the elephant during the evening, he used to messages its body at that time, and gives food then. Slowly and slowly the elephant obeyed the trainer, started loving him. The already trained elephants used to escort the novice for bathing; in front one trained elephant used to move, the novice then follows, another trained elephant remains at back. The hind legs of the first elephant would be chained with front legs of the novice, and again the hind legs of the untrained one would be chained to the front legs of another trained elephant at the back, the elephant had no chance of escape. Initially the captured elephant showed a lot of reluctance, the other elephants beat it by their trunks, then only it moved forward. Slowly and slowly it obliged, it followed instructions with due diligence, slowly and slowly the elephants played with each other and the training period continued for months.

Once the authorities were satisfied with the training progress, the elephant was given more independence, the trained Kharsel elephant was kept in the Chandka Wildlife sanctuary for several months, its behaviour was watched keenly by the mahouts and the trainers. After long probation, the elephant was due for its regular posting in forest department and it was decided to shift it to Sambalpur for the protection duty and Nila was selected as its Mahout in the new assignment. Since the Kharsel elephant was fully trained, so it was decided to transfer it in a closed truck, many apprehended in view of its earlier reluctance, but the process of shifting went on. The ramp was created, the truck was kept at the same height, Nila the mahout sat on the elephant and commanded it to board the truck, the elephant was reluctant, but the mahaout went on giving command, so the elephant boarded the truck. And once inside the truck, the back of the truck was closed and now the elephant was in a closed environment. Suddenly it behaved differently, didn't obey any command and tried to jump out of the truck. Everybody now sensed danger, the elephant would break the truck, may topple it, and above all in the process would hurt itself, then he directedhe directed the operators to open the truck hoodback, the elephant disembarked immediately to the relief of everybody.

They tried to search for the reason of such behaviour the elephant from the beginning was blind on the left eye, so the left was dark for it. Once inside the closed truck, the right portion of the world also turned dark, and it increased the apprehension in of the elephant, resulting in erratic behaviour. The group earlier observed that the elephant was apprehensive for any activity on its left side, and it can be the only reason for its not boarding the truck during the initial transportation, however it accepted the fate in the trailer truck as there was no obstruction to visibility in view of its open structure. The next alternative was to walk the entire length, trailer truck was not thought for transportation for the simple reason that it would draw unnecessary attention of from so many quarters. Walking to the distained place might take few weeks. There was a great challenge, cooling the temper for the entire period, here the walk is continuous not like the begging elephants as talked earlier who used to take months together to cover a distance of say 100- 200 kilometer. Search for the right mahout went on, nobody dared to take the challenge in view of vagaries involved on the way, people, forest, long walk, and little or no rest, all can be potential causes of failure, the elephant might draw itself to its wild days. Finally a retired mahout was called, the old man after great persuasions agreed to control the animal for the entire journey, he had a strange vow, he wouldn't sit on the back of the elephant, the reason – he survived the tame elephant fury and at that time he vowed before the deity not to ride on the back of the elephant. Even though he was the most adept in elephant handlerhandleing, still he lived with strange beliefs; probably this kind of belief gave them courage to handle the mightiest land animal on the earth.

At around 4 a.m. in the early hours of the day the long journey started, a distance of around 350 kms would be covered. Many rules need to be followed strictly, the elephant would walk till 8 a.m. in the morning and take rest for the whole day, then in the evening it would walk for few some distances, and the rule were followed, it was seen that on an average the elephant crossed around 30 kilometers a day. All precautions were taken during the entire journey, proper food, water and rest were provided, during the journey through the jungles it was ensured that the wild elephant herd were not found nearby; the commoners were kept away too from the elephant. After 12 days it reached Samabalpur, and the elephant took rest for few days in the deer park, a place to acclimatise the elephant with the conditions of Sambalpur. Finally Kharsel elephant was sent to the Debrigarh wildlife sanctuary, located around the Hirakud reservoir over river Mahanadi, for protection duty, Nila remained as its mahout. The protection staffs used to ride on the elephant during their patrolling; they caught many wood cutters with ease, the wood smugglers freeze at the sight of charging elephant. The elephant was also happy for being inside a forest, it used to be let off with trailing chains in the evening and it eats throughout the night, the mahout following the mark of the trailing chain and used to reach the elephant in the morning and a new day used to start in the forest protection.

Posting of an elephant for protection duty was a new concept in Odisha. The forest of the sanctuary is mostly filled with bamboo crop, is a haunting ground of the locals as they mostly consume bamboo shoot, a delicacy in Samabalpur; as a result the bamboo crop has been damaged there. The Kharsel elephant now moves around, trumpets, the mahout sits on the elephant, direct the elephant to charge at the trespassers, and bamboo clump collectors. It covers all vulnerable places, difficult places, the thieves couldn't group and attack the forest guards any more, and the forest is safe now.

Many interesting events are were associated with this elephant, and since it killed many persons, so elimination order came three times, but fortunately the shooters couldn't kill the elephant during the permit periods, one such event was described at the beginning of the story. Few legal cases were filed by animal activists in the court of law for chining of the elephant, tranquilizing it too. In Bolangir court an advocated filed a case on chaining the animal, which to him was hurting his religious sentiments and as per the contempt the elephants too was not treated properly. The officials produced evidences before the court, the court was convinced that the elephant was given the best available treatment in the state, the zoo veterinarians who were the best wildlife doctors had taken care of the animal, and the district veterinarian of the district had helped him. Later the same lawyer also filed an appeal to know about the state of health of the elephant in its present duty, the man at the direction of the court was taken to the Debrigarh wildlife sanctuary. He was convinced on the well-being of the elephant, he withdrew his petition. Another case was filed in the High court on the cruelty to animals during handling, later the petitioner was also convinced about the well being of the animal and he withdrew the case. The chaining of the animal was painful, definitely hurt gave pain to the animal, but it was rogue, the chaining was better than eliminating, and later it enjoyed a fruitful life, the answer given by the authorities were satisfying, convincing.

It was a long story, I looked at the Sal forest, the birds were chirping, cool breeze was blowing, a tranquil state, he started reciting the Sholka for Lord Ganesh

Ekadanta Mahakaya ....

(I sing praises of the Lord Ganesh, Who has one tusk of elephant, Who has a huge body, Who is resplendent like heated-gold, Who has a huge belly, and Who has big beautiful eyes.

Those who sing this blissful mantra on Ganesh, with an ocean of devotion inside, having liberated from all their sins, go towards the Rudra-Loka)

His words were reverberating from all the sides. The Sal forests were reverbertingated with the mantras of Ganesh, the birds started singing the songs of Ganesh.

The Forest Guards

"Can't we find a solution to this?" the field director asked the group of forest officials sitting silently before him. He was baffled at the turn of the events; deep lines on his forehead were showing his anxiety, the sweat drops were showing the turmoil in his mind. He was deeply worried over the incidents, scores of elephants had been killed over last five years, the forest officials, police couldn't get any clue. Now the press, the electronic media were crying foul, the government machinery had been shaken, but no result, the big tuskers of Similipal forest were vanishing, the herd population had been depleted, around 450 numbers left now, a small figure for such a large habitat. Everybody was concerned; the common man too has been moved by these ghastly acts. The green mountains, the vast Sal forests were not regularly getting thundered any more, Similipal was losing its glorious wards; trumpets along the riverside were getting silenced.

The audiences were equally perplexed, the next course of action – nobody was having a definite answer, and there were so many ifs and buts, no conclusion in the horizon. It appeared, they were fighting a losing battle, the enemy hidden somewhere was doing his work so stealthily that there was not a line of clue to track him. Elephants in the Similipal Tiger Reserve were dying constantly. The tuskers, the male elephants with long tusks were targeted regularly, their tusks were removed each time, and the corpse were found inside the deep forest, almost in the core of the prestigious tiger reserve. The culprits always vanished into thin air. And the group of protectors, they were in fact, could not get any hint about the persons involved in the act.

The officials of the Tiger Reserve, as well as other senior forest officials of the nearby divisions and the range forest officers were sitting in the chamber of the field director. The field director was a man with broad forehead, trimmed beard covered his face, his sharp eyes were glowing behind the glasses and he was almost at the wits end.

"The informers, we need to culture the informers," the DFO Baripada suggested meekly.

"Can't we further strengthen our network; Similipal is such a vast area, it is virtually impossible to track every movement of a culprit with present strength of the protection staff at our disposal," his voice was getting inaudible, as if he was talking to himself. The audiences were well versed with the problem before them, their eyes were glued to the big map of the Similipal and the areas around.

The director stood from his chair, went near the map, lifted a stick from the corner, and put it over the map, over it red circles were marked all over showing the hot zones – the sites where the elephants were killed and also other sensitive areas from wildlife vulnerability angle. He didn't utter a single word, moved the tip of the stick on different red circles, other members were watching him continuously.

Then he moved his eyes from the map, lifted the news papers from his table and looked at it; newspaper cuttings, letters were laying scattered all over his table, everywhere there was news of the deaths of elephants from the tiger reserve. Similipal, the pride of the Odisha conservation, was doomed into the gloomiest world.

"We have to be proactive; we have to find out a solution." Those official words were not new to anybody, the same words used to be repeated when a problem comes up. The responsibility finally comes to the range officers; in the forest set up, the range officers are considered to be the central pillars on which the entire forest structure is framed, it is the ground executive to perform the job. The range officers were sitting on the opposite side in a group; little away from the senior officials, they all were in khaki uniforms, and their heads were down, they didn't have the answer too.

"What happened to you all? Why can't you mobilize your staff, improve your own network?" the field director was not shouting, he could have done that in view of the problem having such magnitude, but he knew the limitation of the forest officials and the shortcomings in getting concrete information. The logistics was always a problem, no improvement, the staffs were aging and they were only few, the number of vehicles available for the protection job always remained insufficient and above all the forest officials used to remain deep interior with little facilities, malaria always remained a cause of worry.

"Raybabau, now you have groomed into a full forester, the youth is with you, the experience is with you, find out the solution; your Nilagiri Range is on the National Highways, you are sitting with the hidden forest mafias, look for the clue and after all many killing too occurred in your area. Catching the culprit will be a challenge to you," the field director was giving responsibility to Raybabu; the direction came in a subtle manner.

Raybabu was a man in his early thirties, a short and dark complexioned person with sharp eyes, his look showed his strong determination. Listening the words of the director the eyes of Raybabu glittered, he was not fresher to the job, a range officer with almost 10 years of experience and had enough knowledge of forest and modus operandi of the forest criminals; only in this case the culprits were working more fugitively, to know their modus operandi would be big challenge. He was mentally prepared for the job, knew his responsibility well, as a relative young man he was longing for the new adventure, new thrill and challenge.

At this juncture it is essential to know a little about Similipal forests, with an aim to understand the gravity of the situation better. The Similipal National Park is located in the district of Mayurbjanj, the area is 2,750 km^2; in the forest animals like tigers, elephants, deer, leopards, bison, sloth bears, sambar, wild boar, four horned antelope, giant squirrel etc. are found. The reptile species include Python, King Cobra, Monitor Lizard, Black Turtle, etc. The Mugger crocodile are found in good numbers on the banks of Khairi River. Big mahasheer fishes are also found in the streams. The elephants are also found in good numbers. Similipal elephant population is the main surviving concentration of the Central-Indian elephant population. In this forest about 94 species of orchids, 3000 species of other plants, including 2 species of endemic orchids, 8 endangered plants, 8 plant species with vulnerable status and 34 other rare species of plant are found in this forest. Many of the orchids are rare or endemic like Eria meghasaniensis and Tyna hookeriena, Bulbophyllum panigrahianum is also found in Similipal. The Oryza officinalis paddy, believed to be found in Kerala, was first collected in Odisha from Similipal near Khejuri hills in the late 1980s. Another paddy species called Oryza granulate, previously recorded from South Odisha was also found in Similipal.

Many rivers, rivulets originate from the forests of Similipal, prominent among them are Burhabalanga, Palpala Bandan, Kahairi and Deo. There are also few important waterfalls such as, Joranda and Barehipani

On the backdrop of Similipal, we again come back to the main story. Raybabu came back to his office in Nilagiri through the Kuchha roads of Similipal in his old jeep; the long drive on the rough road was almost breaking his back. The staffs were waiting anxiously for his arrival; nobody has the courage to ask him about the meeting, they all knew the gravity of the situation. He did not look at the staffs, even though all came out when his jeep stopped at the gate, instead he went straight into his room and brought the thick yellow file named "Forest offences" from the wooden rack at the corner on, the file gives instant information on the past offences in the range. The dust had gathered on the file, the pages were twisted at the corners, he cleaned the dust and started reading the papers keenly; if any clue could be collected, he had records for solving many complicated forest cases successfully.

The forest watcher came noiselessly into the room with a glass of water, he used to accompany his range officer in his field visits, he used to keep a close watch on his officer. Raybabu used to forget a lot of personal articles, even forgets his meal. The Range officer was not lifting his eyes from the file; his hands were moving like machine, pages were moving fast, no clue was found. The dust from the file was suffocating him, his eyes were getting fatigued, his room was not having proper lighting; the tungsten lamp hanging over his head was not giving enough light. He moved his chair near to the window and looked at the road. The road outside was clam, the rural folk were moving occasionally on the road, his office after all was not located on the busy highways.

Samar, the forest watcher came inside and put the glass of water on the table, almost noiselessly. Raybabu could feel his presence; he knew the caring habit of Samar. His hands moved, eyes did not, it were zoomed into the words hidden inside the file. After some time he picked up the glass and drank the water in one go, took a long breathe, the tiredness was closing his eyes.

"How can we know the movement? How can we know about them?" he murmured. He was not finding the answer.

Samar understood the confusion in the mind of his officer, after all they spent so many years together, went for trekking, inspection, and on raids on so many occasions. He knew, as all the other staffs, the department was in turmoil due to the constant killings.

"Can't we ask Kalu, the infamous wood cutter? Samar suggested to Raybabu.

Raybabu knew Kalu, he was a wood smuggler, had a habit of cutting the trees illegally and selling it to the illegal mills. Every forest guards knew about him, but he was never caught, he was a swift mover in the forest, knew all the corners of the Nilagiri forest very well; many a times the guards closed on him, but he always gave them a slip.

Raybabu, under normal circumstances, had never thought of using a culprit to catch a culprit, the method was new to him. He had no other means to find out the elephant killers, the proposal to him appeared to be the way only out. The killers were working so stealthily, no one was getting slightest advance trace. The forest staffs used to get the information through their own staffs or from persons who were close to them; many a times they fail to provide information in time, advance information are almost absent, the preemptive action are almost nonexistent in the forest set up. To solve complex situation like this, new methodology had to be developed, new techniques need to be followed, the killers were on the elephant's trail, were waiting to kill another bull elephant, another male would be floored, and the Similipal hills would not hear the heavy trumpets any more.

He recollected the details of last elephant killing in his range, after getting the news he went to the place, the elephant was lying on the ground at Dalki area under his range. The tusker was middle-aged, was without the tusks, its built up healthy body was lying still, deep pain was seen on its forehead, the trunk was twisted, saliva was spitted on the ground, the last moments of the elephant was painful, the bushes, small trees were broken everywhere, the sign of agony, the sign of pain. It was a terrible sight, he could not digest the scene; after all he always loved the elephant herds, the tuskers. He recounted one incident which he witnessed in the Similipal forests, the big tusker was throttling at full speed, its tails raised, the trunks raised, the legs were flying, the husky skin was glowing in the yellow sun, the red-yellow dust cloud of the Similipal was dancing with the moving legs of the elephant; it was such a spectacular scene, inked permanently in his mind.

He remembered that herd, they had visited the nearby hamlet inside Kuladiha Wildlife sanctuary, inside the Similipal Tiger Reserve project area; people shouted at the herd, others called it an invasion, the elephants raided the village, damaged the huts and ate the crops; but he felt the herd visited their home ground, ate because they were hungry, after all man had encroached upon the land of the elephants, and the elephants had nowhere to go. He was so fond of those big creatures, he named it as Sonari group, he found them near the Sonari nallah for the first time, it was the name given by him and everybody knew that group as Sonari group. He knew them for years, every member of the group. They were sixteen in numbers, one big tusker, three makhnas, and rest females, young and old, and the group was so jovial, they used to dance, play, run, swim, make sound, make love, they liked each other so much. He had spent years with them; he knew them as his own children.

Last month Samar informed about the arrival of the group near Simlimunda village. He was thrilled then, he wanted to see them so eagerly. But Samar didn't tell the sad part of the story, the group was without the big elegant and awesome tusker, they were not running anymore, not playing anymore, sorrow, no joy was in their behaviour. He rushed to the hamlet, saw his own group, it was his very own, his own children, he could not believe his eyes, the leader was no more, and the big bull was no more, the killer had taken the toll, the killer had killed his child for the tusk. That day he moaned, the tears didn't roll from his eyes, the sorrow filled his heart, his chest was choked, Similipal forest would not be dancing any more at the thunderous trumpet of the big tusker of Sonari group.

He was doomed into his thought, the killing of the tusker was continuously pricking him, so he decided to take the help of infamous wood smuggler named Kalu, there was no alternative, it was the only way out. He had already got the direction, more than direction the killings of his own children were hurting him; ways needs to be found out, inroads into the killing arena need to be made. He nodded his head, sorrow was in his heart, but the culprits need to be put behind bars, he can't see leader big leaders getting butchered by the killers.

Samar then sent the message to Kalu, he came in the evening, no other got the news, the plot was discussed. Surprisingly Kalu, the man who moved in the forest so fearlessly, did not have concrete idea about the killings. The killers were smart people, not leaving the traces of clue in behind.

"But what about sale, they must be selling somebody, what they would do with the tusk, after all they must be killing the tuskers for money only." Raybabu was telling Kalu, Samar was the lone listener apart from Kalu. And for Kalu, he was a wood cutter, but he didn't like the killing of the elephants, he used to worship the animal. He didn't have idea about the methods of killing. Getting information about the sale, there was a possibility, the news came; the informers were pressed into service.

The later events were quick. Kalu informed the Range officer about Guman, the man closely associated with the killers for the hiding and subsequent selling the tusks. But Guman didn't come to Nilagiri range; the reason killers might be having close watch on the Nilagiri staffs and visit of Guman to forest officers would raise suspicion, so he was asked to come to Baripada and meet the field director. As per the plan the meeting of the informer and the field director was fixed at Baripada on Sunday afternoon, it being a holiday there would be few people around, would be relatively safe.

He hurried up on that Sunday, the journey from his headquarter at Nilagairi to Baripada was long, about 100 kms travel along the periphery of the Similipal, on Kuchha road. He arrived at the director's office in the late afternoon, nobody was there in the corridor and except for the lights in the visitor's room, there was almost no light, the office was sunk into darkness, the PA was nowhere seen; Raybabu understood the reason of such silence. The orderly came from a dark corner and escorted him to the chamber of the field director.

"Raybabu sit here." The field director's voice was almost inaudible. The room too was not much lighted, except for the reading lamp; all the lights were switched off. The faint light was creating more shadows, than lighting the room itself.

Raybabu looked at the other persons present in the room, his DFO was sitting right in-front, one man, a thin and black coloured man, a local tribal, was standing at one corner. He was the lone outsider, he was the Guman. The orderly brought cups of steaming lemon tea, a favorite of the field director and the officers started sipping the tea, Guman too took tea.

"Finally, some clue came." The director spoke to the gathering, looking at the lone stranger, and nodded his head, satisfaction was there on his face.

It was agreed upon earlier that Raybabu would take the lead, because of his cunning approach and capability to handle difficult situations; there would be a lot of uncertainties; the root of the crime could be deep.

"Tomorrow, there will be a deal. The tusks will be sent to the market in Balasore. You need to rush to Balasore immediately." The DFO told the Rage Officer, the director was nodding his head, a symbol of approval. The man on the corner was also moving his head slowly. His eyes were fixed on the man, on whose shoulder; the task would be there to lead the game.

"We got definite clue from Gumun, the stranger you are finding here; he is part of the gang who were into the business of killing the elephants, but his accomplices betrayed him badly, so he wants to take revenge, wants to teach them a lesson." The DFO was telling Raybabu, cunning smile was flashing on his face, the sharp eyes, and the deep husky voice spoke about of the command the person had over his job.

Raybabu bowed his head, he knew the task, and the direction had already come. He looked at Guman and moved his hand, the time to depart, plan for tomorrow. They moved, Guman first, then Raybabu.

"Raybabu be careful, it could be a trap, and they are highly cunning people." The field director was cautioning him. Guman had already left the room, was waiting for Raybabu outside. Raybabu bowed his head, smile was on his face and the challenge had the shadow on his face.

They didn't wait long at Baripada, the headquarter of the field director. Raybabu changed his clothes, dressed himself as a merchant, a half washed grey safari covered his body, he put few golden rings on the fingers, a golden earring was hung from the left earlobe, half polished half shoes was put on the feet and he carried a small suitcase, scratch marks on it showed about the rough use, on his right hand. He was looking like a small businessman from Odisha Bihar border, the type of people who always looks for opportunities to earn big bucks in shortest time; all means are acceptable, no business ethics followed. Baripada, Balasore, being border towns of Odisha, were the hunting grounds of this kind of businessman. A white ambassador car was parked outside; Raybabu, Samar and the Guman were occupants of the vehicle. They moved, it was partially dark, hardly anybody was outside. After around three hours of journey, the party arrived at Balasore and stayed at hotel Balasore Inn, the hotel where the transaction would take place.

It was still dark, Raybabu could hardly sleep further, he looked at the watch, time was 4 in the morning, the darkness was still there, but the expected knock was not coming. He tried to close his eyes, no sleep, he in fact had spent the whole night without sleep; the anxiety had snatched his sleep. Samar, was anxious like him, he too was looking outside, in the darkness they were sitting in the room, waiting for Guman to return. In their plan, they were to wait in the hotel in the guise of a customer, and Guman, their accomplice were to go to the bus stand and bring the tusker sellers to the hotel for the deal. The sellers were to come early in the morning, the buyers were to bargain instantly, and the transaction needed to be finished immediately.

Expected knock came at 5.00 am, Samar opened the door; three people including Guman silently came inside and the door was immediately closed on their back. Raybabu looked at the sellers; the sellers were looking at him too, buyers and sellers were gauging each other. The sellers, both in their mid thirties, one little older, both local tribal, were giving rustic look, clothed with un-ironed pant and shirt, had anxiety in their eyes.

"Brought the sample?" Raybabu asked the seller. One of the seller nodded his head, opened his small cotton bag, brought a small box and the tusk sample was placed on the table. The sample, in the shape of a one rupee coin, resembled a carom striker, and it would be difficult to gauge the size of the tusk from this small piece. Raybabu brought out a small torch from his pocket, looked at the sample through a magnifying glass in the faint light of the torch. It was a good quality tusk. His eyes gleaned, the real stuff was there in front of him. He then moved the sample, and Samar was examining it closely. The sellers were gauging their interest.

"Price," his voice was low.

"Five thousand rupees per kg" the seller quoted the price.

"Too high, you know there is a lot of risk in transportation, everyone needs to be satisfied, and money will be distributed to many." Raybabu was creating a transaction atmosphere. Then he paused a little and tried to create a further grave situation.

"Everywhere there are guards, police on the way, the forest check gates, the octrai posts and interstate check gates, there is a great risk." Raybabu was influencing the sellers.

"I can't give more than two," he was bargaining. He looked at the sellers, anguish in their eyes, frustration in their eyes, they looked at each other. Raybabu could instantly gauge their feeling; further bargain has to be done.

"Two thousand five hundred rupees," Raybabu didn't want to distract them; they should be involved in the deal.

The sellers moved their heads, looked at each other, and looked at Guman. There was irritation in their eyes, they were angry, the price was too low for them; they anticipated more. One man lifted the sample and put it inside the bag.

"You are so angry, so disgusted, agreed, you too had laboured hard, but twenty five hundred per kg is a fair price, is not it?" Raybabu tried to impress the sellers, but they moved their head, gesture of disapproval, and one man tried to open the door.

"Three thousand, I can't give more." Raybabu tried to save the dealing.

The advancing legs stopped, one man turned back, looked at Raybabu, moved his head again, still disapproval, and then almost opened the door.

"Three thousand and five hundred rupees a kg, I can't give you more," Raybabu was showing his desperation, he had perfected his acting, the sellers were getting convinced. They agreed to the deal.

"But when can I see the sample," Raybabu asked.

"Come at 2 pm in the afternoon to our village, tomorrow, the tusks will be handed over there. Come with full money." It was the deal, the kind words of the tusk sellers and they vanished.

More information needed to be collected, the tusks needed to be seen, further action needed to be planned. Raybabu reached the hamlet right in time, the sun was still over the head; probably he was a little early. They moved in a motorcycle, the vehicle went right into the village through the narrow roads, and parked it at the outskirts of the hamlet. Seeing them, Guman came out followed by other two persons; they looked at Raybabu, searched his motorcycle, no articles of suspicion. One man carefully looked at the forest; in came the sound of a bird, another bird called from a different corner. The message came, nobody was following; tusk could safely be shown to the buyers. They escorted Raybabu to the hamlet through narrow roads and stopped in front of a hut, roof thatched, the walls made of soil and bamboo, the wall was coloured red and few designs were drawn on it; the hut was typical tribal hut. One man came out, called the buyer to the courtyard on the back, and he went to a paddy heap of around six feet height, removed paddy hay a little, and brought a tusk. Raybabu looked at the tusk, it was clean, white in colour, had good grains and lusture, a good stuff, would definitely fetch high value in appropriate market.

Raybabu looked at the tusk, lifted it, heavy, around ten-fifteen kilogram, curved a little towards end. The other tusk too was presented before him, almost equal weight, from the same elephant of course. The elephant must be a strong and healthy bull of around forty five-fifty years of age, prime age for reproduction; the elephant herd must have been affected by this killing. Raybabu was feeling sorry, he almost felt like crying, wanted to beat those scoundrels, he loved those tall creatures so much. He didn't show his emotion, restrained himself, else the game would fail miserably.

"Fifteen kilogram each, both would be thirty kilogram." Raybabu was telling to himself, the sellers were looking at him, their sharp eyes were the eyes of the hunters, trying find the weak links, weak moments, to hound at Raybabu. But Raybabu was playing his part very well.

"I shall come at this hour with full money, tomorrow," Raybabu told them. On the way back Raybabu looked at the mountains; the red sun was turning orange, was sinking, the forest was tanned red, the red blood on the soil, the soil of Similipal was soaked in the blood of innocent elephants.

In the next evening he met the director at his residence, the DFO was there, both were waiting for him anxiously, they wished to know the developments. Raybabu told about the happenings in details; they were pleased at his achievement. Further plan, the next step, now the information about the tusk had come.

"Why can't you raid the village, recover the tusk straightway and arrest the culprits?" asked the director, looking at the Range officer. Raybabu looked at his DFO, he thought that the director would take more risk.

"With all possibility, we might not get the tusk there, they must have hidden the stuff somewhere by this time, and you know Sir, they are a notorious group, expert in this type of deal," Raybabu was explaining.

His DFO was appreciating the remarks of his Range Officer, it would be difficult, next to impossible to recover tusk from that hamlet, in view of the location, from the hill top one could track the movement of outsiders. Mass movement of staffs would cause suspicion, and the tusk would never surface; the director understood the complexity of the issue.

"You in fact did a marvelous job, we never expected them to arrive so easily, discuss with you so freely, but further action," he was not finding a solution.

He looked at the DFO; the DFO was also not having any answer. Arranging two lakhs of rupees was not that easy in those years.

“We have to purchase the tusks, then will catch them red handed,” Raybabu suggested.

“Money, where will we get that much of money?” the field director asked the Range officer.

“Even if we arrange, what is the guarantee that the money will not vanish, these culprits outwitted the whole forest machinery for so long, may now play further trick; a little suspicion, they would kill the Range Officer, will vanish with money? No, we can’t take that much of risk.” He was trying to explain to himself, only other people could listen his murmuring.

“Agreed Sir, we can outwit them so easily, we will not hand over the cash.” The DFO was supporting the range officer.

A lot of risk was involved, the matter could take ugly turn, the director was not giving any sign, the biggest one is of course money. The DFO understood the turmoil in the mind of the director; it would not be easy to enter to their den with money.

“We will have real currency in one suitcase and in another identical one we will put fake currencies and the fake currencies will be handed over to the culprits,” he was explaining to director, eagerness was in his voice, so also determination. The director was getting convinced, there is no other way out, and risk has to be taken.

Fake notes, the director could not believe his ears, his own DFO was putting an unethical plan before him, was pleading to break the law to catch a culprit, his eyebrows raised, anxiety in his face.

“If they understood our trick, then there might be attack, there might be human causalities. Who will take that risk,” the director was talking to himself, in the innermost corner of his mind there was opposition. He didn’t utter a single word, lost to him for a while; others also didn’t utter a single line, waited for the reaction, for the confirmation from the director.

“Go ahead,” was the faint direction, an uncertain direction came.

The action team returned from the Director’s office, and gathered at the DFO residence. Raybabu, would remain in the same guise of the businessman, Samar would be the jeep driver, and other people would wait at the entry point into the sanctuary. If Raybabu would be late for more than three hours, subsequent action would start, the hamlet would be raided with full force.

Accordingly the message for alertness passed, the staffs were asked to remain in readiness for the visit of the DFO, no further detail was given. The vehicle was a problem, departmental vehicle can't be used, the killers would be suspicious, and others should not be involved, the taxi should not be hired, Raybabu had the answer; his own friend's old jeep would be used.

The DFO agreed for the money, it was the greatest stumbling block, getting one lakhs of rupees that time was not that easy, it was a big money when this incident took place, the salary of the officers were meager and asking for money from many quarters would create suspicion.

"Use the Cash Advance available with you, there is no other way out," was the answer, was the direction from the DFO. The forest department has a system of cash advance for carrying out works in field in view of remoteness of locations, the works are carried out departmentally, the labourers are paid directly, not through banks. The DFO suggested using this official money as bait for a day.

The fake currency was a great challenge, where to get those fake currencies.

"I shall manage it, leave it to me Sir, we would use the printed notes of the game "Business" and put those fake notes between the real notes in such manner that nobody would suspect, and after all the stay would be for a short time.." Raybabu told his DFO. The CA cheque was given to the Range Officer, he encashed the amount the same day and got his team readied for the operation.

Next day work would be hectic; the Range Officer was to get his act perfect – the money, the suitcases, the driver, the vehicle were ready. The place where the dealings would take place was around one hour journey on the bumpy road from the entry point to the sanctuary and was located deep inside the forest. That area was notoriously known for the wood mafias; the team had to be extremely careful.

When they arrived, the sun was setting behind the tall hills of the Similipal. The hamlet Baniabasa was located in the foot of hill ranges, was surrounded by thick forest, a rivulet was passing nearby. The jeep halted outside the village, they were standing approximately half a kilometer away from the huts, a safe distance to escape. Raybabu came out of the jeep, stood next to the jeep, brought out a cigarette box from pocket, and started smoking. Samar was anxiously waiting inside, both of them were armed with Govt. revolvers, in the case of exigency the firearms would be used for self defence.

Cool bridge was blowing from the Hills on the back; the day birds were returning to their nests slowly, the day was exiting. Raybabu looked at the hamlet, a few thatched huts, low in height, and with thick soil walls. The huts were not very close, rather scattered, tamarind, Mahula trees and bamboo bushes were standing all around. A small narrow footpath, covered with bushes from the sides, was running to the village from the relatively wide forest road, through the cultivation fields in steps, with irregular bunds, which too continued to the edge of the hamlet, and further forest on the back of the hamlet was around hundred meter away. These open patches, though not a barrier, still acted as barrier against the tigers and leopards, the big cats could be sighted more easily. The dogs, usual lives in the tribal villages, were moving here and there, the hens and the cocks were running, smoke was coming from the roofs, symbolizing life in the hamlet, but there was no human voice, no cry of the children. It was strange. Raybabu knew, the whole village was prepared to pounce on him his vehicle would be covered with sharp arrows from unseen bows, his body would be torn to pieces, it was not known where those people were hiding, behind which bush, which stone, on which tree.

He was waiting there for more than half an hour, so he was moving restlessly, to show his anxiety to the hidden eyes, the culprits were gauging his movement. After sometime two people came, one was Guman, the other was one of the tusk sellers. They were coming through the small paddy fields, they arrived, cigarettes were offered, and they smoke.

"Brought the money?" was the question.

Raybabu quietly tuned back, opened the back door of the jeep, opened the small suitcase, it was filled with hundred rupees bundles. The man looked inside, took one bundle, saw it closely, was happy; his face glowed in the fading sunlight.

"Brought the tusk?" Raybabu asked the man.

"Wait my friend is bringing," was the answer. Raybabu then closed the suitcase, locked it, and handed over the keys to the sellers with an intention to create more faith on him. These groups of people never speak much, they confine themselves to their thought and are highly suspicious. Raybabu opened a bag and brought out two bottles of cheap whisky and handed over the same to them, they were happy, the evening would be interesting, there would be a lot of guests, there would be a lot of dance and singing, money and liquor, both would be available.

The man then moved quickly towards a bush nearby and the other man emerged from the back of a big Sal tree. Raybabu looked at the man, his hands moved quickly, the suitcase with real notes was changed and the suitcase with fake notes took its place. He then looked at the coming legs, they were coming fast, smile moved on his lips, a cunning one. They were also laughing, talking to themselves in their dialect, cheer in their words.

“I couldn’t arrange the full money, my money lender could give me fifty thousand rupees only, he would take a day to arrange rest money.” Raybabu was apologetic, he was playing a trick. The sellers looked at each other, displeasure in their faces.

“You will get one tusk, the other one you will get after we get the full money” was their decision. Raybabu nodded his head, he pretended to be shameful.

“Right, my money lender was extremely careless, but he promised me to hand over the money today, I shall certainly manage the money. Please come tomorrow to the same hotel, in the morning.” Raybabu tried to convince them, he was perfect in his acting.

The other man again went to that bush, opened the branches slightly and brought out a thick cotton bag and came back to Raybabu who took the bag from him, it was heavy, after all fifteen kilogram of tusk was there, the tusk was cut to three pieces. He took the bag, handed over the fake suitcase. The last man suddenly nodded his head in disapproval, he was not thoroughly convinced.

“Full deal, we need full money and then only the tusks will be handed over to you,” the other man was giving direction, the first man too nodded his head in approval, he returned the suitcase; Raybabu’s job was getting unfinished, there would be more uncertainties.

“Tomorrow in the morning we will meet in the same hotel at Balasore.” Raybabu told the sellers. The vehicle was in the start condition he came back, and drove away, a dust cloud was created on the back.

The job was yet to be over, the sellers were convinced, but they were highly cunning people; but they now started believing Raybabu, the most satisfying part of the effort so far. He reported the development to the DFO, met the field director along with him. All were satisfied, the plan was clicking, the bait was perfect, and the fish was biting it slowly, a few more hours, clear picture would emerge.

Raybabu then rushed to his Range in the same night, prepared his team, they all came to Balasore in their office vehicle. Samar stayed with the team, he knew the culprits, and the leader Raybabu was in the guise of the businessman remained in the hotel. His team members remained in another place, were waiting for the direction from the Range Officer. He looked outside, the room was facing the road, in front there was a tea stall and a snacks shop. His members would stay there in civilian dress, a few meters away the other group would to be in uniform. To give symbol, the range officer would come to the window and would smoke there, it would be the symbol of arrival of the seller. When the deal would be made, the Range Officer would come to the window, would open the windows further, then would smoke the cigarette. The team would act, the officers outside would give signal to the men in uniform and they would capture the seller.

In the morning at around 7 a.m. the usual knock came, one man was standing outside with the bag, Guman was not there, Guman was hinted by the Range Officer not to accompany.

"Brought the tusk," was the immediate question Raybabu put to the man. He nodded his head, Raybabu was very happy, brought a cigarette, then went to the window to smoke, it was rather the direction, and his group became alert.

"I couldn't bring, the bag was heavy, the police is everywhere. We will collect it from my friend." The man too did not believe Raybabu fully; in this business of mistrust no one is trustworthy. Raybabu then went to the window, smoked there continuously, the whole group was to be alerted, and the time for action had come.

Raybabu took the currency in one bag, followed the man. They walked outside, the usual morning crowd was there in front of the tea shop, some were standing, some were sipping hot tea. They waited there and sipped hot tea, Raybabu could see the anxious faces of his men, they were in plain clothes and were very close. He nodded the head, the symbol to follow, and the group hurried up. Raybabu walked for almost fifty meters with the seller, they found a man, the second seller, standing behind a bus, Raybabu came closer, the plainclothes men were close, and the men in uniform were also somewhere hiding.

"I couldn't bring the tusks, there is security everywhere, come to Betanati village, on Baripada – Udala road at eight, we will hand over the tusks there." The other man said, rudeness in his talk, the foul smell of Handia, the country liquor called in the local language, was coming from his mouth. Raybabu looked at the man, he was in dirty clothes, his eyes were red and blurred, teeth yellow, the man looked like a rogue. Raybabu understood, the sellers were getting alerted, they were bringing goons to the forefront now the challenge would be tougher.

Both man then boarded the bus for Udala, the bus sped way, and the forest party remained confused, uncertain.

Further planning was made, Raybabu with the driver would move in the same white ambassador car in the evening, the raiding party would arrive in the spot in two groups in two different cars from different sides, one from Udala side, and the other from Baripada side, the vehicles would reach the spot at one time and would raid the sellers on the road. Raybabu would engage the sellers for fifteen minutes, and the raiding party would jump at the sellers.

As per the plan, Raybabu started for the destination, the attire of the businessman was on his body, the driver too was dressed like a Bihari driver, straight mustache, red vermillion on the forehead, hair oiled. They reached the spot at 8.15 p.m. The sellers were waiting there, they were now five people, two of them were earlier seen by Raybabu, and other three were unknown. Raybabu was fearful, the sellers were not behaving properly, and arrogance was on their faces. They were standing below a big sal tree, little away from the village stop.

"Got the tusk?" Raybabu asked to the known one.

He nodded his head, two cloth bag was brought from the nearby bush, and was kept before him, but the same was not handed over to him.

"Brought the money?" was the instant question from the sellers.

Raybabu nodded his head in approval; the smile came to face of the sellers. Raybabu opened his suitcase, their eyes were glittering, their yellow teeth in their dark faces were turning them to demons.

"We need to measure," Raybabu told the sellers, the anxious eyes agreed, the deal had to be fair.

Raybabu then brought a measuring scale and weights from the car, handed over the same to the known seller. He took the scale and weight and other saw it keenly. The ivory was then brought from the bags, the tusks were in six pieces. Raybabu raised the scale, put the weights on one side, the ivory was kept in another side. He was measuring slowly, he wanted to delay the sale, was also getting anxious, his friends were not seen, the drama was turning dangerous. If they were late, then the whole play would be a great failure, after all there is only a thin line between success and failure, success matters, not failure and at the end everybody would say it was an ill planned exercise.

Then came the lights of coming vehicles, the vehicles were coming from both sides of the road, the sellers looked at the lights, but they didn't suspect it to be a foul play, both the vehicles came nearer, and at one time, they crossed the parked ambassador car, both went ahead in opposite direction, stopped at around fifteen feet away in their respective directions. The action team came out, scuffles took place, Raybabu in the meantime sped away, and the scale and the tusks remained scattered on the ground. The drama reached the final scene, the fleeing of Raybabu was a perfect scene, much better than the apprehending of the culprits, the culprits wouldn't suspect the informer or the buyer.

Same evening the arrest message was passed to the director, to the DFO too. The culprit were brought to the Range Office at Nilagiri for interrogation. The culprits didn't open their mouth initially, but broke after three days of captivity.

The DFO looked at his Range Officer; Raybabu had finally caught the tusk sellers. They were sitting in the residence of their director and the morning sun was pleasant, the steaming tea was highly relaxing, refreshing too, the hard work of previous days had bore the right fruit as desired.

"Are you sure?" those are the words from the DFO.

"Yes Sir, the Nepalis are involved in the killing," Raybabu was elaborating his findings to his senior, about the involvement of the outsiders in this crime.

"Yes Sir, the tusk seller in our custody revealed the story, initially like you, I couldn't believe, but they were repeatedly telling the same story. They were not the killers, were mere a conduit, agents for selling the tusks in the market, only they would get some commission," he was explaining the matter.

The DFO also couldn't believe the story, outsiders like Nepalis, who are so conspicuous, could stage manage the killing show for such a long period, it was unthinkable.

"Where are those Nepalis?" the question of the director.

"Here, under our nose, right in Baripada," Raybabu almost ignited the explosive.

The DFO and the field director could not believe, couldn't recite a word for minutes, it was a shock, how could the Nepalis with distinctly different physical features from the locals, operate for so long from Baripada, the headquarters of forest and police.

Raybabu looked at his seniors; they were dumbfounded, speechless too, he remembered, the news of the presence of the Nepalis in Baripada and their involvement in killing had made him deaf and dumb earlier for almost half an hour. He simply couldn't digest this fact; the Neapalis could operate with so impunity and kill his elephants inside the sanctuary.

The field director took a long sigh, looked at the big Sal tree standing in his bungalow, the birds were still chirping, some life was still left in Baripada, not everybody was thunderstruck like him. The time had come for action perfect, crafts matching the stealth of the Nepalis, revenge reflected in his eyes, but he controlled his emotions.

"What was the modus operandi of the killers?" the director was trying to understand the matter properly.

"The Nepalis would contact the tribal who reside inside through their accomplice at Baripada. The gun used for the purpose would come from some retired army people. They use aconite, the herbal poison from North East to kills the elephant within hours." Raybabu was explaining the killing details.

The DFO and the director knew about the use of aconite in immobilizing and subsequent killing of the wild animals by the north eastern tribal. The tribal there lace the arrow with aconite paste, dry it, and then shoots the arrow at the animal. As soon as the poison comes into the contact of the blood stream, drowsiness comes; the animal gets immobilized slowly and finally dies. Aconite is a herb with beautiful blue flower, usually found near the streams, hanging from the rocks; one could see it in plenty in high hills of Himalayas.

Raybabu, without waiting further started telling the accounts he had collected from those arrested men.

"These Nepalis are ex army or police men, have an accomplice here in Bariapda, whom they meet at Siliguri, and were in constant touch with him for several years. At the request of the local man they came here, and the local man arranged their hideouts and also the put his informers around, to track the movements of elephants, foresters also. Once the movements of the tuskers were confirmed, those people then come out from their hides and move to the site of the prey. They put aconite laced iron arrow tip over the rifle bullet, inside the muzzle, and fire at the elephant. The elephant, even if not grievously hurt, still is killed due to the aconite poison. Then, over the root of the tusk, they pour acid and the flesh burns and the bone gets exposed and the tusks are cut from the root. These un-cleaned tusk used to be to buried in pits for some days so that the flesh melts away fully, and then they bring out the tusk, clean it again by acid and water, and the tusk is ready for the market" Raybabu was telling to his seniors.

"See how intelligent they are, and with what impunity they are working!" the director was telling his DFO. The morning sun had moved further, hurting the body, a crow started calling Ka, Ka.

"The market, where they get the market?" was the immediate, but expected question, unless there is a good market, there is no need to kill the elephants.

"They take the tusks mostly to Siliguri near Indian border, in north east, sometimes to the border by themselves, but when the money is the immediate need, the local helps are asked for to go to the market, they avoid the local market. Balasore is a flourishing centre for the illegal wildlife market, because of rail, and road connectivity, sometimes the materials are transported through river route. After all the town was once a port town during the period of the Britishers." Raybabu was explaining. They never expected the root of the crime to be so deep, extends to the borders of India.

"But why they were trying to sell the tusk right this time here at Balasore, instead of taking it to Darjeeling?" the DFO asked.

"They were trying to explore the market, want to see the rate, the response; also they need immediate money for payment to their informers and collaborators," was the reply. He had already completed his home work.

The crow again called Ka, Ka, the locals believe, if the dark crow called Damarakau, sits on the roof of some house and calls from there then some guest will come to that house. The director again looked at the calling crow; it was hopping in the open space in front of the house.

The day was increasing, the plan was to be made immediately, and an emergency meeting was called. The arrested person had already revealed the location of the house, nearby there were no houses. Baripada still was an old town that time, the roads were not parallel, serpentine, narrow, the town too was not thickly populated, had both urban and rural touch together; and sometimes the houses located in the fringe areas of the town could be the den of the criminals. The reconnaissance was made, the house was located near a small earthen tiled building, itself was a mud plastered thatched house, not appearing as the dwelling place for criminals of such stature, and the house was found locked. Gloom again shadowed over their enthusiasm, the birds of no feathers flew from the nest, and probably the message of arrest of their accomplice had been leaked to them.

However, it was decided to keep a constant watch for some days, and after two days news came, good news, movements had been noticed. The raiding team consisting of two ACFs, four Range Officers and twenty five foresters and forest guards were mobilized, and they raided the house at 2 a.m in the night. There was stiff resistance from the five Nepalis, who were actually turned out to be Manipuris, but finally they were overpowered and were arrested and handcuffed. The news of arrest of the Manipuris flashed in the Baripada town, the roads were jam-packed to see the elephant killers, the Manipuris. Seeing the crowd around it was decided to take the accused away from Baripada, and also there was need to get the clear picture, interrogation in the presence of the tusk sellers was required.

The team started for Nilagiri in the evening, were moving in four vehicles along with the culprits. They halted at a forest check gate on the Baripada-Balasore highway; the gate keeper merrily offered them cups of tea, the forest officials were relaxed. Suddenly the jeep in which the Manipuris were kept, started moving, the forest officials on the ground shouted, but the jeep did not stop, and the vehicle started getting speed. They jumped on the other waiting jeeps and started chasing the first jeep. The chase was not long, the first jeep went off track, out of the national highway into a side road, a kuchha one. After a brief distance, the vehicle suddenly stopped, other vehicles were around 100 meters away, the Manipuris fled into the forest, they were given a chase, but couldn't find them in the darkness. In the jeep, when the team saw inside couldn't believe their eyes, two range officers were bleeding profusely, the driver was almost strangulated, the arrested group, taking the advantage of night, and also relaxed attitude of the range Officers, charged at them and overpowered the officers, beat them thoroughly in their handcuffs, and tried to strangulate the driver, and then vanished into the forest at the first opportunity.

The news of the escape reached Nilagiri as well as the forest headquarters at Baripada. The forest officials were ashamed, helplessness was reflected on their faces, the usual fault finding, accusations about the laxity, the stern warning of the director came, now the time had come to act swiftly. The police was contacted, all the stations on the highway were briefed about the escape of the Manipuris. The forest vehicles moved in the villages, announcements were made, the rewards were declared, if anybody could help in re-arresting the culprits, then he would be suitably rewarded. News about the sighting of Manipuris came frequently, but when people came closer they used to vanish into the forest. The handcuffs were found, but the killers couldn't be apprehended. They, even though adept in hiding inside the forest, but could be easily identified due to their distinct feature, also. their accomplices in different villages though alerted, were not in a position to provide them help directly. After five days, the news of two Manipuris came, the local police rushed to the site along with the forest officials, but they were not the easy catch, rather they showed aggression, tried to attack police; so armed police was called and they were apprehended. No news about the other three came; those men vanished into thin air. The police officers handed the two Manipuris to the forest Range Officer Raybabu for further proceedings. The culprits were to be kept for the evening, and in the next day, after interrogation, they were to be presented before the magistrate at Udala for trial. They then were shifted to the Range office, the forest officials remained very alert, both of them were locked inside a room, and from outside the door was locked and four forest guards attended the sentry duty.

Raybabu then looked at the arrested persons, a ray of contentment flashed on his face, the older man was in his late forties and the younger one was around thirty, may be less than that, they rather looked like father and son.

Those Nepalis, any man from mongoloid race, are called as Nepalis, were of short stature, heavily built, had strong arms, heavy legs, the chests were full with muscles, eyes were glowing like burning stars, the look resembles that of a tiger, as if the tiger was waiting to pounce. He looked at his ageing force, the foresters and the forest guards at his disposal were in their late forties and fifties were not a match to the swift Manipuri. The locals, though nimble footed, still would not match the physical strength of these people. The arrested seller was produced before the Manipuri, he was not in handcuff, but on ropes, and these people were in handcuffs, they roared, and the seller pointed at them. But they didn't shout, grumble, feeling of anger came out from their throat, from their eyes, treachery means death.

Raybabu wanted to bring more information out of them, so wanted to pacify them, offered tea, which they gladly drank. They made gesture for cigarette, and the Range Officer offered them cigarette, they were very happy, after all somebody was treating them better. Raybabu was also equally hopeful, his good behaviour was winning the criminals, probably he would get some clue about the transit route of the tusks. He directed his guards to be kind to the culprits, hesitantly they agreed to the order. They were allowed to take food with open hands, the guards were guarding all around and the local people formed the outer ring, were outside, waiting to get a glimpse of the killers. They smiled at the onlookers, waived their hands, and started eating. The onlookers too, looking at their behavior of the Manipuris couldn't believe their eyes, the ferocious group who had brutally assaulted the Range Officers, dodged police, forest officials for five days, could be so humble, so polite. There was no sign of resistance from them, all signs of cooperation.

"How many elephants you have killed?" Raybabu asked the Manipuris.

"Seventeen elephants," the older man replied, his voice was normal, no sign of regret in it, he was not repentant of such killings.

Raybabu recollected, the elephant killings were going on in the Similipal for several years, but without any trace, except this one.

"Where from you get the firearm, or the poison?" Raybabu wanted to know further.

The men had the stamp of their early service, they were replying instantly.

"The gun comes from the local friend, he used to escort us to the forest, we aim at the elephant and kill them. The cartridge and poison are supplied by us; we collect the poison from Nepal.

"Since how long you have been killing the elephants in Similipal?" Was the question from Raybabu.

"Since last six years, we used to come to Baripada during winters, camp there and kill the elephants when opportunity comes." He was replying, no hesitation in his mind, both of them were normal, no sign of vacillation in their speech, no incoherence.

Raybabu didn't ask further questions. He was tired, the night was getting dense. He looked at the culprits, even though their hands were not handcuffed, for the reason of security, strong ropes were tied to their waists at one end, the other ends were strongly tied to the door frame. The accused finished their food, drank water, attended nature's call, and then smiled at the forest officials for their good behaviour and the forest officials locked them inside the room. Four forest guards stood as sentry, others left the place for food, the Range Officer went to his house for food, the onlookers retreated to their respective houses, the Range Office was giving a deserted look, the eclectic bulbs were creating the shadows on the road and in open spaces. The place was getting calm, the owls were calling from the nearby mango trees; the mice were screaming at the sound of the owl, the night was getting thicker and thicker.

Suddenly the light scream, the moan and goofing sound alerted the sentries, the sentry called for the Range Officer loudly. Other forest guards, Range officers rushed to the room, the room was locked from outside, but moaning was coming from the room, Something untoward had happened, the Range officer prayed to the God, the prisoners should be safe. With trembling hands the sentry opened the room, the sight was unimaginable, the forest officials who used to deal with petty criminals, never encountered hardened criminals, couldn't believe their eyes. The older Manipur had caught the naked electric wire in his right hand and in his left hand he was holding the younger Manippuri. The younger fellow was trying to free himself from the clutches of the older man, but so determined he was that he was not leaving him, also not leaving the electric wire, he was shivering, but not leaving the electric wire. The main line was disconnected, the man felled unconscious, the younger man was panting. Both of them were rushed to the government hospital, the younger man was released after minor treatment, but the older man was not getting sense, his hands were burnt. The younger man looked at the older man, hatred in his eyes, and he left the hospital quietly.

The younger man was presented in the court, the magistrate sent him to jail. The older man regained sense after three days. In between rumors flew around, dangerous, hair raising, the Manipuris were coming in groups, to take the older man away from hospital to free him from the foresters. Armed police, forest guards guarded the older man throughout, but there was no attack. He was too produced in the court immediately, the forest officials were not enthusiastic to keep him for an hour in their custody. During the trial the man laughed a hearty laugh.

"Why this offender is laughing?" the magistrate was furious. He expected the culprit not to give answer.

"He will be jailed for seven years for killing the elephants inside the Similipal," the magistrate was passing the order.

The culprit looked at the roof, a sigh of relief came and he laughed again, laugh was louder, thunderous.

"Oh! I didn't know, I am being trialed here for killing an elephant and being sent to jail for seven years. I was a fool, was killing myself, killing my dear friend too, I think something else. God saved me," he spoke to himself, to the audience in clear Hindi. The court, with full house inside, turned silent.